DR. SLUMP VOL. 2
The SHONEN JUMP Graphic Novel Edition

STORY AND ART BY
AKIRA TORIYAMA

English Adaptation & Translation/Alexander O. Smith
Touch-up Art & Lettering/Walden Wong
Design/Sean Lee
Editor/Yuki Takagaki

Managing Editor/Elizabeth Kawasaki
Director of Production/Noboru Watanabe
Vice President of Publishing/Alvin Lu
Vice President & Editor in Chief/ Yumi Hoashi
Sr. Director of Acquisitions/Rika Inouye
Vice President of Sales & Marketing/Liza Coppola
Publisher/Hyoe Narita

Some art has been modified, including nudity, underage drinking scenes and underage smoking scenes, from the original Japanese edition. The stories, characters and incidents mentioned in this publication are entirely fictional.

Printed in the U.S.A.

Published by VIZ, LLC
P.O. Box 77010
San Francisco, CA 94107

10 9 8 7 6 5 4 3 2 1
First printing, June 2005

www.viz.com

PARENTAL ADVISORY
DR. SLUMP is rated T for Teen. Contains suggestive themes. Recommended for ages 13 and up.

THE WORLD'S MOST POPULAR MANGA
SHONEN JUMP GRAPHIC NOVEL
www.shonenjump.com

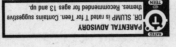

I am truly a bumpkin. Country livin', all the way. I never took much to the big city, where there's more people than trees!

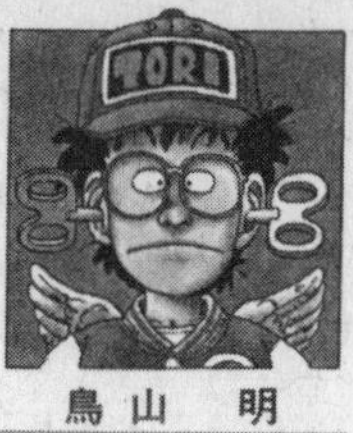
TORI

鳥山 明

No, it's the country for me...Mothra flitting in the spring, Gamera taking a walk along the sea in the summertime, Angirus in the fall, snowball fights with the mammoths in the winter... What the heck kind of country is this!? Morning has come to Penguin Village. My eyes still hazy with sleep, I grab the wheel and barely make it to the airport alive. Local produce, delivered straight to your door.

Whatever. Just read the manga!

—Akira Toriyama, 1980

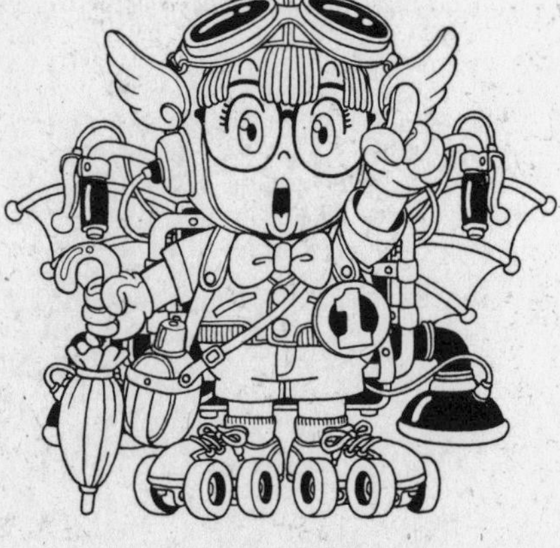

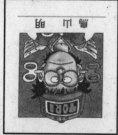

Akira Toriyama's first weekly series, **Dr. Slump**, has entertained generations of readers in Japan since it was introduced in Shueisha's **Weekly Shonen Jump** magazine in 1980. A few years later, he created his wildly popular **Dragon Ball** series, which brought him international success. Toriyama is also known for his character designs for video games, including **Dragon Warrior, Chrono Trigger** and **Tobal No. 1**. He lives with his family in Japan.

SHONEN JUMP GRAPHIC NOVEL

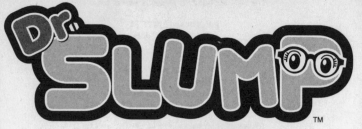

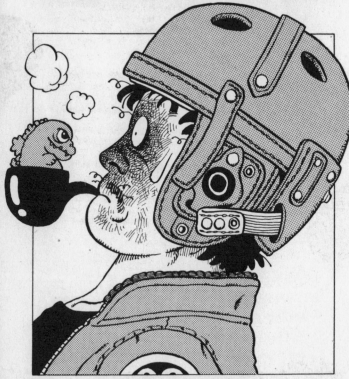

Story & Art by
Akira Toriyama

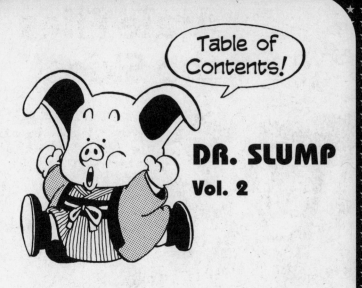

Table of Contents!

DR. SLUMP
Vol. 2

Arale Flies the Skies!

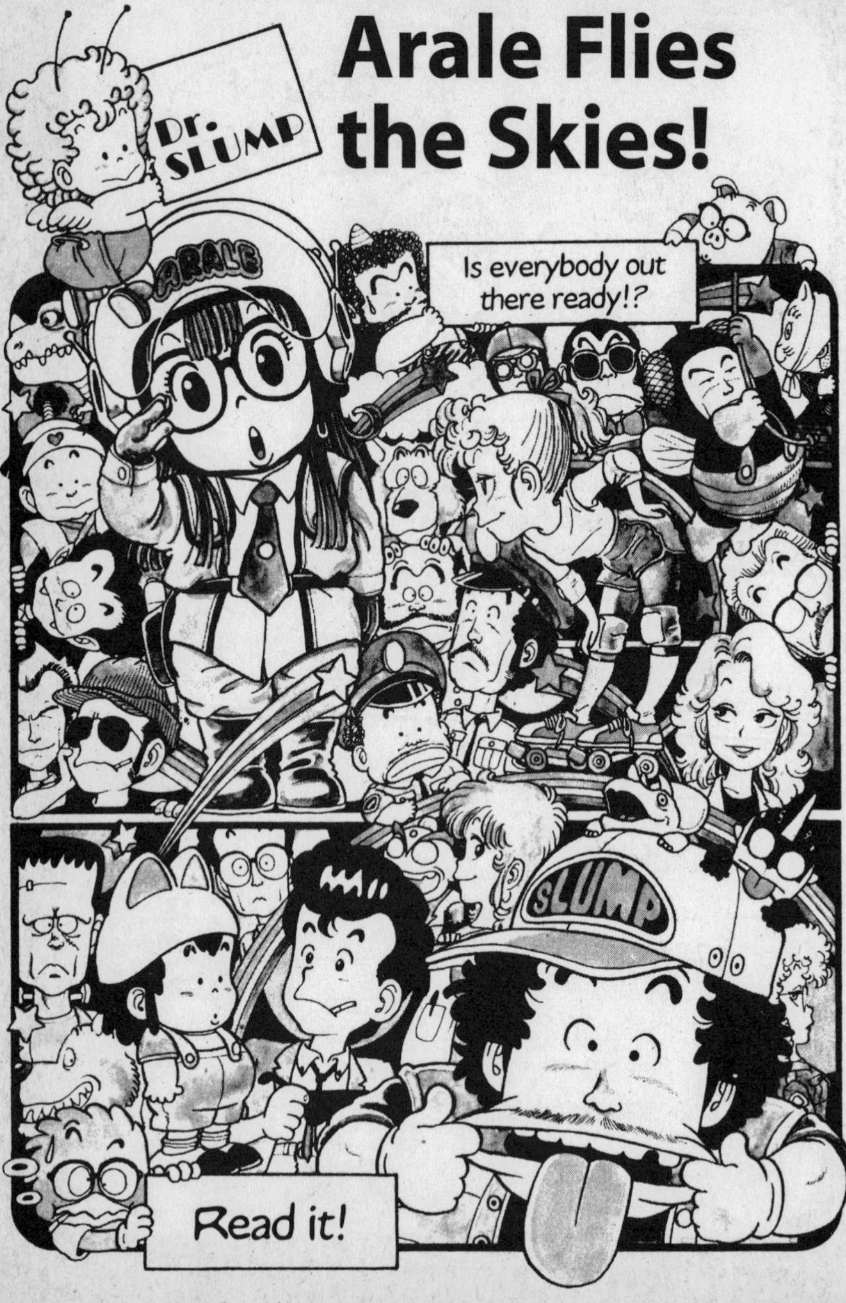
Dr. SLUMP
ARALE
Is everybody out there ready!?
SLUMP
Read it!

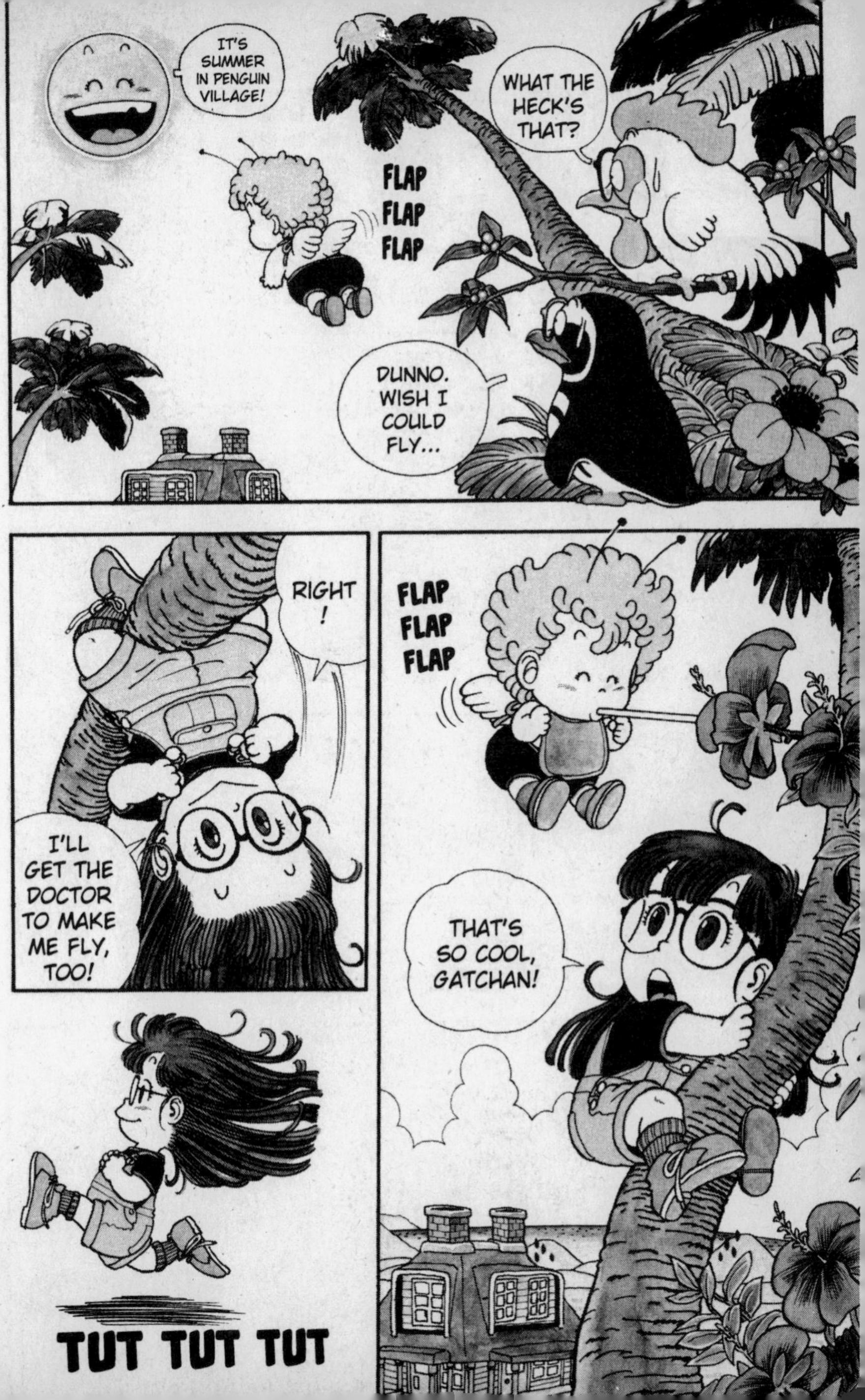
WHAT THE HECK'S THAT?
IT'S SUMMER IN PENGUIN VILLAGE!
FLAP FLAP FLAP
DUNNO. WISH I COULD FLY...
FLAP FLAP FLAP
THAT'S SO COOL, GATCHAN!
RIGHT!
I'LL GET THE DOCTOR TO MAKE ME FLY, TOO!
TUT TUT TUT

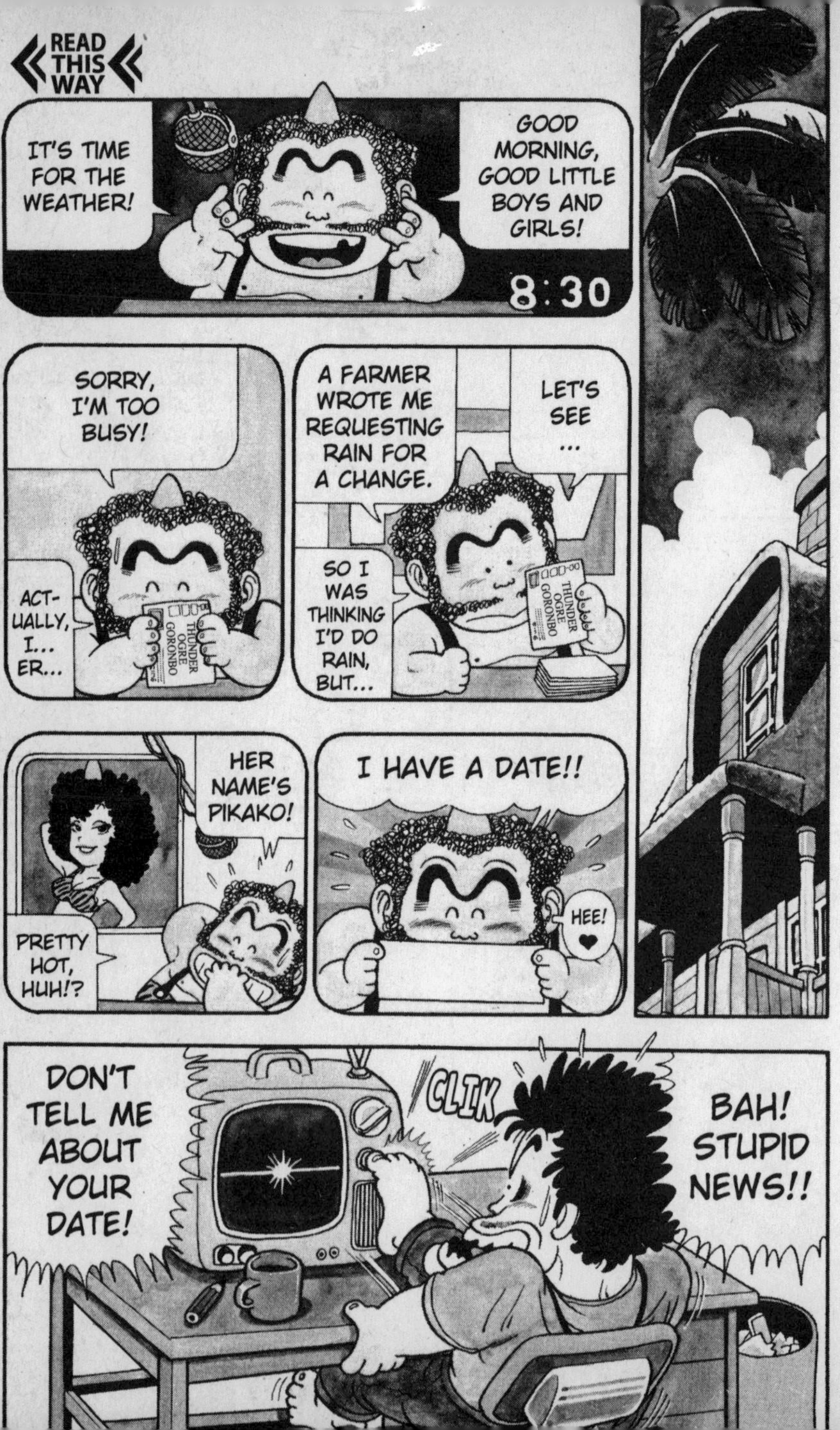
READ THIS WAY
GOOD MORNING, GOOD LITTLE BOYS AND GIRLS!
IT'S TIME FOR THE WEATHER!
8:30
LET'S SEE ...
A FARMER WROTE ME REQUESTING RAIN FOR A CHANGE.
SO I WAS THINKING I'D DO RAIN, BUT...
THUNDER OGRE GORONBO
SORRY, I'M TOO BUSY!
ACT-UALLY, I... ER...
THUNDER OGRE GORONBO
I HAVE A DATE!!
HEE! ♥
HER NAME'S PIKAKO!
PRETTY HOT, HUH!?
BAH! STUPID NEWS!!
CLIK
DON'T TELL ME ABOUT YOUR DATE!

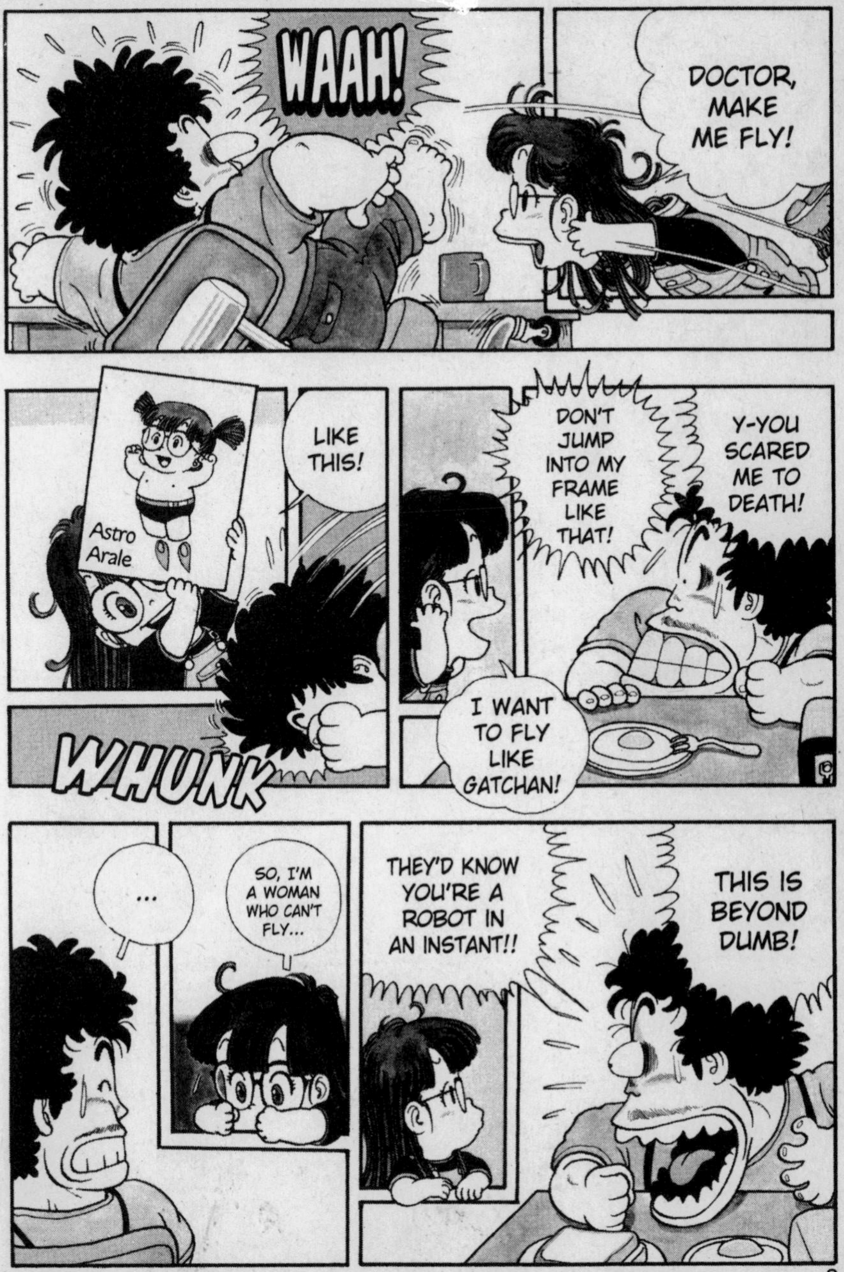
DOCTOR, MAKE ME FLY!
WAAH!
Y-YOU SCARED ME TO DEATH!
DON'T JUMP INTO MY FRAME LIKE THAT!
I WANT TO FLY LIKE GATCHAN!
LIKE THIS!
Astro Arale
WHUNK
THIS IS BEYOND DUMB!
THEY'D KNOW YOU'RE A ROBOT IN AN INSTANT!!
SO, I'M A WOMAN WHO CAN'T FLY...
...

READ THIS WAY

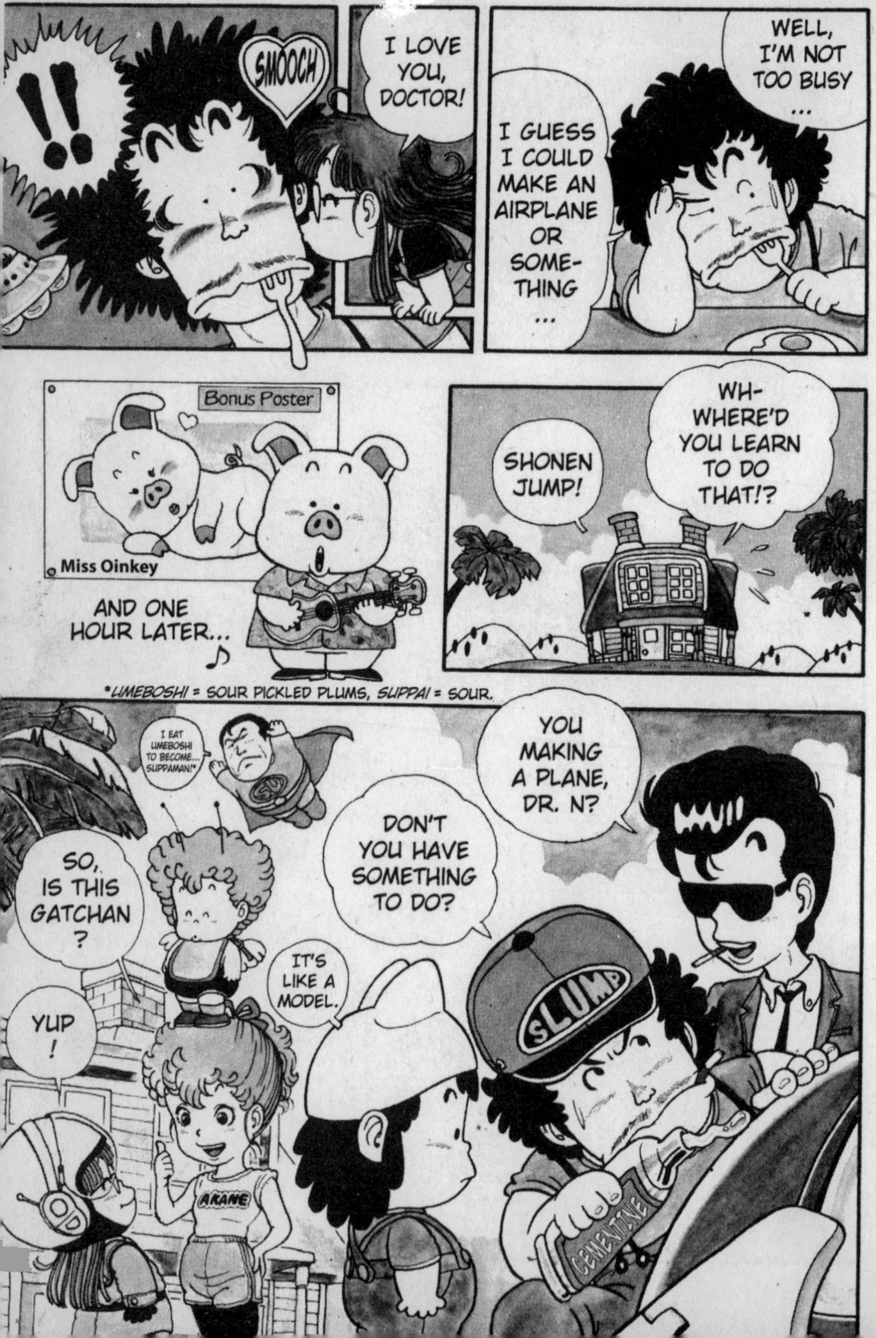
WELL, I'M NOT TOO BUSY ...
I GUESS I COULD MAKE AN AIRPLANE OR SOMETHING ...
I LOVE YOU, DOCTOR!
SMOOCH
!!
WH- WHERE'D YOU LEARN TO DO THAT!?
SHONEN JUMP!
Bonus Poster
Miss Oinkey
AND ONE HOUR LATER...
*UMEBOSHI = SOUR PICKLED PLUMS, SUPPAI = SOUR.
YOU MAKING A PLANE, DR. N?
DON'T YOU HAVE SOMETHING TO DO?
SLUMP
CEMENTINE
IT'S LIKE A MODEL.
I EAT UMEBOSHI TO BECOME... SUPPAMAN!*
SO, IS THIS GATCHAN ?
AKANE
YUP !

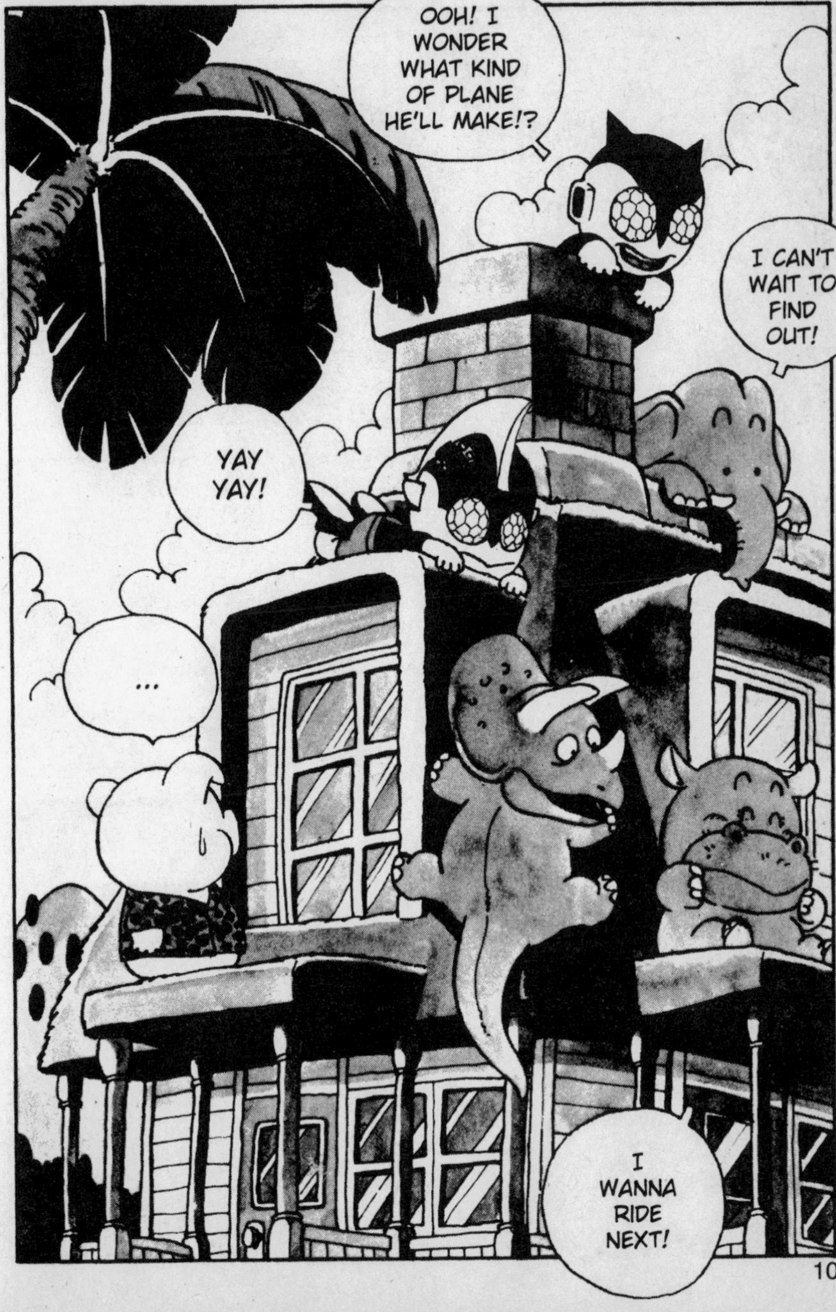
OOH! I WONDER WHAT KIND OF PLANE HE'LL MAKE!?
I CAN'T WAIT TO FIND OUT!
YAY YAY!
...
I WANNA RIDE NEXT!

READ THIS WAY

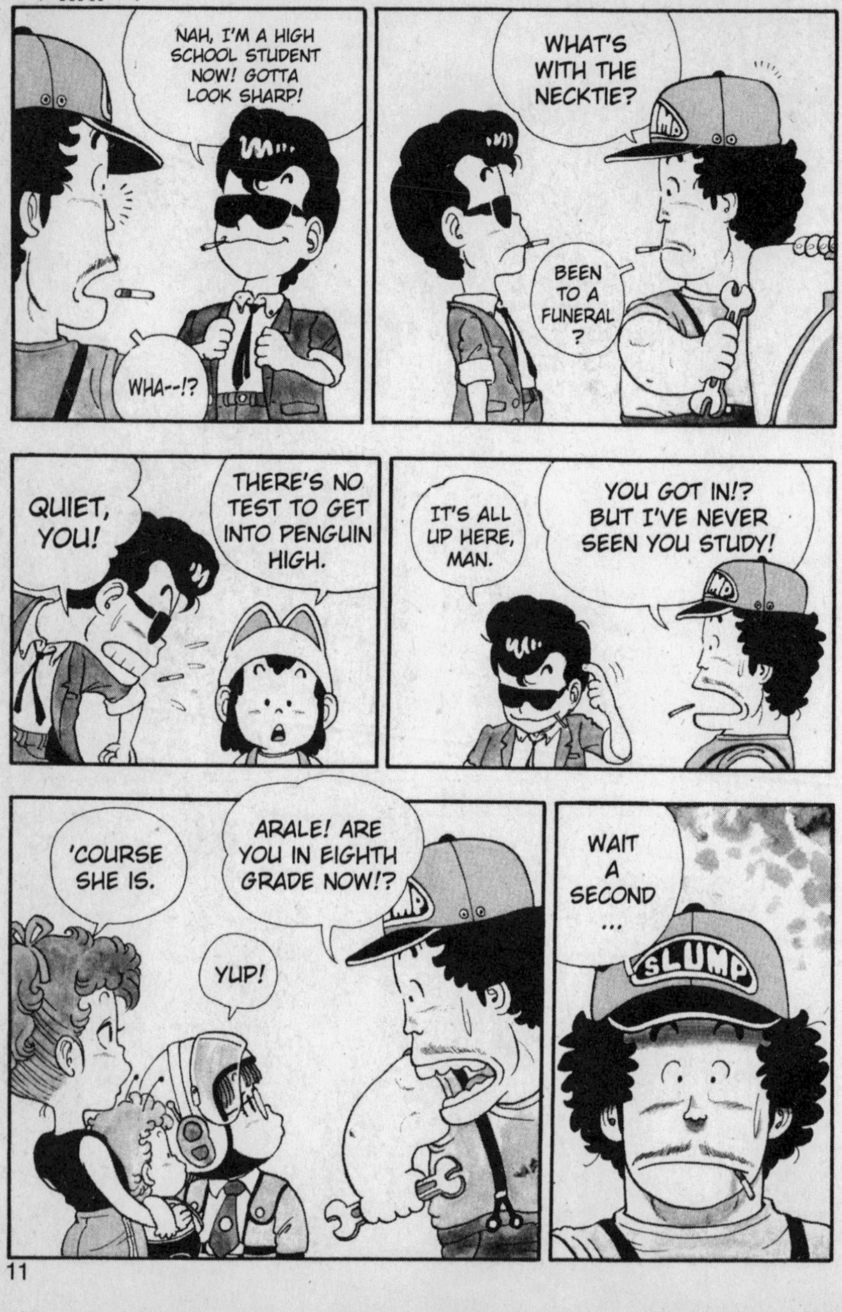
WHAT'S WITH THE NECKTIE?
BEEN TO A FUNERAL?
NAH, I'M A HIGH SCHOOL STUDENT NOW! GOTTA LOOK SHARP!
WHA--!?
YOU GOT IN!? BUT I'VE NEVER SEEN YOU STUDY!
IT'S ALL UP HERE, MAN.
THERE'S NO TEST TO GET INTO PENGUIN HIGH.
QUIET, YOU!
WAIT A SECOND ...
SLUMP
ARALE! ARE YOU IN EIGHTH GRADE NOW!?
'COURSE SHE IS.
YUP!

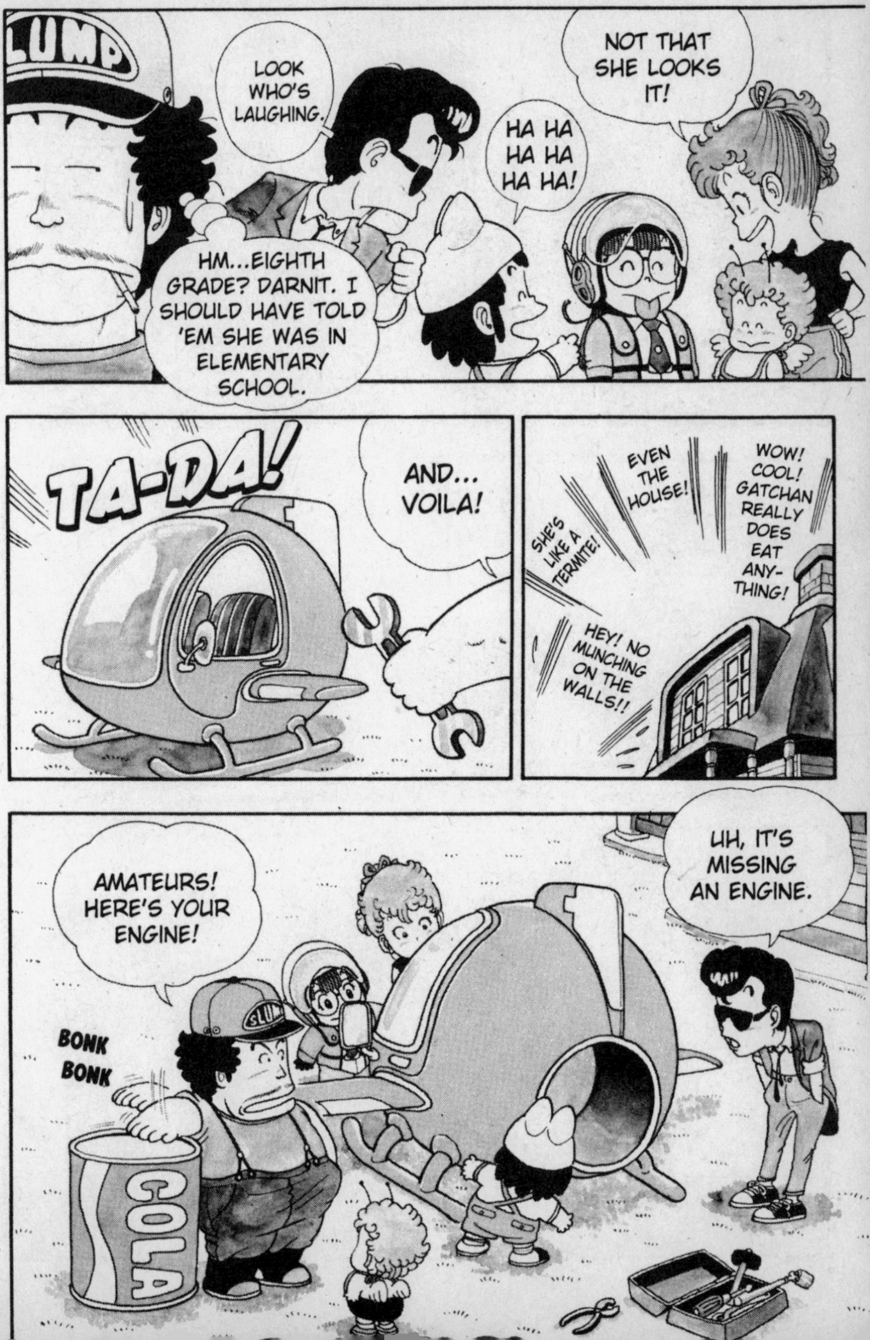
NOT THAT SHE LOOKS IT!
HA HA HA HA HA HA!
LOOK WHO'S LAUGHING.
HM...EIGHTH GRADE? DARNIT. I SHOULD HAVE TOLD 'EM SHE WAS IN ELEMENTARY SCHOOL.
WOW! COOL! GATCHAN REALLY DOES EAT ANY-THING!
EVEN THE HOUSE!
SHE'S LIKE A TERMITE!
HEY! NO MUNCHING ON THE WALLS!!
AND... VOILA!
TA-DA!
UH, IT'S MISSING AN ENGINE.
AMATEURS! HERE'S YOUR ENGINE!
BONK BONK
COLA

READ THIS WAY

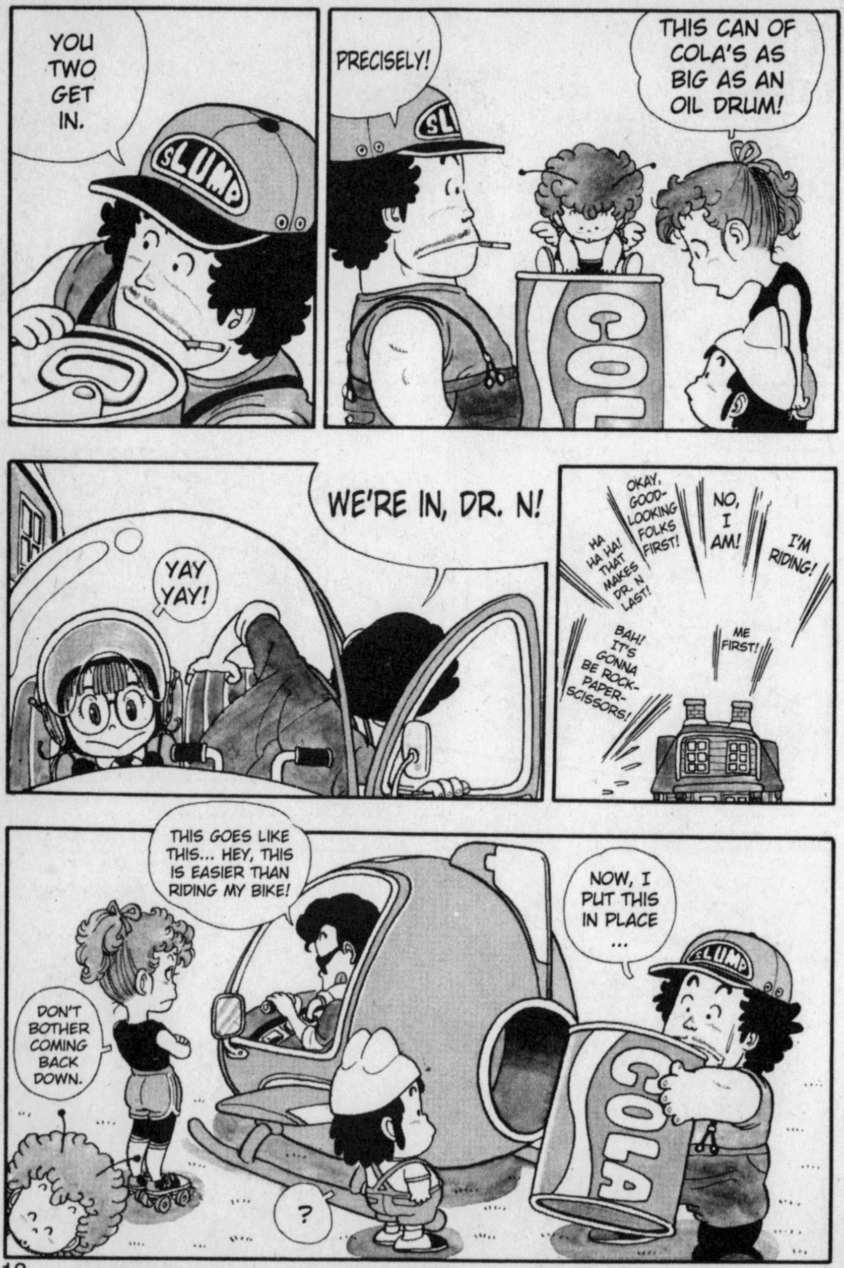
THIS CAN OF COLA'S AS BIG AS AN OIL DRUM!
PRECISELY!
YOU TWO GET IN.
I'M RIDING!
NO, I AM!
OKAY, GOOD-LOOKING FOLKS FIRST!
HA HA HA! THAT MAKES DR. N LAST!
ME FIRST!
BAH! IT'S GONNA BE ROCK-PAPER-SCISSORS!
WE'RE IN, DR. N!
YAY YAY!
NOW, I PUT THIS IN PLACE ...
THIS GOES LIKE THIS... HEY, THIS IS EASIER THAN RIDING MY BIKE!
?
DON'T BOTHER COMING BACK DOWN.

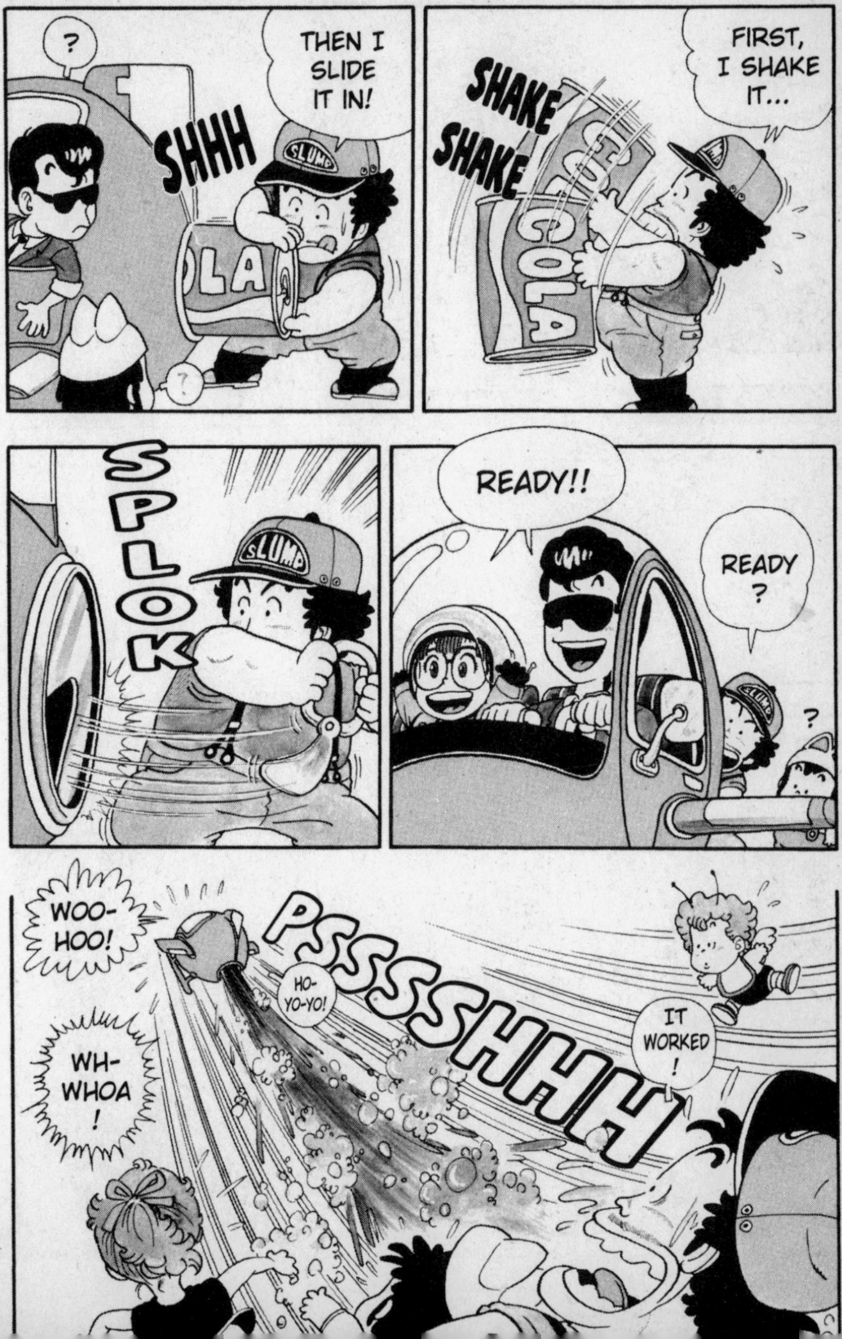
FIRST, I SHAKE IT...
SHAKE SHAKE
COLA
THEN I SLIDE IT IN!
SHHH
?
?
SLUMP
READY?
READY!!
?
SPLOK
SLUMP
IT WORKED!
PSSSSHHHH
HO-YO-YO!
WOO-HOO!
WH-WHOA!

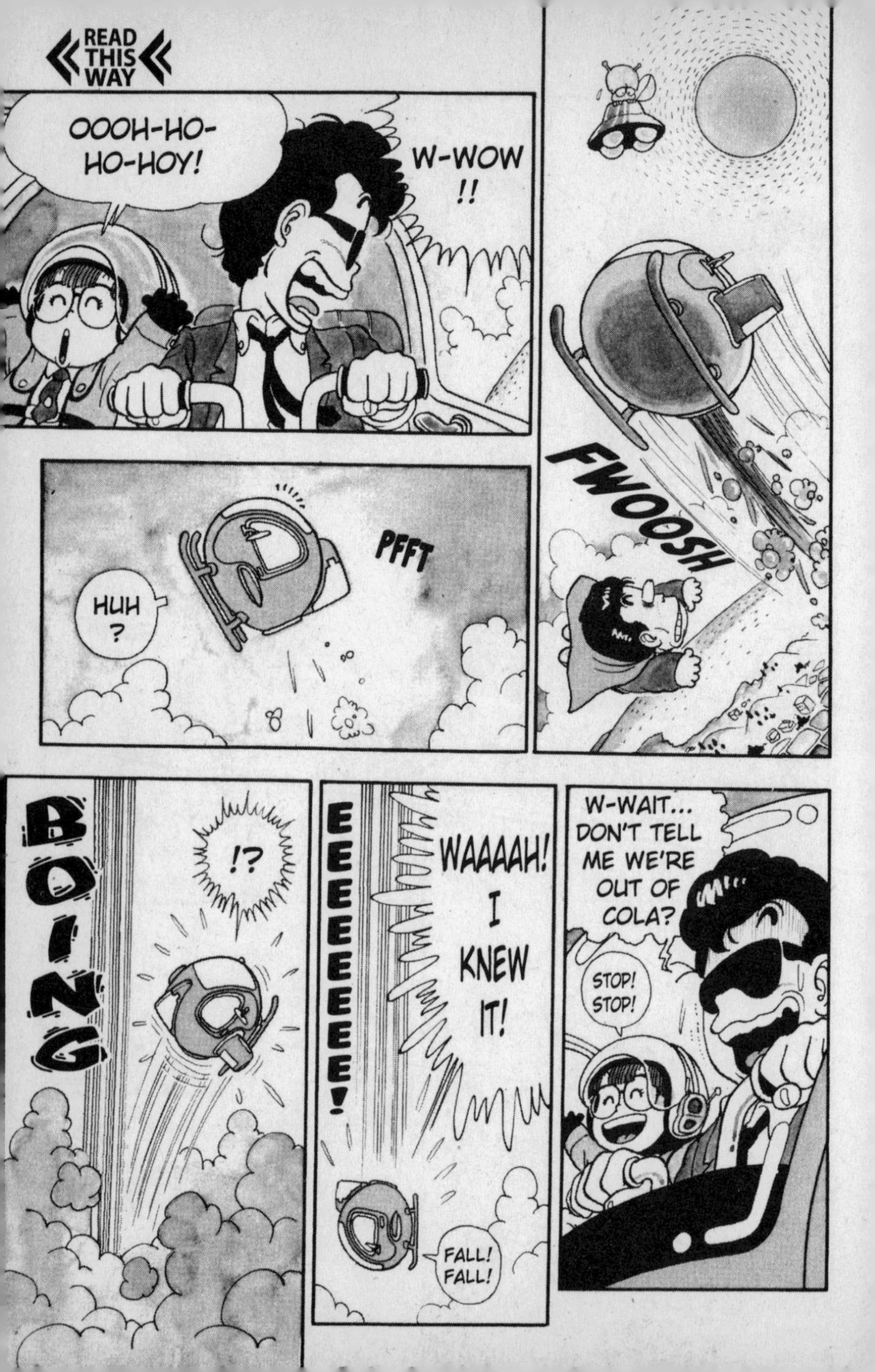
READ THIS WAY
FWOOSH
W-WOW !!
OOOH-HO-HO-HOY!
PFFT
HUH ?
W-WAIT... DON'T TELL ME WE'RE OUT OF COLA?
STOP! STOP!
WAAAAH! I KNEW IT!
EEEEEEEEEEE!
FALL! FALL!
!?
BOING

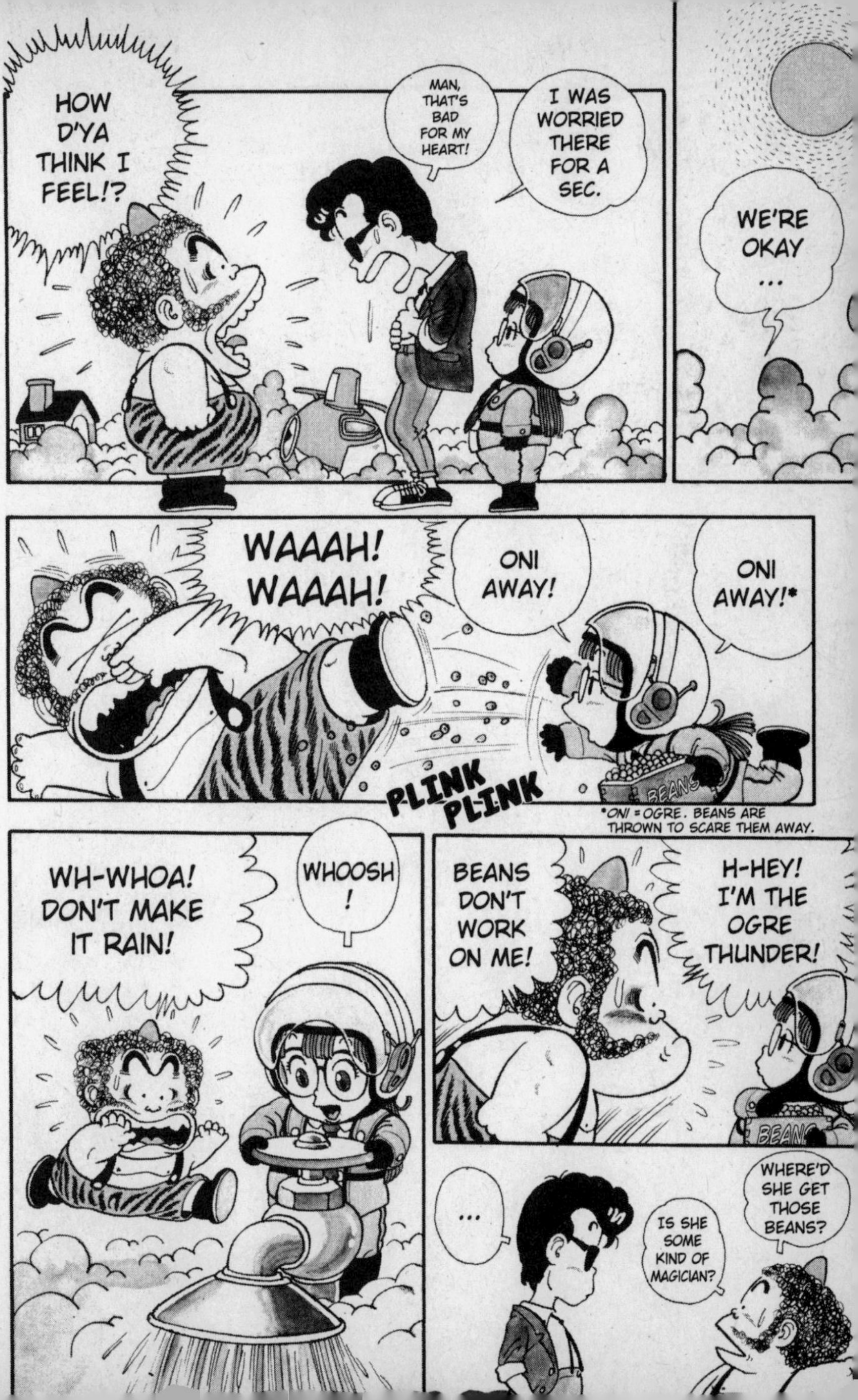
WE'RE OKAY ...
I WAS WORRIED THERE FOR A SEC.
MAN, THAT'S BAD FOR MY HEART!
HOW D'YA THINK I FEEL!?
ONI AWAY!*
ONI AWAY!
WAAAH! WAAAH!
BEANS
P-LINK PL-INK
H-HEY! I'M THE OGRE THUNDER!
BEANS DON'T WORK ON ME!
BEANS
WHERE'D SHE GET THOSE BEANS?
IS SHE SOME KIND OF MAGICIAN?
...
WHOOSH!
WH-WHOA! DON'T MAKE IT RAIN!

*ONI = OGRE. BEANS ARE THROWN TO SCARE THEM AWAY.

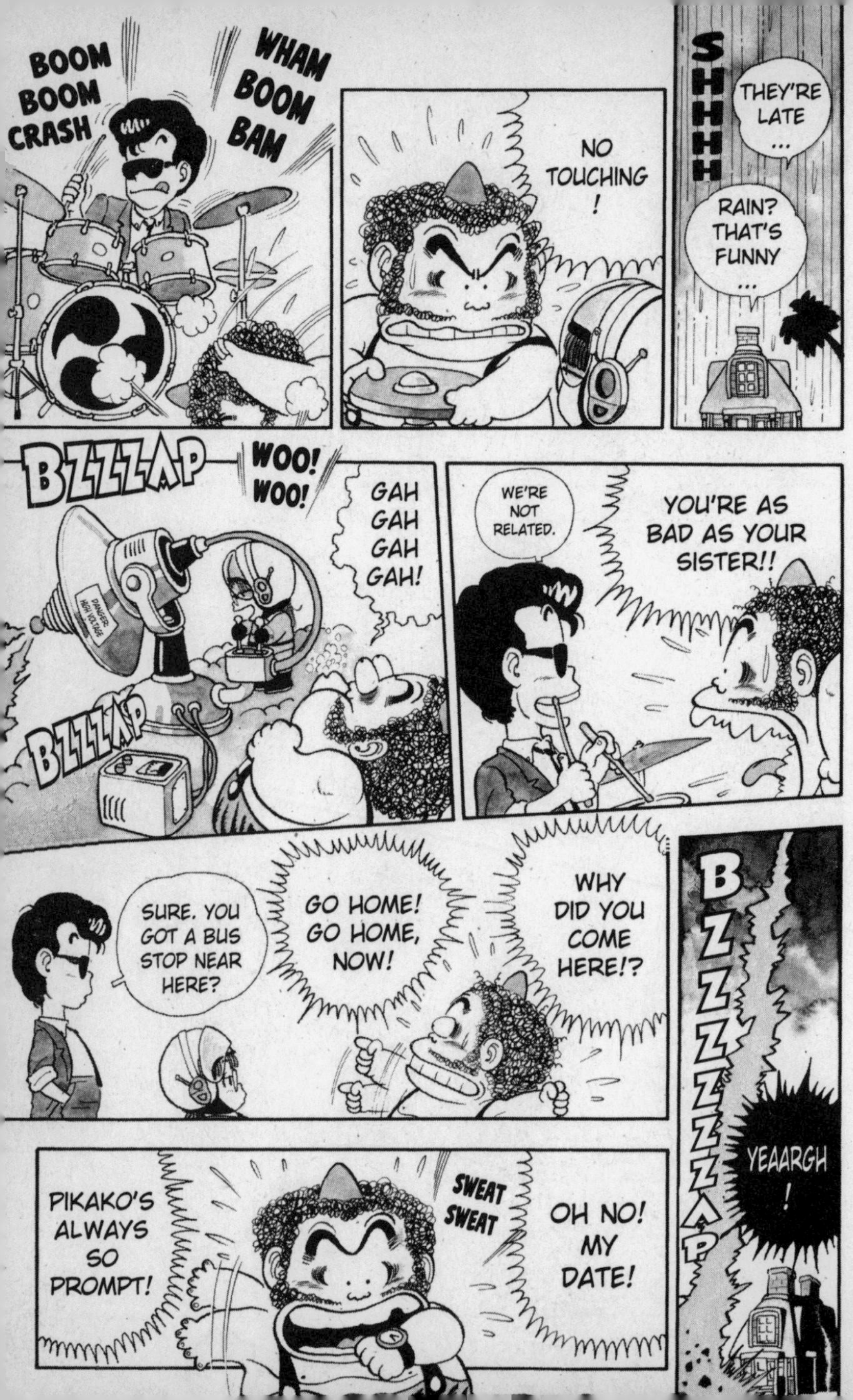
SHHHH
THEY'RE LATE ...
RAIN? THAT'S FUNNY ...
NO TOUCHING !
BOOM BOOM CRASH
WHAM BOOM BAM
YOU'RE AS BAD AS YOUR SISTER!!
WE'RE NOT RELATED.
GAH GAH GAH GAH!
WOO! WOO!
BZZZAP
DANGER HIGH VOLTAGE
BZZZAP
BZZZZZZZAP
YEAARGH !
WHY DID YOU COME HERE!?
GO HOME! GO HOME, NOW!
SURE. YOU GOT A BUS STOP NEAR HERE?
OH NO! MY DATE!
SWEAT SWEAT
PIKAKO'S ALWAYS SO PROMPT!

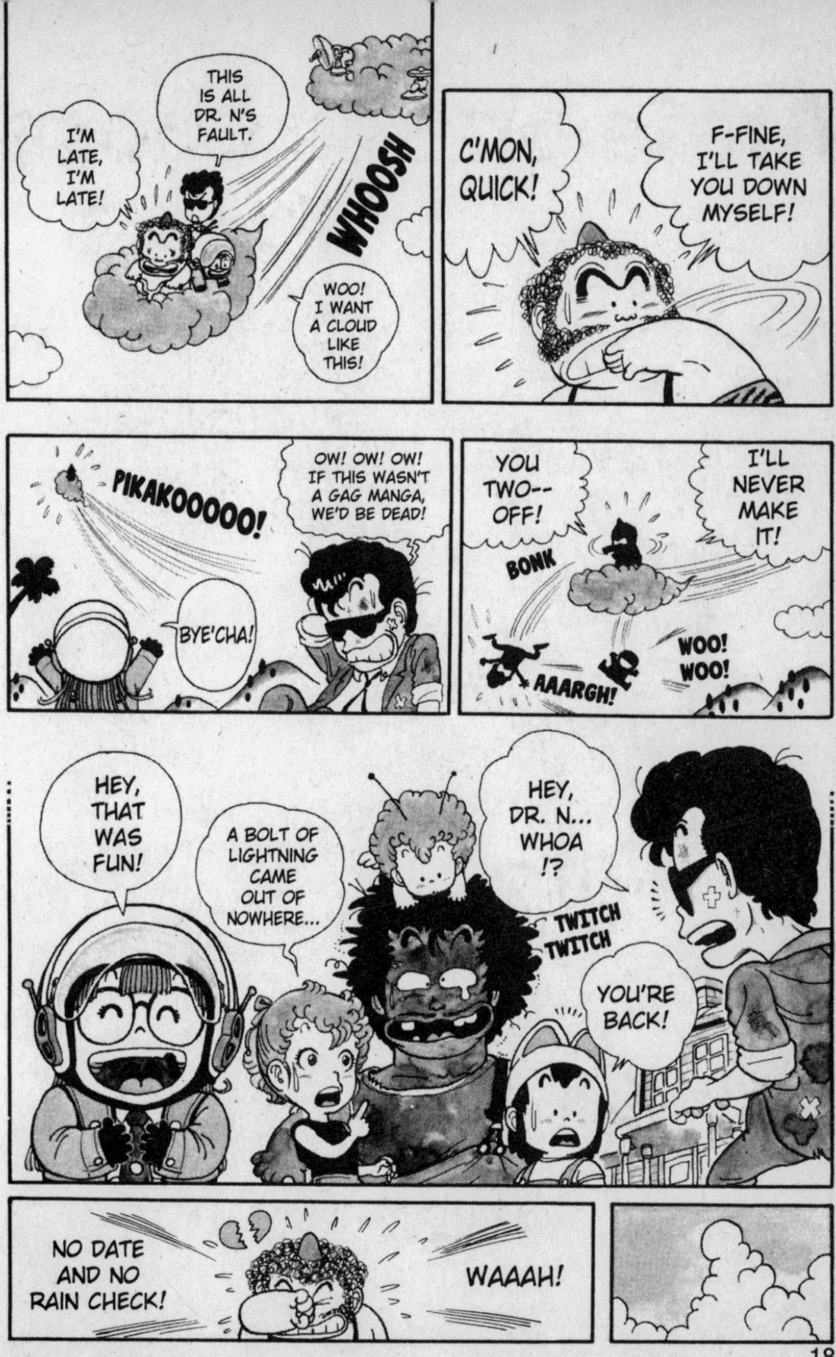

F-FINE, I'LL TAKE YOU DOWN MYSELF!
C'MON, QUICK!
THIS IS ALL DR. N'S FAULT.
I'M LATE, I'M LATE!
WHOOSH
WOO! I WANT A CLOUD LIKE THIS!
I'LL NEVER MAKE IT!
YOU TWO-- OFF!
BONK
WOO! WOO!
AAARGH!
OW! OW! OW! IF THIS WASN'T A GAG MANGA, WE'D BE DEAD!
PIKAKOOOOO!
BYE'CHA!
HEY, DR. N... WHOA !?
TWITCH TWITCH
YOU'RE BACK!
A BOLT OF LIGHTNING CAME OUT OF NOWHERE...
HEY, THAT WAS FUN!
WAAAH!
NO DATE AND NO RAIN CHECK!

Arale on the Loose Part 1

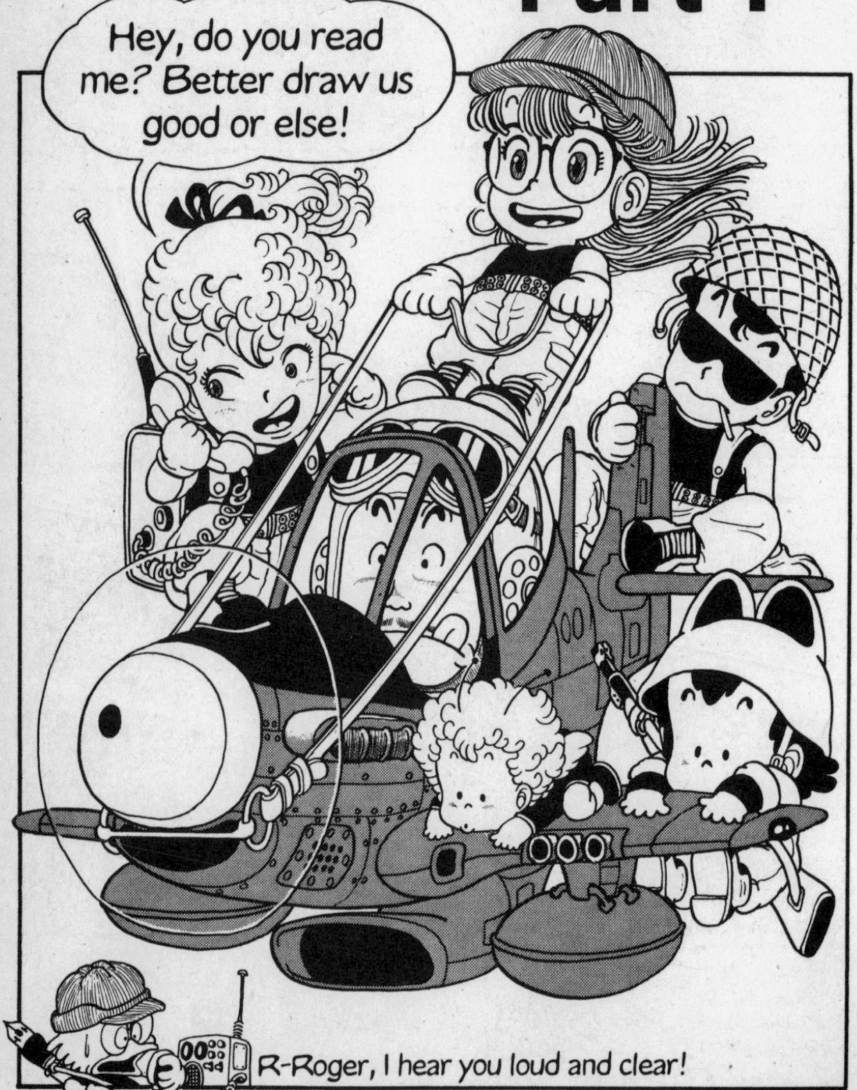
Hey, do you read me? Better draw us good or else!
R-Roger, I hear you loud and clear!

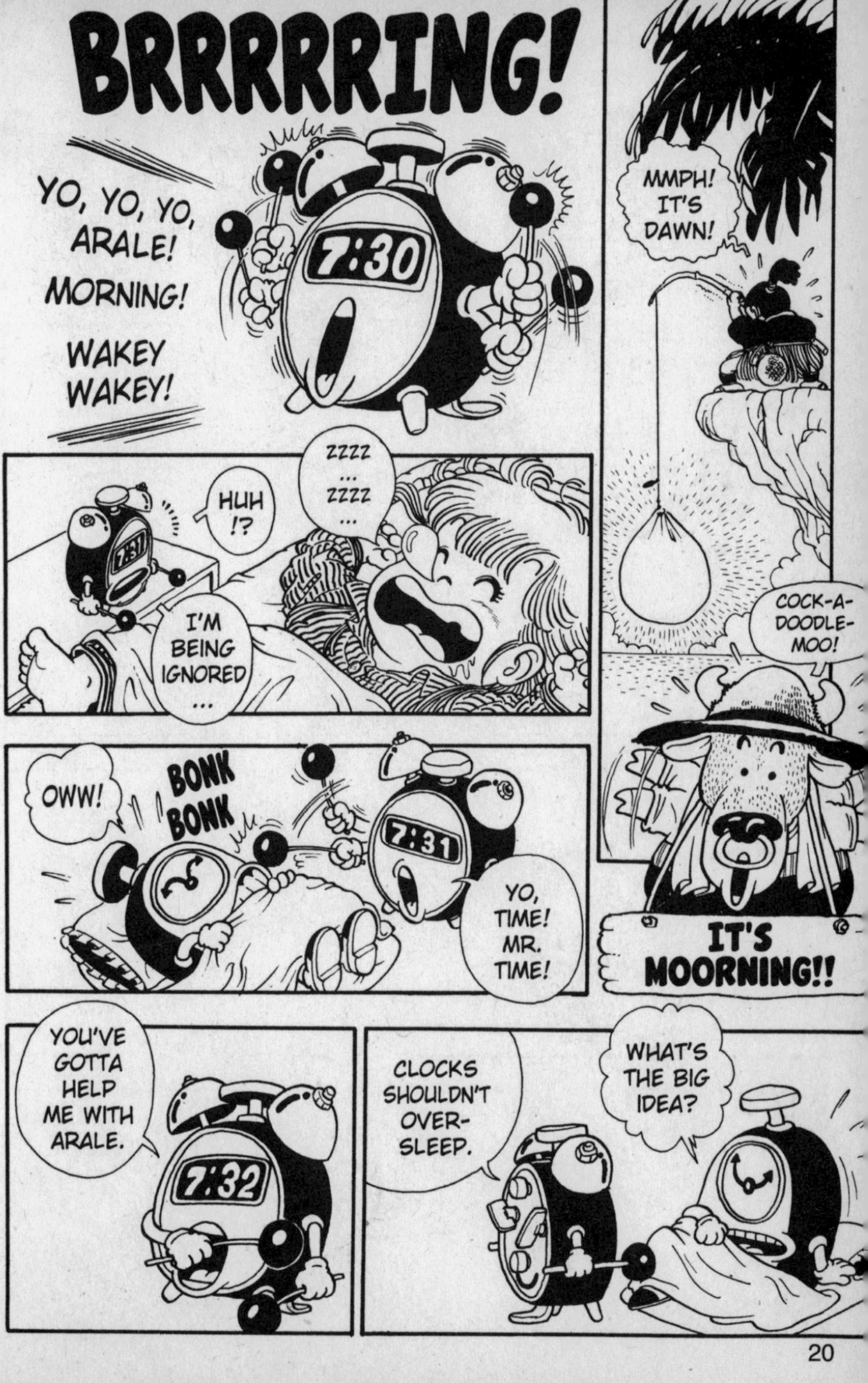
MMPH! IT'S DAWN!
COCK-A-DOODLE-MOO!
IT'S MOORNING!!
BRRRRRING!
YO, YO, YO, ARALE!
MORNING!
WAKEY WAKEY!
ZZZZ ... ZZZZ ...
HUH !?
I'M BEING IGNORED ...
YO, TIME! MR. TIME!
BONK BONK
OWW!
WHAT'S THE BIG IDEA?
CLOCKS SHOULDN'T OVER-SLEEP.
YOU'VE GOTTA HELP ME WITH ARALE.

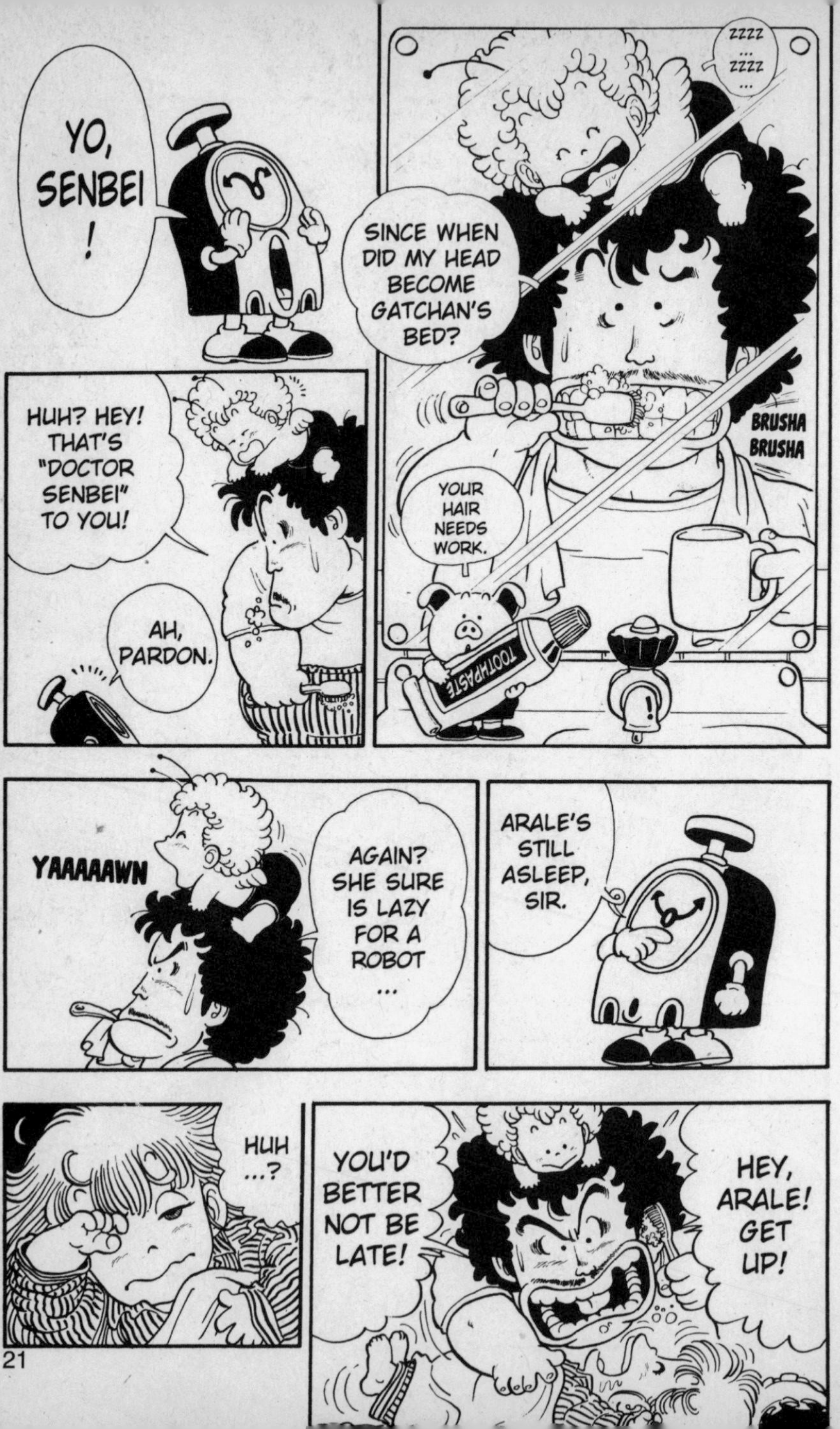
ZZZZ ... ZZZZ ...
SINCE WHEN DID MY HEAD BECOME GATCHAN'S BED?
BRUSHA BRUSHA
YOUR HAIR NEEDS WORK.
YO, SENBEI!
HUH? HEY! THAT'S "DOCTOR SENBEI" TO YOU!
AH, PARDON.
ARALE'S STILL ASLEEP, SIR.
AGAIN? SHE SURE IS LAZY FOR A ROBOT ...
YAAAAAWN
HEY, ARALE! GET UP!
YOU'D BETTER NOT BE LATE!
HUH ...?

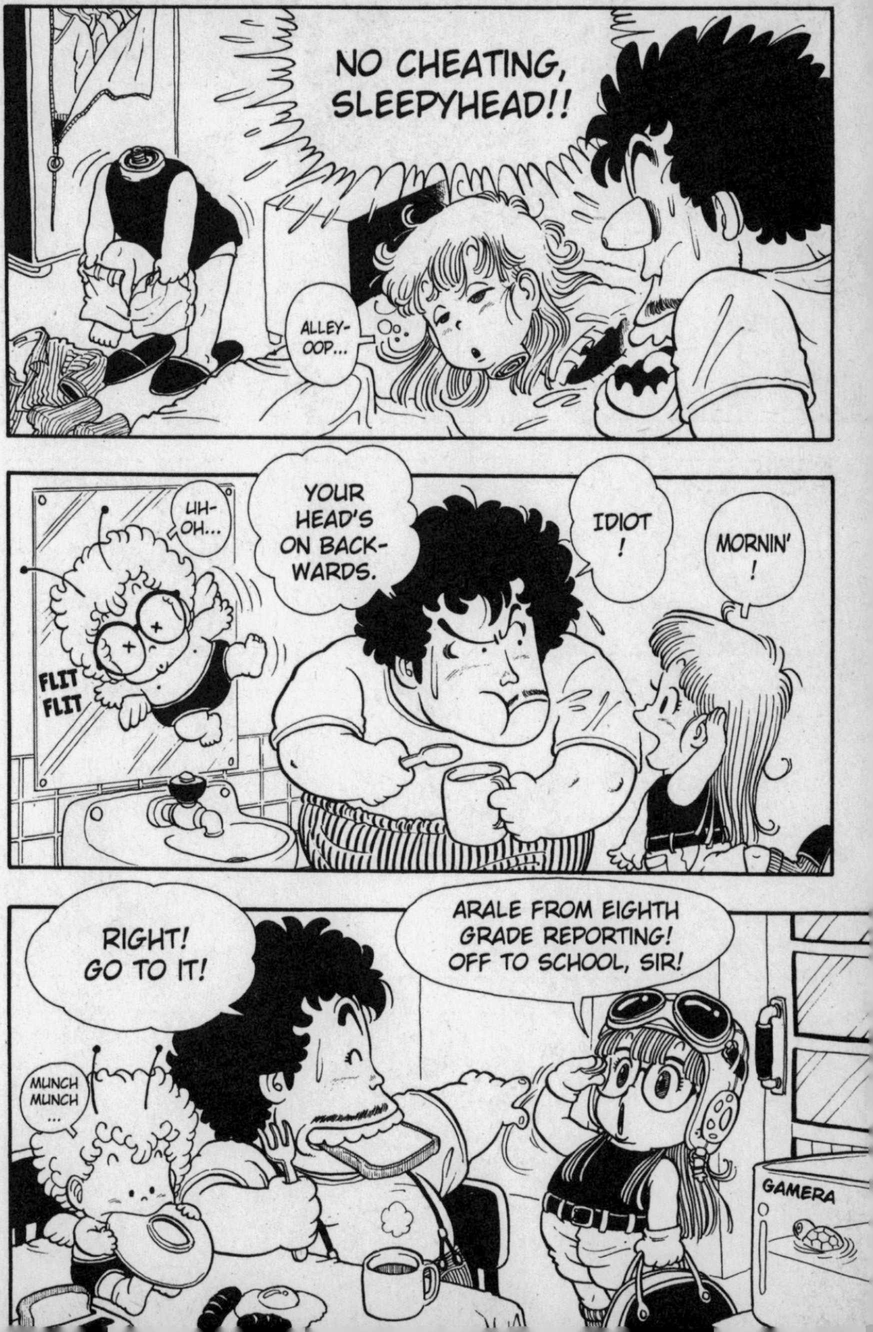
NO CHEATING, SLEEPYHEAD!!
ALLEY-OOP...
MORNIN'!
IDIOT!
YOUR HEAD'S ON BACK-WARDS.
UH-OH...
FLIT FLIT
ARALE FROM EIGHTH GRADE REPORTING! OFF TO SCHOOL, SIR!
RIGHT! GO TO IT!
GAMERA
MUNCH MUNCH ...

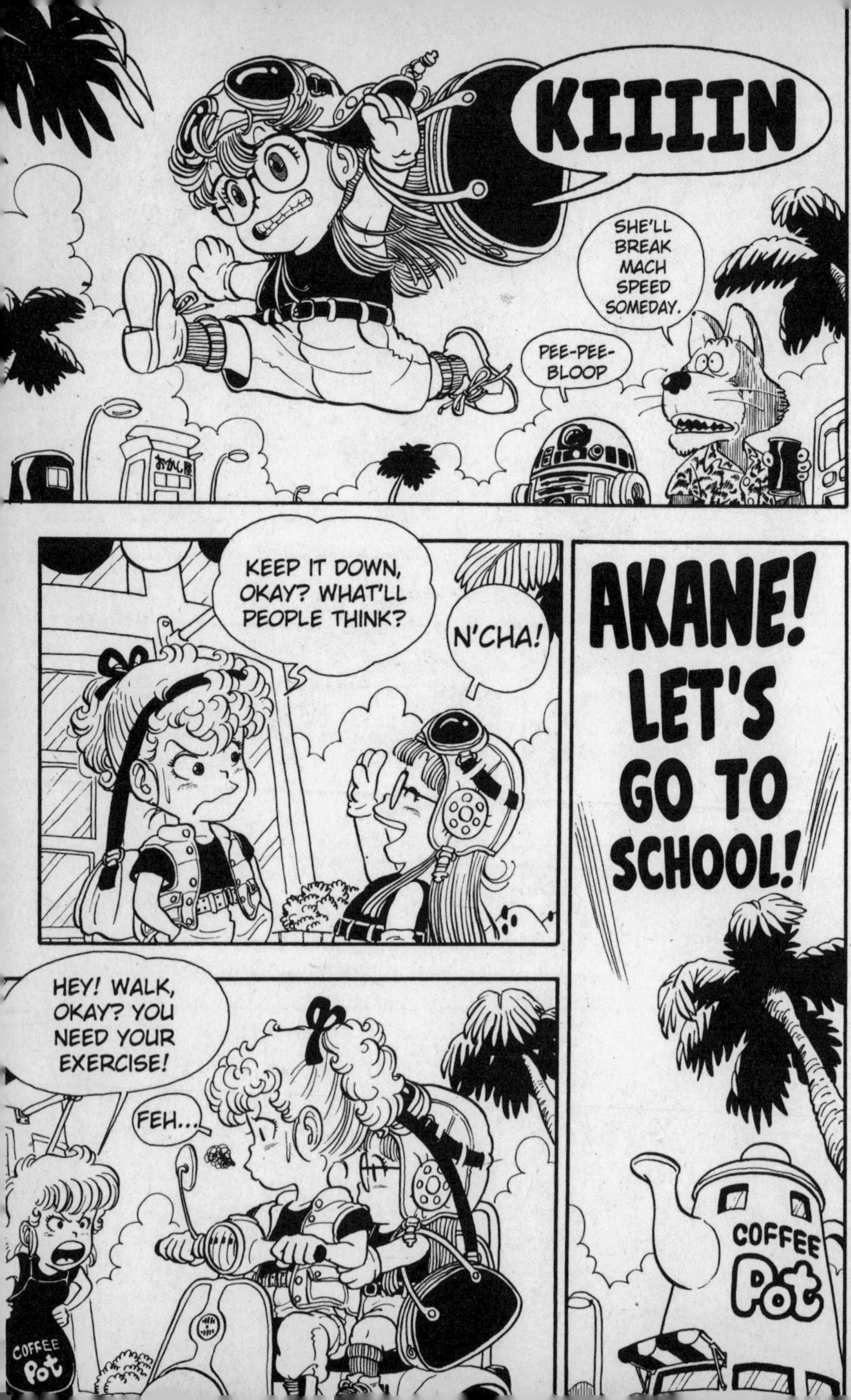

KIIIN
SHE'LL BREAK MACH SPEED SOMEDAY.
PEE-PEE-BLOOP
おかし屋
AKANE! LET'S GO TO SCHOOL!
COFFEE Pot
KEEP IT DOWN, OKAY? WHAT'LL PEOPLE THINK?
N'CHA!
HEY! WALK, OKAY? YOU NEED YOUR EXERCISE!
FEH...
COFFEE Pot

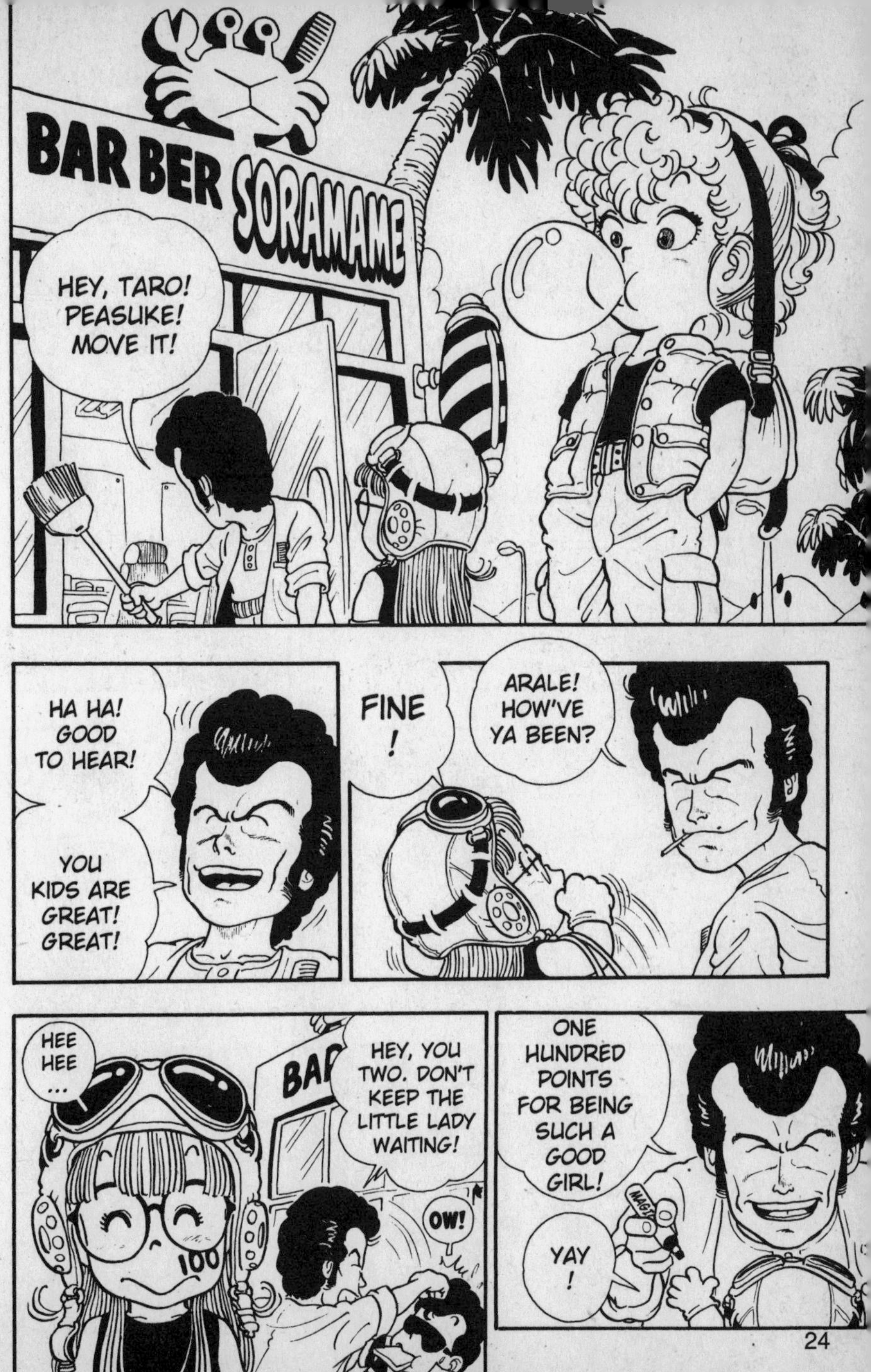
BAR BER SORAMAME
HEY, TARO! PEASUKE! MOVE IT!
ARALE! HOW'VE YA BEEN?
FINE!
HA HA! GOOD TO HEAR!
YOU KIDS ARE GREAT! GREAT!
ONE HUNDRED POINTS FOR BEING SUCH A GOOD GIRL!
YAY!
HEY, YOU TWO. DON'T KEEP THE LITTLE LADY WAITING!
HEE HEE ...
OW!
100

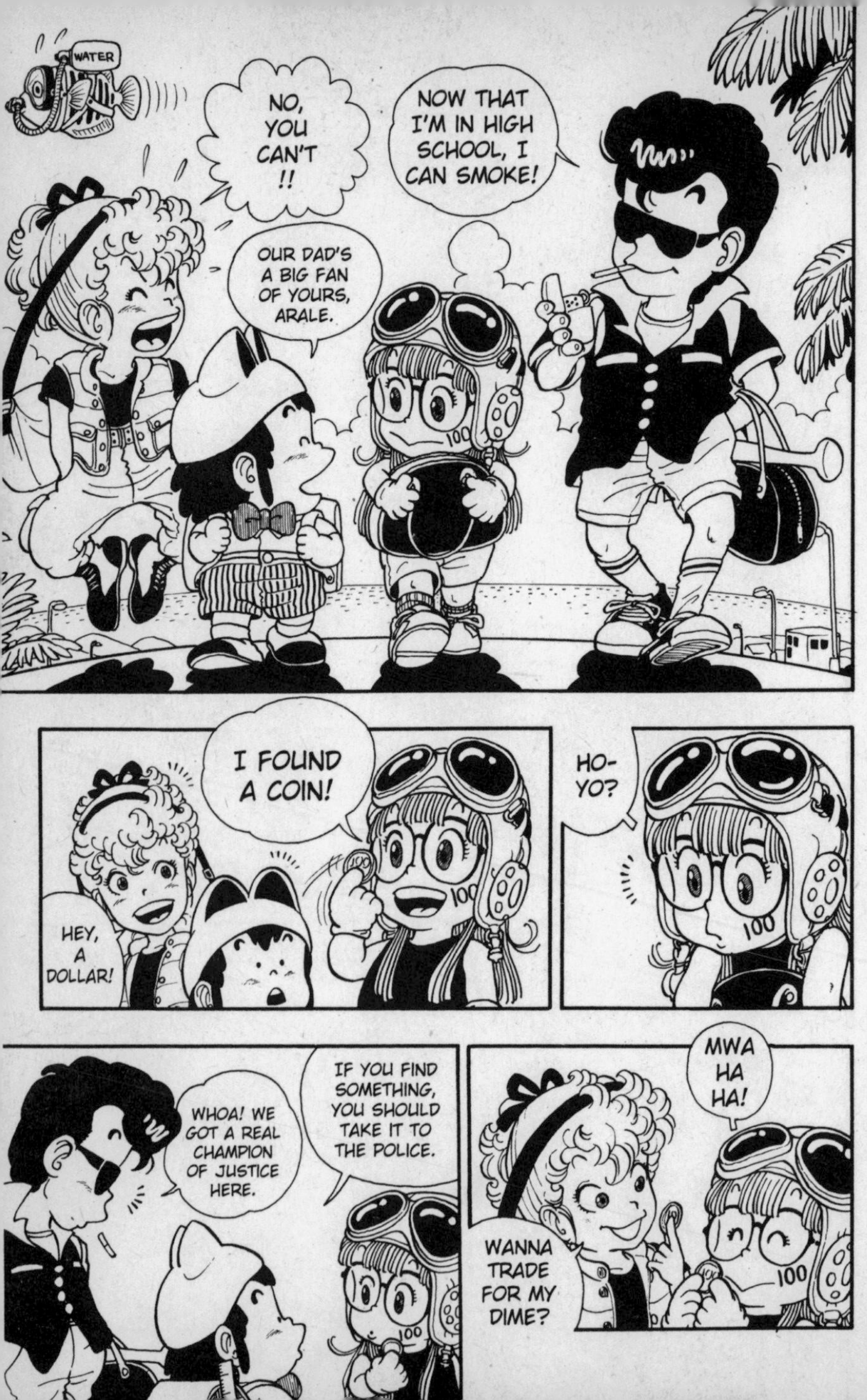
NOW THAT I'M IN HIGH SCHOOL, I CAN SMOKE!
NO, YOU CAN'T !!
WATER
OUR DAD'S A BIG FAN OF YOURS, ARALE.
HO-YO?
I FOUND A COIN!
HEY, A DOLLAR!
MWA HA HA!
WANNA TRADE FOR MY DIME?
IF YOU FIND SOMETHING, YOU SHOULD TAKE IT TO THE POLICE.
WHOA! WE GOT A REAL CHAMPION OF JUSTICE HERE.

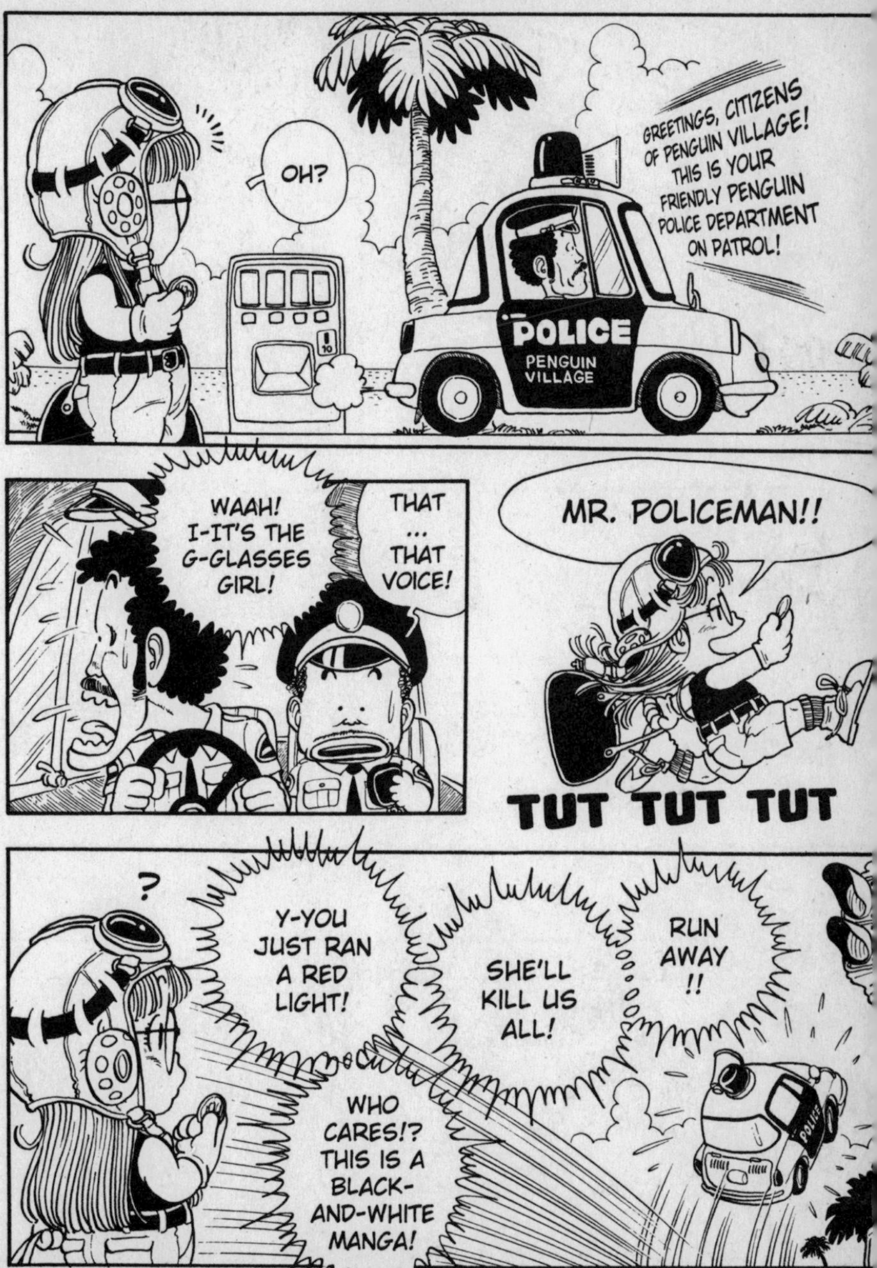
GREETINGS, CITIZENS OF PENGUIN VILLAGE! THIS IS YOUR FRIENDLY PENGUIN POLICE DEPARTMENT ON PATROL!
POLICE
PENGUIN VILLAGE
OH?
MR. POLICEMAN!!
TUT TUT TUT
THAT ... THAT VOICE!
WAAH! I-IT'S THE G-GLASSES GIRL!
RUN AWAY !!
SHE'LL KILL US ALL!
Y-YOU JUST RAN A RED LIGHT!
WHO CARES!? THIS IS A BLACK-AND-WHITE MANGA!
?

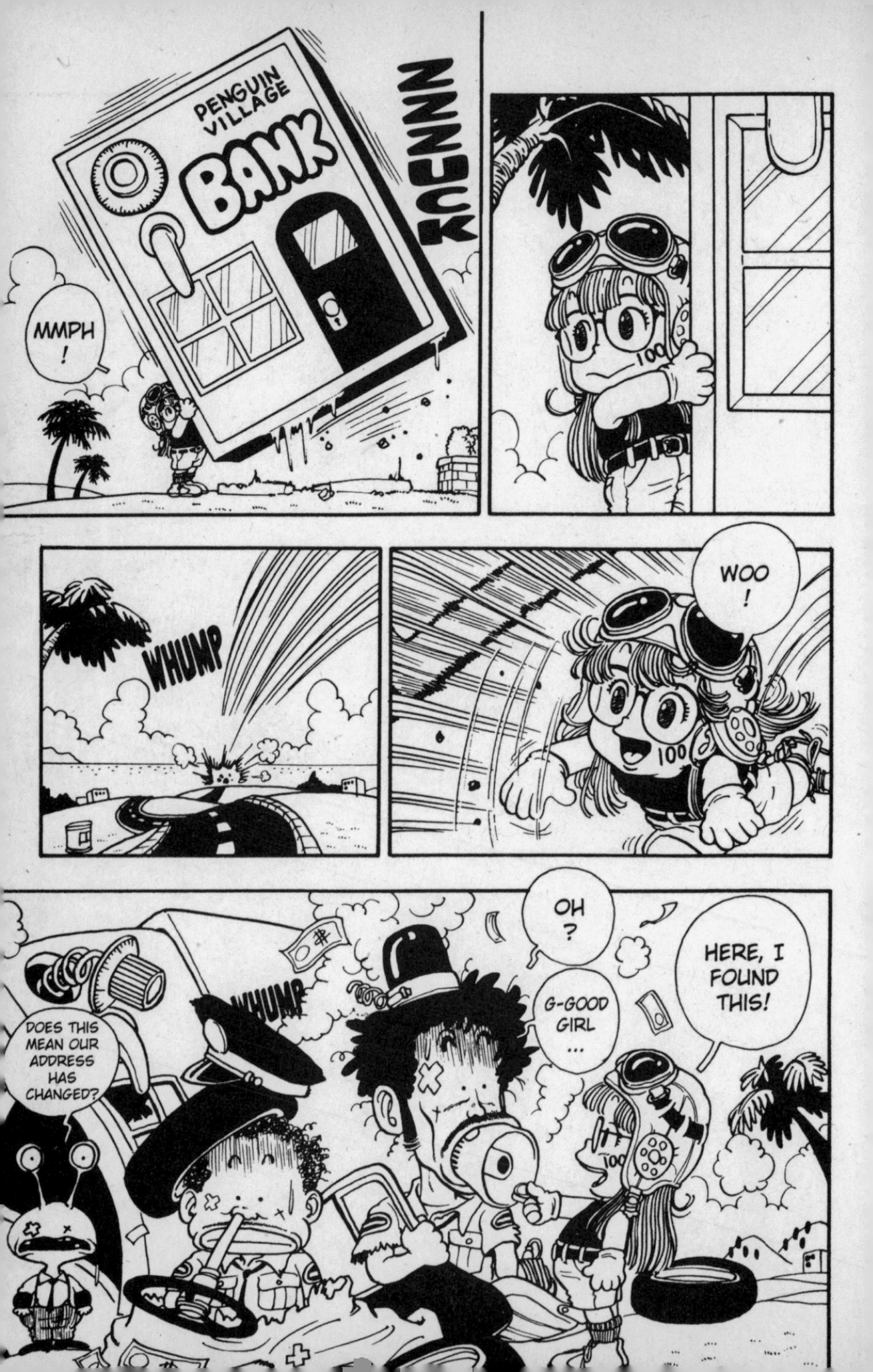
PENGUIN VILLAGE
BANK
MMPH!
WOO!
WHUMP
HERE, I FOUND THIS!
OH?
G-GOOD GIRL...
WHUMP
DOES THIS MEAN OUR ADDRESS HAS CHANGED?

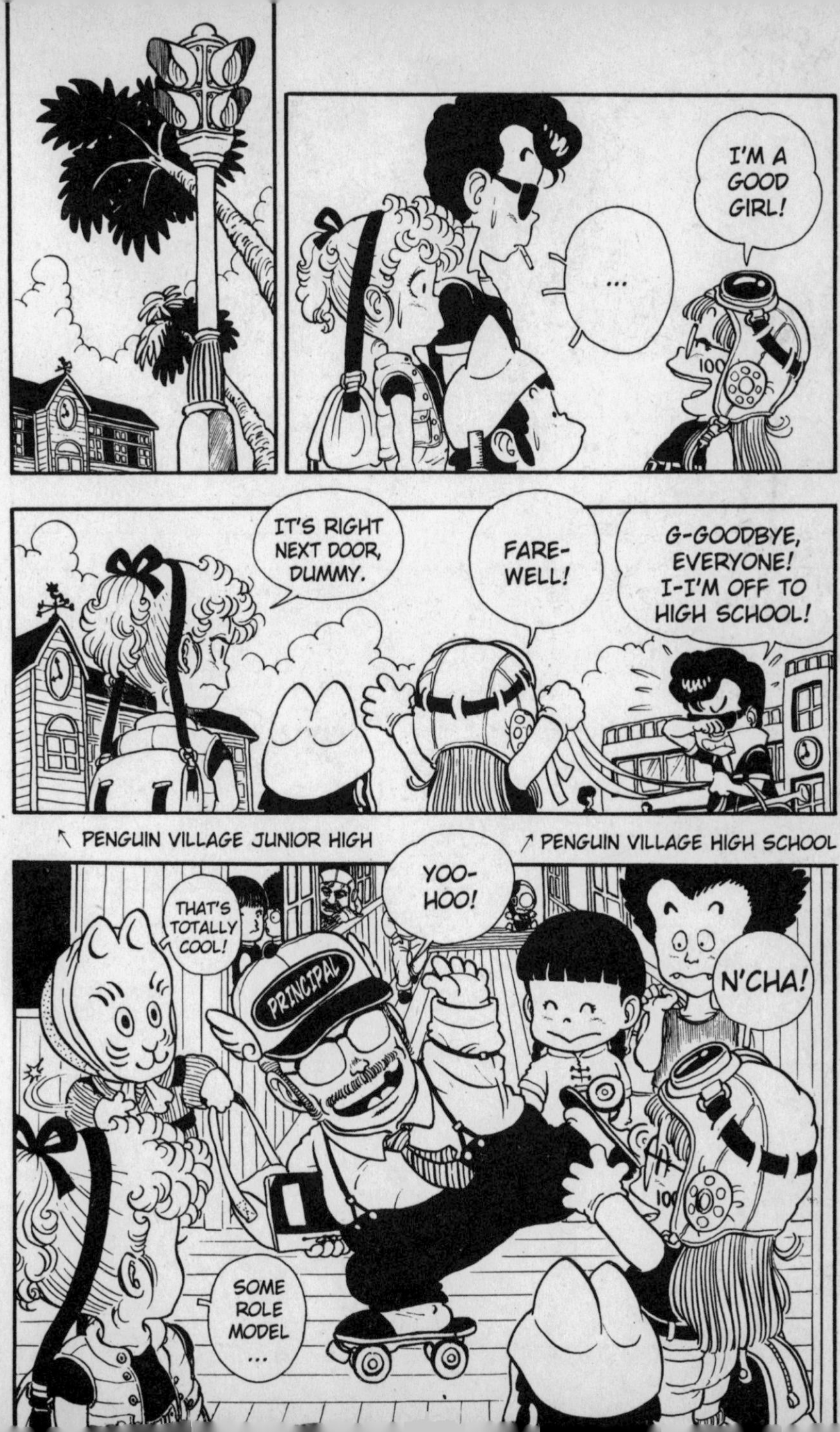
I'M A GOOD GIRL!
...
G-GOODBYE, EVERYONE! I-I'M OFF TO HIGH SCHOOL!
FARE-WELL!
IT'S RIGHT NEXT DOOR, DUMMY.
↗ PENGUIN VILLAGE HIGH SCHOOL
↖ PENGUIN VILLAGE JUNIOR HIGH
N'CHA!
YOO-HOO!
THAT'S TOTALLY COOL!
PRINCIPAL
SOME ROLE MODEL ...

READ THIS WAY

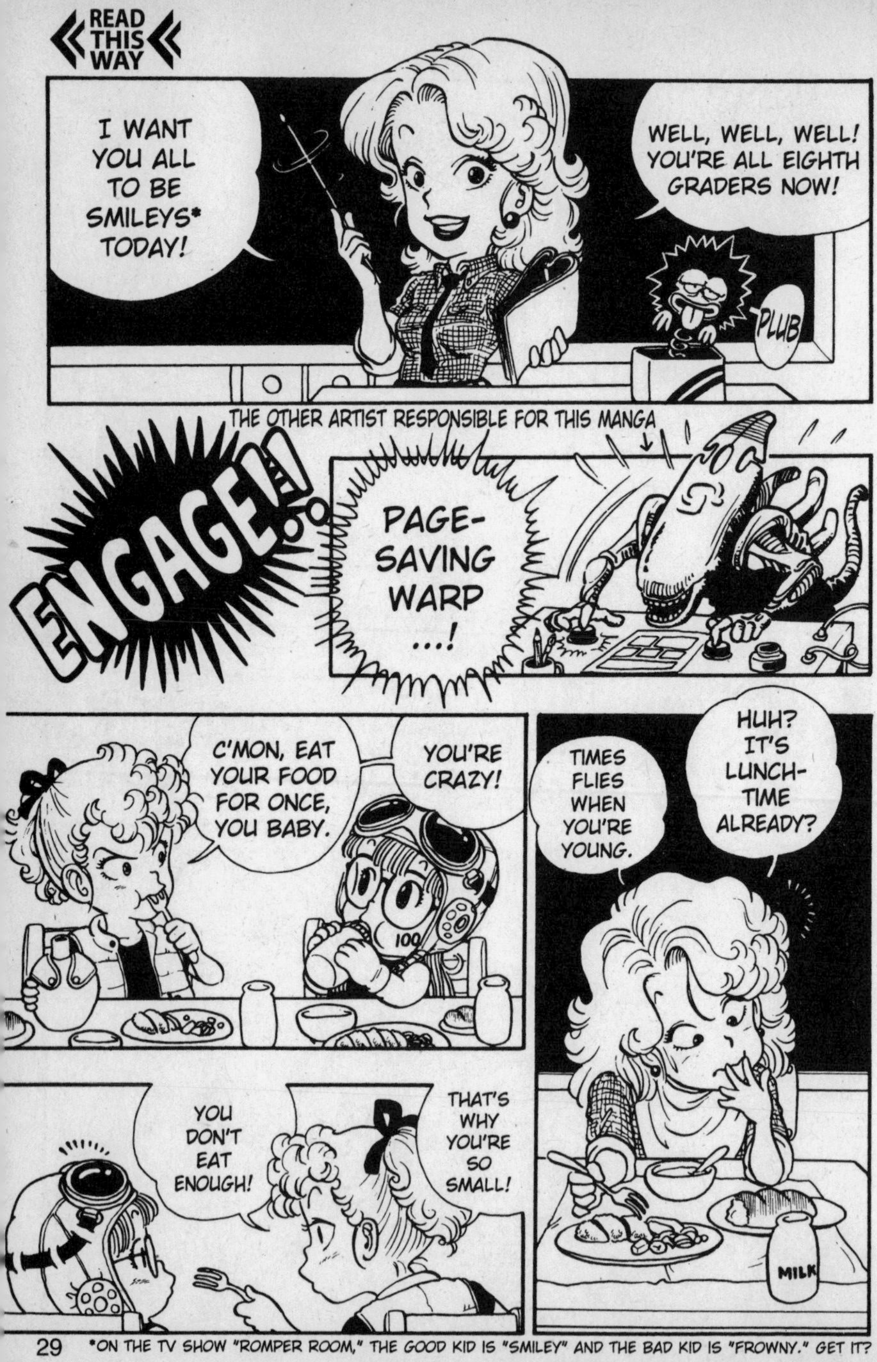
WELL, WELL, WELL! YOU'RE ALL EIGHTH GRADERS NOW!
I WANT YOU ALL TO BE SMILEYS* TODAY!
PLUB
THE OTHER ARTIST RESPONSIBLE FOR THIS MANGA
PAGE-SAVING WARP ...!
ENGAGE!!
HUH? IT'S LUNCH-TIME ALREADY?
TIMES FLIES WHEN YOU'RE YOUNG.
MILK
YOU'RE CRAZY!
C'MON, EAT YOUR FOOD FOR ONCE, YOU BABY.
THAT'S WHY YOU'RE SO SMALL!
YOU DON'T EAT ENOUGH!
100

*ON THE TV SHOW "ROMPER ROOM," THE GOOD KID IS "SMILEY" AND THE BAD KID IS "FROWNY." GET IT?

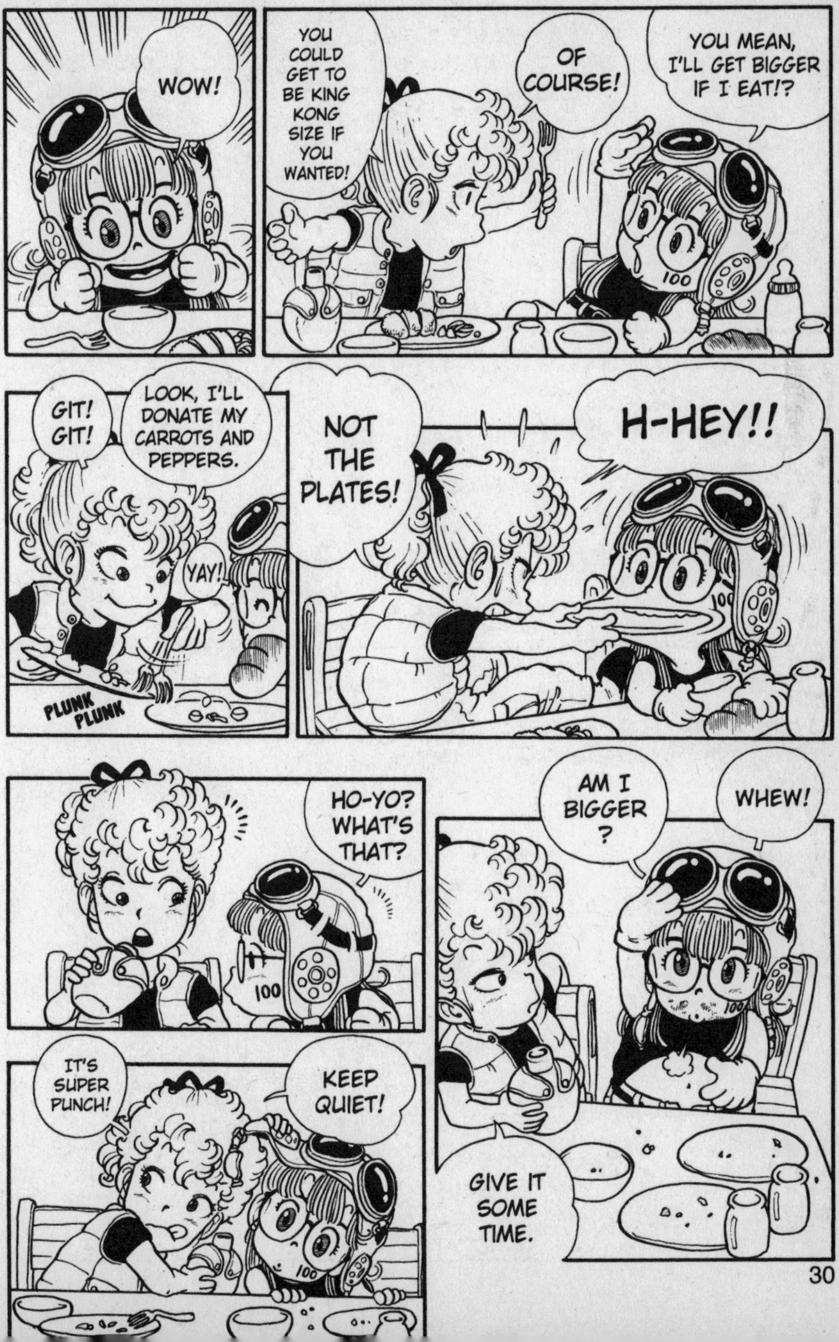
YOU MEAN, I'LL GET BIGGER IF I EAT!?
OF COURSE!
YOU COULD GET TO BE KING KONG SIZE IF YOU WANTED!
WOW!
H-HEY!!
NOT THE PLATES!
LOOK, I'LL DONATE MY CARROTS AND PEPPERS.
GIT! GIT!
YAY!
PLUNK PLUNK
WHEW!
AM I BIGGER ?
GIVE IT SOME TIME.
HO-YO? WHAT'S THAT?
KEEP QUIET!
IT'S SUPER PUNCH!

READ THIS WAY

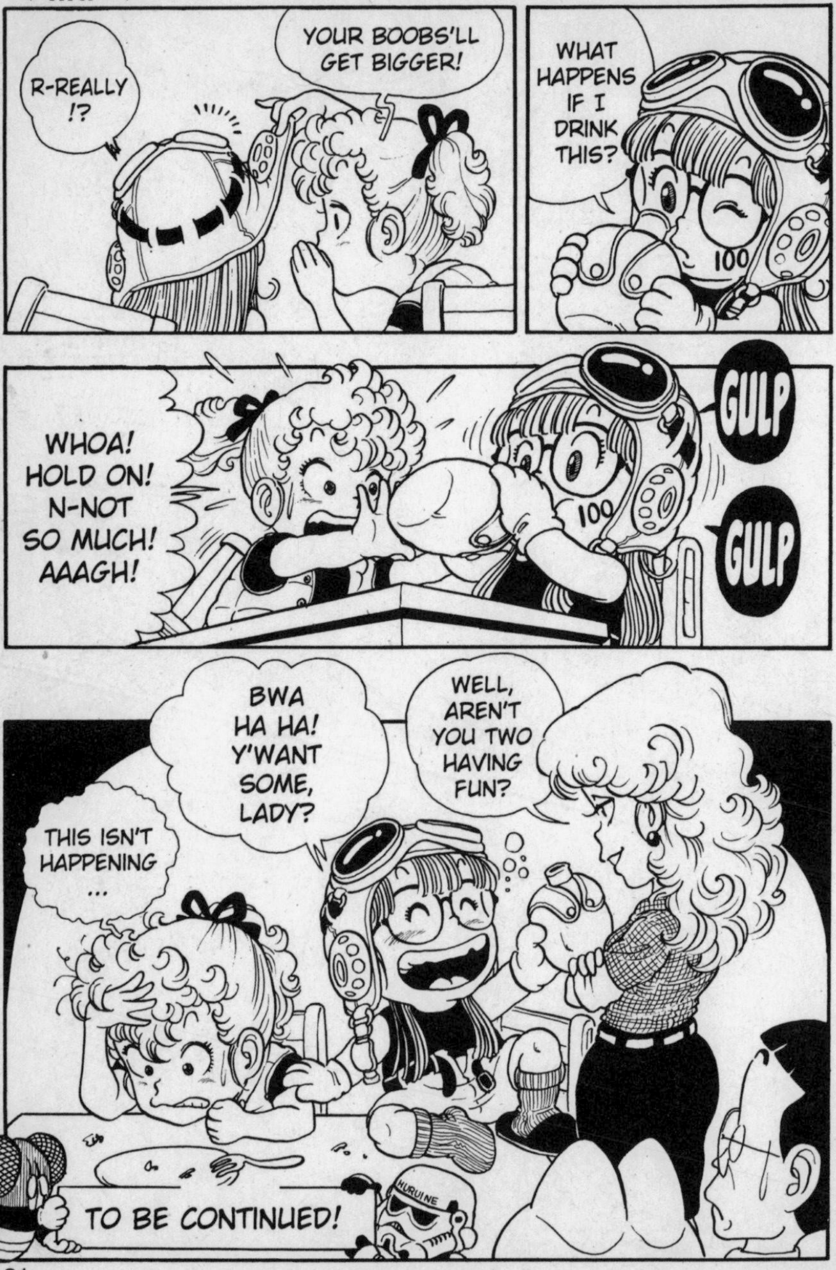
WHAT HAPPENS IF I DRINK THIS?
YOUR BOOBS'LL GET BIGGER!
R-REALLY !?
GULP
GULP
WHOA! HOLD ON! N-NOT SO MUCH! AAAGH!
WELL, AREN'T YOU TWO HAVING FUN?
BWA HA HA! Y'WANT SOME, LADY?
THIS ISN'T HAPPENING ...
HURUINE
TO BE CONTINUED!

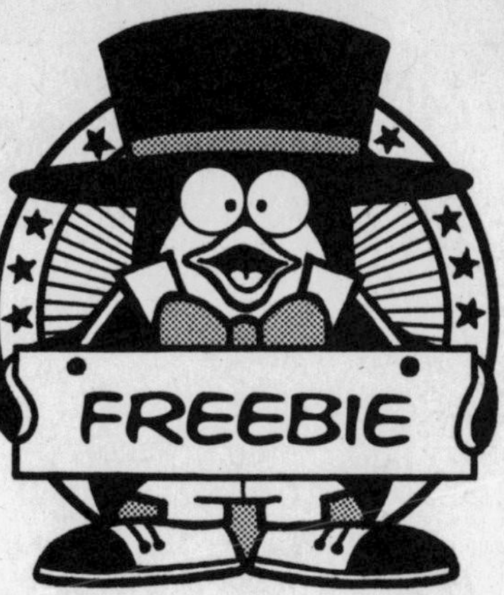
FREEBIE

Color Me

Color us in as you see fit.

I sincerely believe colored pencils would work best.

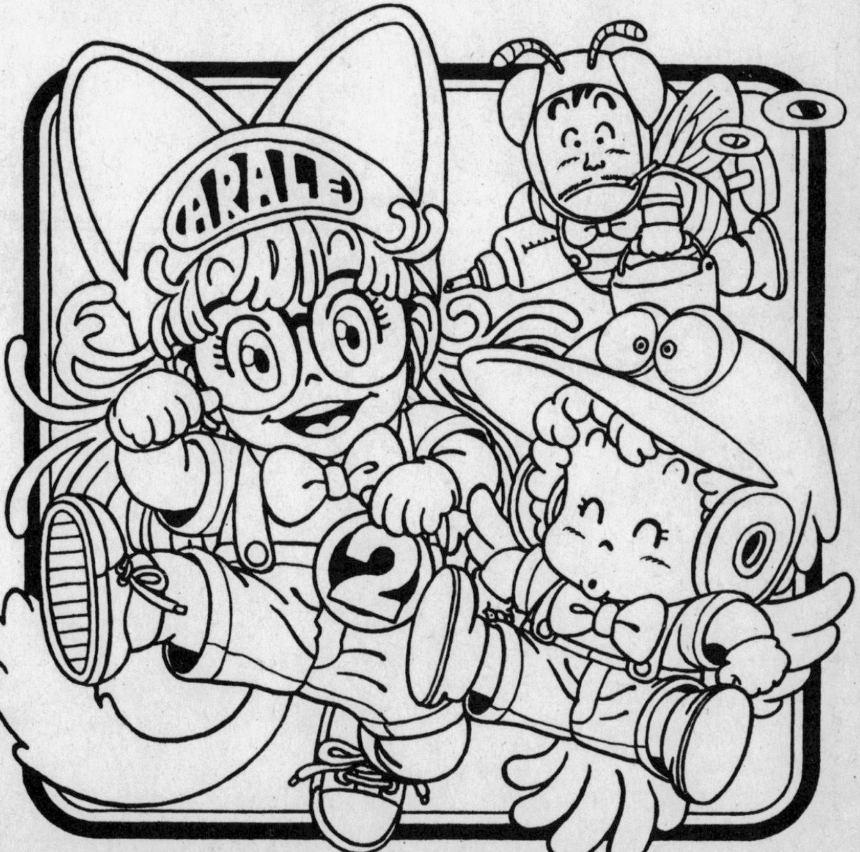

Arale on the Loose Part 2

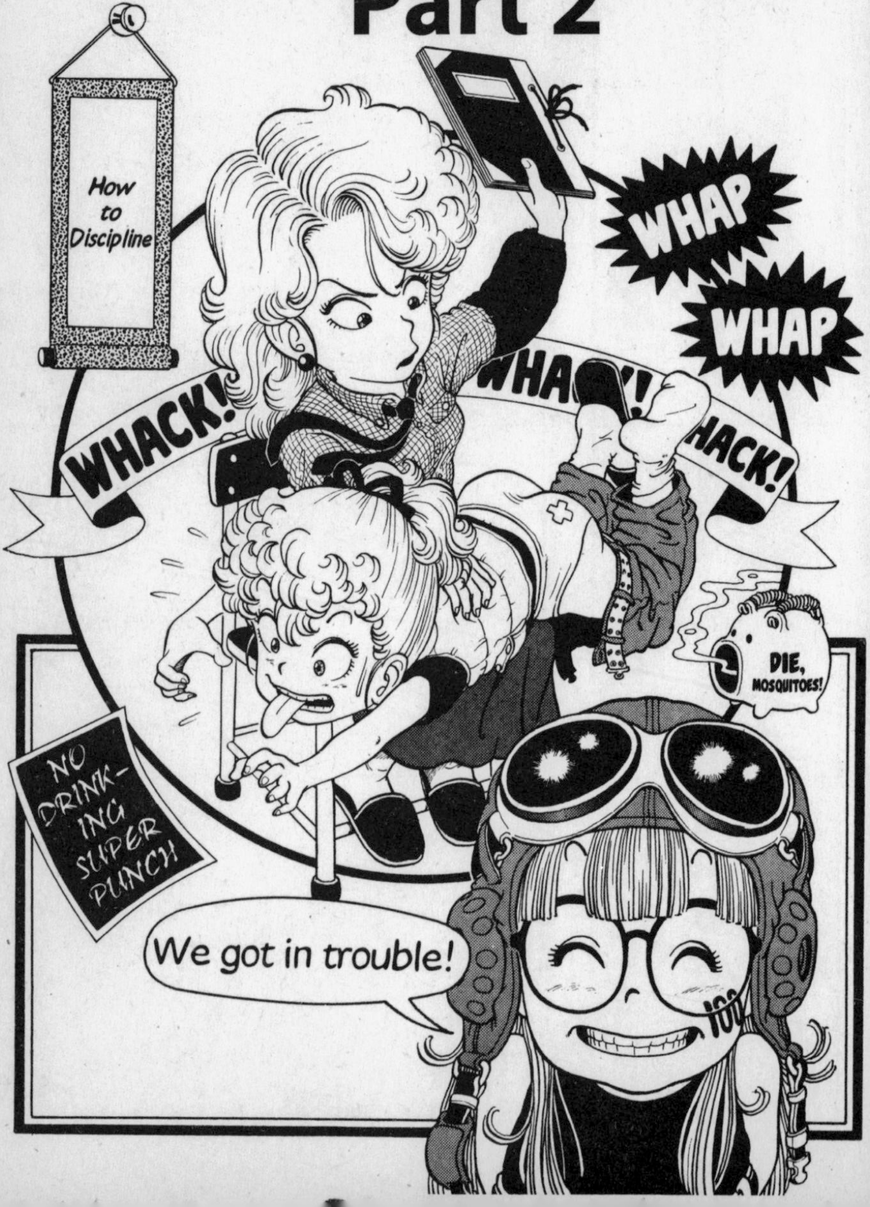
WHAP
WHAP
How to Discipline
WHACK!
DIE, MOSQUITOES!
NO DRINK-ING SUPER PUNCH
We got in trouble!

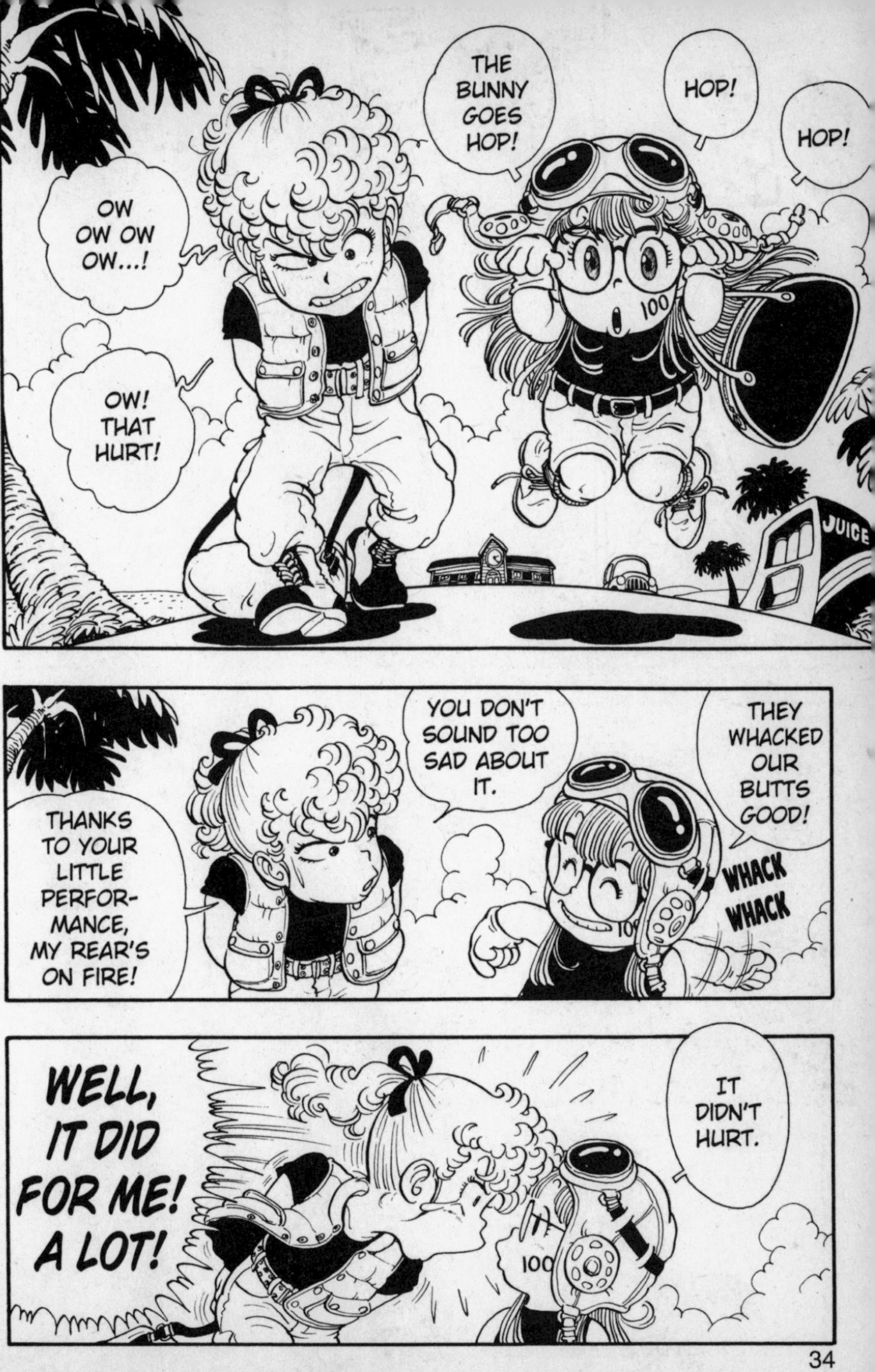
HOP!
HOP!
THE BUNNY GOES HOP!
OW OW OW OW...!
OW! THAT HURT!
JUICE
THEY WHACKED OUR BUTTS GOOD!
WHACK WHACK
YOU DON'T SOUND TOO SAD ABOUT IT.
THANKS TO YOUR LITTLE PERFORMANCE, MY REAR'S ON FIRE!
IT DIDN'T HURT.
WELL, IT DID FOR ME! A LOT!

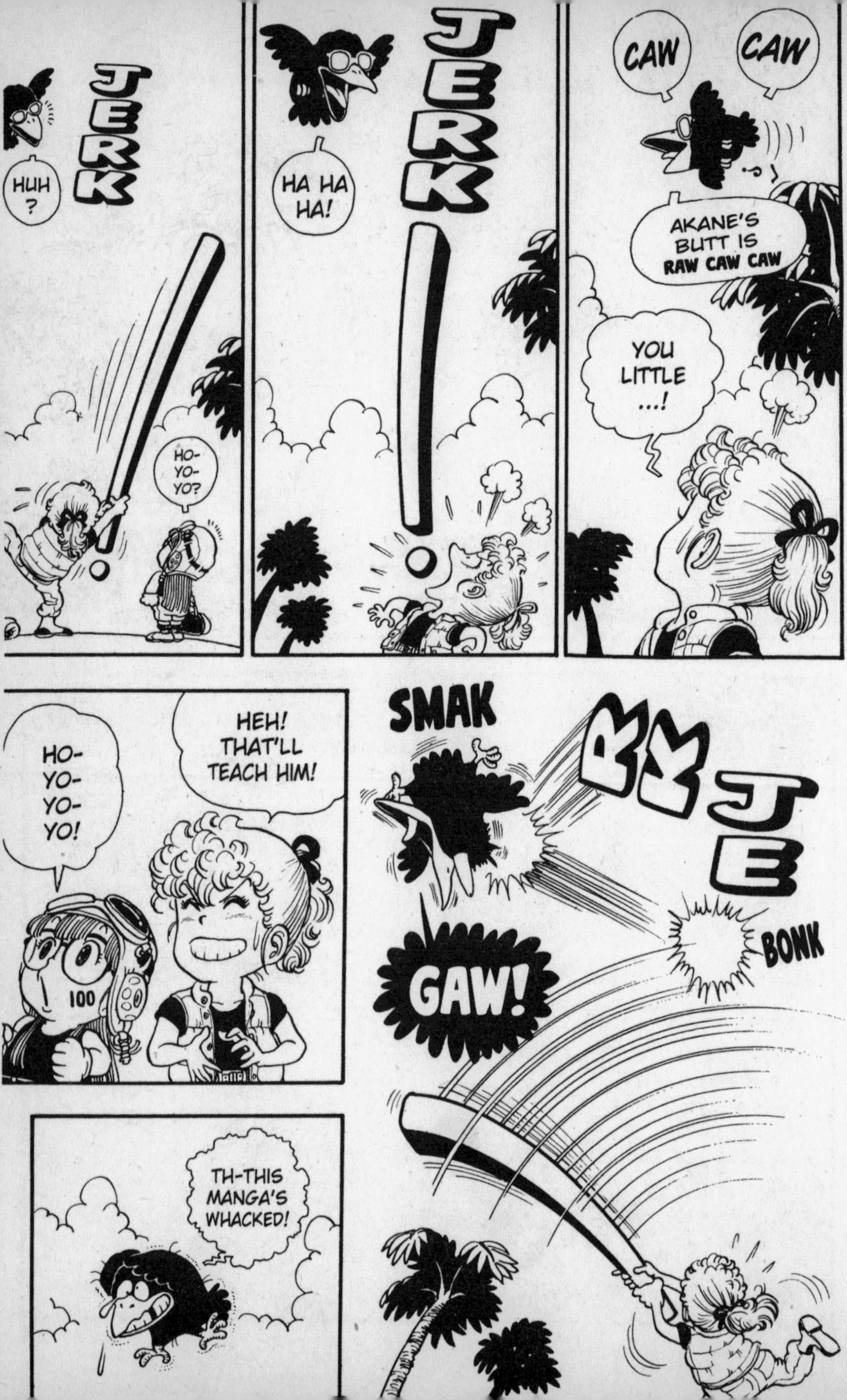

CAW
CAW
AKANE'S BUTT IS RAW CAW CAW
YOU LITTLE ...!
JERK
HA HA HA!
JERK
HUH ?
HO-YO-YO?
SMAK
JERK
GAW!
BONK
HEH! THAT'LL TEACH HIM!
HO-YO-YO-YO!
100
TH-THIS MANGA'S WHACKED!

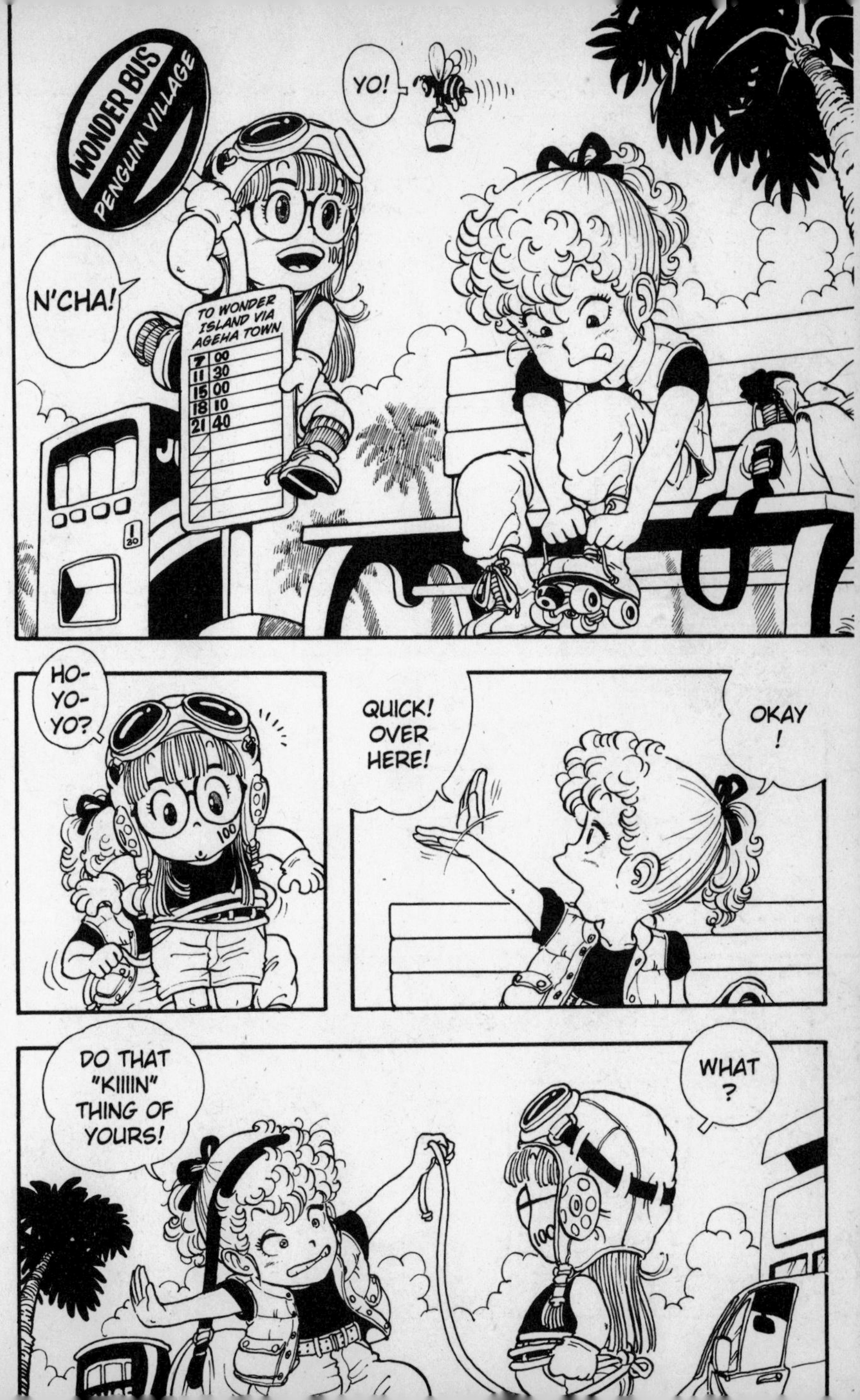
YO!
WONDER BUS
PENGUIN VILLAGE
N'CHA!
TO WONDER ISLAND VIA AGEHA TOWN
7 00
11 30
15 00
18 10
21 40
OKAY!
QUICK! OVER HERE!
HO-YO-YO?
WHAT?
DO THAT "KIIIIN" THING OF YOURS!

READ THIS WAY

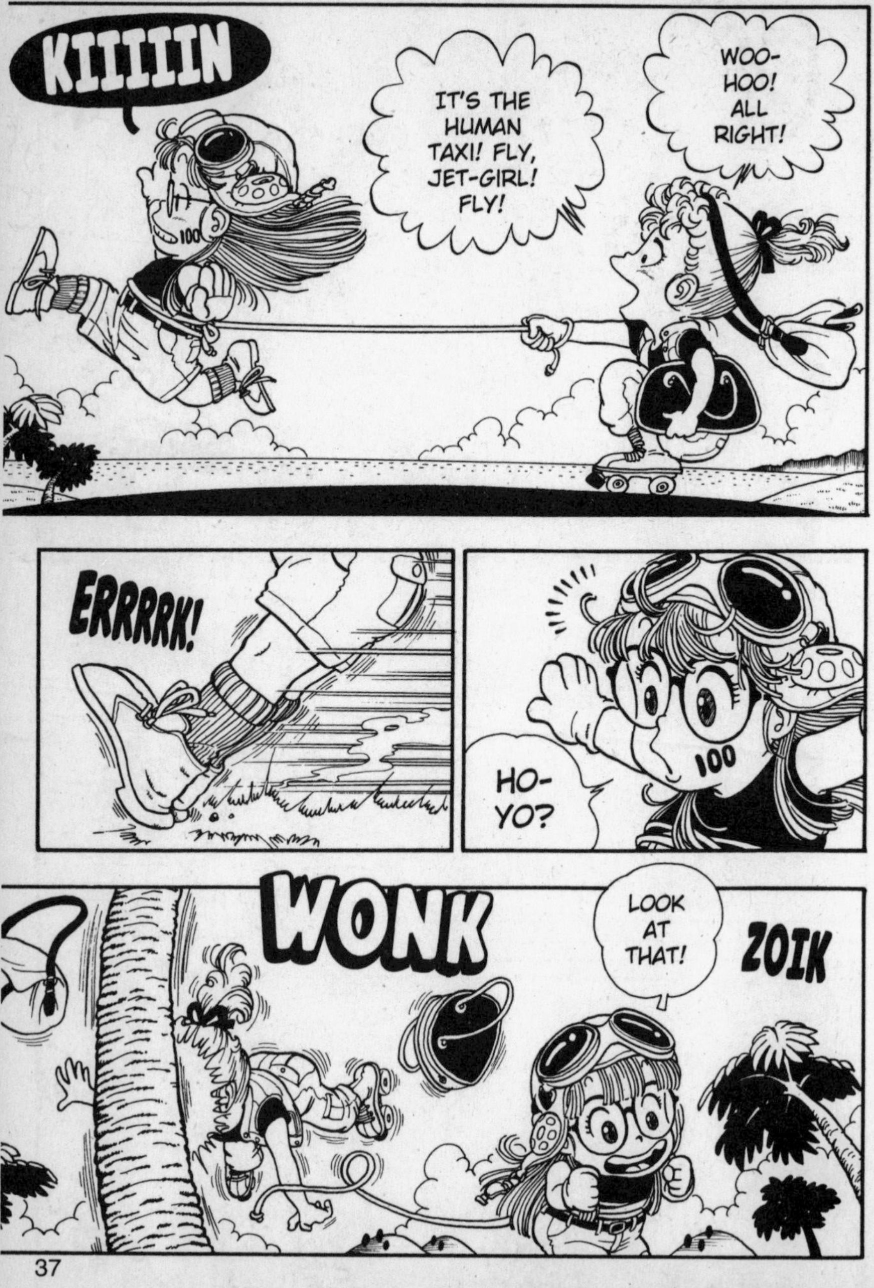
WOO-HOO! ALL RIGHT!
IT'S THE HUMAN TAXI! FLY, JET-GIRL! FLY!
KIIIIIN
HO-YO?
ERRRRK!
ZOIK
LOOK AT THAT!
WONK

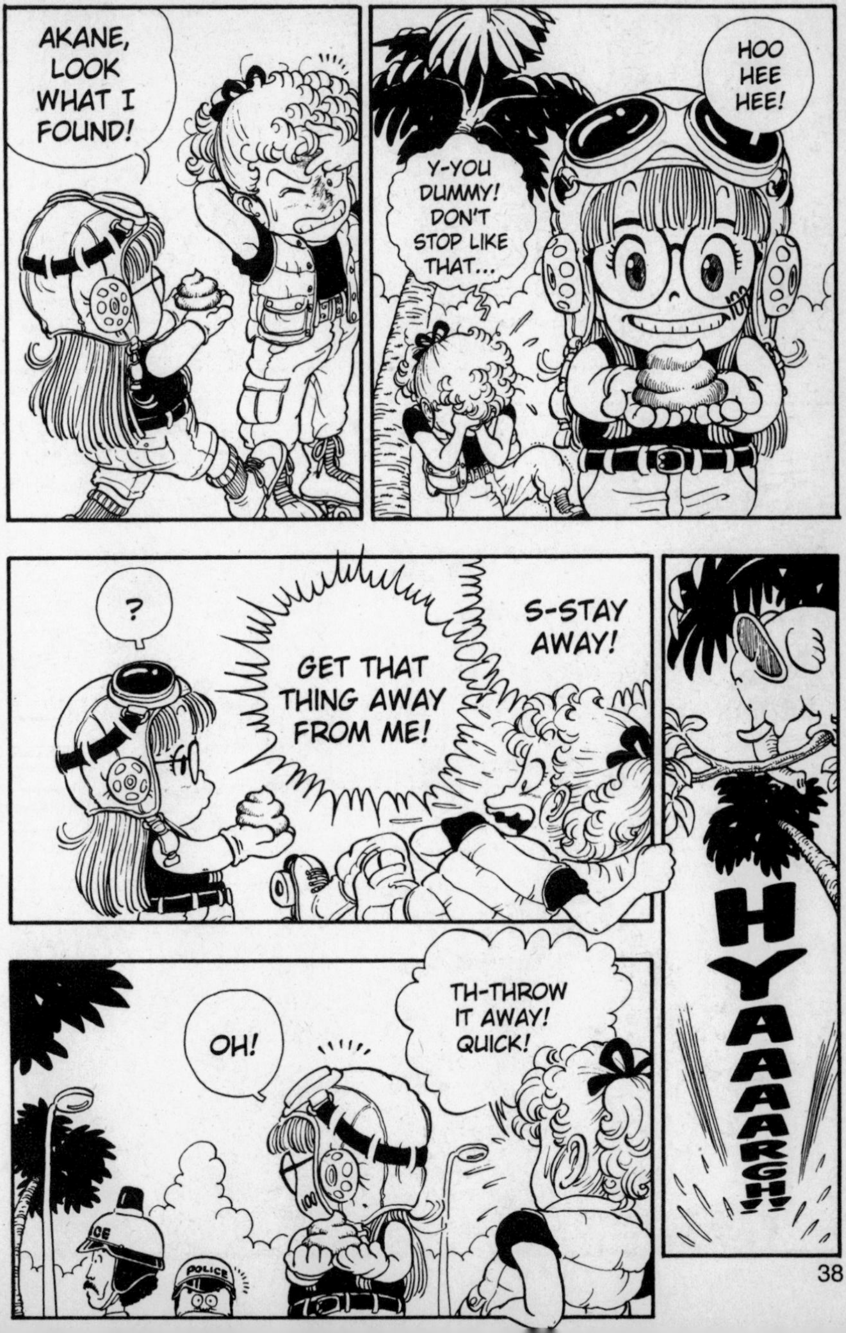
HOO HEE HEE!
Y-YOU DUMMY! DON'T STOP LIKE THAT...
AKANE, LOOK WHAT I FOUND!
HYAAAARGH!!
S-STAY AWAY!
GET THAT THING AWAY FROM ME!
?
TH-THROW IT AWAY! QUICK!
OH!
POLICE

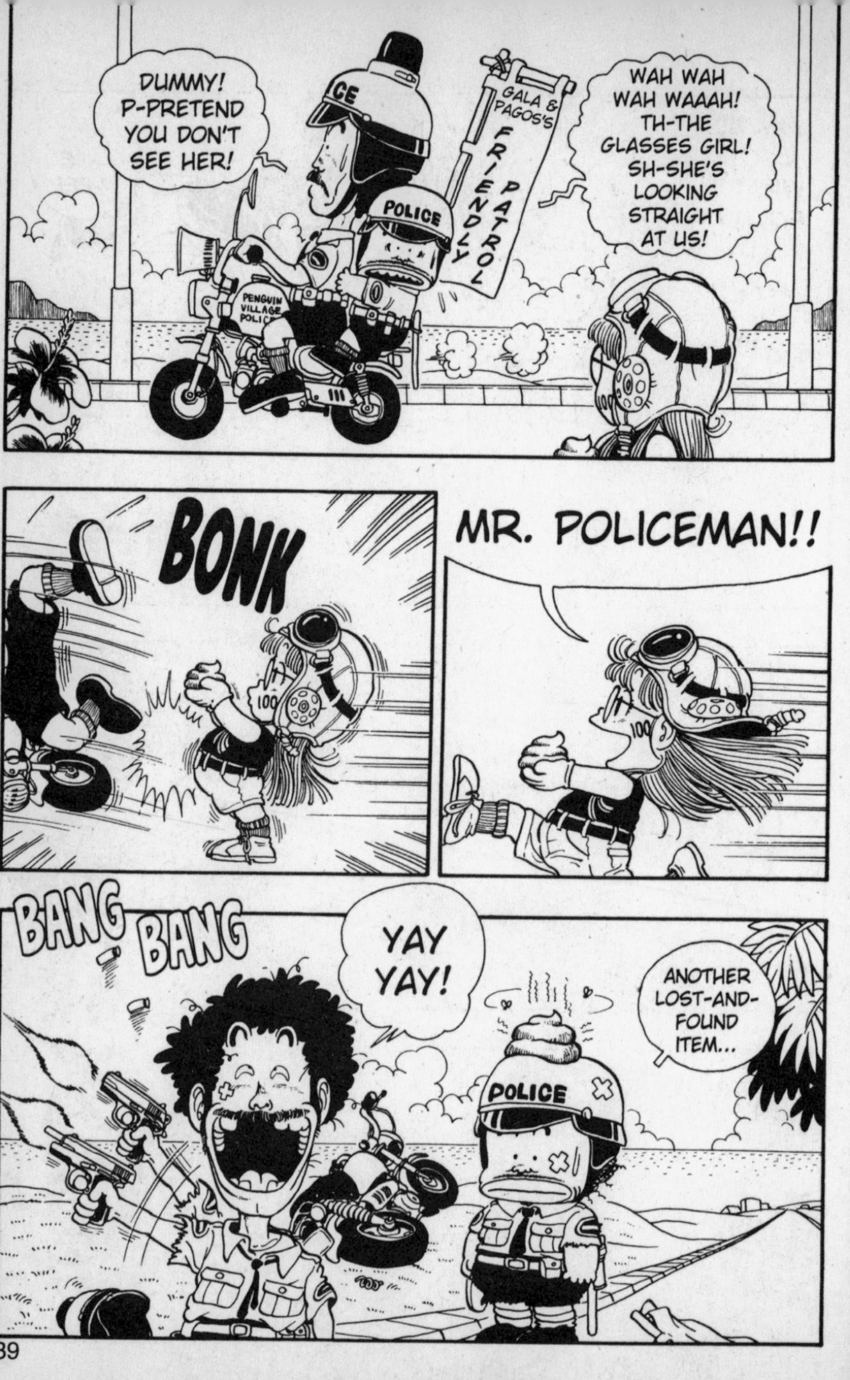
WAH WAH WAH WAAAH! TH-THE GLASSES GIRL! SH-SHE'S LOOKING STRAIGHT AT US!
GALA & PAGOS'S FRIENDLY PATROL
DUMMY! P-PRETEND YOU DON'T SEE HER!
POLICE
PENGUIN VILLAGE POLIC
MR. POLICEMAN!!
BONK
ANOTHER LOST-AND-FOUND ITEM...
POLICE
YAY YAY!
BANG BANG

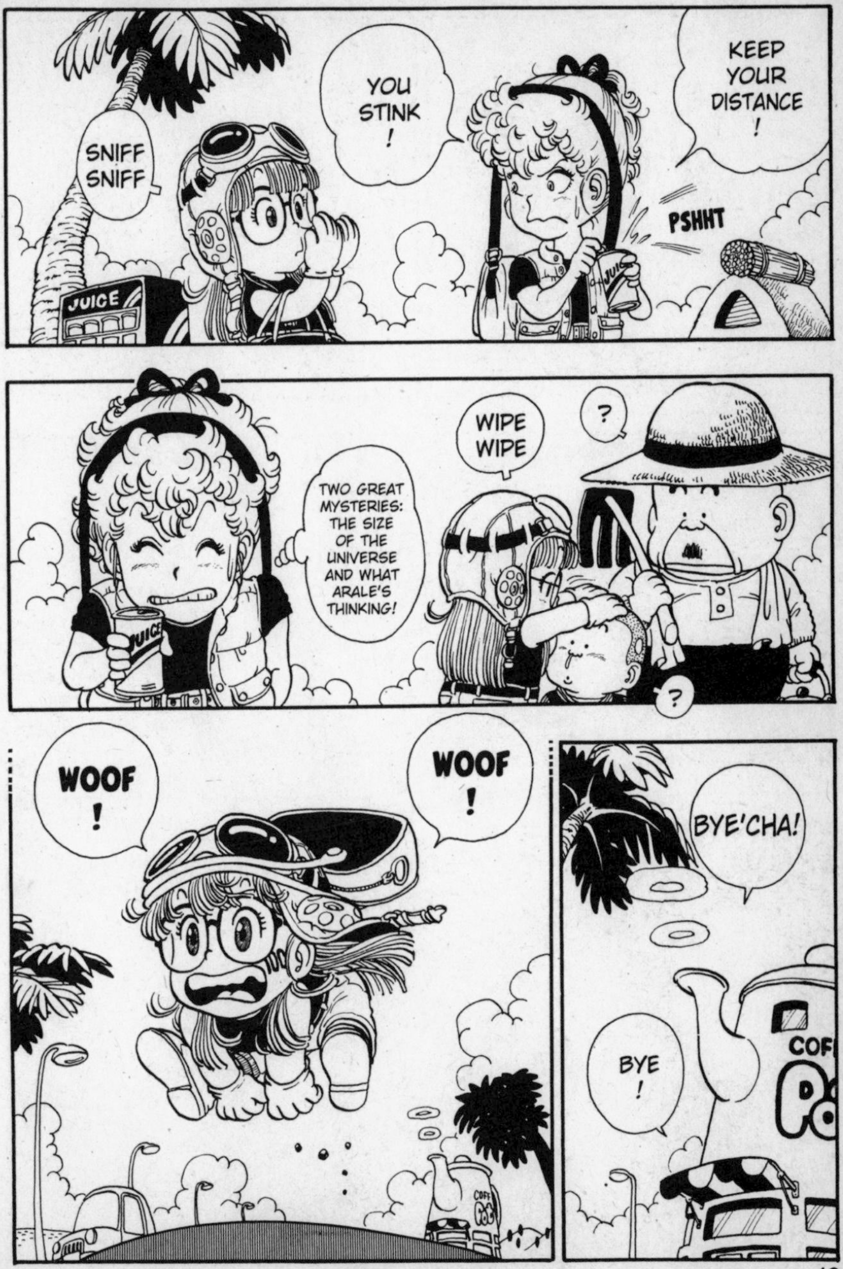
KEEP YOUR DISTANCE !
PSHHT
YOU STINK !
SNIFF SNIFF
JUICE
?
WIPE WIPE
TWO GREAT MYSTERIES: THE SIZE OF THE UNIVERSE AND WHAT ARALE'S THINKING!
JUICE
?
BYE'CHA!
BYE !
WOOF !
WOOF !

READ THIS WAY

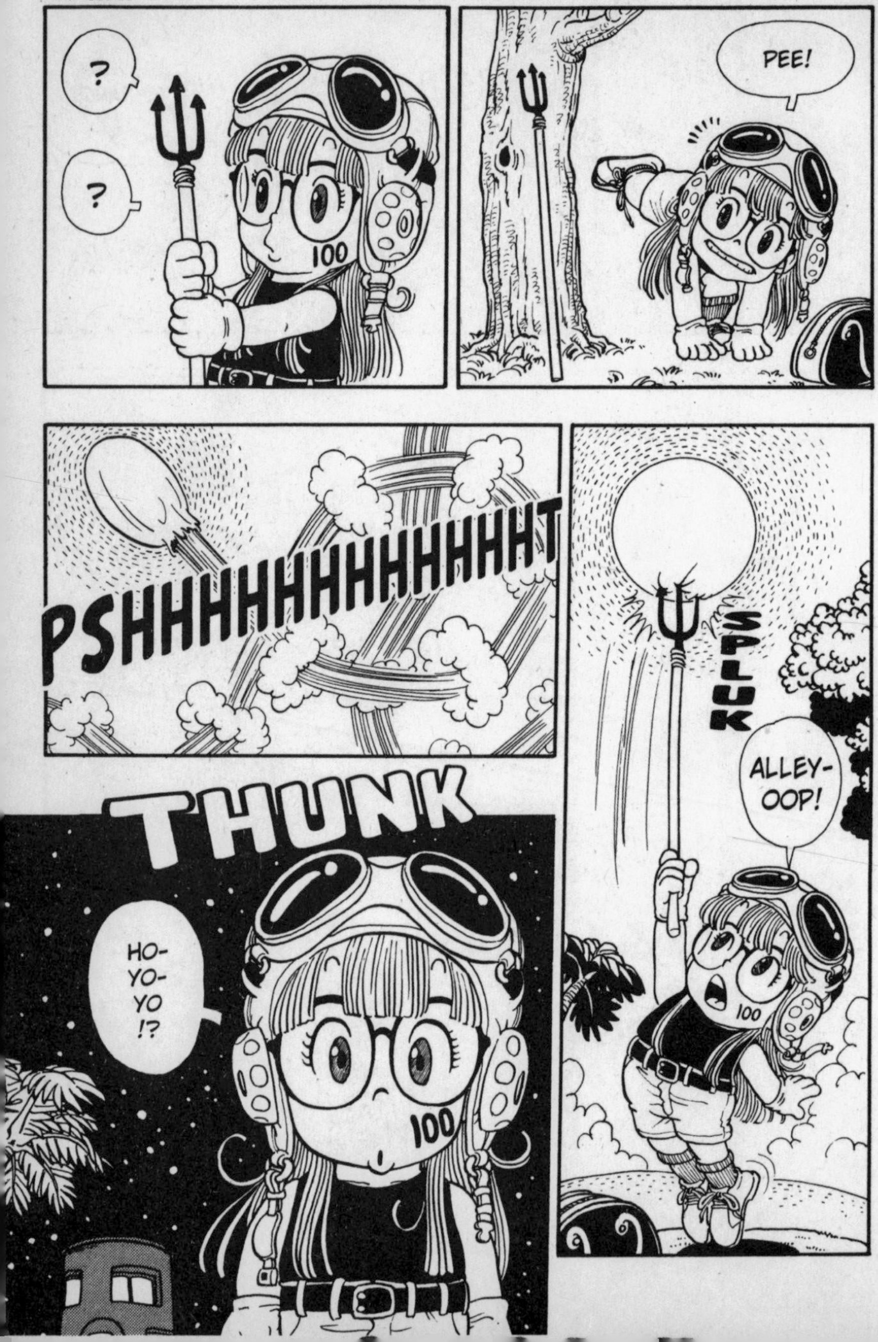
PEE!
?
?
SPLUK
ALLEY-OOP!
PSHHHHHHHHHHHHT
THUNK
HO-YO-YO!?

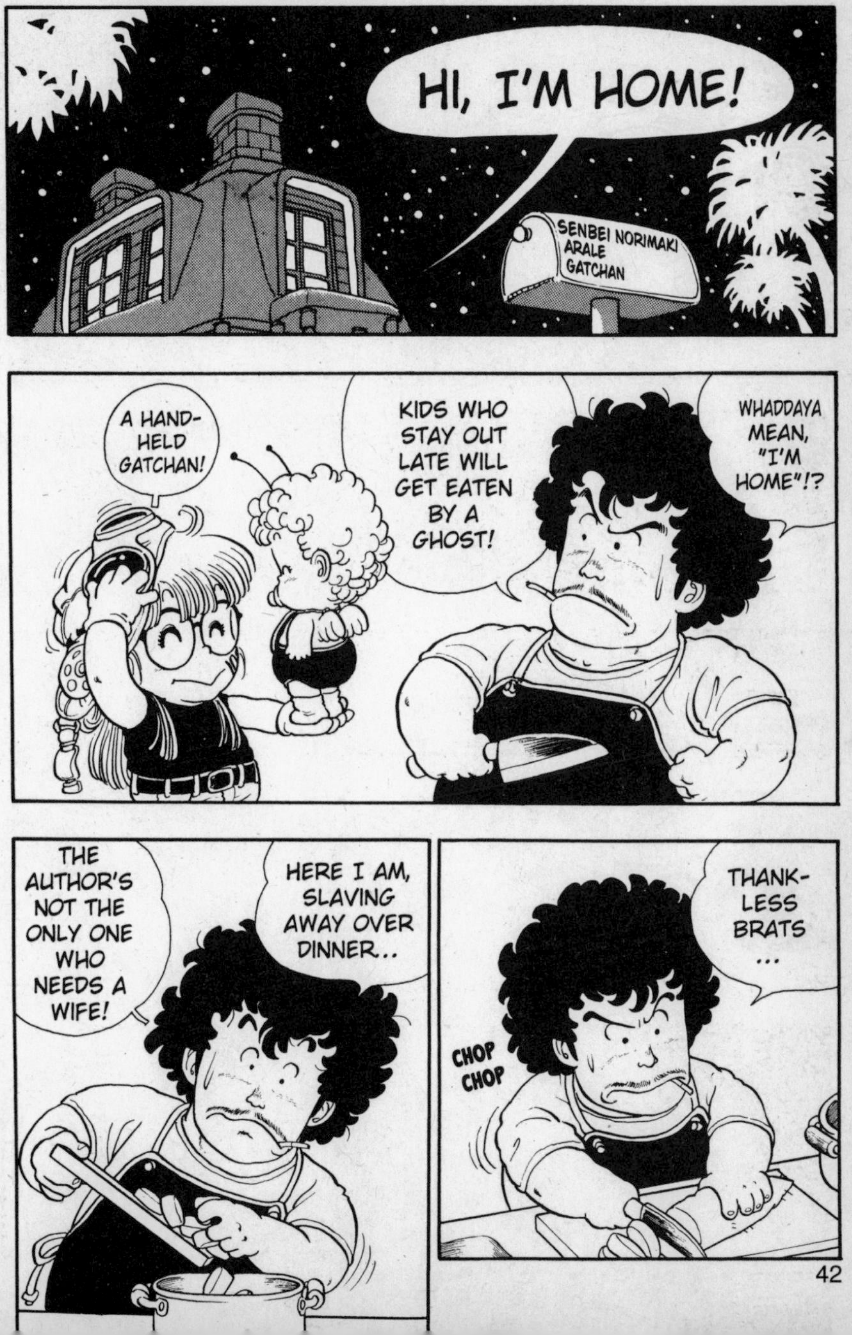
HI, I'M HOME!
SENBEI NORIMAKI
ARALE
GATCHAN
WHADDAYA MEAN, "I'M HOME"!?
KIDS WHO STAY OUT LATE WILL GET EATEN BY A GHOST!
A HAND-HELD GATCHAN!
THANKLESS BRATS ...
CHOP CHOP
HERE I AM, SLAVING AWAY OVER DINNER...
THE AUTHOR'S NOT THE ONLY ONE WHO NEEDS A WIFE!

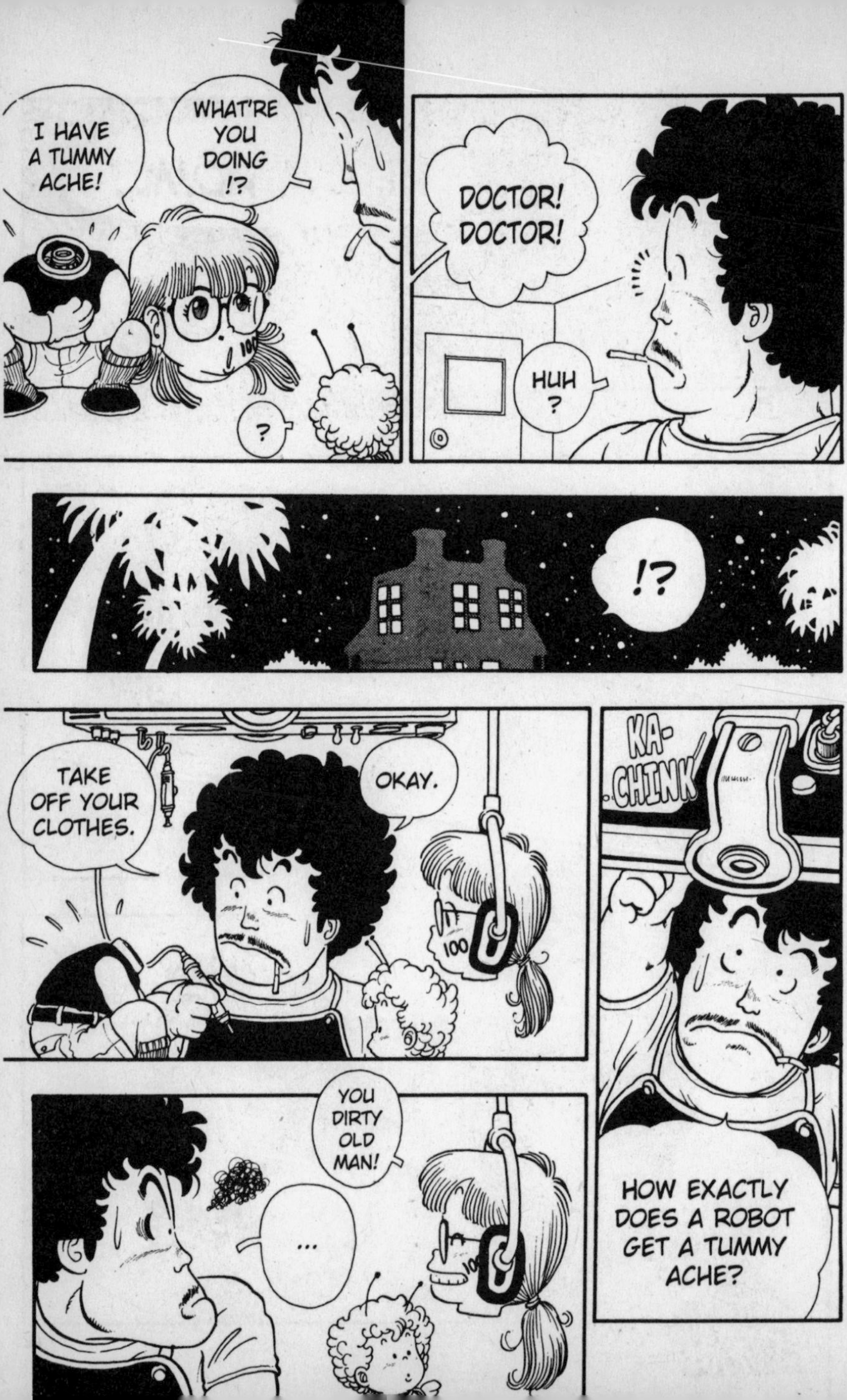
DOCTOR! DOCTOR!
HUH ?
WHAT'RE YOU DOING !?
I HAVE A TUMMY ACHE!
?
!?
KA-CHINK
HOW EXACTLY DOES A ROBOT GET A TUMMY ACHE?
OKAY.
TAKE OFF YOUR CLOTHES.
YOU DIRTY OLD MAN!
...

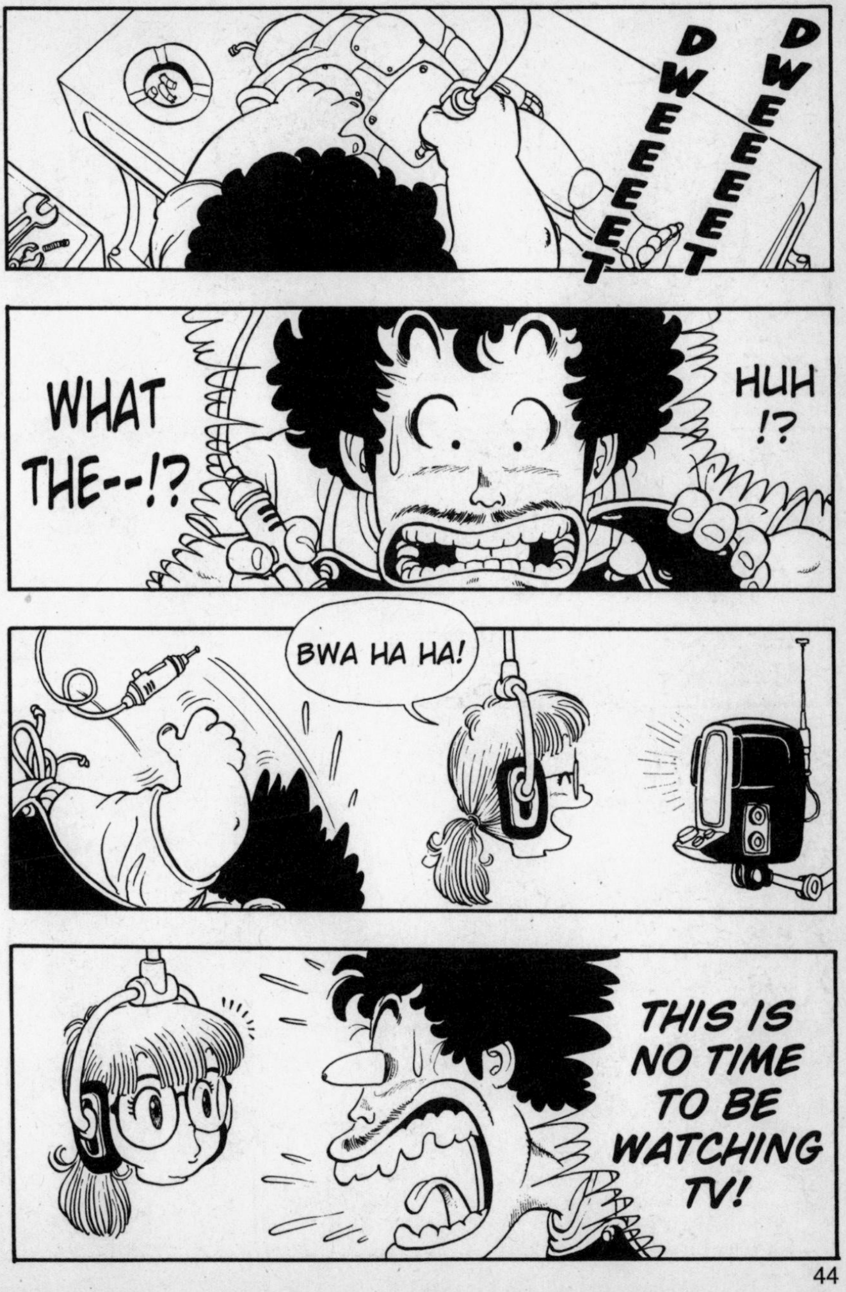
DWEEEEET
DWEEEEET
HUH !?
WHAT THE--!?
BWA HA HA!
THIS IS NO TIME TO BE WATCHING TV!

READ THIS WAY

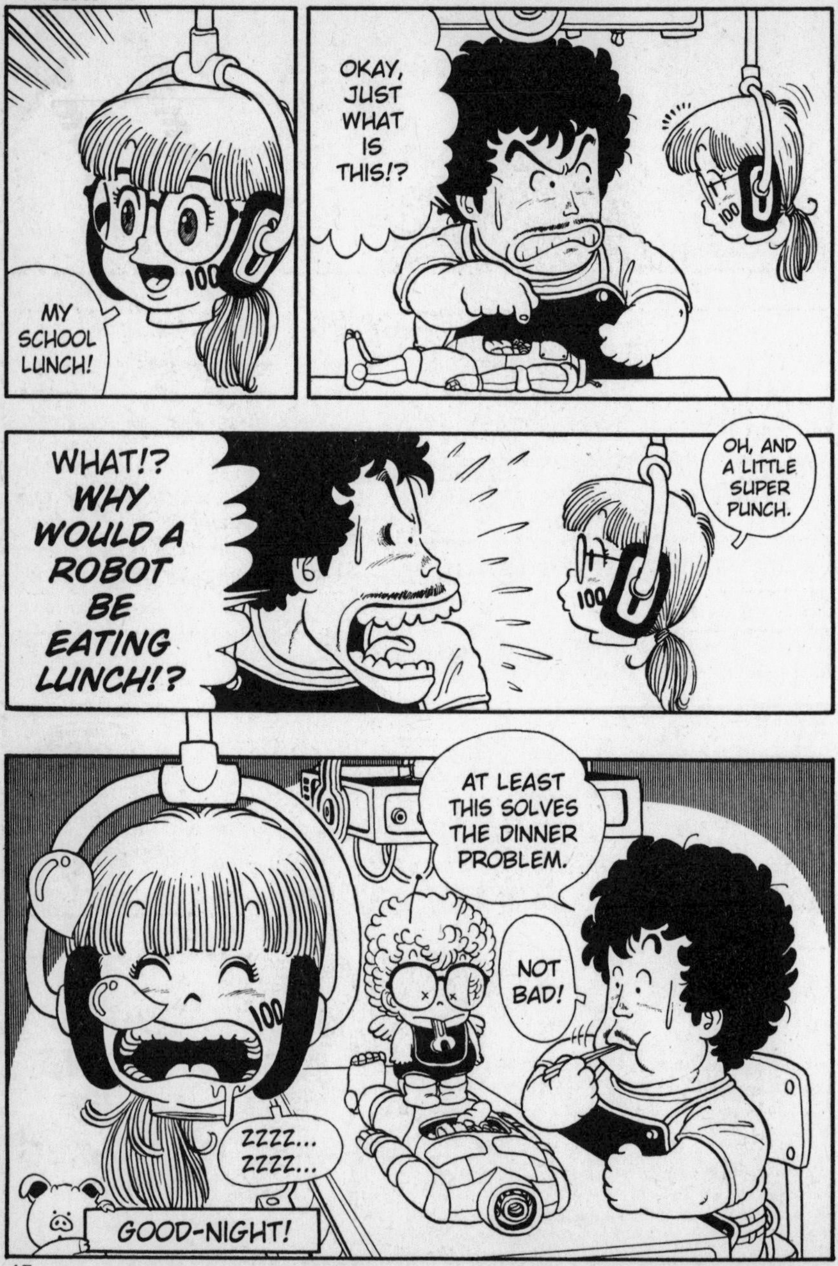

OKAY, JUST WHAT IS THIS!?
MY SCHOOL LUNCH!
OH, AND A LITTLE SUPER PUNCH.
WHAT!? WHY WOULD A ROBOT BE EATING LUNCH!?
AT LEAST THIS SOLVES THE DINNER PROBLEM.
NOT BAD!
ZZZZ... ZZZZ...
GOOD-NIGHT!

HOW TO ENLARGE A PICTURE!

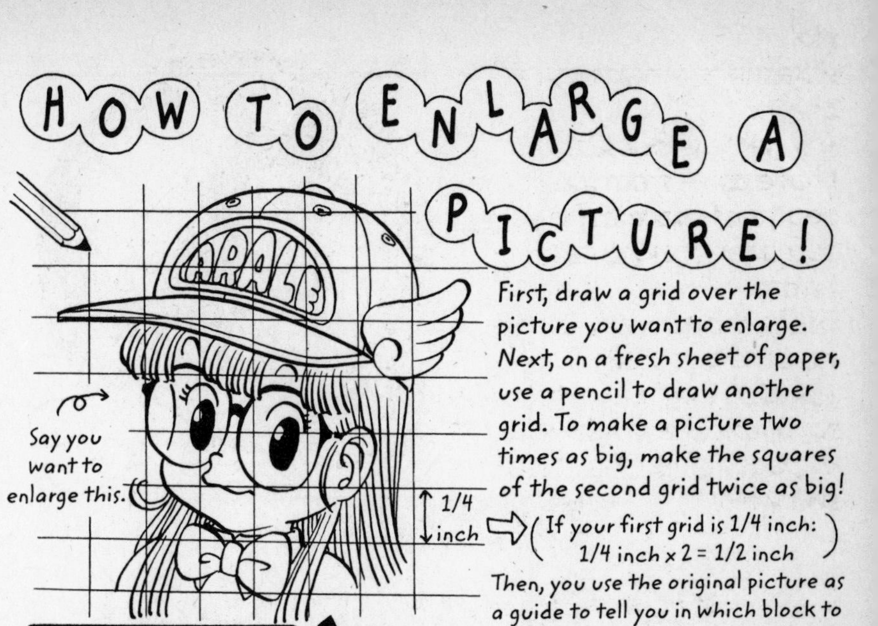
ARALE
Say you want to enlarge this.
1/4 inch

First, draw a grid over the picture you want to enlarge. Next, on a fresh sheet of paper, use a pencil to draw another grid. To make a picture two times as big, make the squares of the second grid twice as big!
(If your first grid is 1/4 inch: 1/4 inch x 2 = 1/2 inch)
Then, you use the original picture as a guide to tell you in which block to draw the nose, the eyes, etc. Use a pencil! Then when you're happy with your enlarged drawing, trace over it with a pen and erase the grid lines, and you're done! (Got that?)

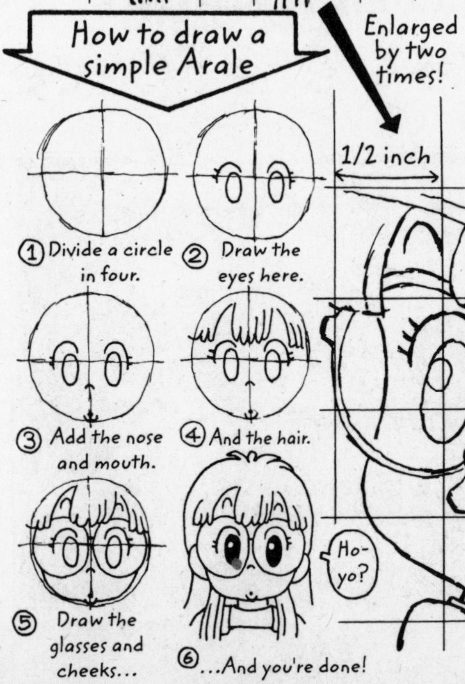
How to draw a simple Arale
Enlarged by two times!
① Divide a circle in four.
② Draw the eyes here.
③ Add the nose and mouth.
④ And the hair.
⑤ Draw the glasses and cheeks...
⑥ ...And you're done!

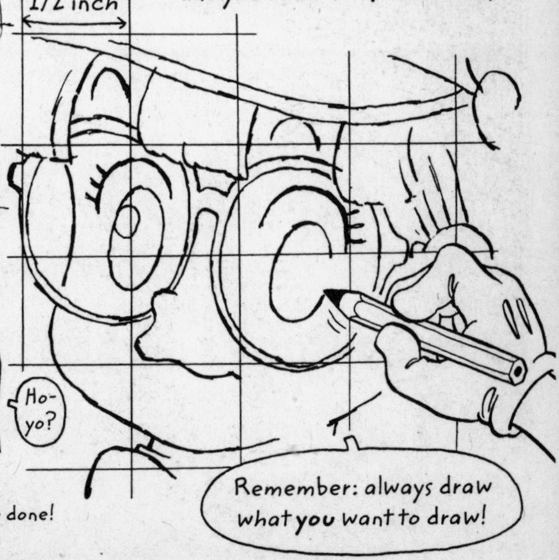
1/2 inch
Ho-yo?
Remember: always draw what you want to draw!

Hullo!
Greetings, weaklings of Earth!
My name is Bubibinman!
I have come from the depths of space to be your defender of peace and justice!
Sit back and watch a real superhero in action!
...And so begins our special sci-fi epic feature spanning 15 pages of glorious black and white!

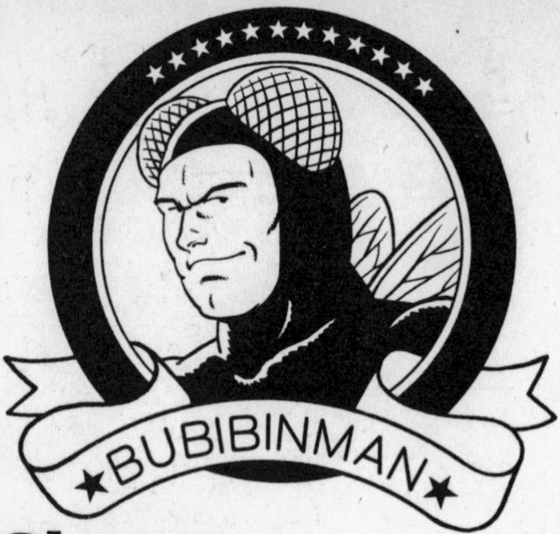
★BUBIBINMAN★

Dr. Slump Ho-yo-yo Special I The Invader from Space

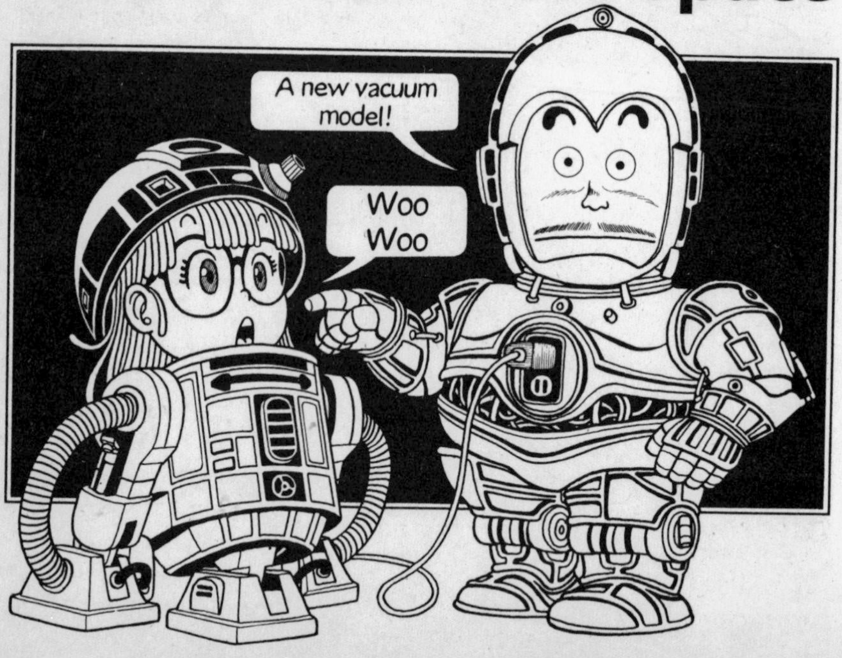
A new vacuum model!
Woo Woo

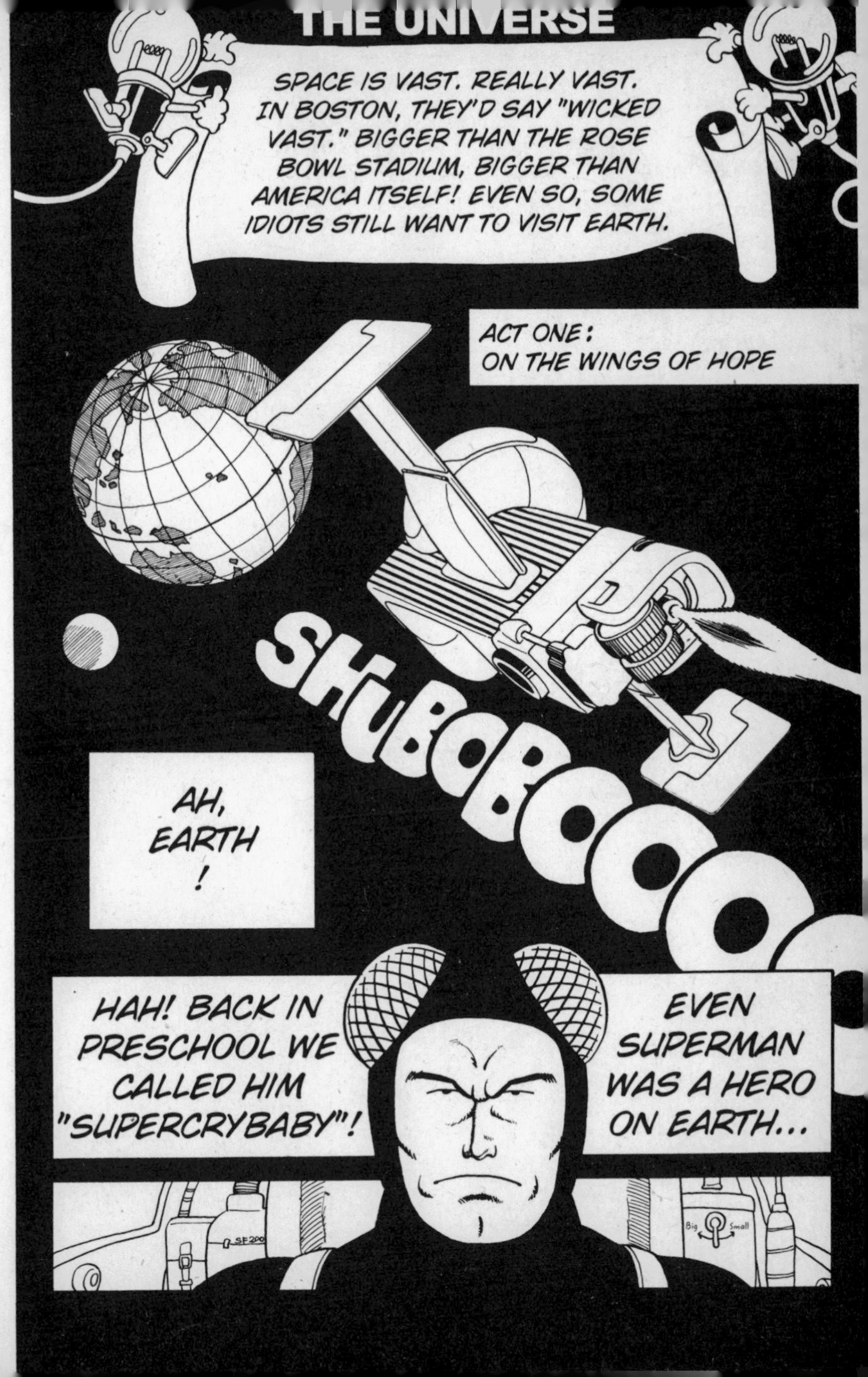
THE UNIVERSE
SPACE IS VAST. REALLY VAST. IN BOSTON, THEY'D SAY "WICKED VAST." BIGGER THAN THE ROSE BOWL STADIUM, BIGGER THAN AMERICA ITSELF! EVEN SO, SOME IDIOTS STILL WANT TO VISIT EARTH.
ACT ONE: ON THE WINGS OF HOPE
SHUBOBOOOO
AH, EARTH!
EVEN SUPERMAN WAS A HERO ON EARTH...
HAH! BACK IN PRESCHOOL WE CALLED HIM "SUPERCRYBABY"!
Big
Small

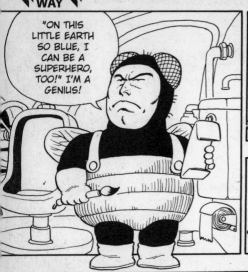

READ THIS WAY

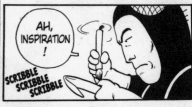

IT JUST PROVES HOW WEAK EARTHLINGS ARE...
AH, INSPIRATION !
SCRIBBLE SCRIBBLE SCRIBBLE
"ON THIS LITTLE EARTH SO BLUE, I CAN BE A SUPERHERO, TOO!" I'M A GENIUS!
ACT TWO: LAND OF MY GLORY
PUT PUT PUT PUT PUT
PSHHHHHT
AT LAST !
THERE'S OXYGEN, RIGHT?
KA-CHUNK KA-CHUNK KA-CHUNK
CLICK
CHECK !
BOOP
YES
NO
HUH?

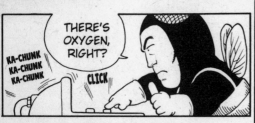

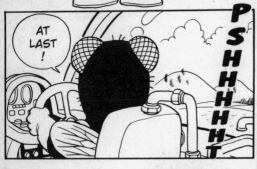

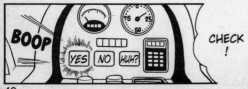

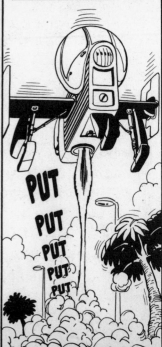

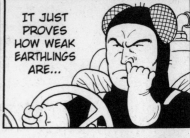

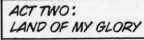

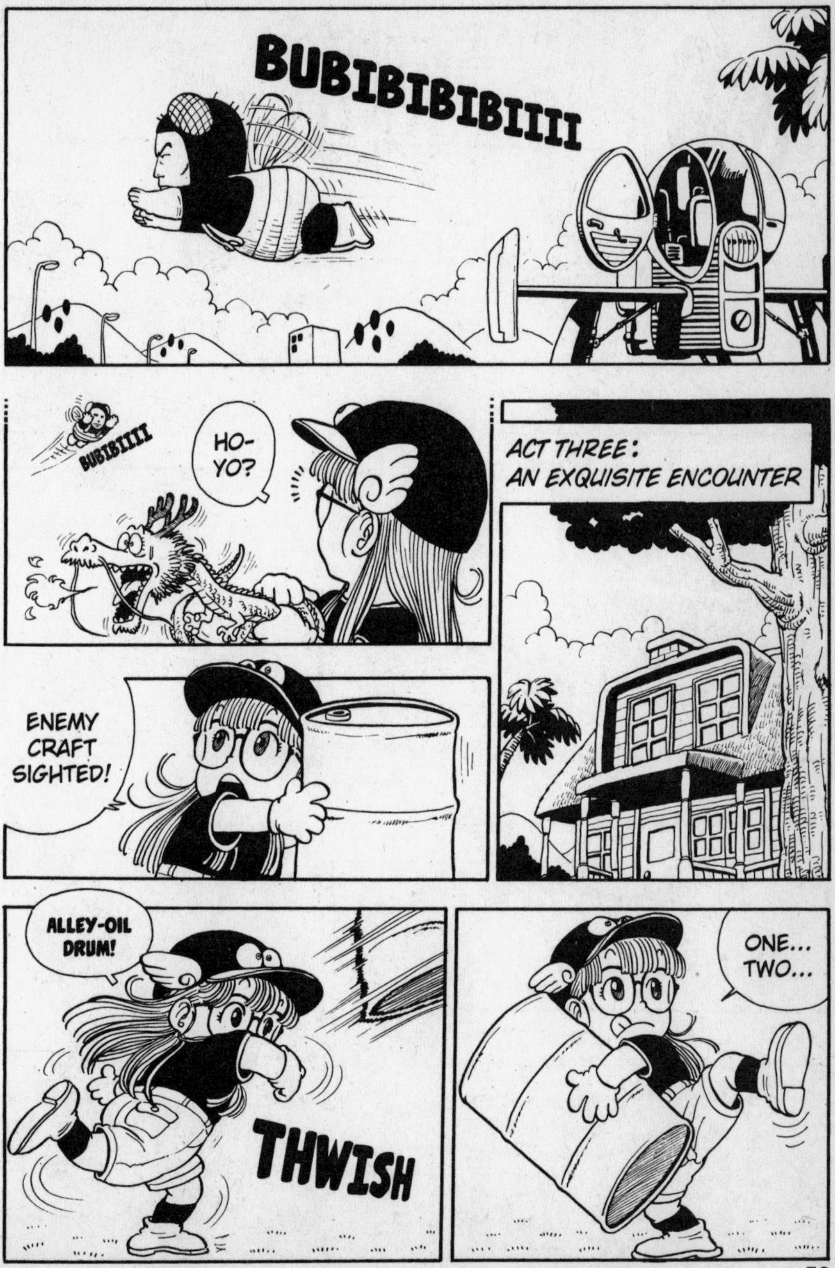
BUBIBIBIBIIII
ACT THREE: AN EXQUISITE ENCOUNTER
BUBIBIIII
HO-YO?
ENEMY CRAFT SIGHTED!
ONE... TWO...
ALLEY-OIL DRUM!
THWISH

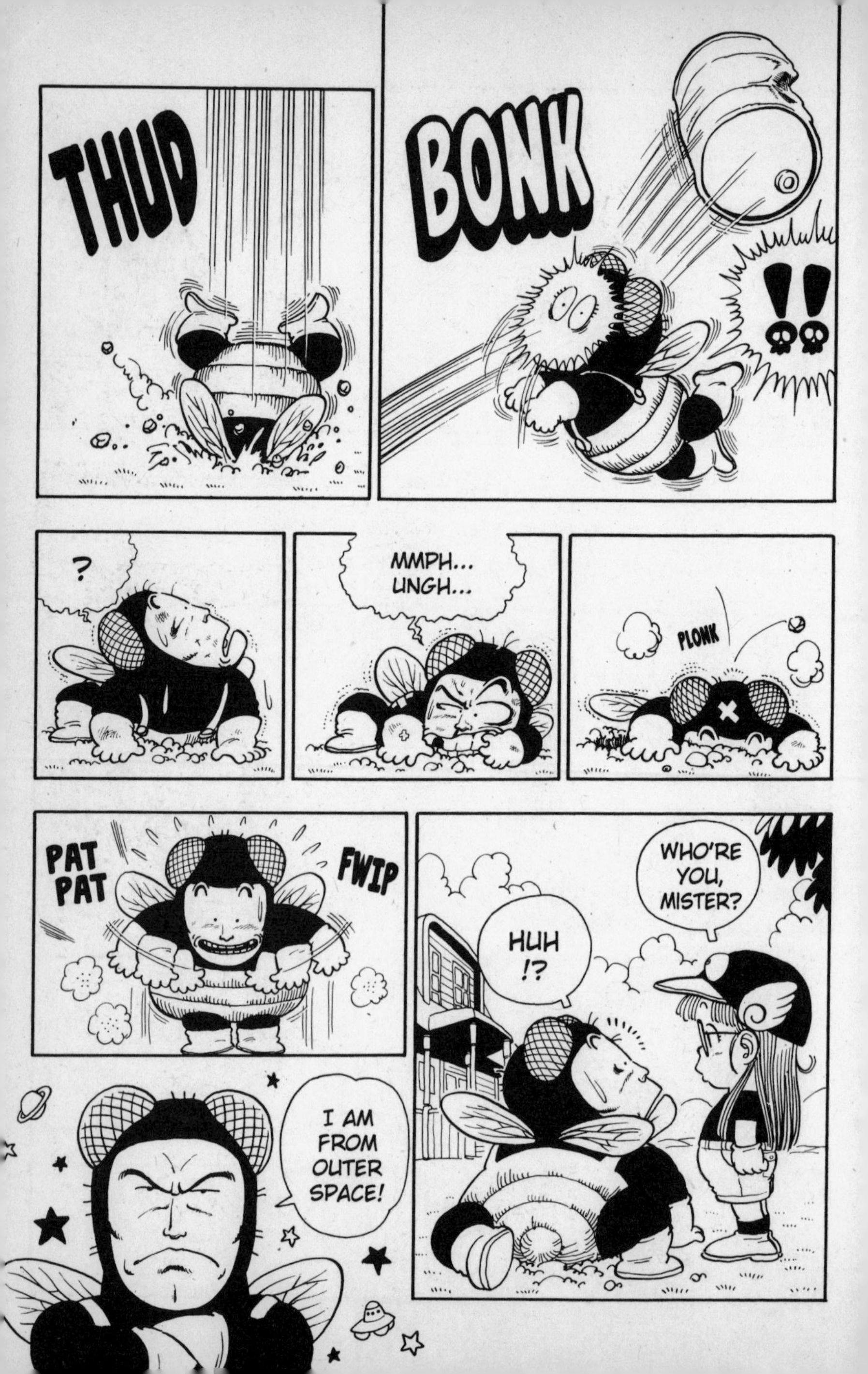
!!
BONK
THUD
PLONK
MMPH... UNGH...
?
WHO'RE YOU, MISTER?
HUH !?
FWIP
PAT PAT
I AM FROM OUTER SPACE!

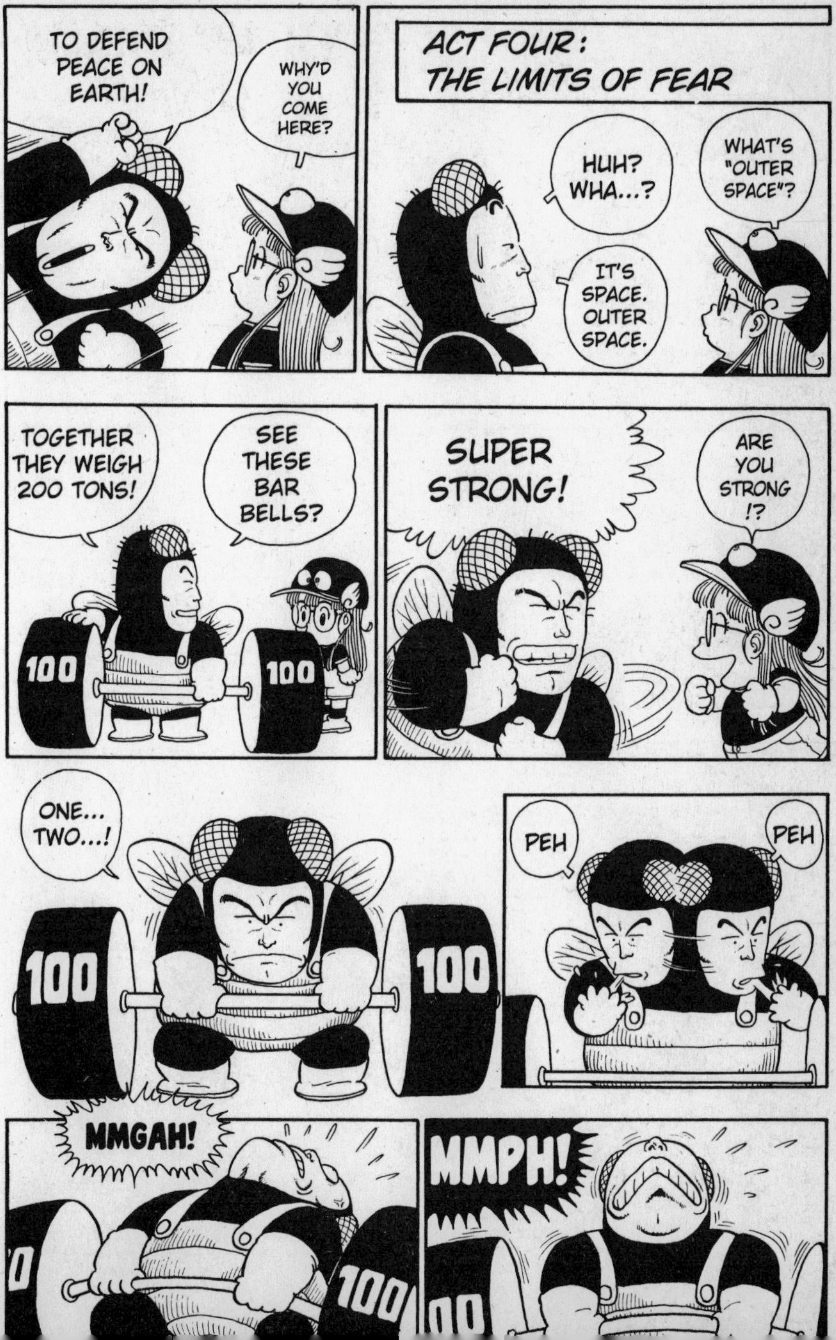
ACT FOUR: THE LIMITS OF FEAR
WHAT'S "OUTER SPACE"?
HUH? WHA...?
IT'S SPACE. OUTER SPACE.
WHY'D YOU COME HERE?
TO DEFEND PEACE ON EARTH!
ARE YOU STRONG !?
SUPER STRONG!
SEE THESE BAR BELLS?
TOGETHER THEY WEIGH 200 TONS!
100
100
PEH
PEH
ONE... TWO...!
100
100
MMPH!
100
MMGAH!
100

READ THIS WAY

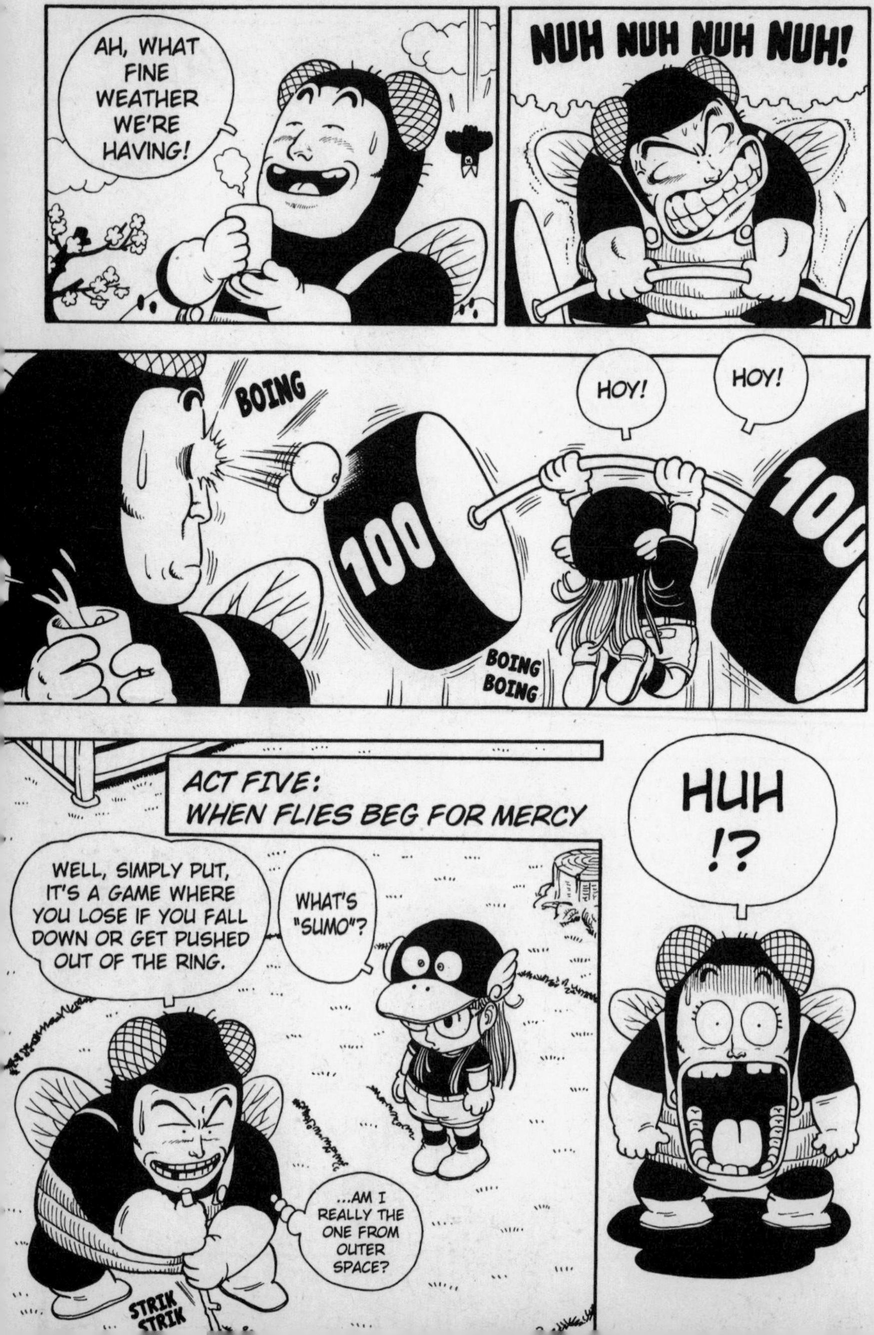
NUH NUH NUH NUH!
AH, WHAT FINE WEATHER WE'RE HAVING!
HOY!
HOY!
BOING
BOING BOING
HUH !?
ACT FIVE: WHEN FLIES BEG FOR MERCY
WHAT'S "SUMO"?
WELL, SIMPLY PUT, IT'S A GAME WHERE YOU LOSE IF YOU FALL DOWN OR GET PUSHED OUT OF THE RING.
...AM I REALLY THE ONE FROM OUTER SPACE?
STRIK STRIK

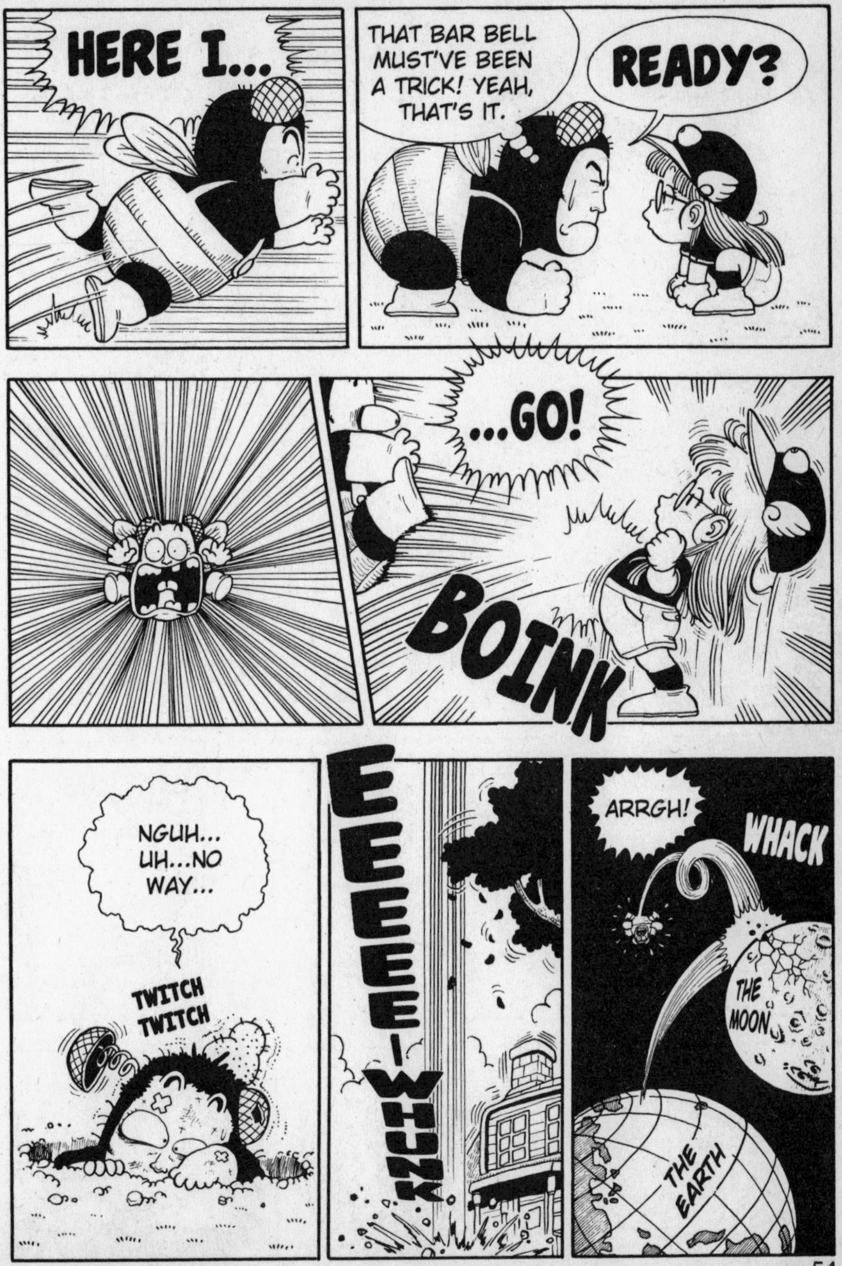
READY?
THAT BAR BELL MUST'VE BEEN A TRICK! YEAH, THAT'S IT.
HERE I...
...GO!
BOINK
ARRGH!
WHACK
THE MOON
THE EARTH
EEEEE-WHUNK
NGUH... UH...NO WAY...
TWITCH TWITCH

READ THIS WAY

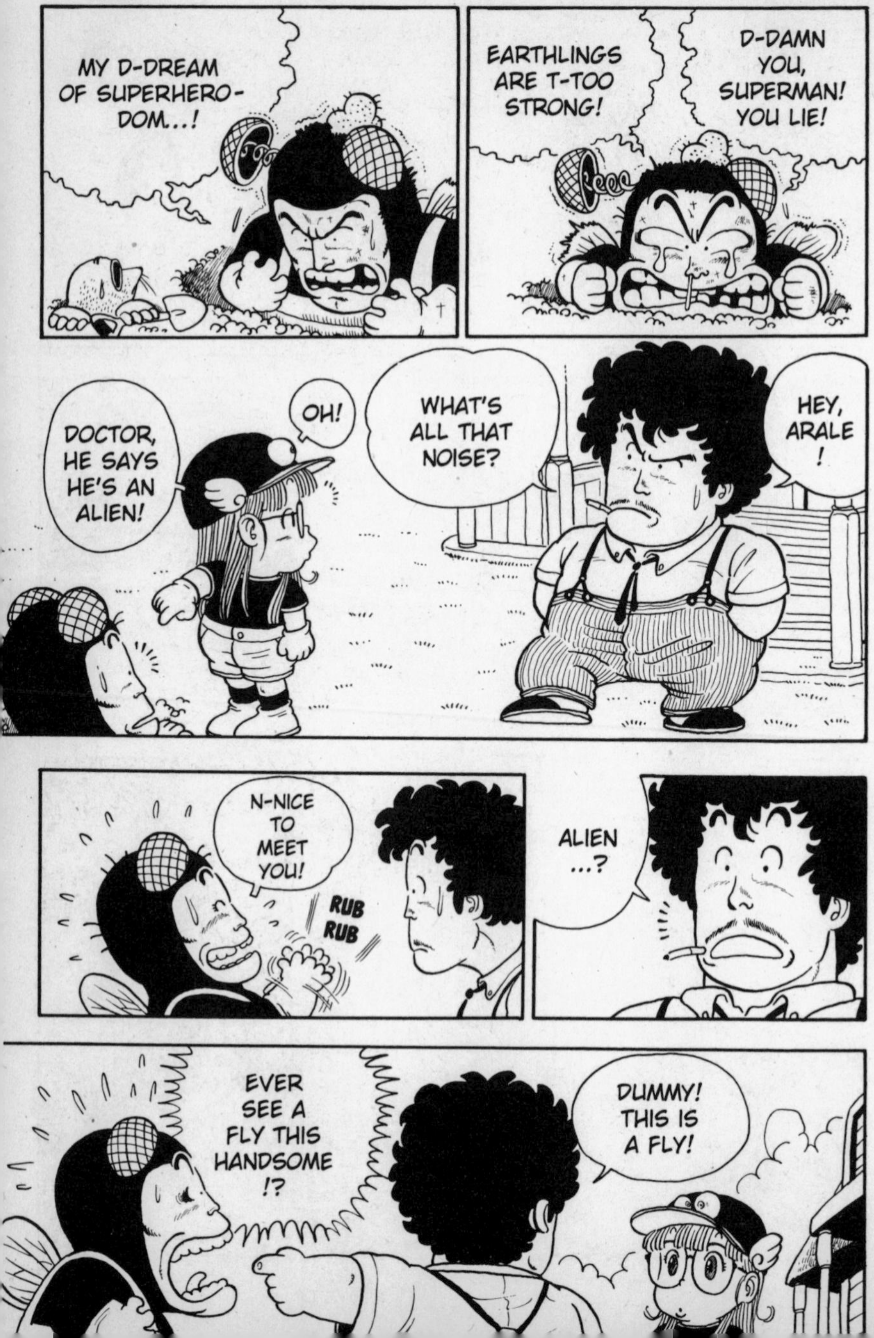
D-DAMN YOU, SUPERMAN! YOU LIE!
EARTHLINGS ARE T-TOO STRONG!
MY D-DREAM OF SUPERHERO-DOM...!
HEY, ARALE!
WHAT'S ALL THAT NOISE?
OH!
DOCTOR, HE SAYS HE'S AN ALIEN!
ALIEN ...?
N-NICE TO MEET YOU!
RUB RUB
DUMMY! THIS IS A FLY!
EVER SEE A FLY THIS HANDSOME !?

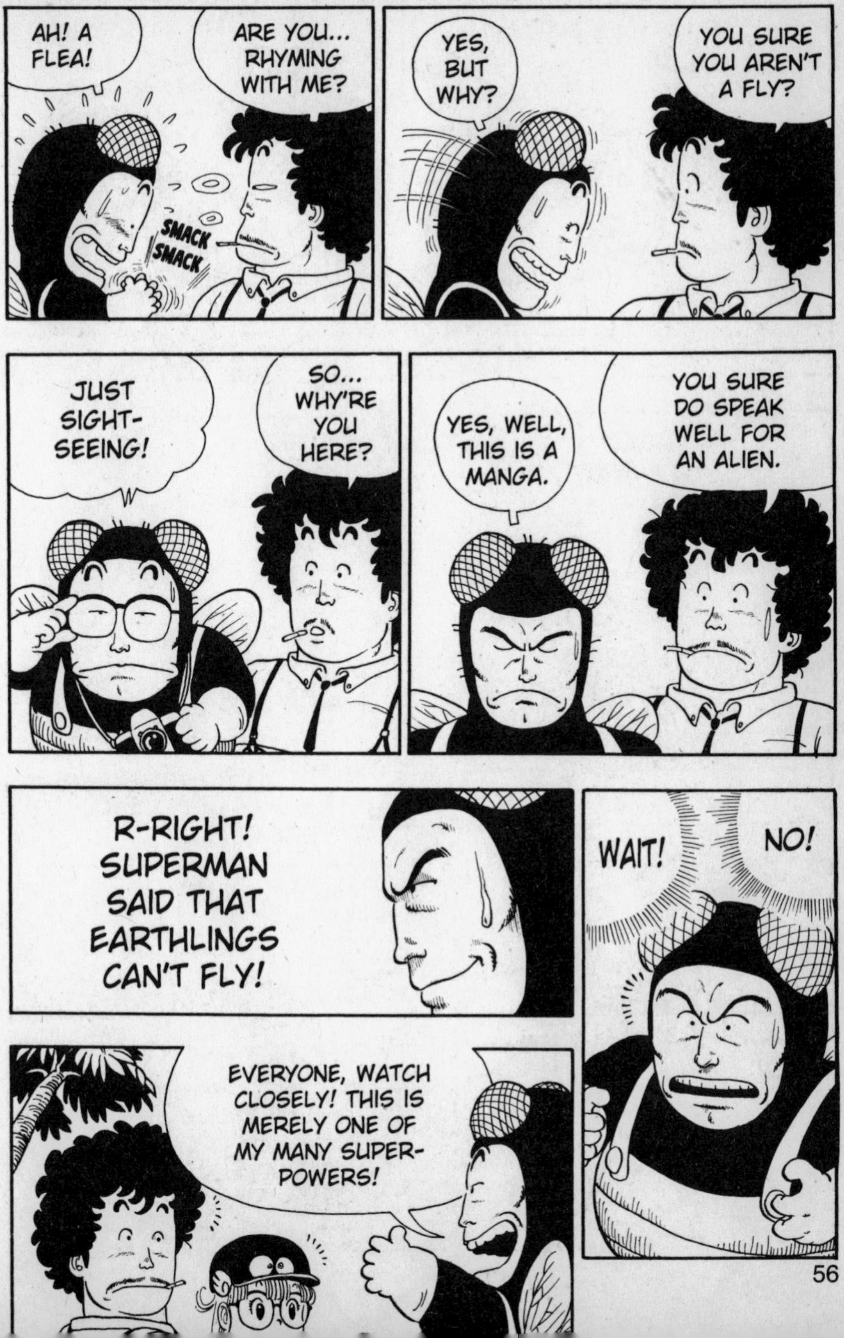
YOU SURE YOU AREN'T A FLY?
YES, BUT WHY?
ARE YOU... RHYMING WITH ME?
AH! A FLEA!
SMACK SMACK
YOU SURE DO SPEAK WELL FOR AN ALIEN.
YES, WELL, THIS IS A MANGA.
SO... WHY'RE YOU HERE?
JUST SIGHT-SEEING!
NO!
WAIT!
R-RIGHT! SUPERMAN SAID THAT EARTHLINGS CAN'T FLY!
EVERYONE, WATCH CLOSELY! THIS IS MERELY ONE OF MY MANY SUPER-POWERS!

READ THIS WAY

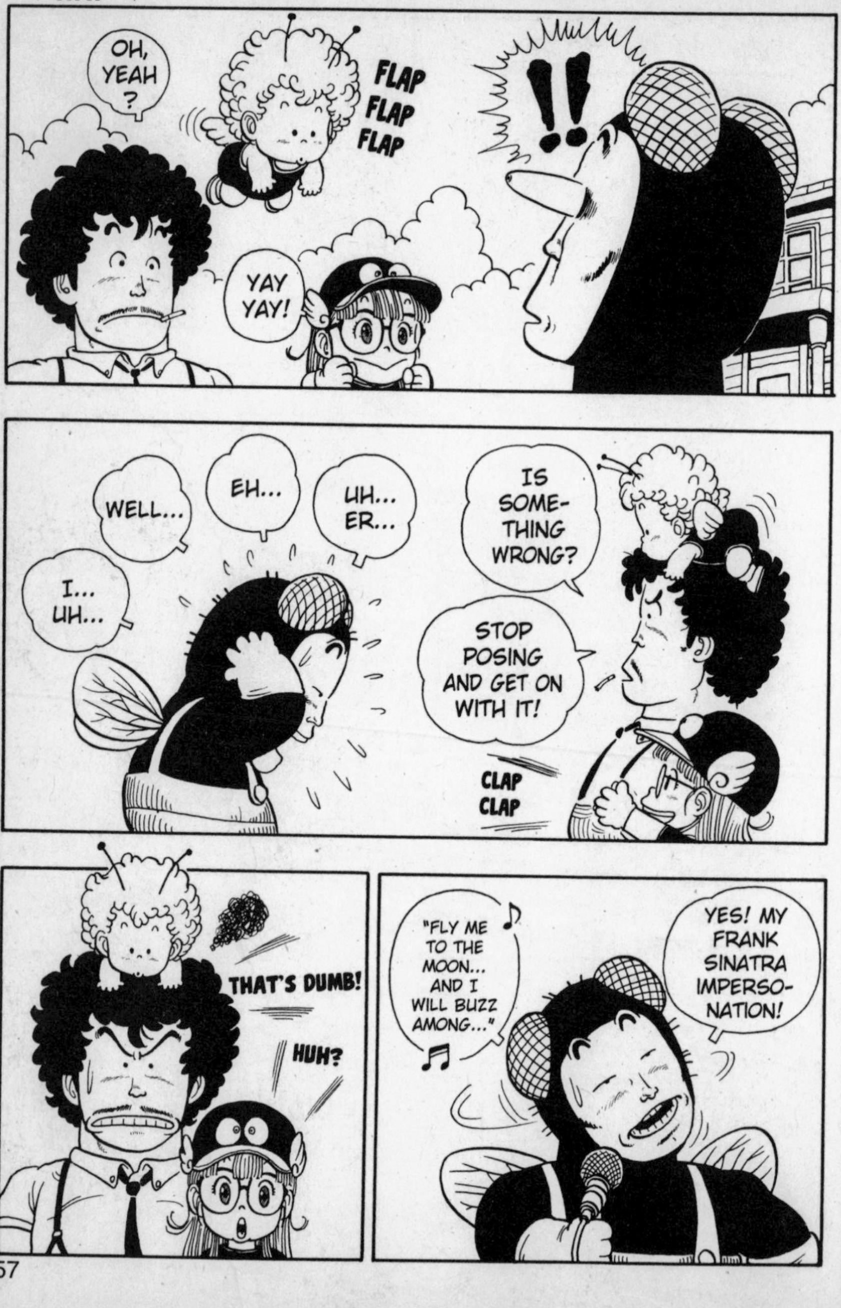
!!
FLAP FLAP FLAP
OH, YEAH?
YAY YAY!
IS SOMETHING WRONG?
STOP POSING AND GET ON WITH IT!
CLAP CLAP
UH... ER...
EH...
WELL...
I... UH...
YES! MY FRANK SINATRA IMPERSONATION!
"FLY ME TO THE MOON... AND I WILL BUZZ AMONG..."
THAT'S DUMB!
HUH?

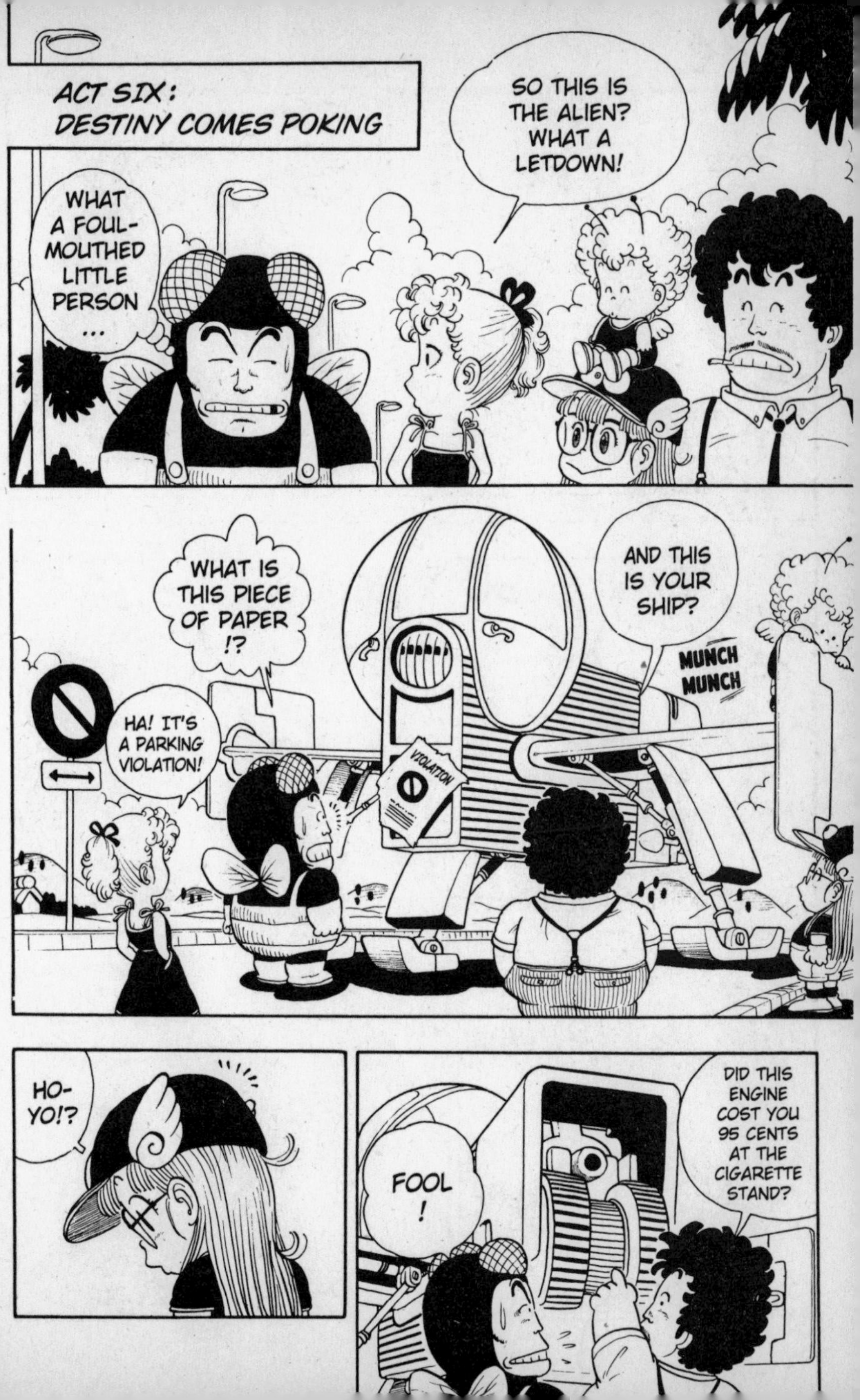
ACT SIX: DESTINY COMES POKING
SO THIS IS THE ALIEN? WHAT A LETDOWN!
WHAT A FOUL-MOUTHED LITTLE PERSON ...
AND THIS IS YOUR SHIP?
MUNCH MUNCH
WHAT IS THIS PIECE OF PAPER !?
VIOLATION
HA! IT'S A PARKING VIOLATION!
DID THIS ENGINE COST YOU 95 CENTS AT THE CIGARETTE STAND?
FOOL !
HO-YO!?

READ THIS WAY

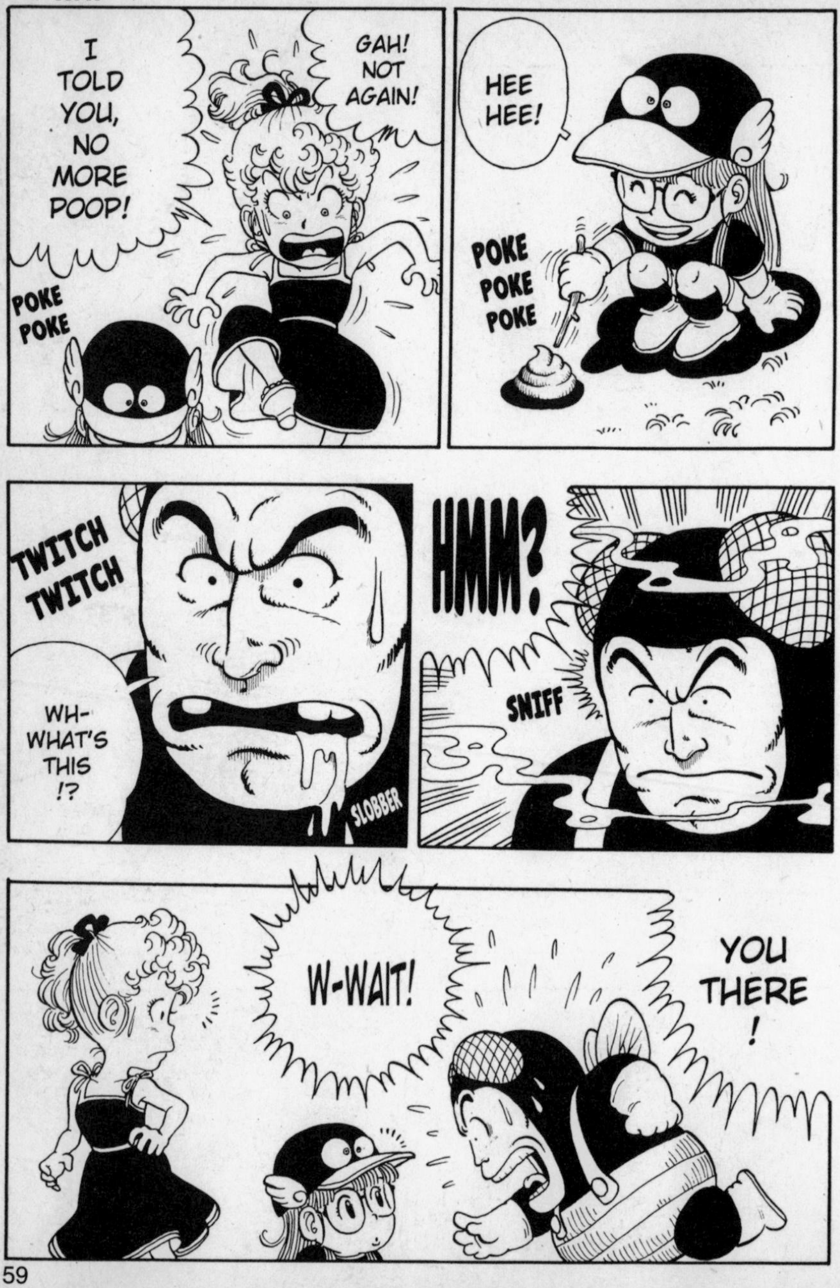
HEE HEE!
POKE POKE POKE
GAH! NOT AGAIN!
I TOLD YOU, NO MORE POOP!
POKE POKE
HMM?
SNIFF
TWITCH TWITCH
WH-WHAT'S THIS!?
SLOBBER
YOU THERE!
W-WAIT!

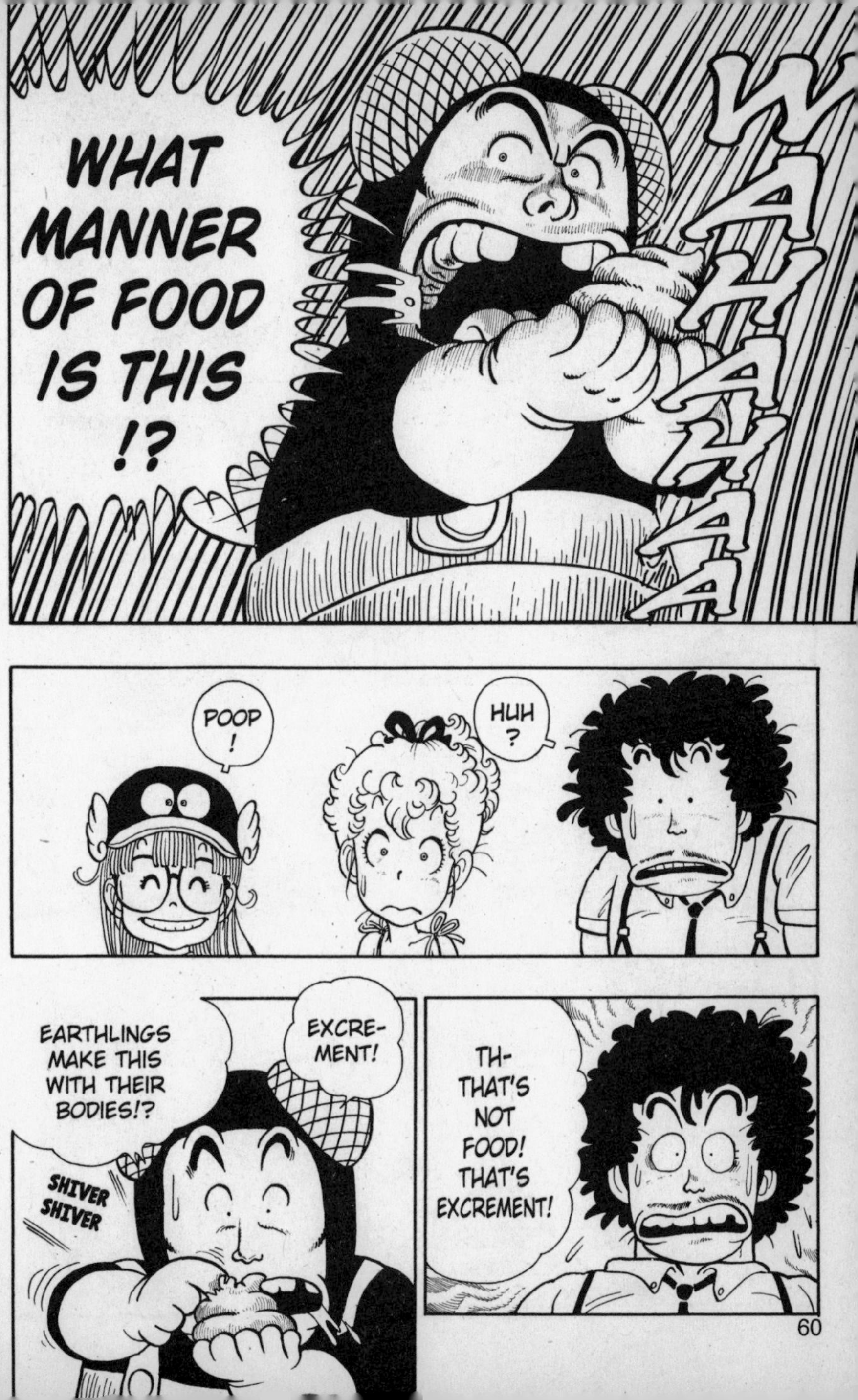
WHAT MANNER OF FOOD IS THIS !?
WAHAHAAA
HUH ?
POOP !
TH- THAT'S NOT FOOD! THAT'S EXCREMENT!
EXCRE- MENT!
EARTHLINGS MAKE THIS WITH THEIR BODIES!?
SHIVER SHIVER

READ THIS WAY

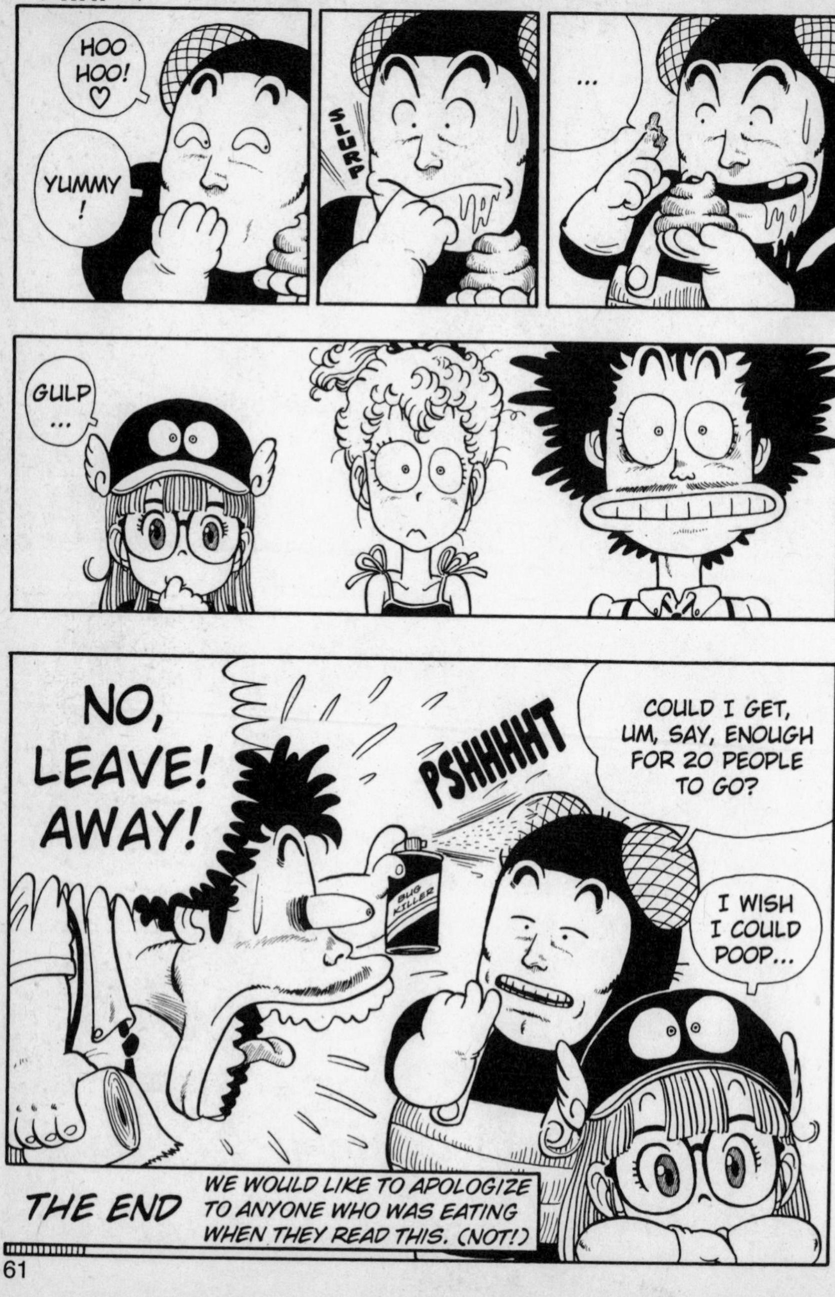

...
SLURP
HOO HOO! ♡
YUMMY!
GULP...
COULD I GET, UM, SAY, ENOUGH FOR 20 PEOPLE TO GO?
PSHHHHT
I WISH I COULD POOP...
BUG KILLER
NO, LEAVE! AWAY!
WE WOULD LIKE TO APOLOGIZE TO ANYONE WHO WAS EATING WHEN THEY READ THIS. (NOT!)
THE END

The Reality Machine

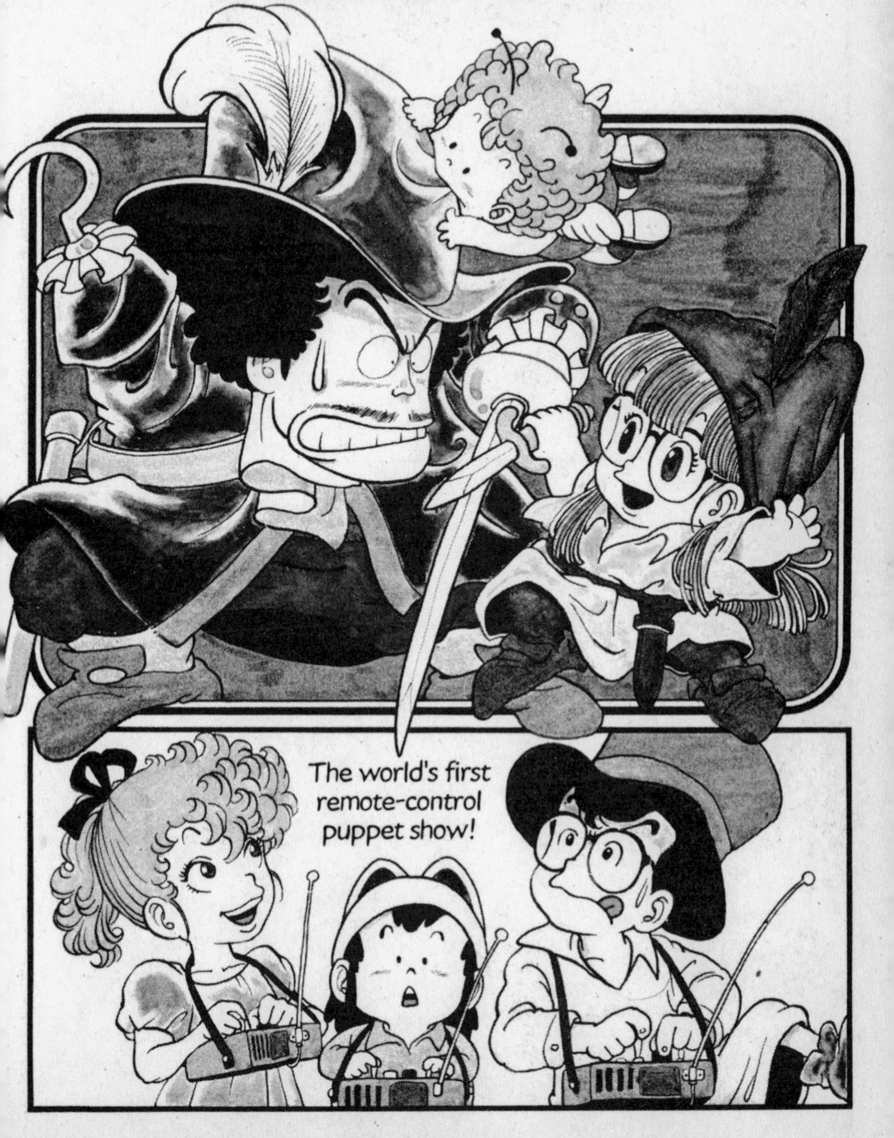
The world's first remote-control puppet show!

READ THIS WAY

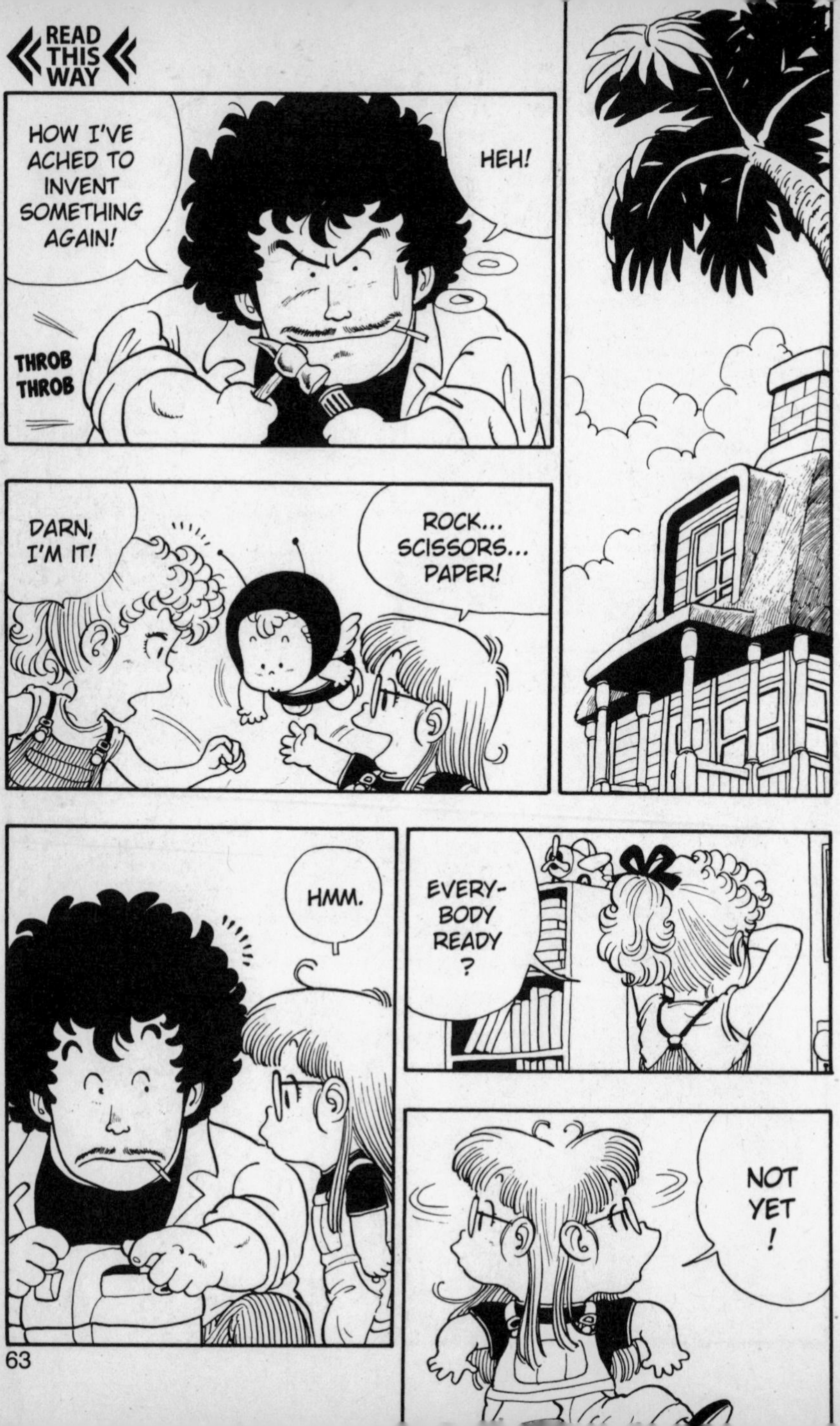
HEH!
HOW I'VE ACHED TO INVENT SOMETHING AGAIN!
THROB THROB
ROCK... SCISSORS... PAPER!
DARN, I'M IT!
EVERY-BODY READY ?
NOT YET !
HMM.

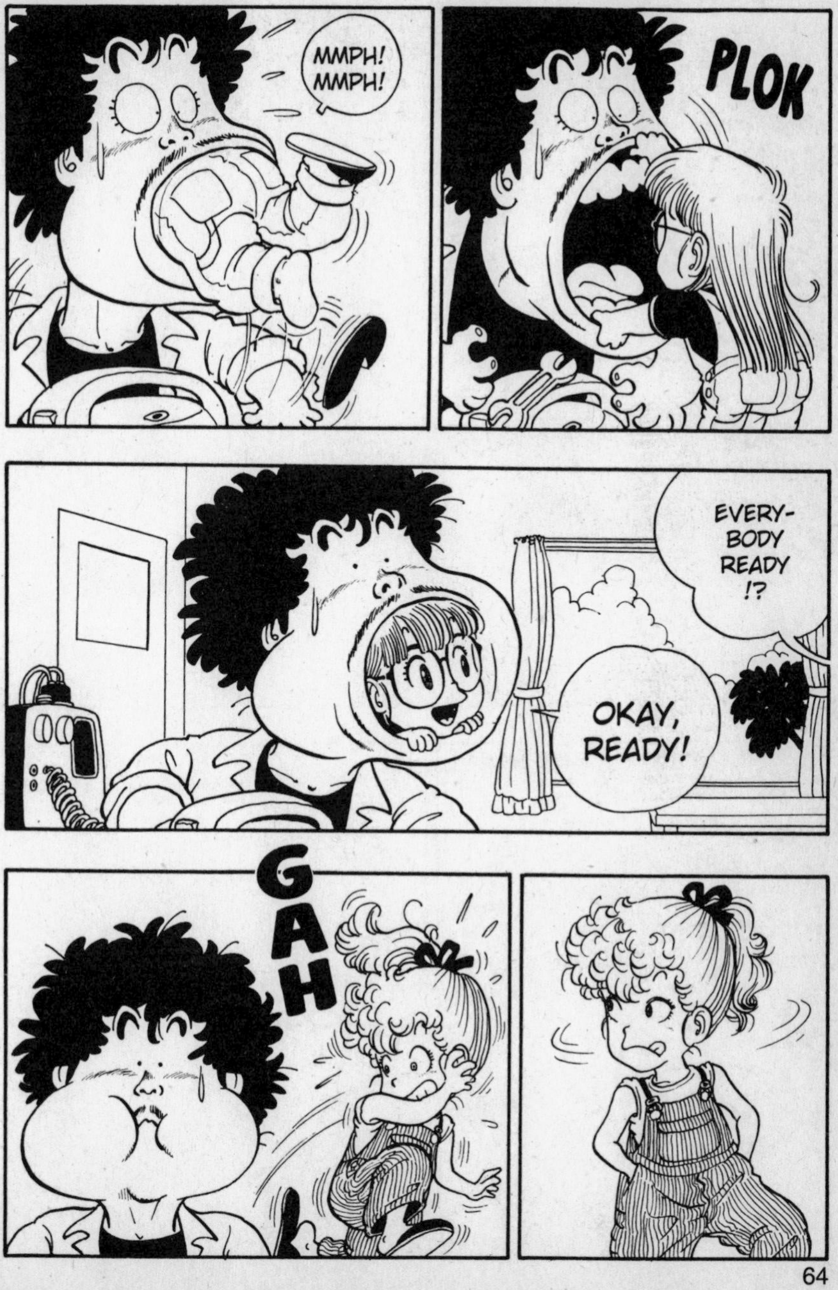
PLOK
MMPH! MMPH!
EVERY-BODY READY !?
OKAY, READY!
GAH

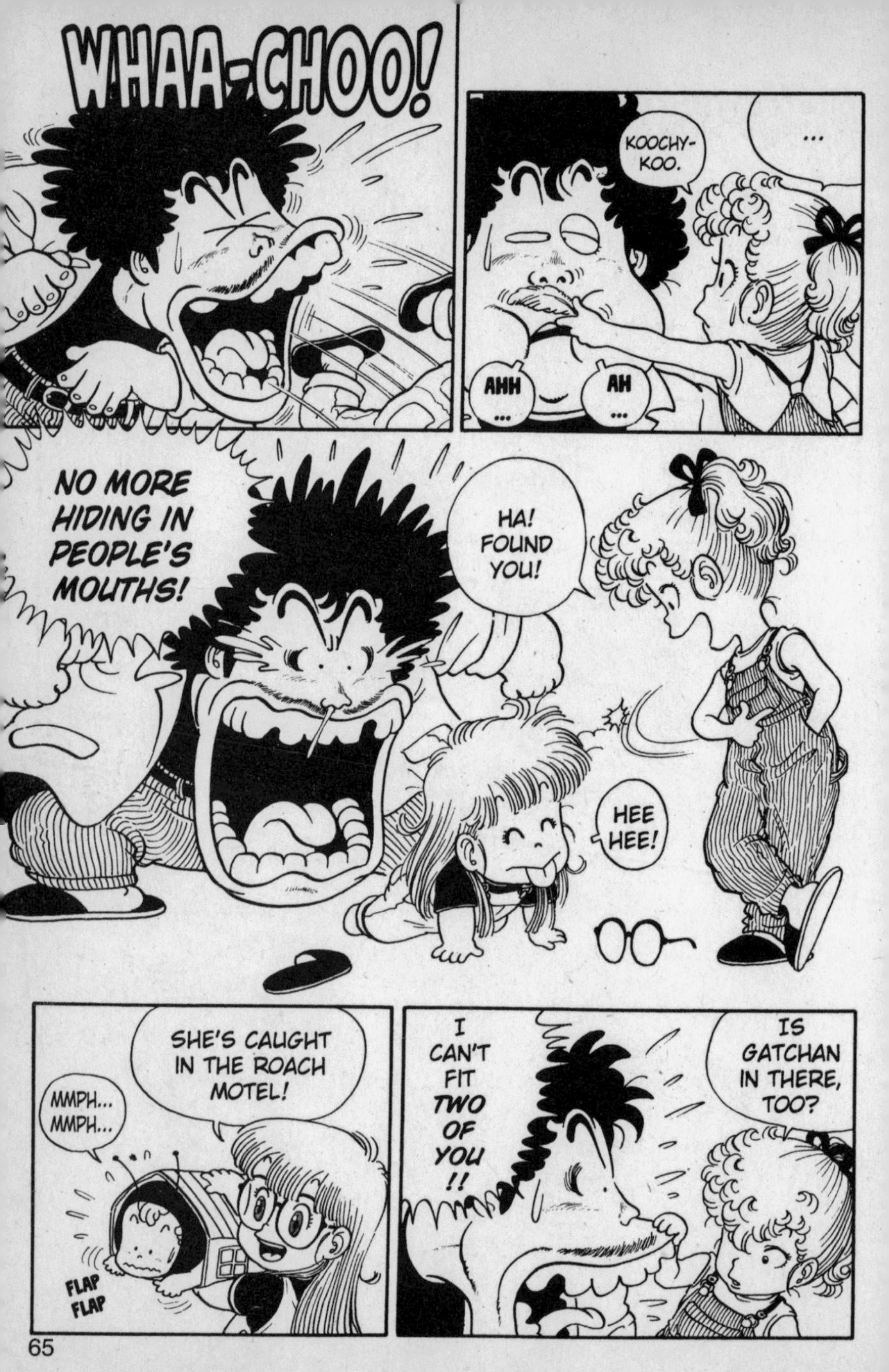
...
KOOCHY-KOO.
AH...
AHH...
WHAA-CHOO!
HA! FOUND YOU!
HEE HEE!
NO MORE HIDING IN PEOPLE'S MOUTHS!
IS GATCHAN IN THERE, TOO?
I CAN'T FIT TWO OF YOU !!
SHE'S CAUGHT IN THE ROACH MOTEL!
MMPH... MMPH...
FLAP FLAP

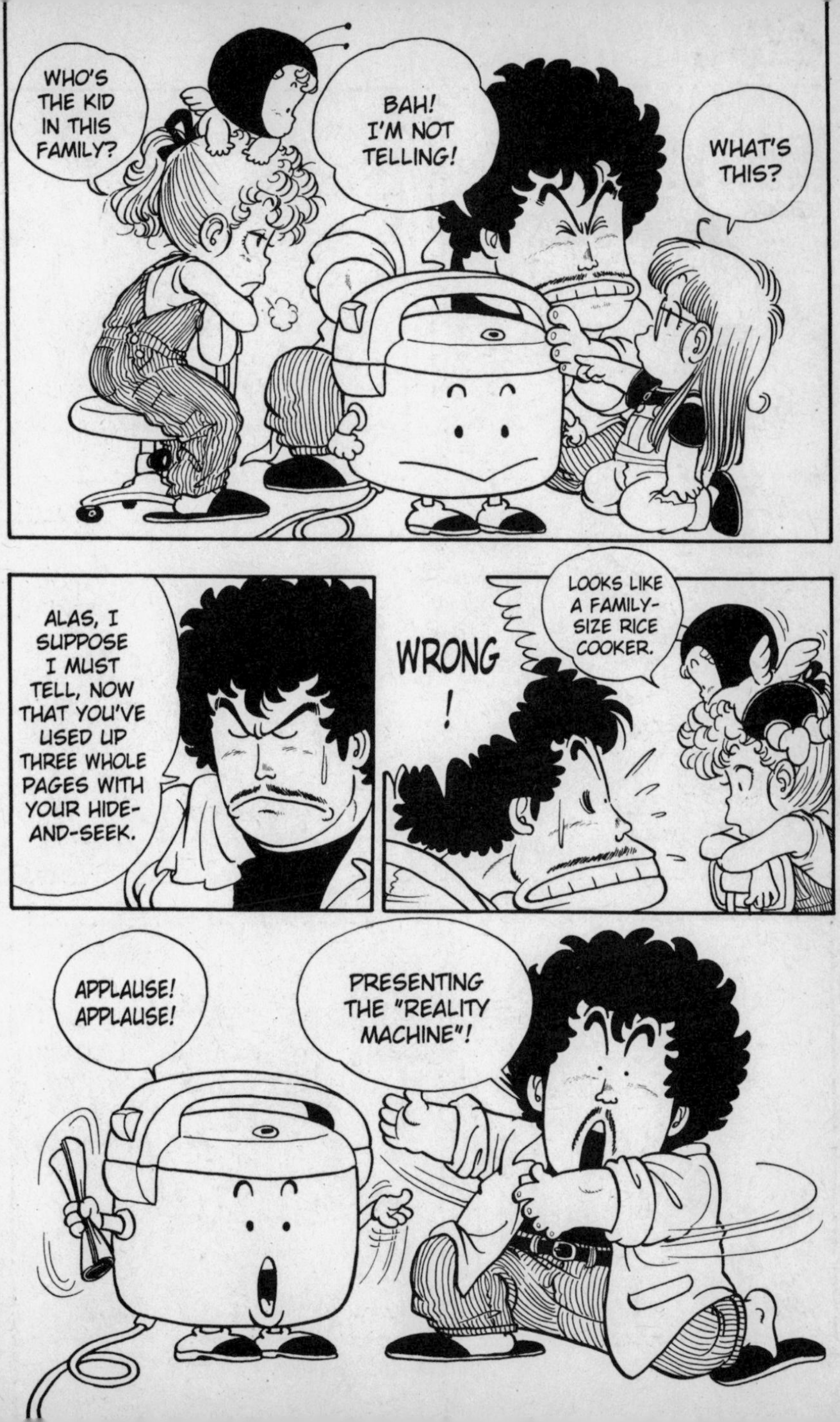
WHAT'S THIS?
BAH! I'M NOT TELLING!
WHO'S THE KID IN THIS FAMILY?
LOOKS LIKE A FAMILY-SIZE RICE COOKER.
WRONG!
ALAS, I SUPPOSE I MUST TELL, NOW THAT YOU'VE USED UP THREE WHOLE PAGES WITH YOUR HIDE-AND-SEEK.
PRESENTING THE "REALITY MACHINE"!
APPLAUSE! APPLAUSE!

READ THIS WAY

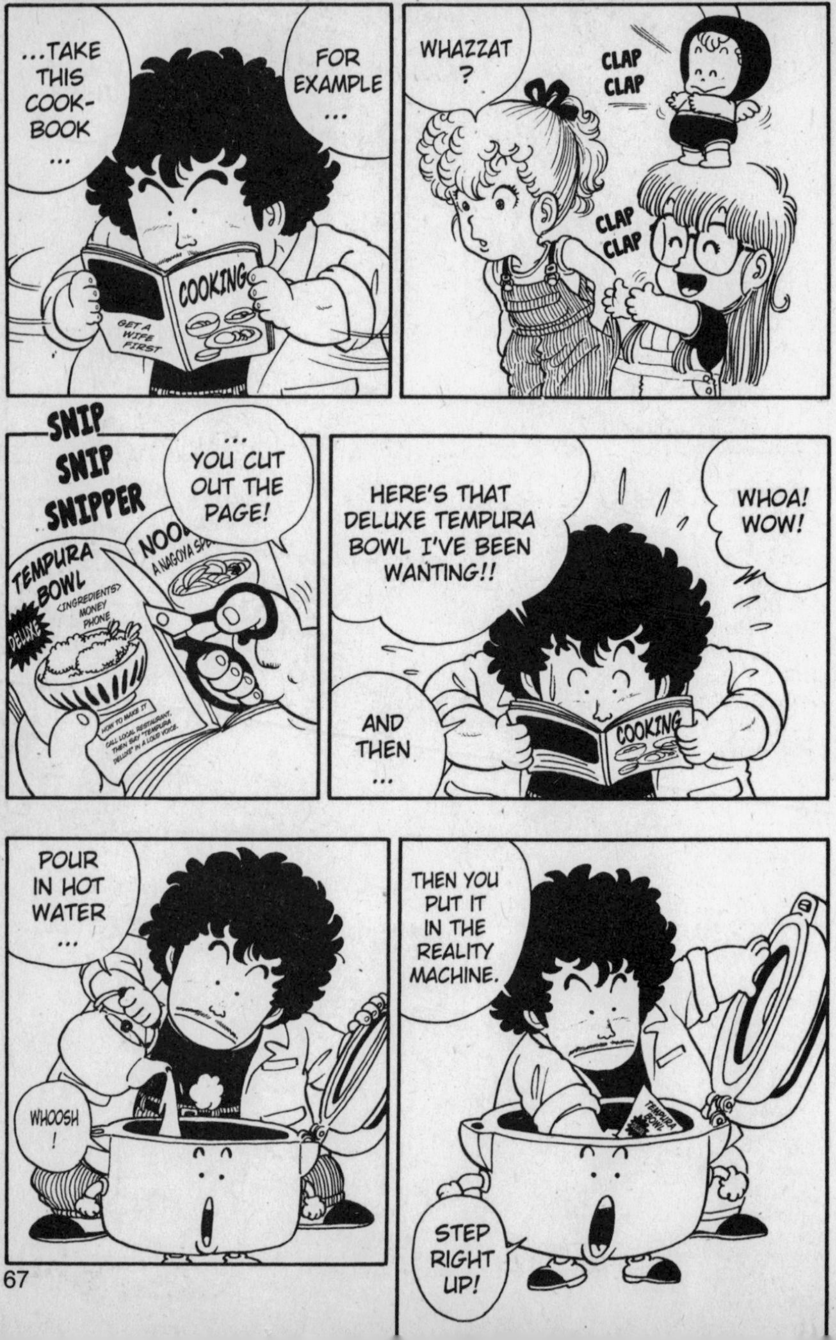
WHAZZAT ?
CLAP CLAP
CLAP CLAP
FOR EXAMPLE ...
...TAKE THIS COOK-BOOK ...
COOKING
GET A WIFE FIRST
WHOA! WOW!
HERE'S THAT DELUXE TEMPURA BOWL I'VE BEEN WANTING!!
AND THEN ...
COOKING
... YOU CUT OUT THE PAGE!
SNIP SNIP SNIPPER
TEMPURA BOWL
DELUXE
<INGREDIENTS> MONEY PHONE
HOW TO MAKE IT CALL LOCAL RESTAURANT, THEN SAY "TEMPURA DELUXE" IN A LOUD VOICE.
THEN YOU PUT IT IN THE REALITY MACHINE.
TEMPURA BOWL
STEP RIGHT UP!
POUR IN HOT WATER ...
WHOOSH !

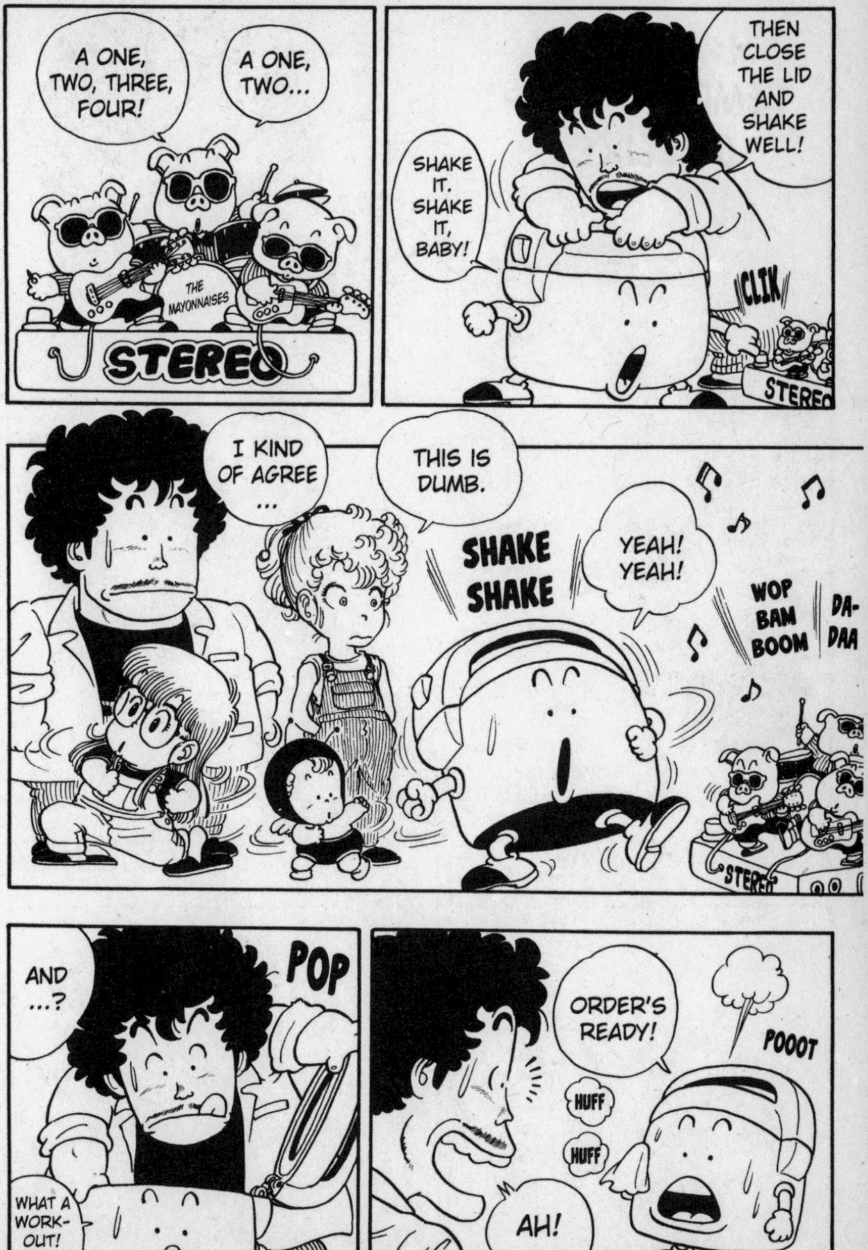
THEN CLOSE THE LID AND SHAKE WELL!
SHAKE IT. SHAKE IT, BABY!
CLIK
STEREO
A ONE, TWO...
A ONE, TWO, THREE, FOUR!
THE MAYONNAISES
STEREO
DA-DAA
WOP BAM BOOM
YEAH! YEAH!
SHAKE SHAKE
THIS IS DUMB.
I KIND OF AGREE ...
STEREO
POOOT
ORDER'S READY!
HUFF
HUFF
AH!
POP
AND ...?
WHAT A WORK-OUT!

READ THIS WAY

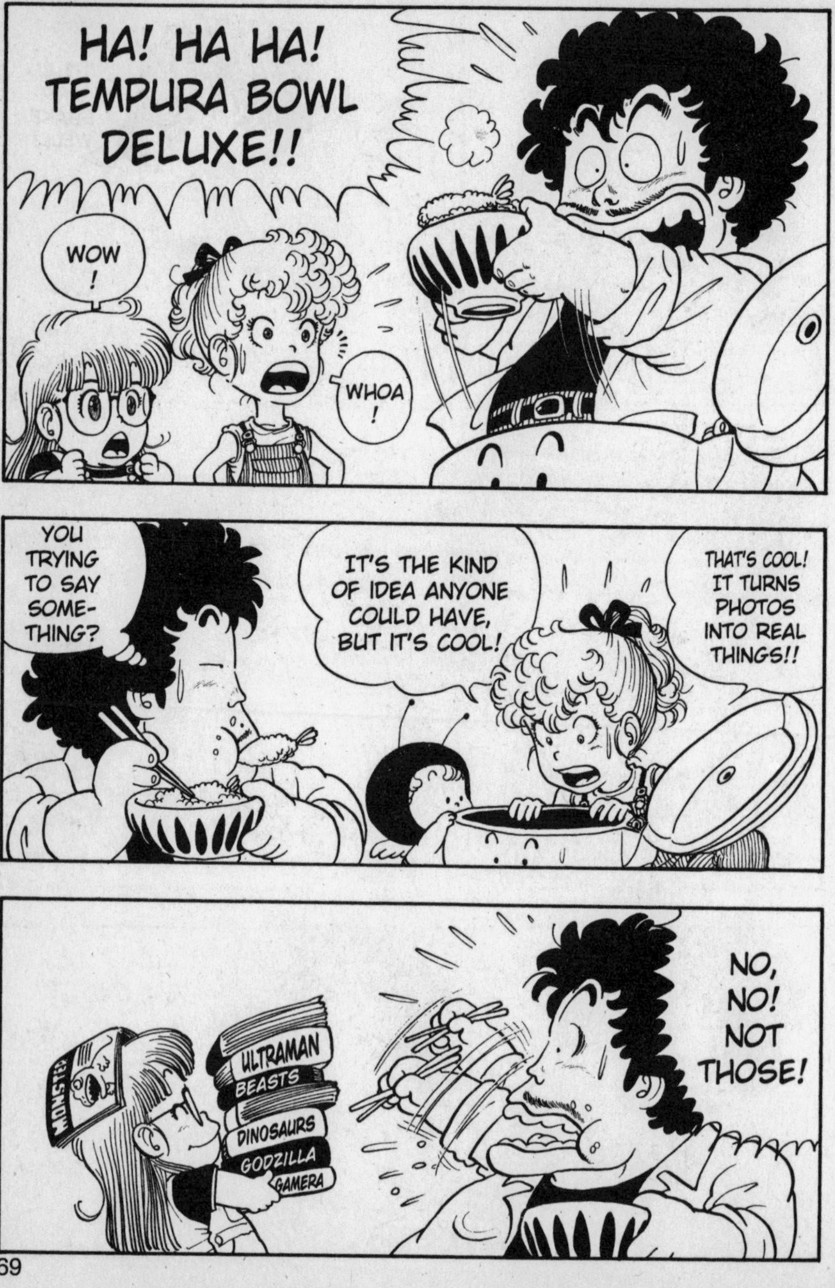

HA! HA HA! TEMPURA BOWL DELUXE!!
WHOA!
WOW!
THAT'S COOL! IT TURNS PHOTOS INTO REAL THINGS!!
IT'S THE KIND OF IDEA ANYONE COULD HAVE, BUT IT'S COOL!
YOU TRYING TO SAY SOME-THING?
NO, NO! NOT THOSE!
ULTRAMAN
BEASTS
DINOSAURS
GODZILLA
GAMERA
MONSTER

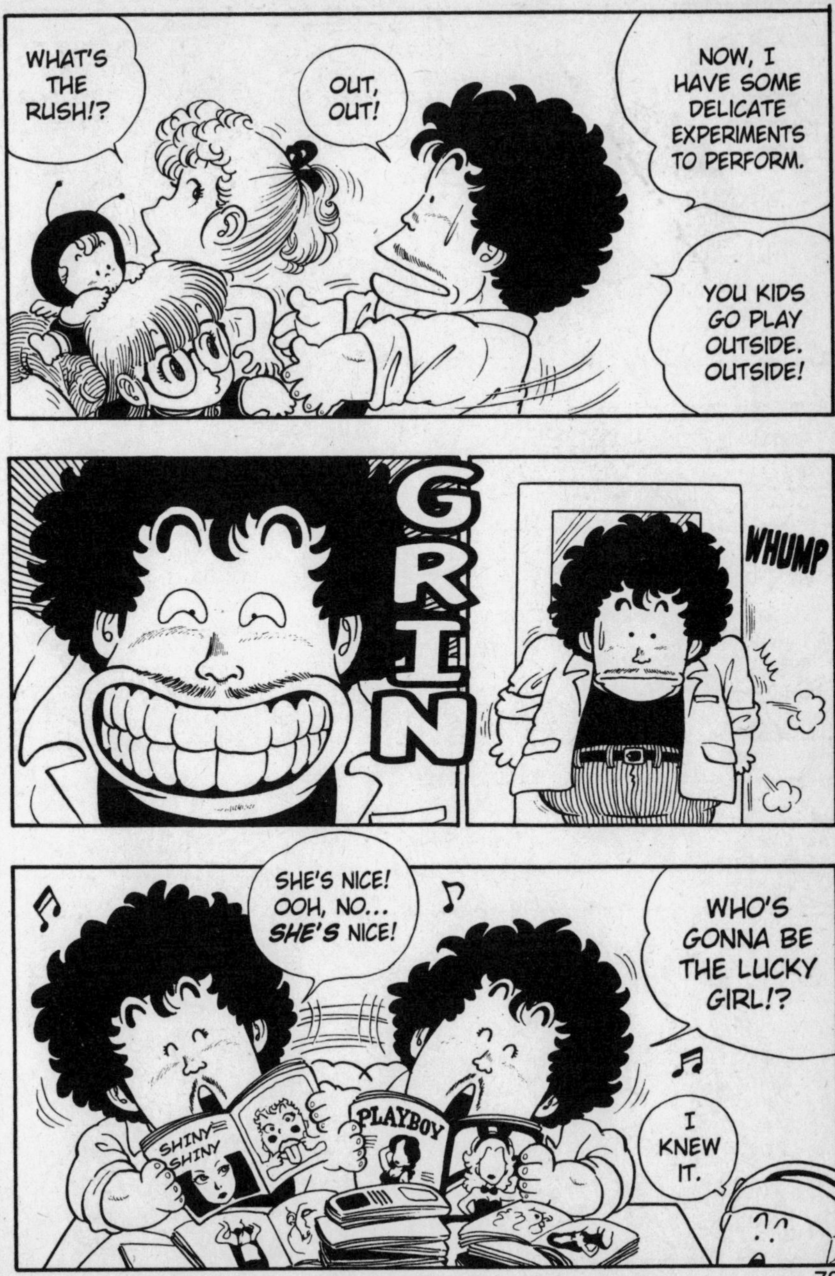
NOW, I HAVE SOME DELICATE EXPERIMENTS TO PERFORM.
YOU KIDS GO PLAY OUTSIDE. OUTSIDE!
OUT, OUT!
WHAT'S THE RUSH!?
WHUMP
GRIN
WHO'S GONNA BE THE LUCKY GIRL!?
SHE'S NICE! OOH, NO... *SHE'S* NICE!
I KNEW IT.
PLAYBOY
SHINY SHINY

READ THIS WAY

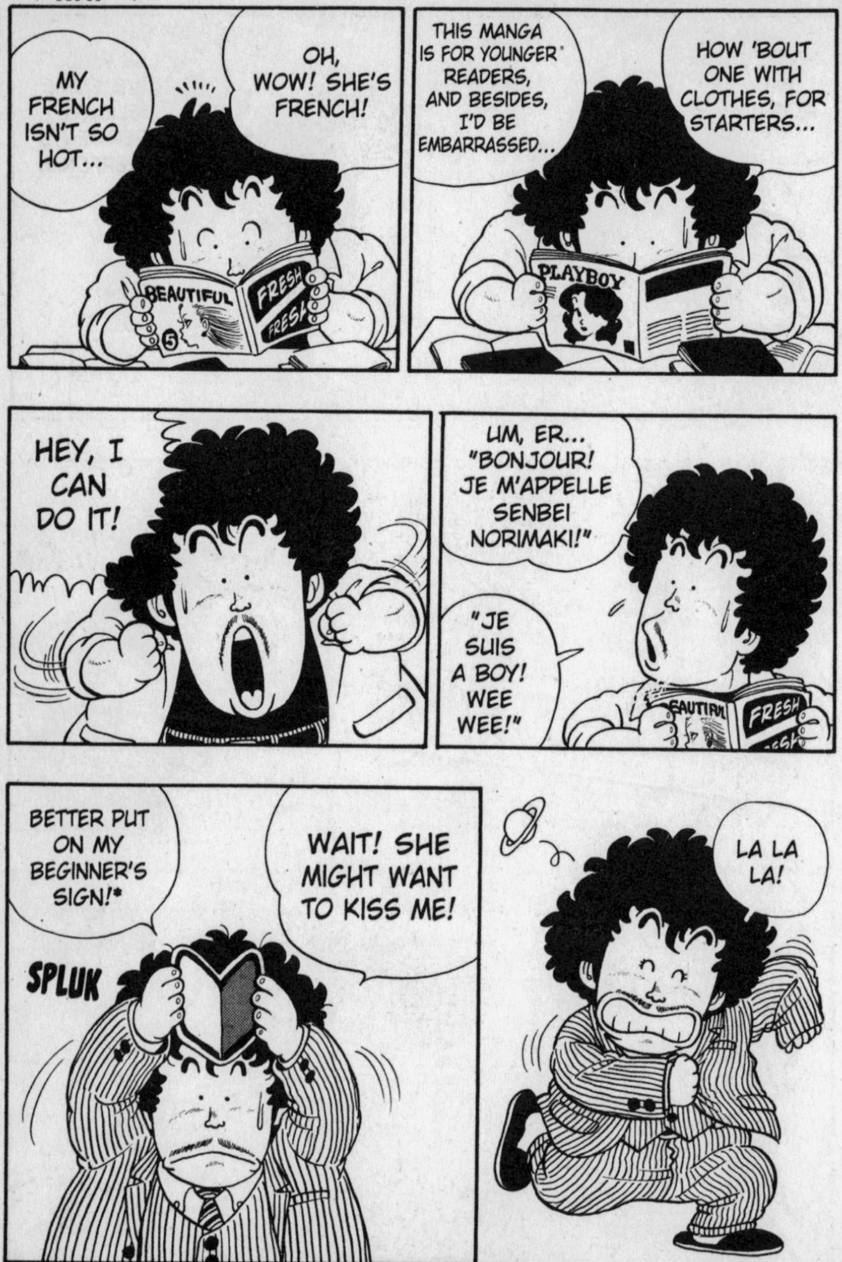
HOW 'BOUT ONE WITH CLOTHES, FOR STARTERS...
THIS MANGA IS FOR YOUNGER READERS, AND BESIDES, I'D BE EMBARRASSED...
PLAYBOY
OH, WOW! SHE'S FRENCH!
MY FRENCH ISN'T SO HOT...
BEAUTIFUL
FRESH
UM, ER... "BONJOUR! JE M'APPELLE SENBEI NORIMAKI!"
"JE SUIS A BOY! WEE WEE!"
HEY, I CAN DO IT!
LA LA LA!
WAIT! SHE MIGHT WANT TO KISS ME!
BETTER PUT ON MY BEGINNER'S SIGN!*
SPLUK

*THE SIGN FOR "STUDENT DRIVER" IN JAPAN

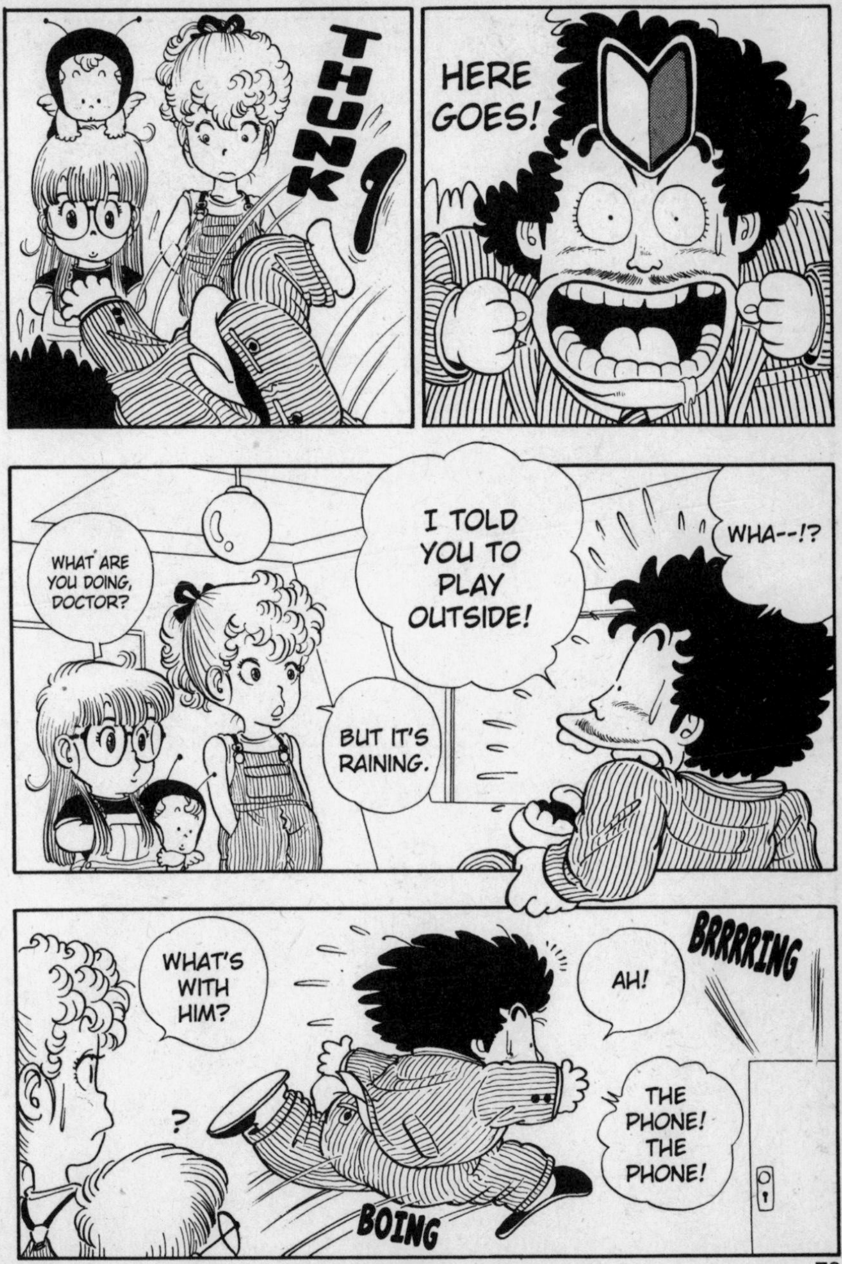
HERE GOES!
THUNK
WHA--!?
I TOLD YOU TO PLAY OUTSIDE!
WHAT ARE YOU DOING, DOCTOR?
BUT IT'S RAINING.
BRRRRING
AH!
THE PHONE! THE PHONE!
WHAT'S WITH HIM?
?
BOING

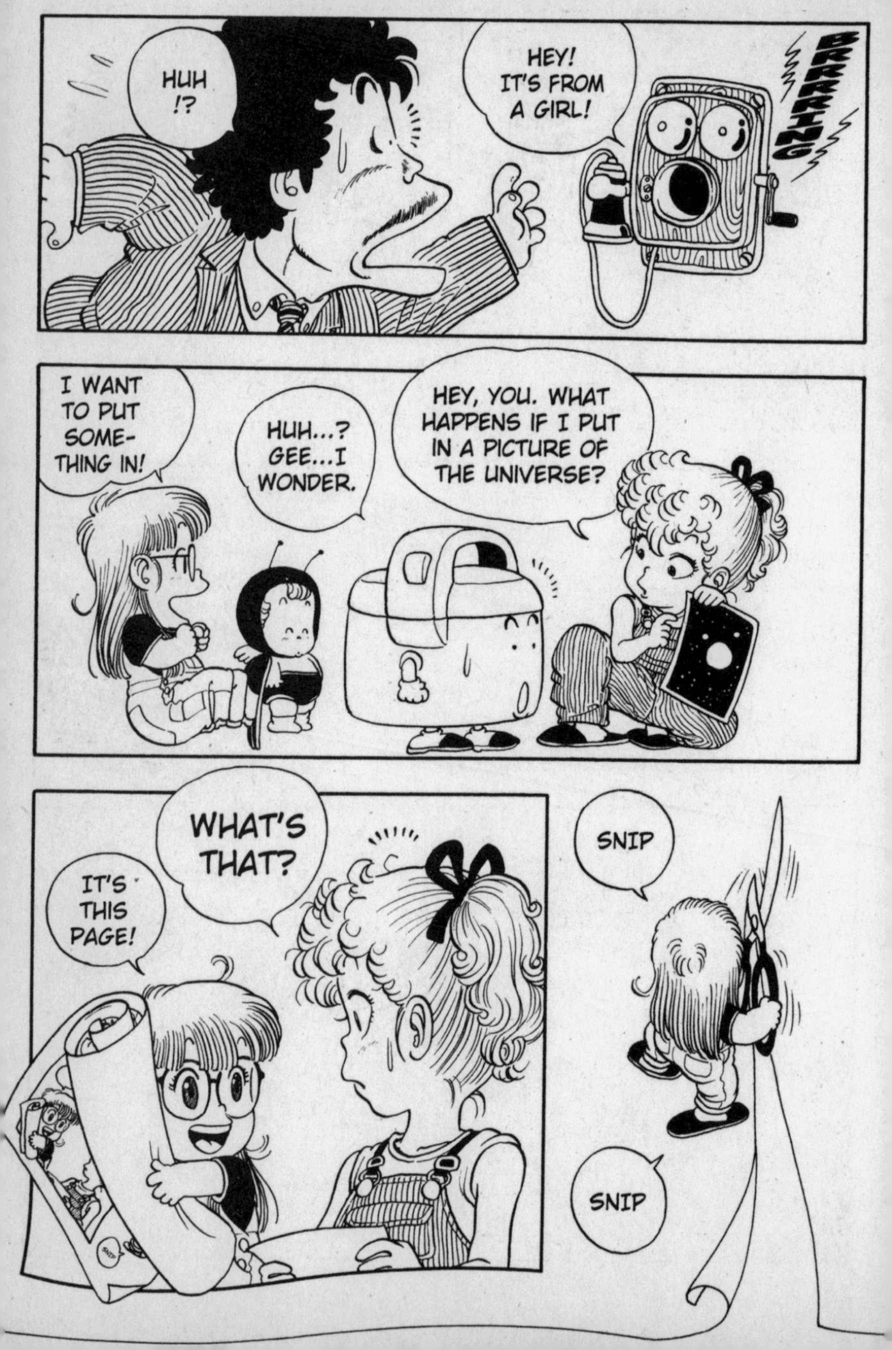
BRRRING
HEY! IT'S FROM A GIRL!
HUH !?
HEY, YOU. WHAT HAPPENS IF I PUT IN A PICTURE OF THE UNIVERSE?
HUH...? GEE...I WONDER.
I WANT TO PUT SOME-THING IN!
SNIP
SNIP
WHAT'S THAT?
IT'S THIS PAGE!

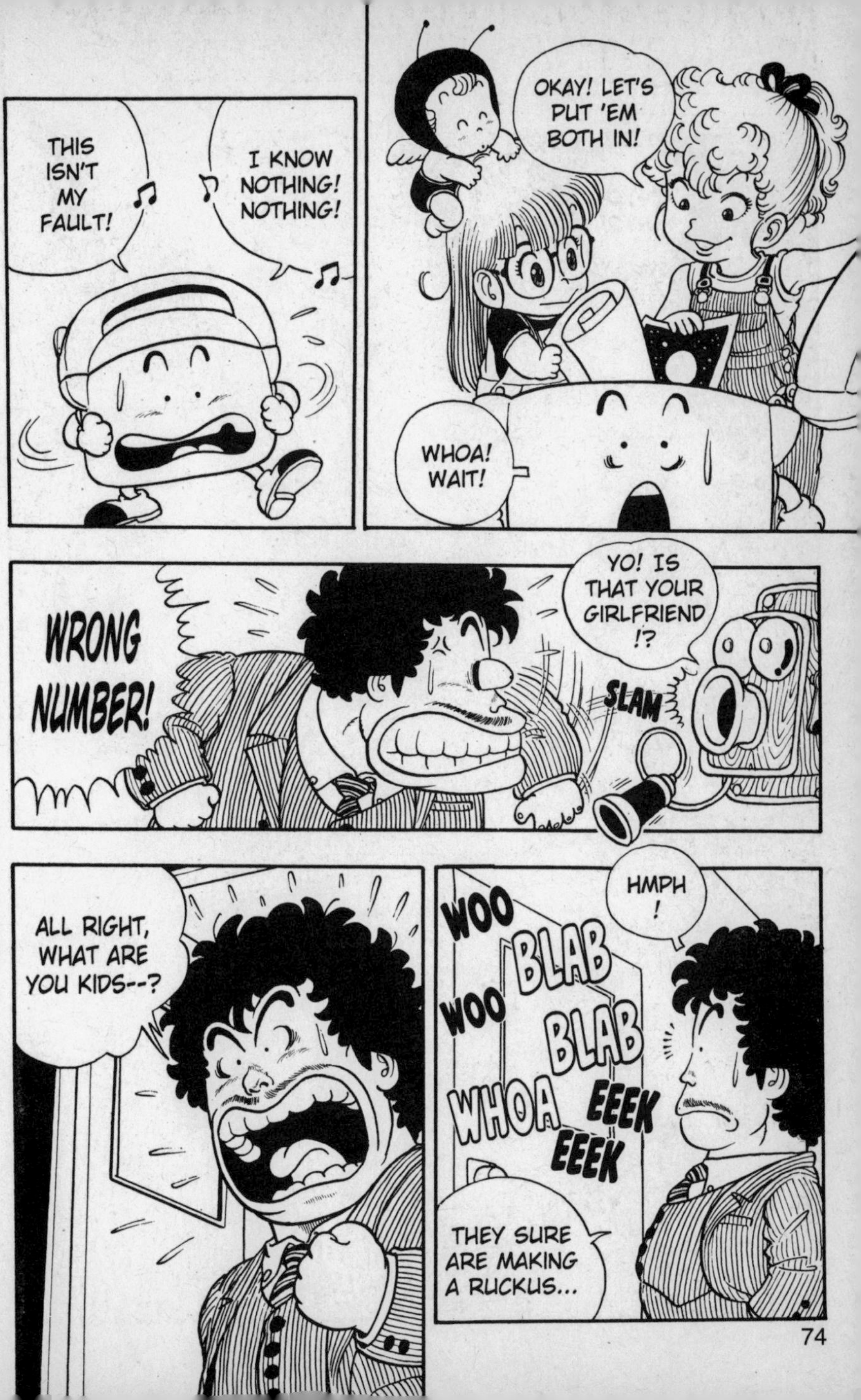
OKAY! LET'S PUT 'EM BOTH IN!
WHOA! WAIT!
I KNOW NOTHING! NOTHING!
THIS ISN'T MY FAULT!
YO! IS THAT YOUR GIRLFRIEND!?
SLAM
WRONG NUMBER!
HMPH!
WOO
BLAB
WOO
BLAB
WHOA
EEEK
EEEK
THEY SURE ARE MAKING A RUCKUS...
ALL RIGHT, WHAT ARE YOU KIDS--?

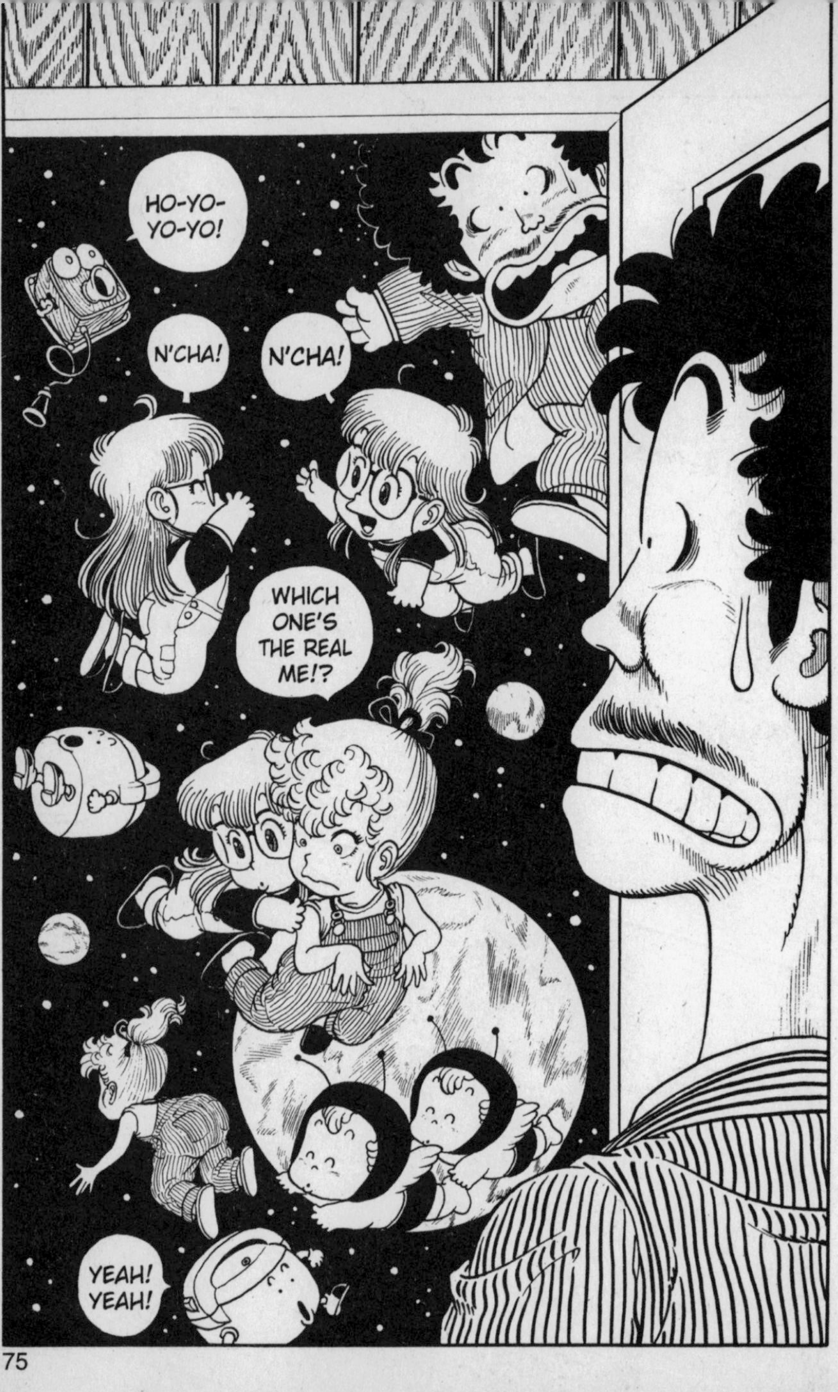
HO-YO-YO-YO!
N'CHA!
N'CHA!
WHICH ONE'S THE REAL ME!?
YEAH! YEAH!

Kidnapped!?

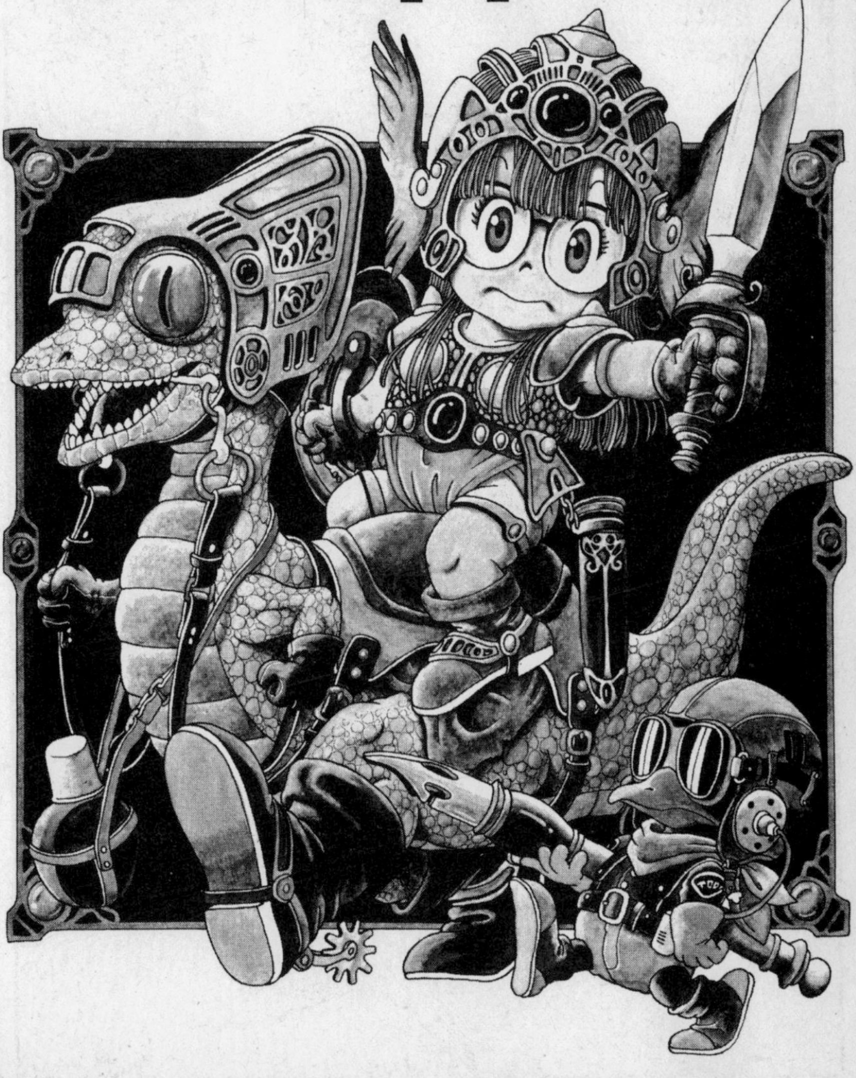

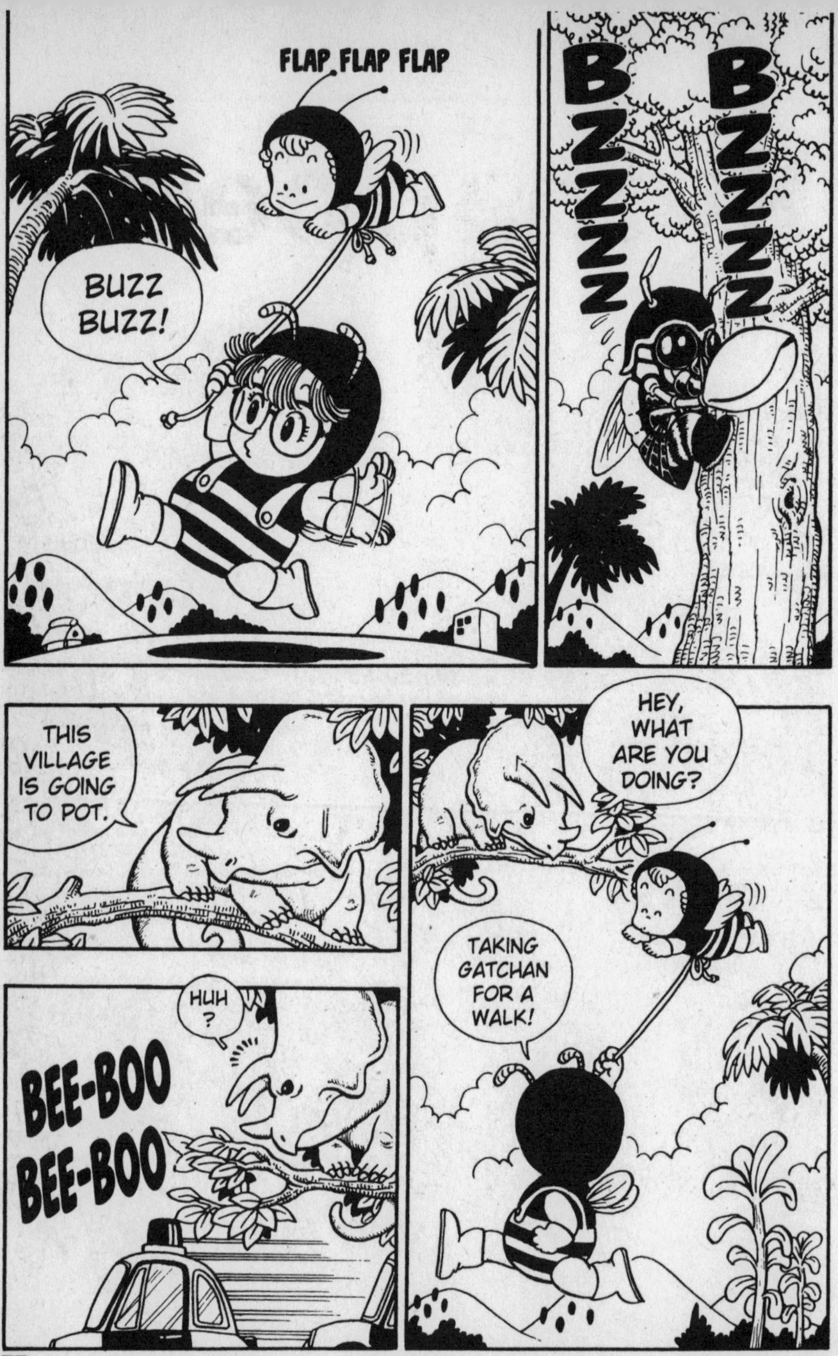
BZZZZ
BZZZZ
FLAP FLAP FLAP
BUZZ BUZZ!
HEY, WHAT ARE YOU DOING?
TAKING GATCHAN FOR A WALK!
THIS VILLAGE IS GOING TO POT.
HUH?
BEE-BOO BEE-BOO

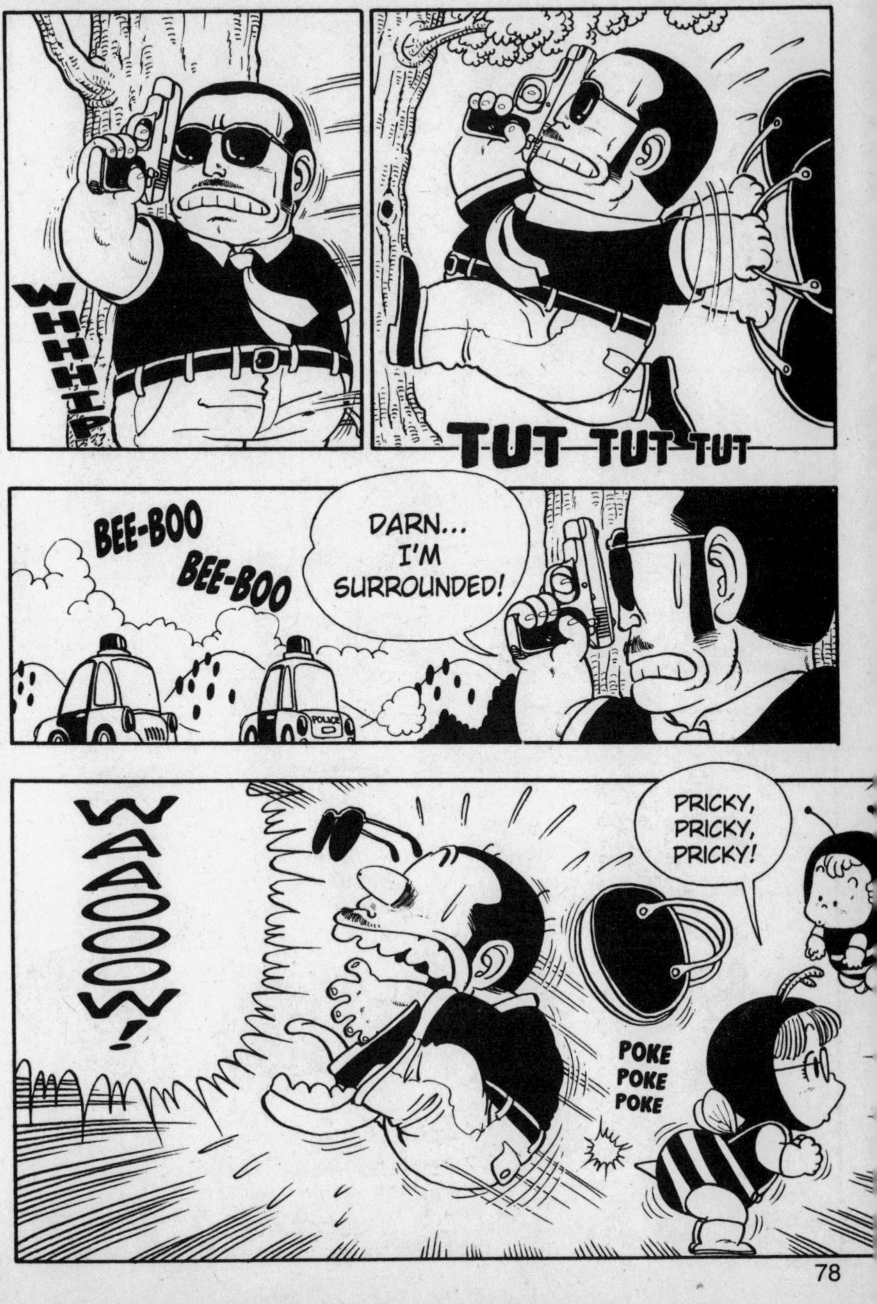
TUT TUT TUT
WHHHIP
DARN... I'M SURROUNDED!
BEE-BOO
BEE-BOO
POLICE
PRICKY, PRICKY, PRICKY!
WAAOOOW!
POKE
POKE
POKE

READ THIS WAY

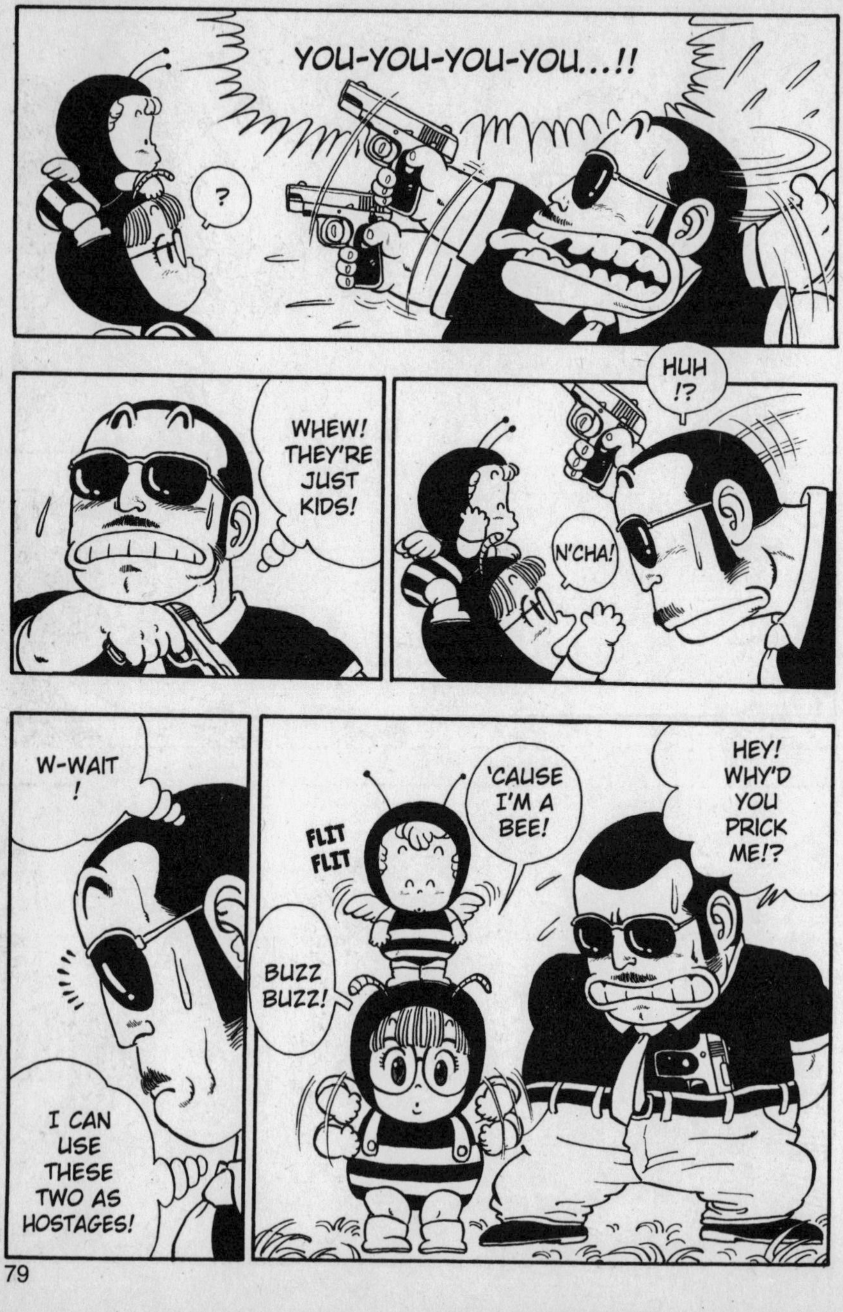

YOU-YOU-YOU-YOU...!!
?
HUH !?
N'CHA!
WHEW! THEY'RE JUST KIDS!
HEY! WHY'D YOU PRICK ME!?
'CAUSE I'M A BEE!
FLIT FLIT
BUZZ BUZZ!
W-WAIT !
I CAN USE THESE TWO AS HOSTAGES!

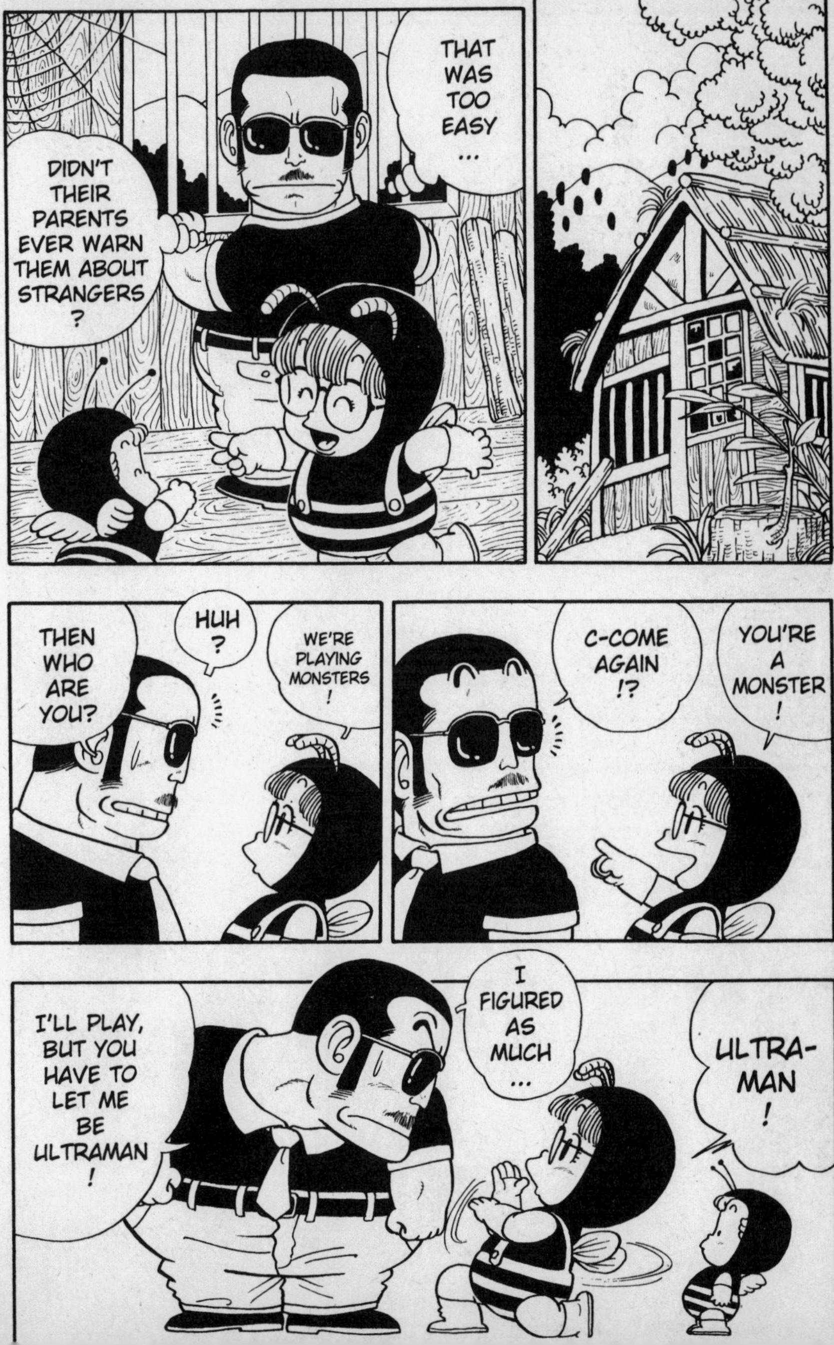
THAT WAS TOO EASY ...
DIDN'T THEIR PARENTS EVER WARN THEM ABOUT STRANGERS ?
YOU'RE A MONSTER !
C-COME AGAIN !?
WE'RE PLAYING MONSTERS !
HUH ?
THEN WHO ARE YOU?
ULTRA-MAN !
I FIGURED AS MUCH ...
I'LL PLAY, BUT YOU HAVE TO LET ME BE ULTRAMAN !

READ THIS WAY

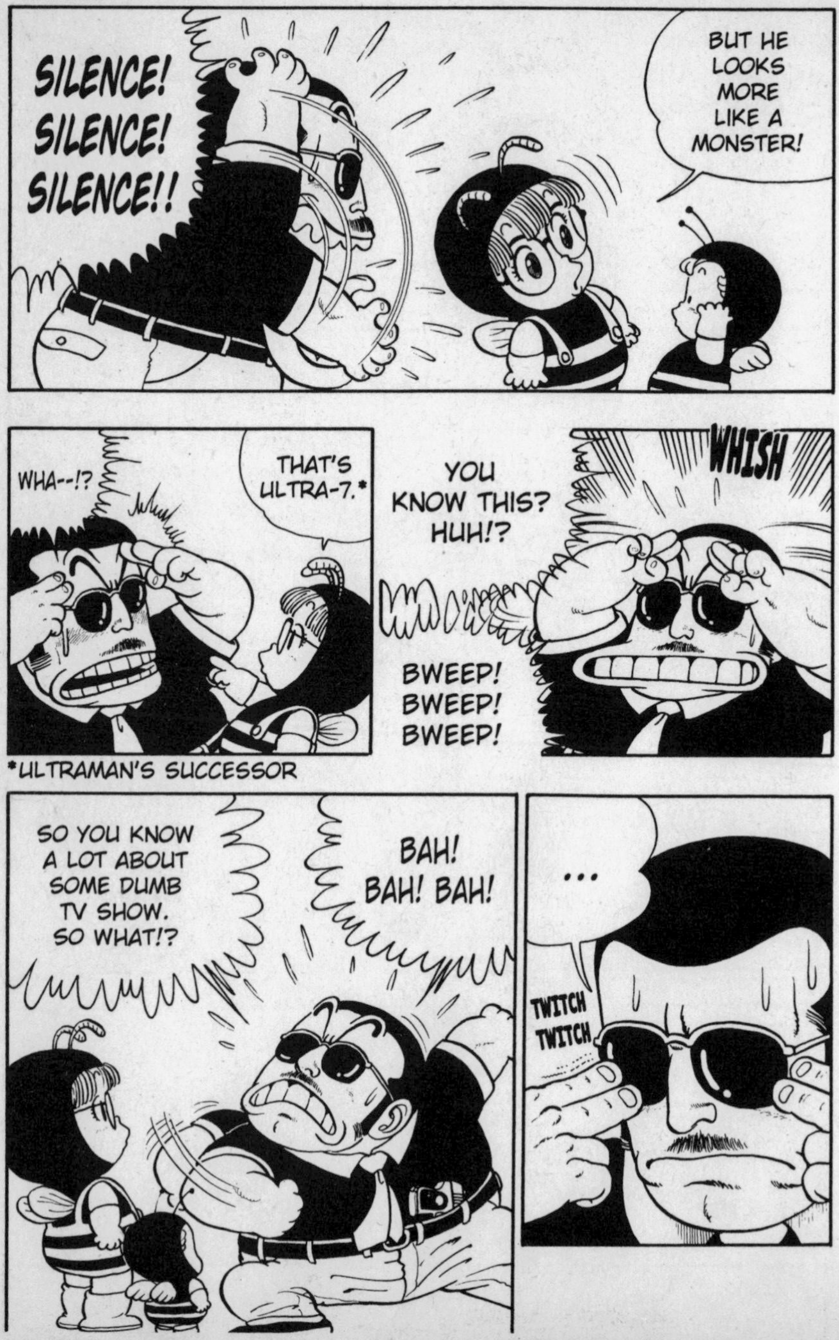

BUT HE LOOKS MORE LIKE A MONSTER!
SILENCE! SILENCE! SILENCE!!
WHISH
YOU KNOW THIS? HUH!?
BWEEP! BWEEP! BWEEP!
THAT'S ULTRA-7.*
WHA--!?
...
TWITCH TWITCH
BAH! BAH! BAH!
SO YOU KNOW A LOT ABOUT SOME DUMB TV SHOW. SO WHAT!?

*ULTRAMAN'S SUCCESSOR

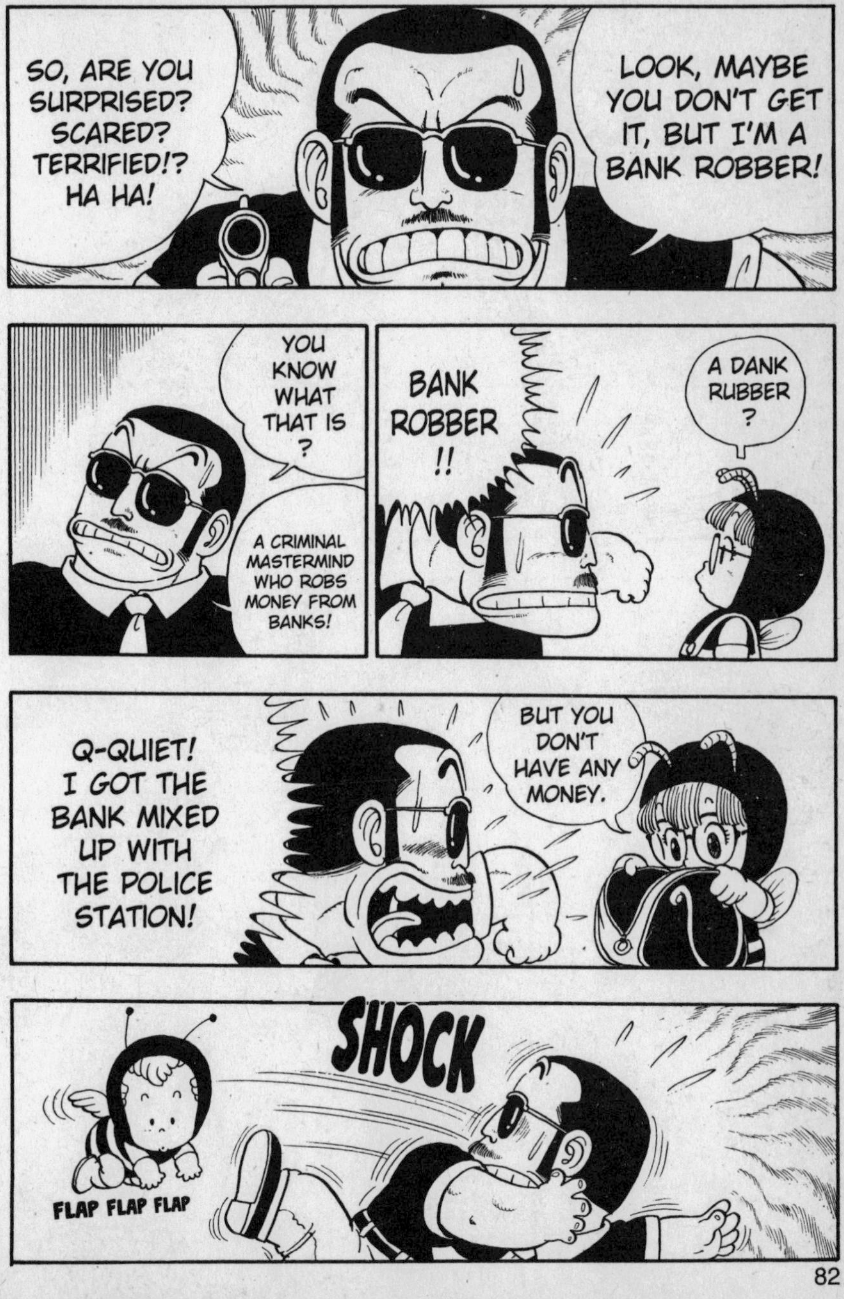
LOOK, MAYBE YOU DON'T GET IT, BUT I'M A BANK ROBBER!
SO, ARE YOU SURPRISED? SCARED? TERRIFIED!? HA HA!
A DANK RUBBER ?
BANK ROBBER !!
YOU KNOW WHAT THAT IS ?
A CRIMINAL MASTERMIND WHO ROBS MONEY FROM BANKS!
BUT YOU DON'T HAVE ANY MONEY.
Q-QUIET! I GOT THE BANK MIXED UP WITH THE POLICE STATION!
SHOCK
FLAP FLAP FLAP

READ THIS WAY

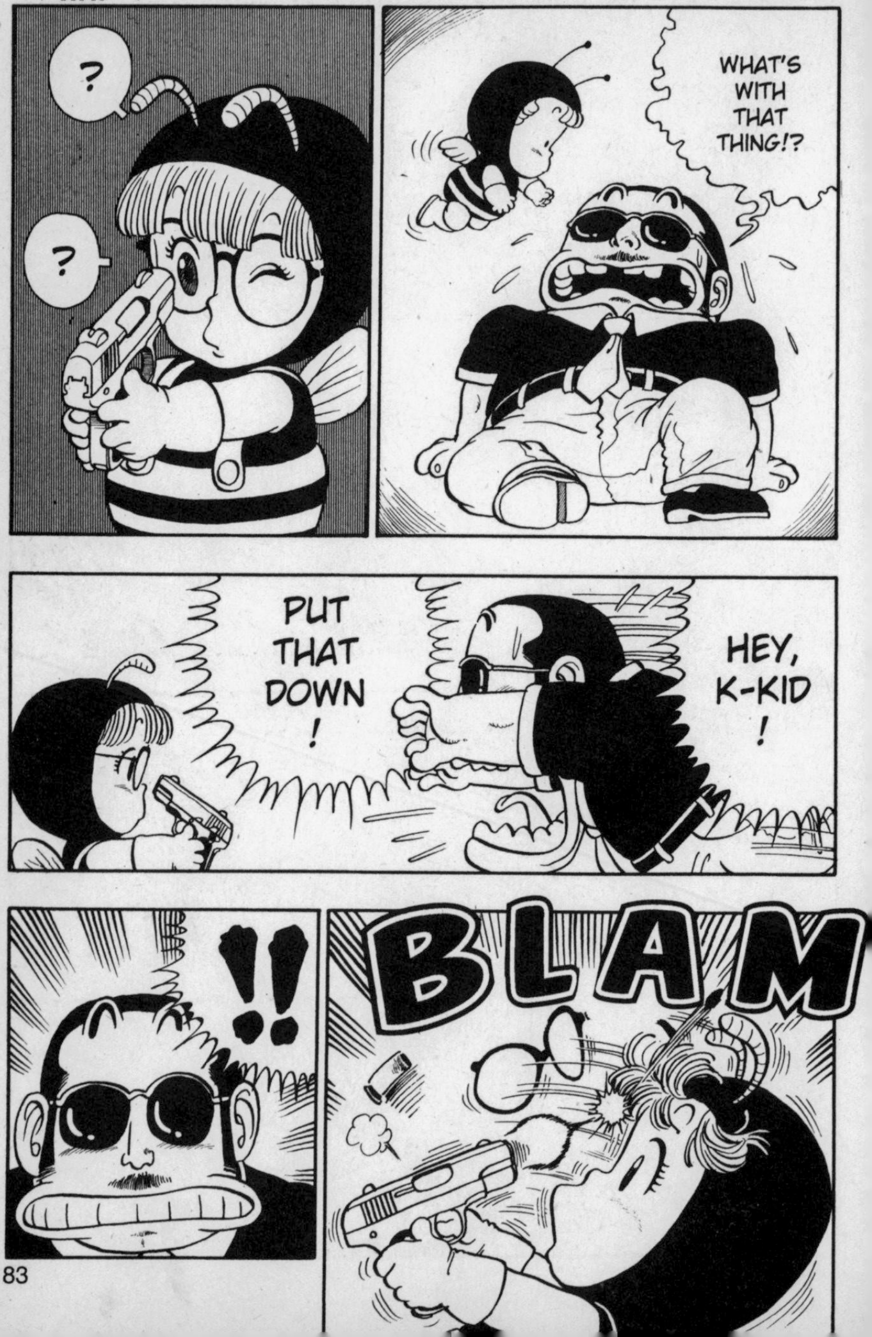
WHAT'S WITH THAT THING!?
?
?
HEY, K-KID!
PUT THAT DOWN!
BLAM
!!

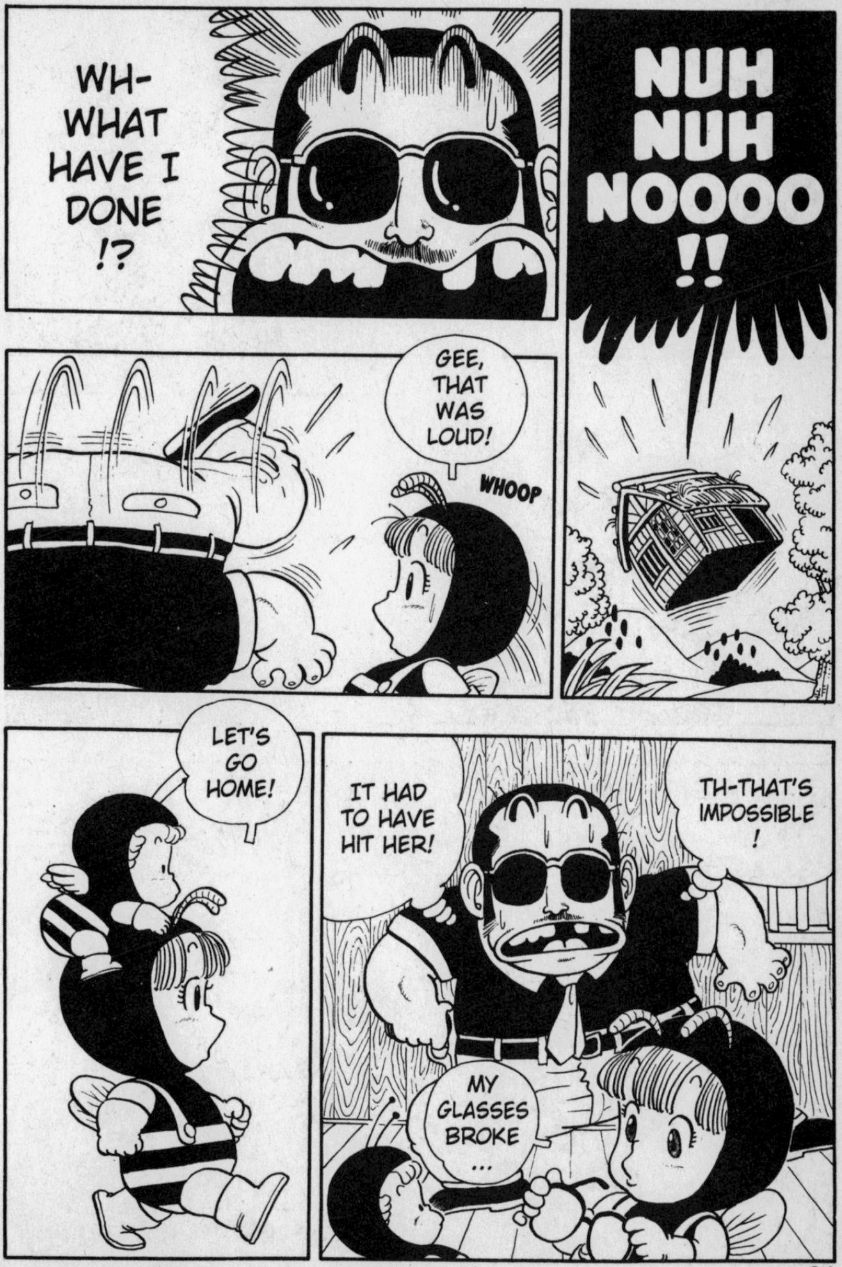
NUH NUH NOOOO!!
WH- WHAT HAVE I DONE!?
GEE, THAT WAS LOUD!
WHOOP
TH-THAT'S IMPOSSIBLE!
IT HAD TO HAVE HIT HER!
MY GLASSES BROKE...
LET'S GO HOME!

READ THIS WAY

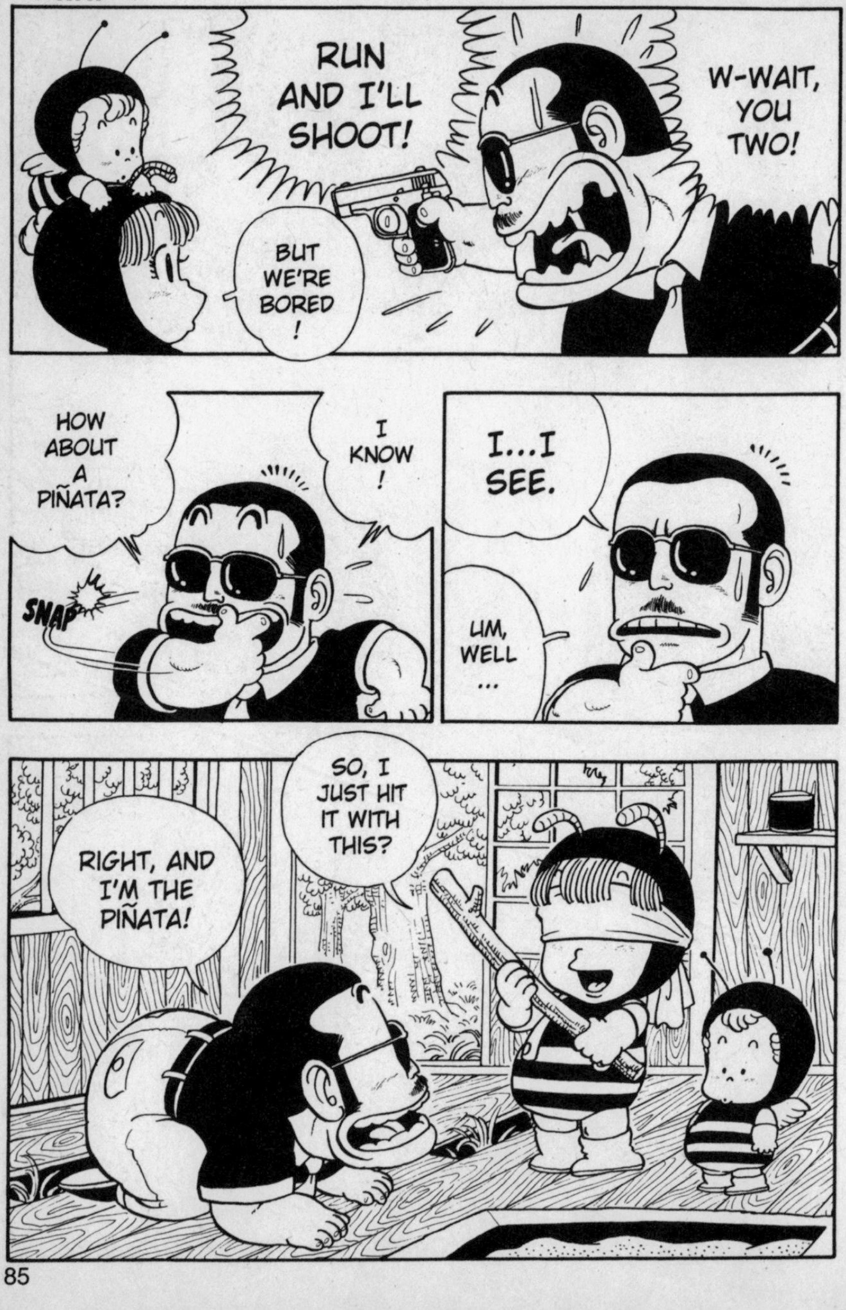
W-WAIT, YOU TWO!
RUN AND I'LL SHOOT!
BUT WE'RE BORED!
I...I SEE.
UM, WELL...
I KNOW!
HOW ABOUT A PIÑATA?
SNAP
SO, I JUST HIT IT WITH THIS?
RIGHT, AND I'M THE PIÑATA!

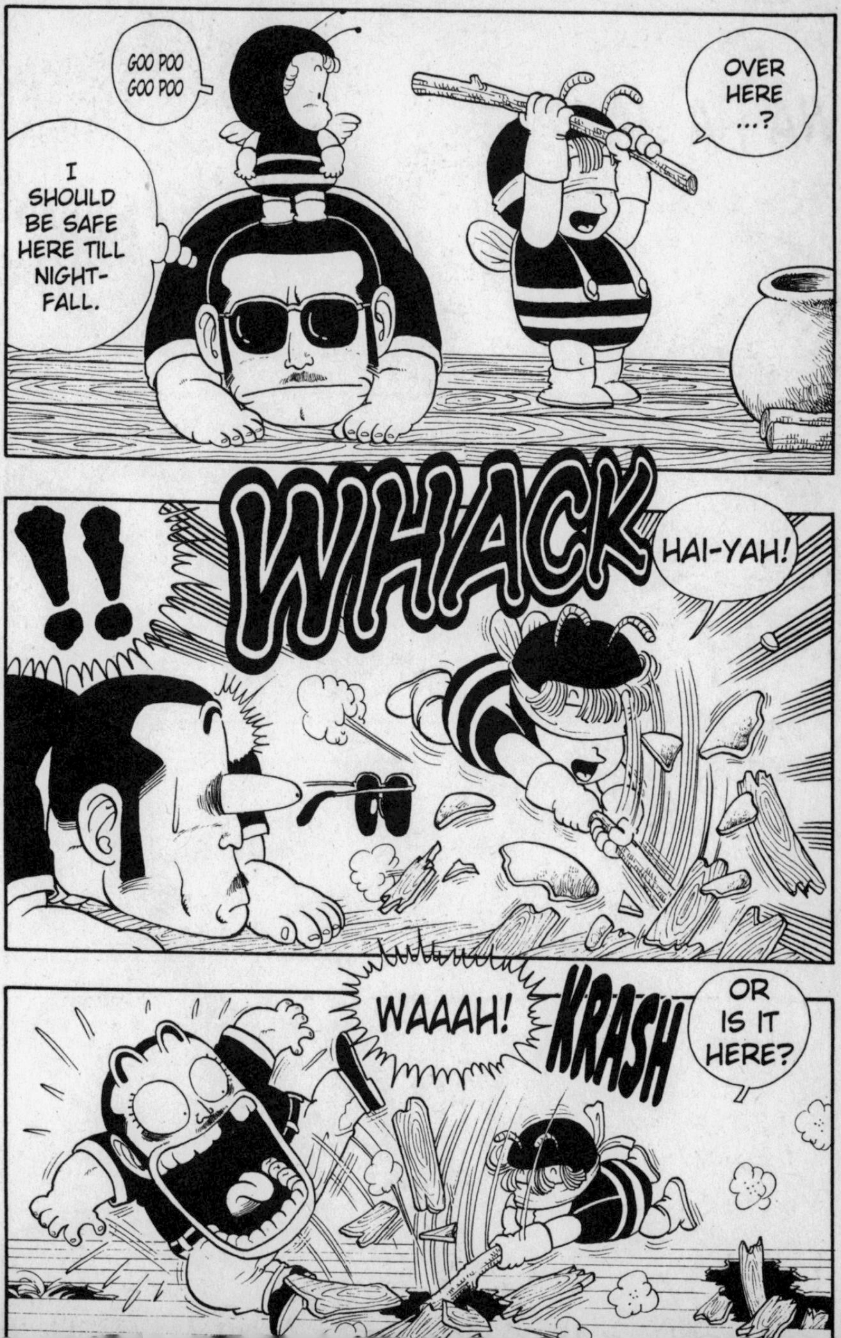

OVER HERE ...?
GOO POO GOO POO
I SHOULD BE SAFE HERE TILL NIGHT-FALL.
HAI-YAH!
WHACK
!!
OR IS IT HERE?
KRASH
WAAAH!

READ THIS WAY

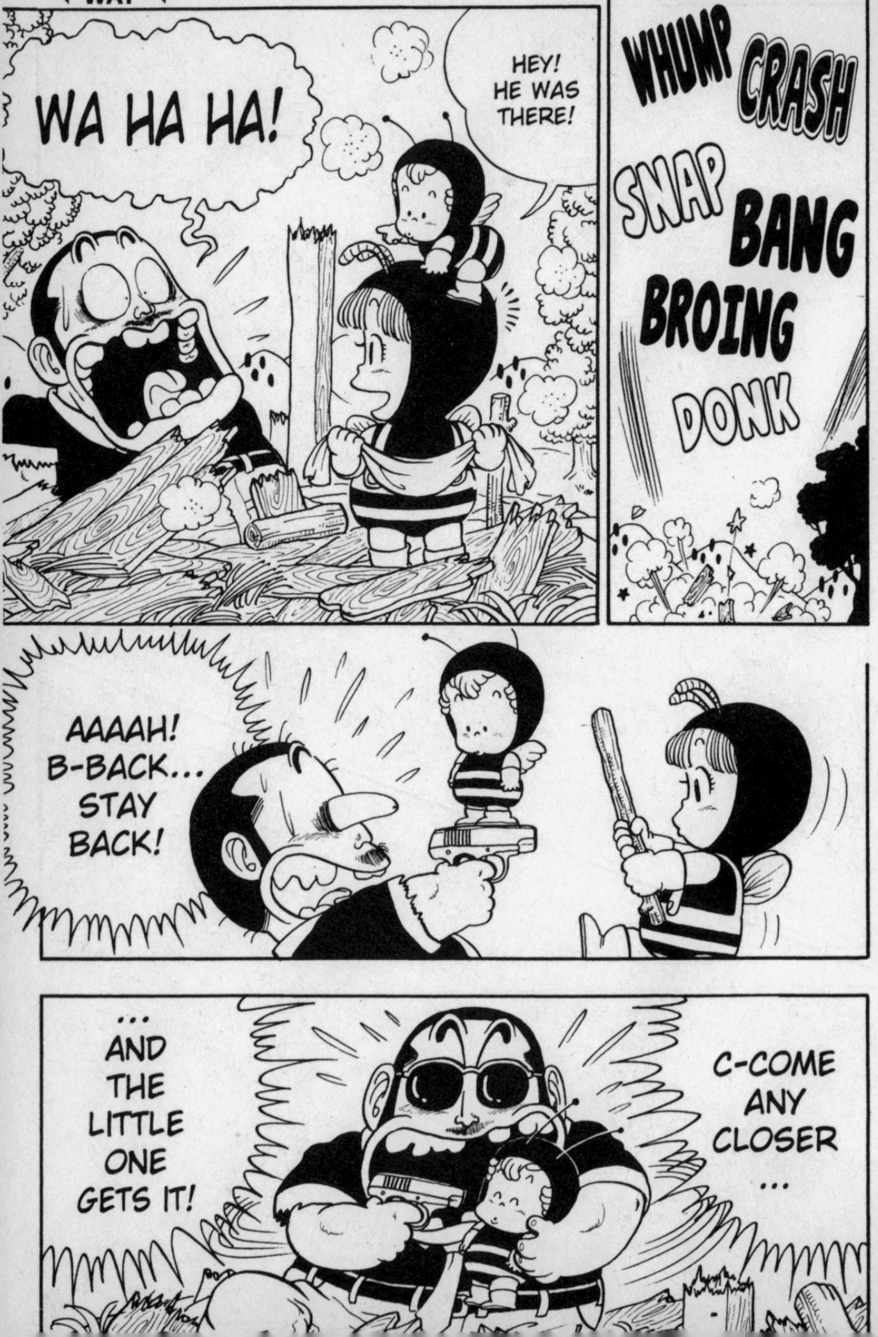
WHUMP
CRASH
SNAP
BANG
BROING
DONK
HEY! HE WAS THERE!
WA HA HA!
AAAAH! B-BACK... STAY BACK!
C-COME ANY CLOSER ...
... AND THE LITTLE ONE GETS IT!

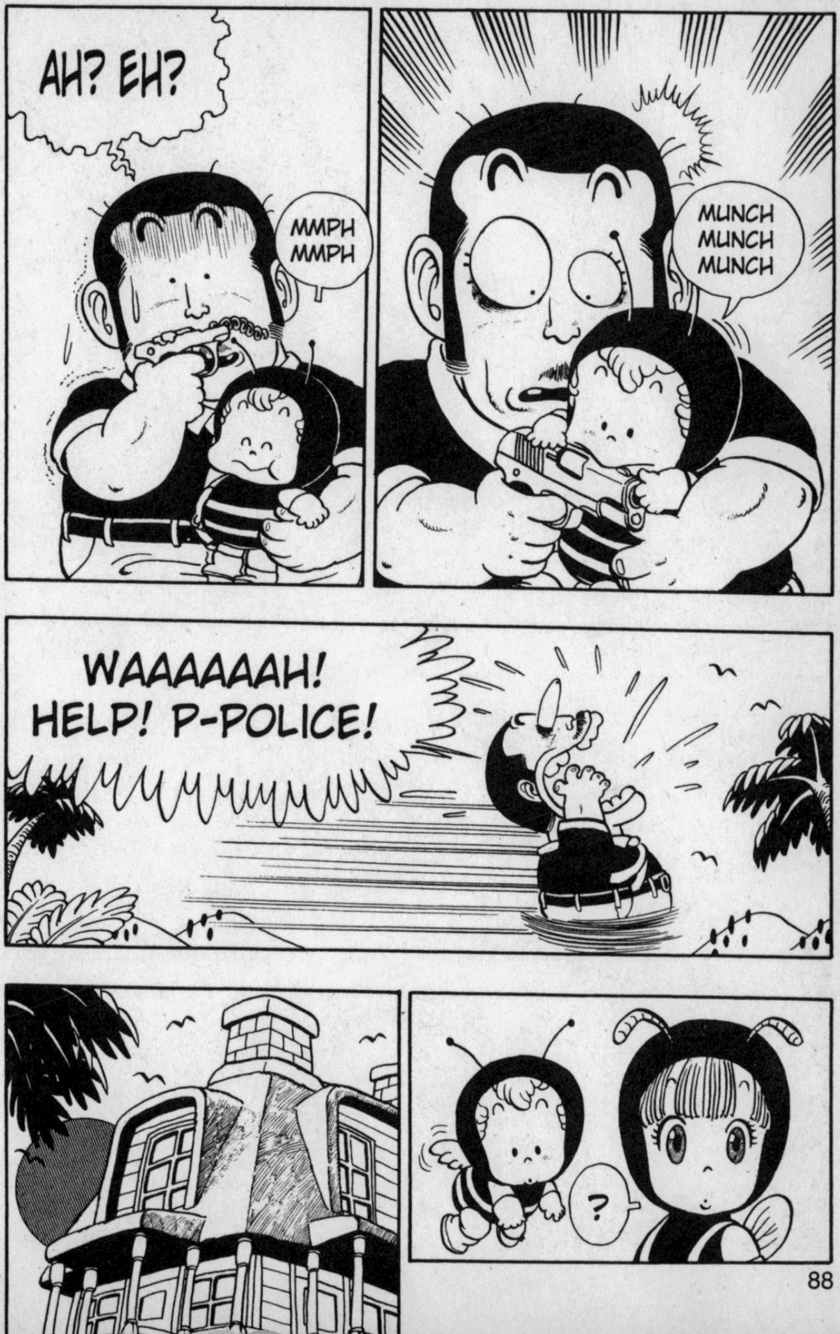
MUNCH MUNCH MUNCH
AH? EH?
MMPH MMPH
WAAAAAAH! HELP! P-POLICE!
?

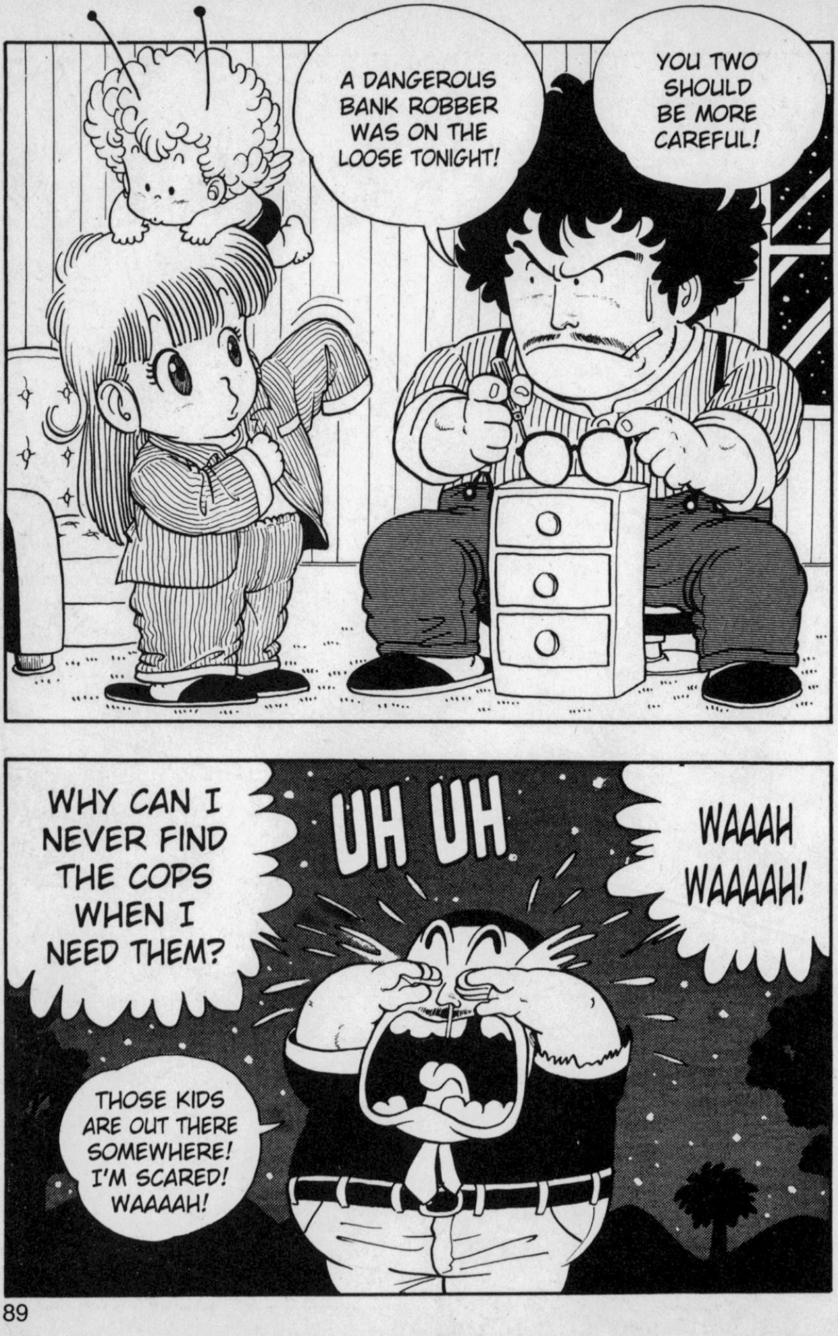
YOU TWO SHOULD BE MORE CAREFUL!
A DANGEROUS BANK ROBBER WAS ON THE LOOSE TONIGHT!
WAAAH WAAAAH!
UH UH
WHY CAN I NEVER FIND THE COPS WHEN I NEED THEM?
THOSE KIDS ARE OUT THERE SOMEWHERE! I'M SCARED! WAAAAH!

Teacher's Coming!

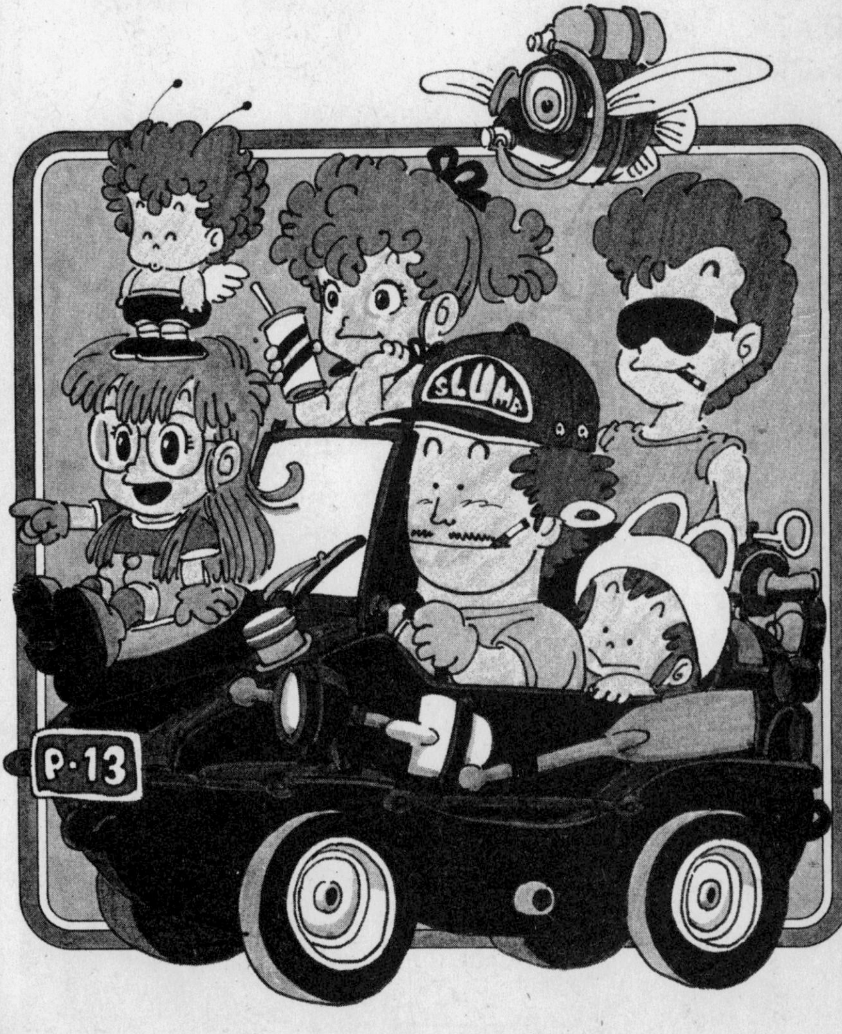
SLUMP
P-13

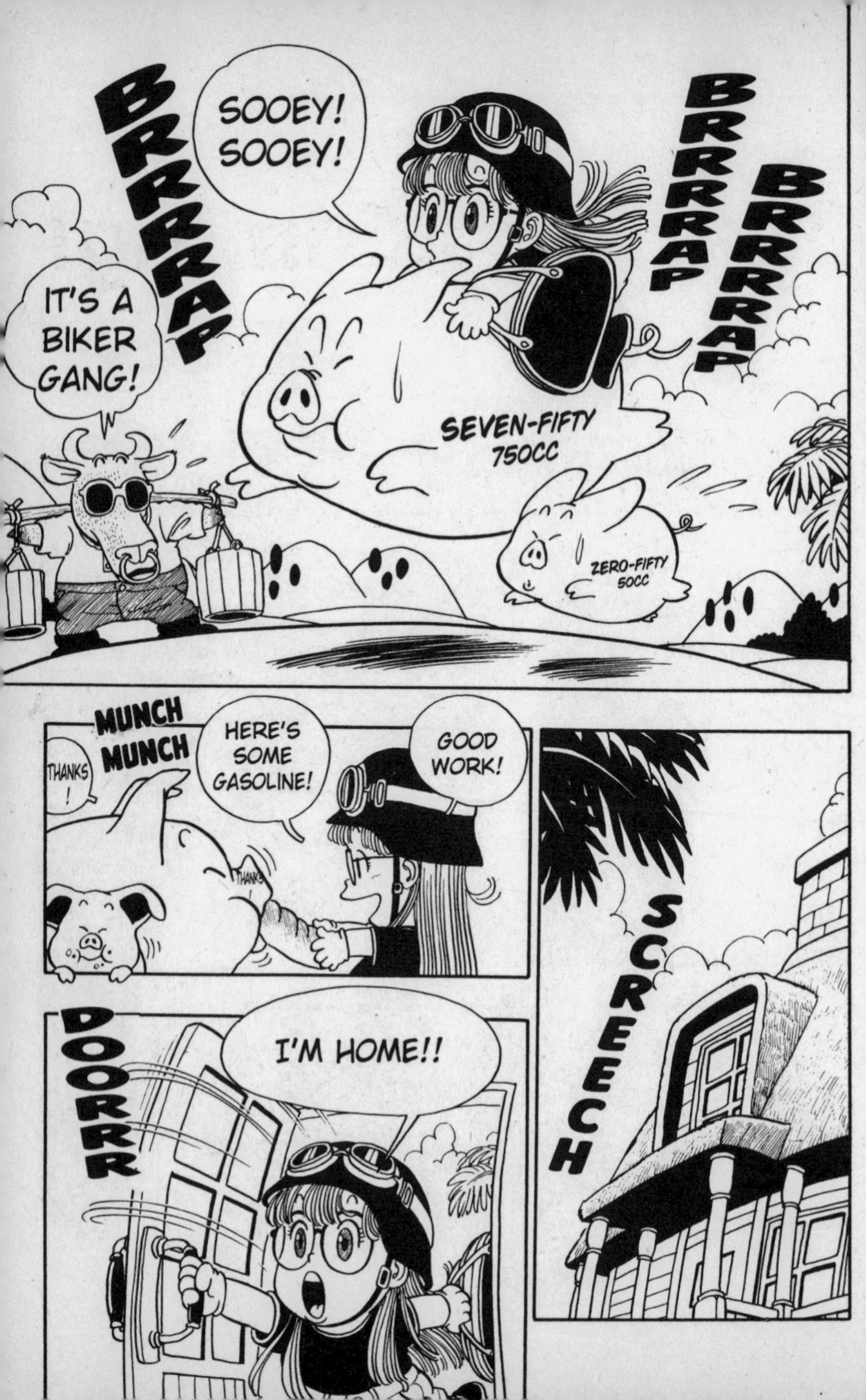
BRRRRAP
BRRRRAP
SOOEY! SOOEY!
BRRRRAP
SEVEN-FIFTY 750CC
ZERO-FIFTY 50CC
IT'S A BIKER GANG!
SCREECH
GOOD WORK!
HERE'S SOME GASOLINE!
MUNCH MUNCH
THANKS!
THANKS
DOORRR
I'M HOME!!

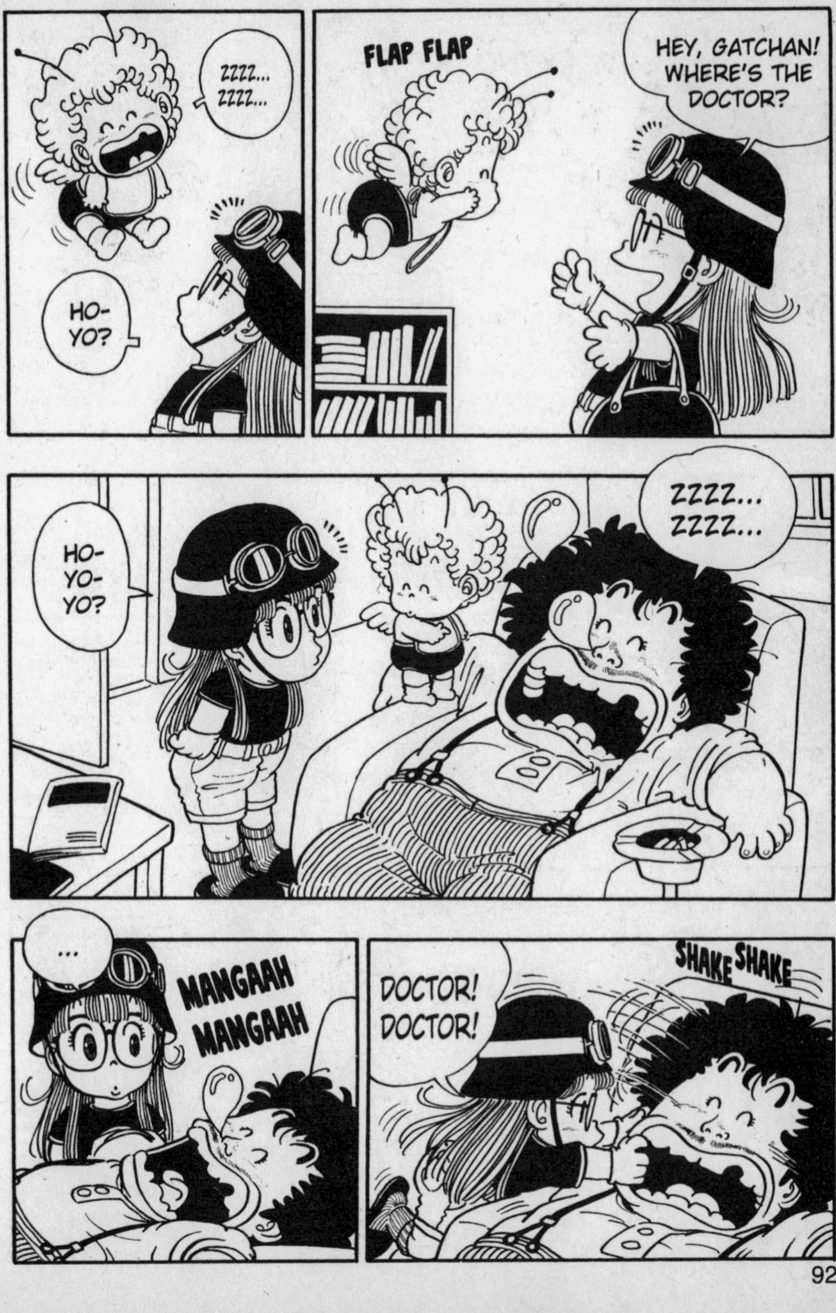
HEY, GATCHAN! WHERE'S THE DOCTOR?
FLAP FLAP
ZZZZ... ZZZZ...
HO-YO?
ZZZZ... ZZZZ...
HO-YO-YO?
SHAKE SHAKE
DOCTOR! DOCTOR!
...
MANGAAH MANGAAH

READ THIS WAY

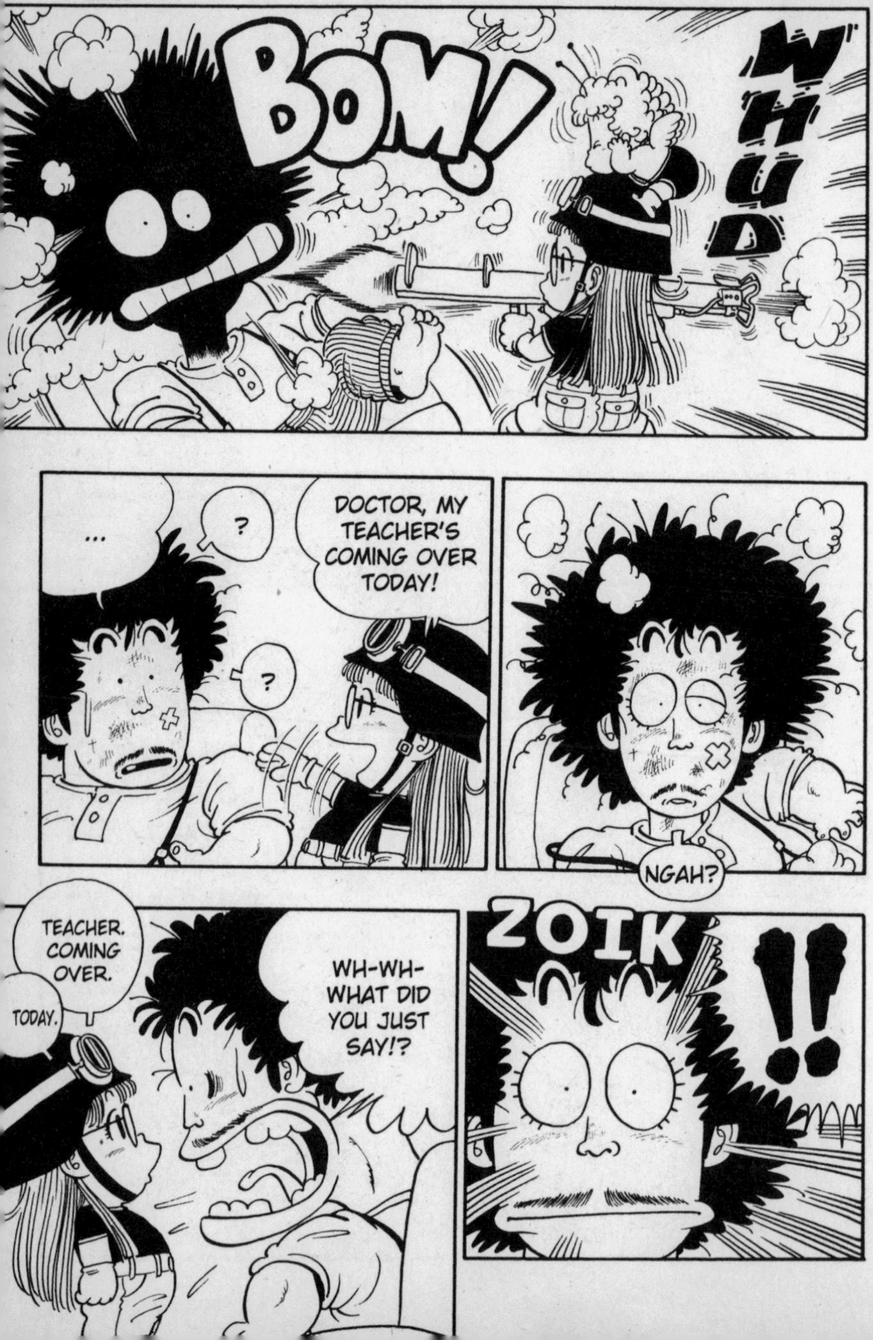
WHUD
BOM!
NGAH?
DOCTOR, MY TEACHER'S COMING OVER TODAY!
?
...
?
ZOIK
!!
WH-WH-WHAT DID YOU JUST SAY!?
TEACHER. COMING OVER.
TODAY.

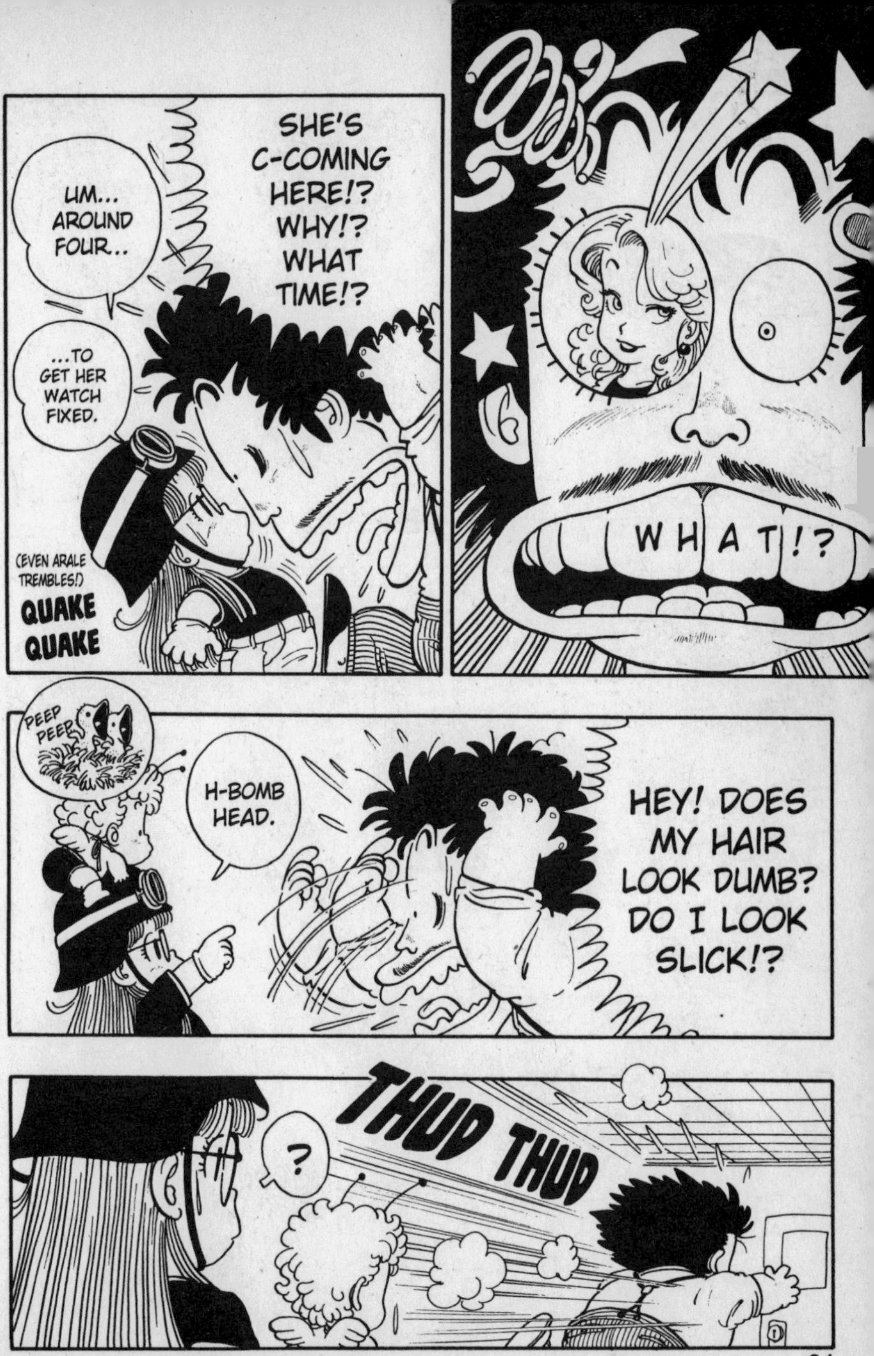
WHAT!?
SHE'S C-COMING HERE!? WHY!? WHAT TIME!?
UM... AROUND FOUR...
...TO GET HER WATCH FIXED.
(EVEN ARALE TREMBLES!)
QUAKE QUAKE
HEY! DOES MY HAIR LOOK DUMB? DO I LOOK SLICK!?
H-BOMB HEAD.
PEEP PEEP
THUD THUD
?

READ THIS WAY

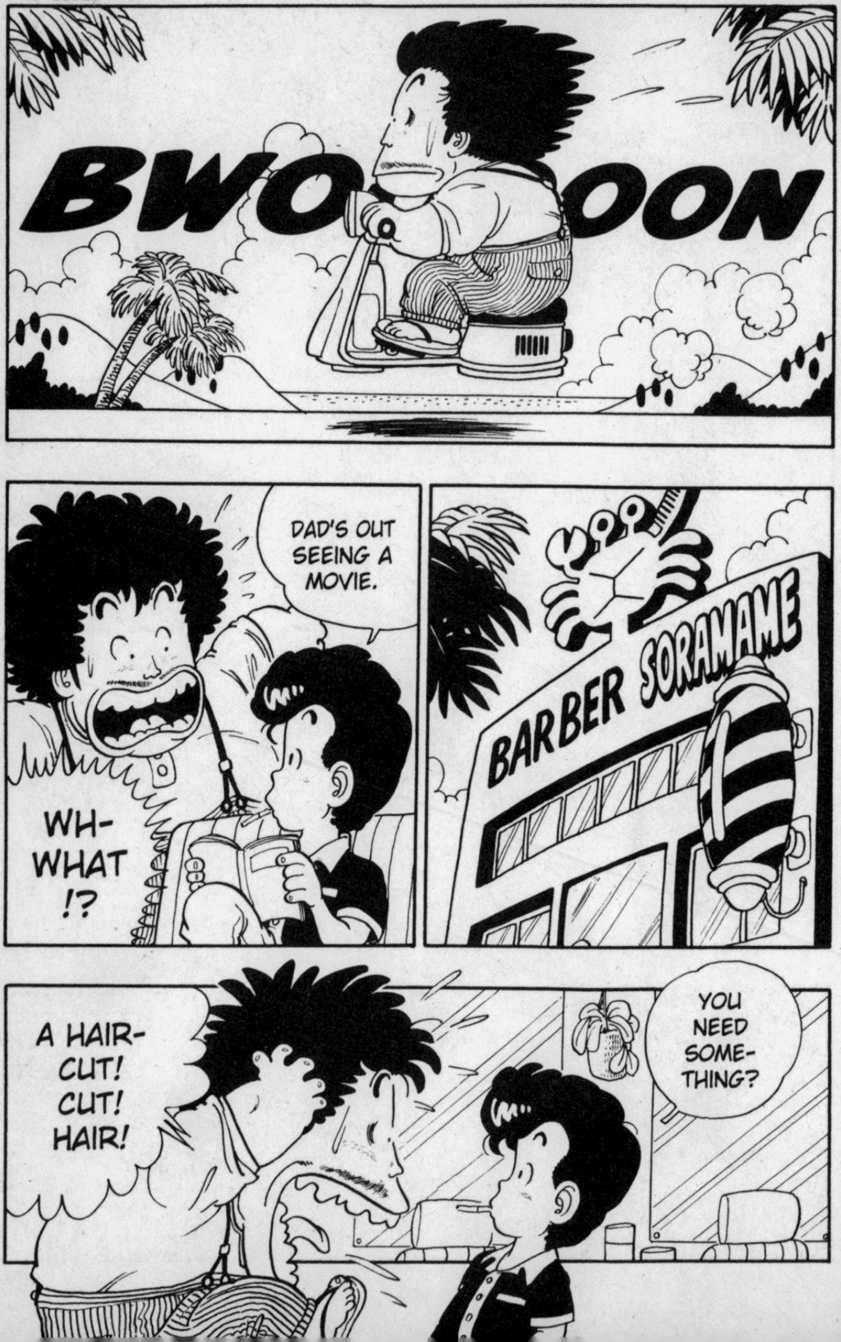

BWOOOON
BARBER SORAMAME
DAD'S OUT SEEING A MOVIE.
WH-WHAT !?
YOU NEED SOME-THING?
A HAIR-CUT! CUT! HAIR!

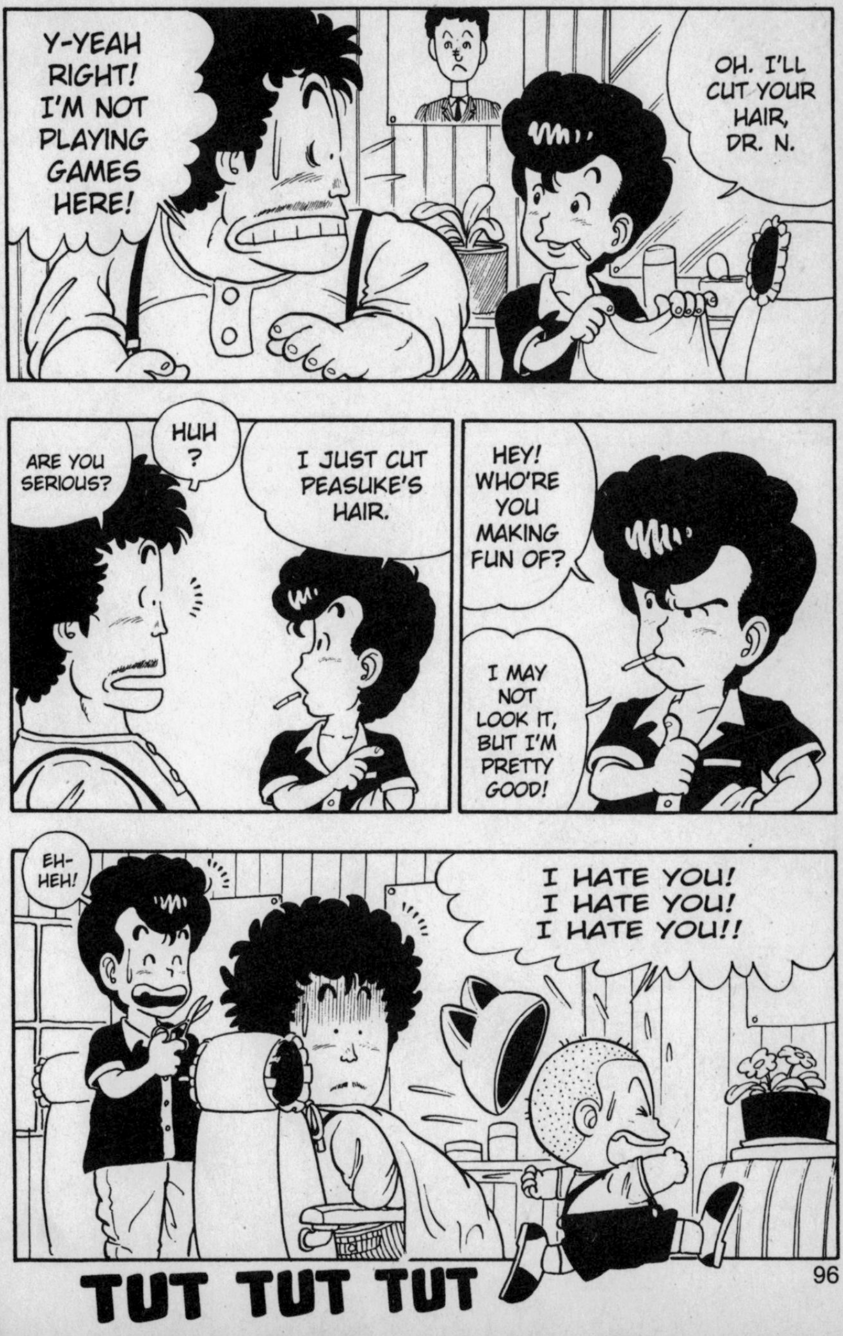
OH. I'LL CUT YOUR HAIR, DR. N.
Y-YEAH RIGHT! I'M NOT PLAYING GAMES HERE!
HEY! WHO'RE YOU MAKING FUN OF?
I MAY NOT LOOK IT, BUT I'M PRETTY GOOD!
I JUST CUT PEASUKE'S HAIR.
HUH ?
ARE YOU SERIOUS?
I HATE YOU! I HATE YOU! I HATE YOU!!
EH-HEH!
TUT TUT TUT

READ THIS WAY

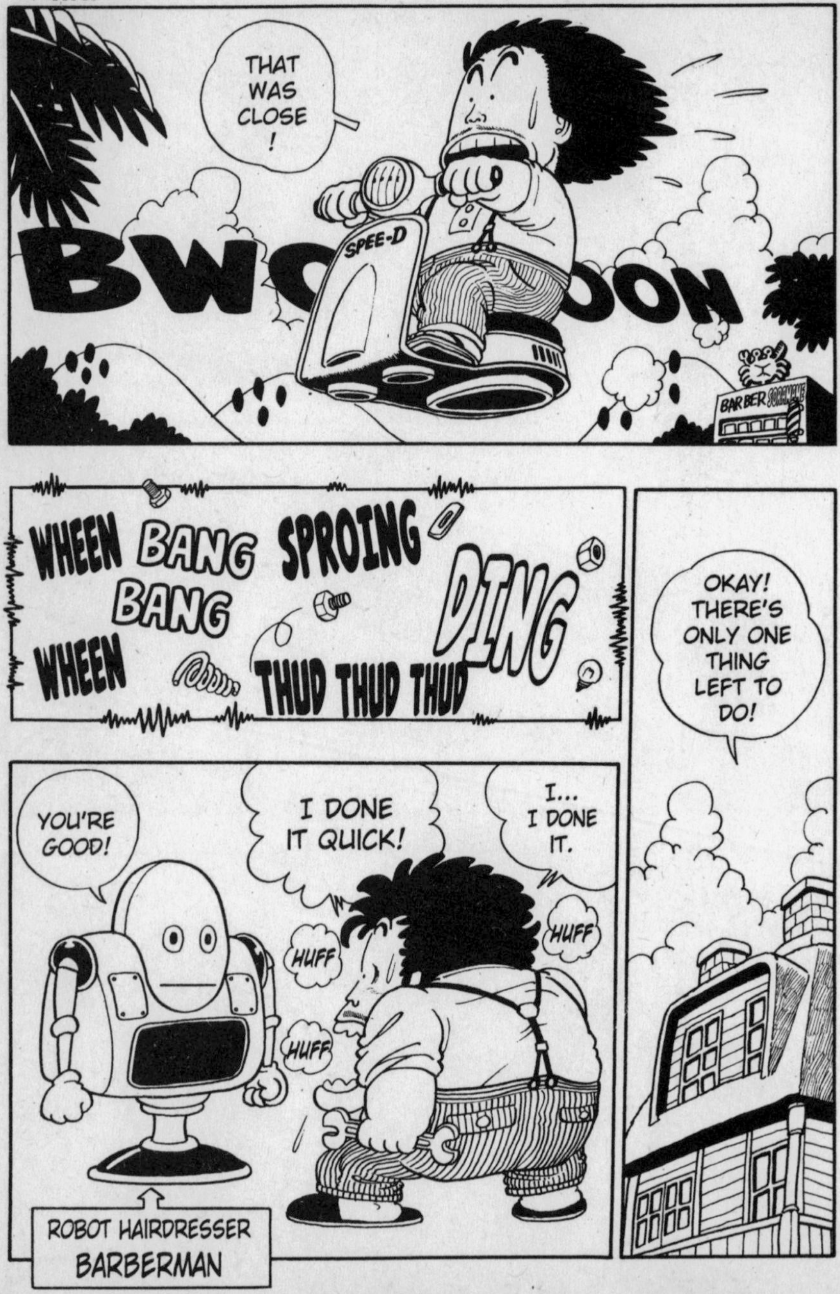
THAT WAS CLOSE !
BWOOOM
SPEE-D
BARBER
OKAY! THERE'S ONLY ONE THING LEFT TO DO!
DING
SPROING
THUD THUD THUD
BANG
BANG
WHEEN
WHEEN
I... I DONE IT.
HUFF
I DONE IT QUICK!
HUFF
HUFF
YOU'RE GOOD!
ROBOT HAIRDRESSER
BARBERMAN

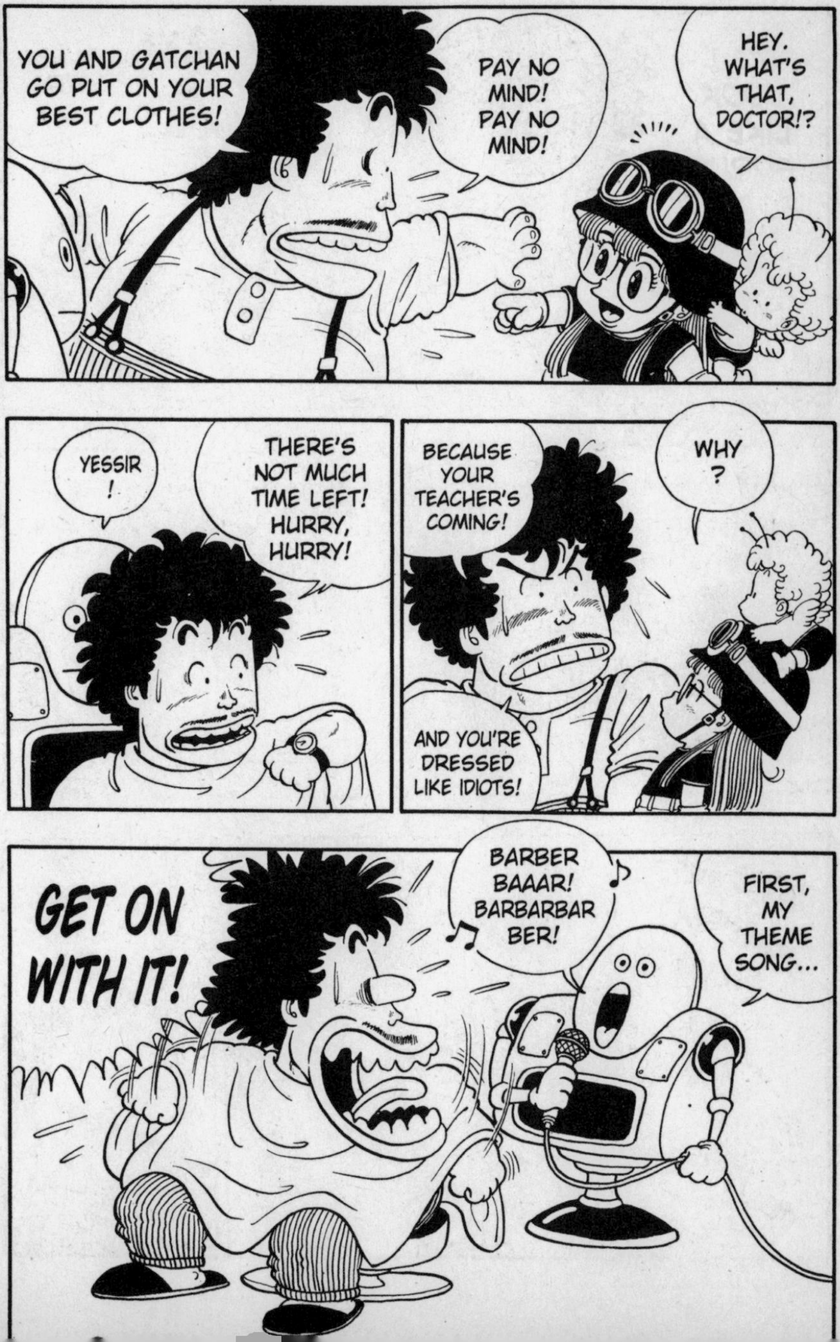
HEY. WHAT'S THAT, DOCTOR!?
PAY NO MIND! PAY NO MIND!
YOU AND GATCHAN GO PUT ON YOUR BEST CLOTHES!
WHY?
BECAUSE YOUR TEACHER'S COMING!
AND YOU'RE DRESSED LIKE IDIOTS!
THERE'S NOT MUCH TIME LEFT! HURRY, HURRY!
YESSIR!
FIRST, MY THEME SONG...
BARBER BAAAR! BARBARBAR BER!
GET ON WITH IT!

READ THIS WAY

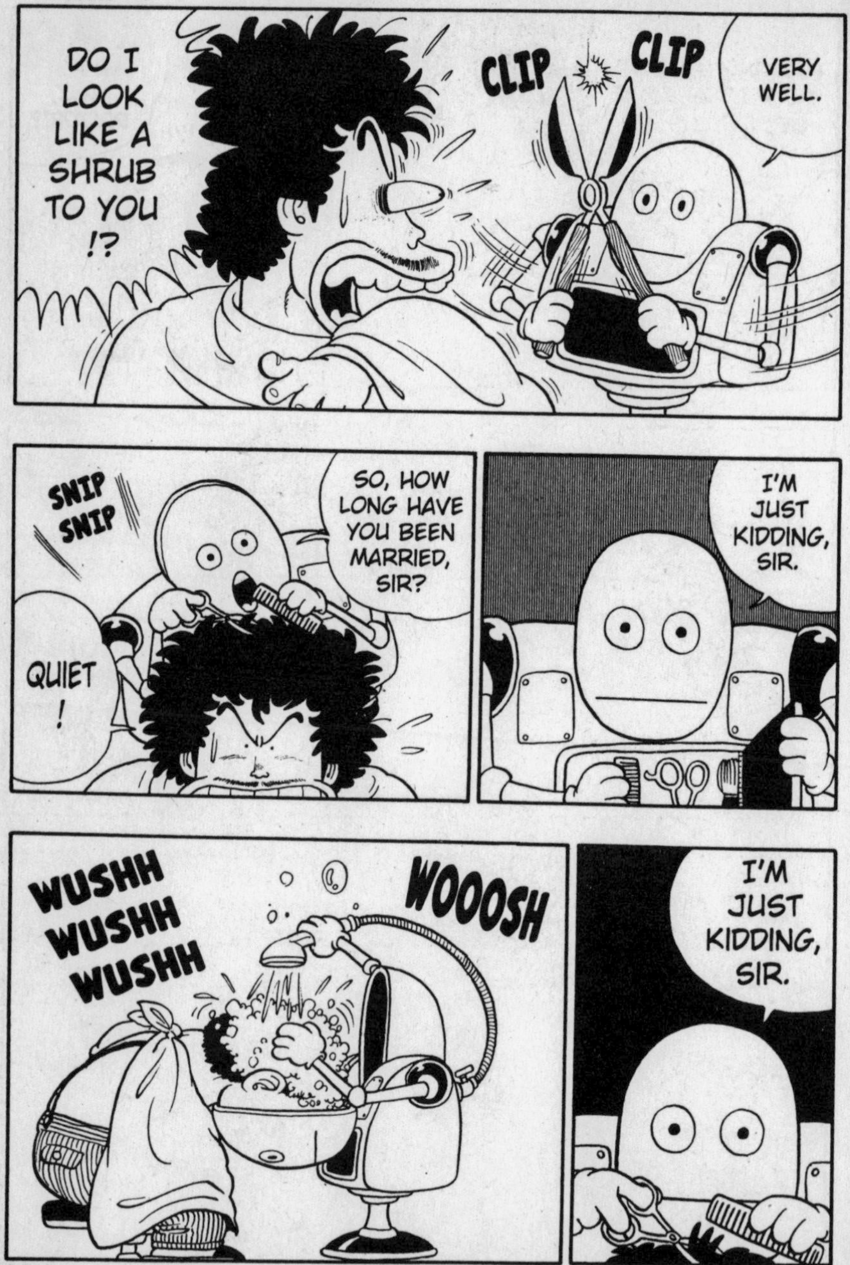
VERY WELL.
CLIP CLIP
DO I LOOK LIKE A SHRUB TO YOU !?
I'M JUST KIDDING, SIR.
SO, HOW LONG HAVE YOU BEEN MARRIED, SIR?
SNIP SNIP
QUIET !
I'M JUST KIDDING, SIR.
WOOOSH
WUSHH WUSHH WUSHH

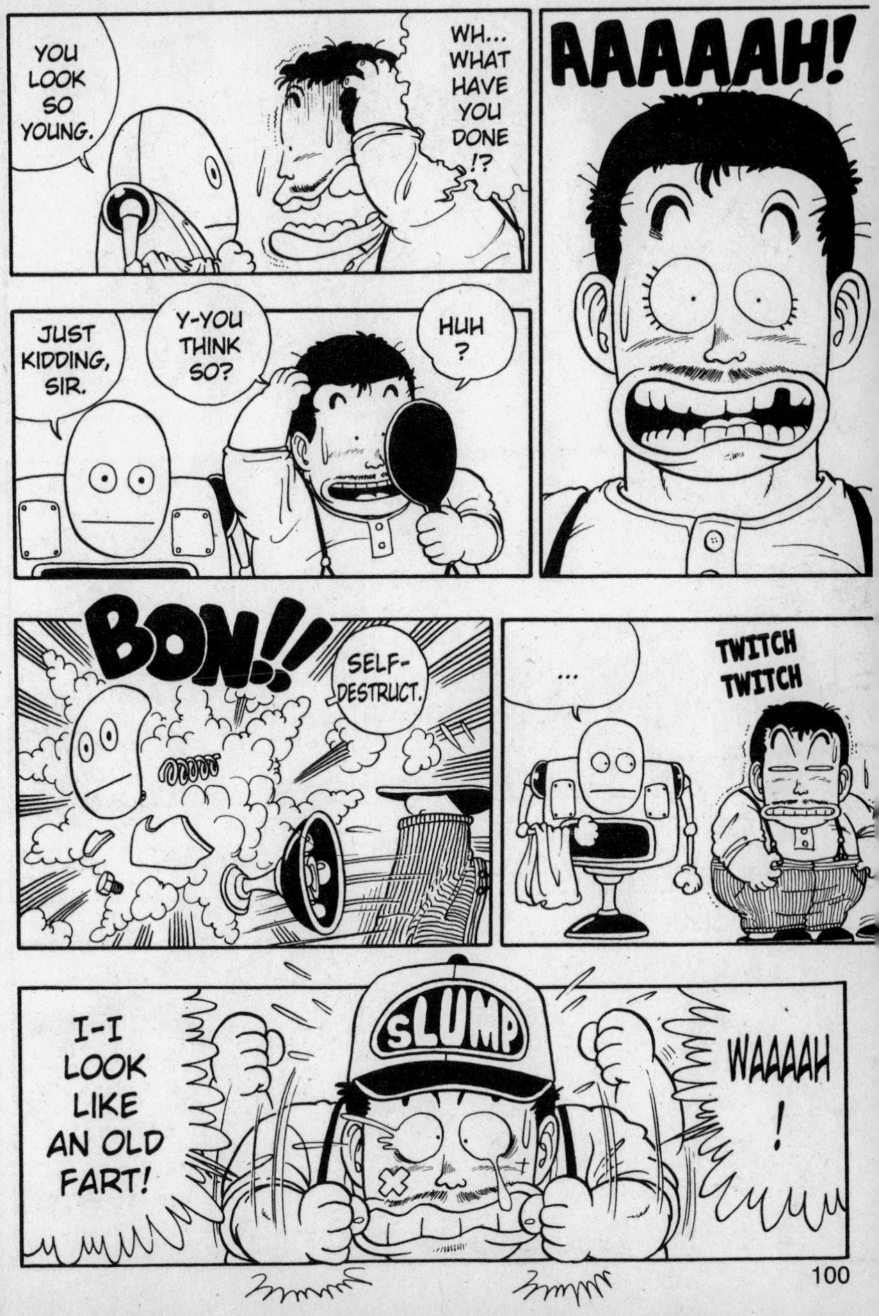

AAAAAH!
WH... WHAT HAVE YOU DONE!?
YOU LOOK SO YOUNG.
HUH?
Y-YOU THINK SO?
JUST KIDDING, SIR.
...
TWITCH TWITCH
BON!!
SELF-DESTRUCT.
WAAAAH!
SLUMP
I-I LOOK LIKE AN OLD FART!

READ THIS WAY

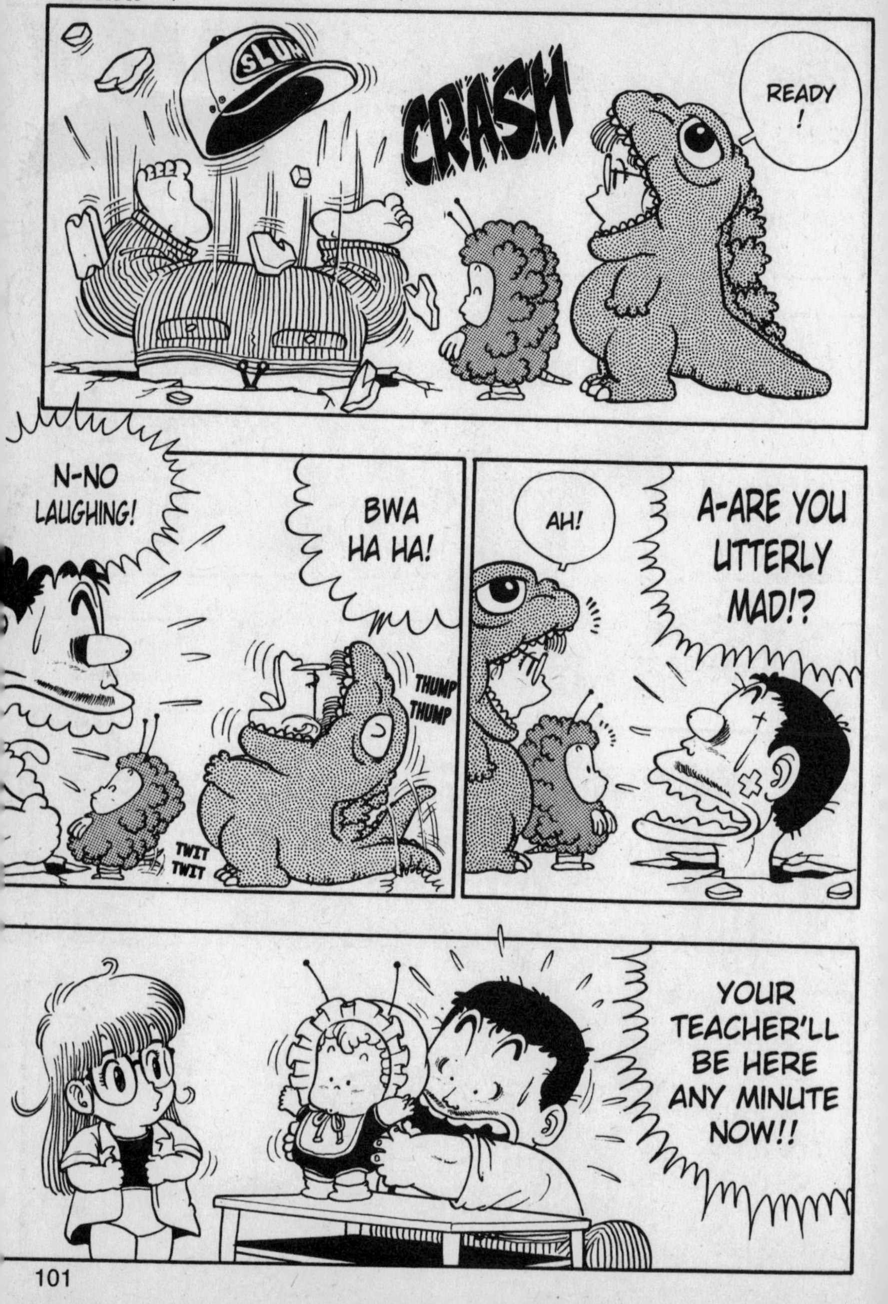
READY!
CRASH
A-ARE YOU UTTERLY MAD!?
AH!
BWA HA HA!
THUMP THUMP
N-NO LAUGHING!
TWIT TWIT
YOUR TEACHER'LL BE HERE ANY MINUTE NOW!!

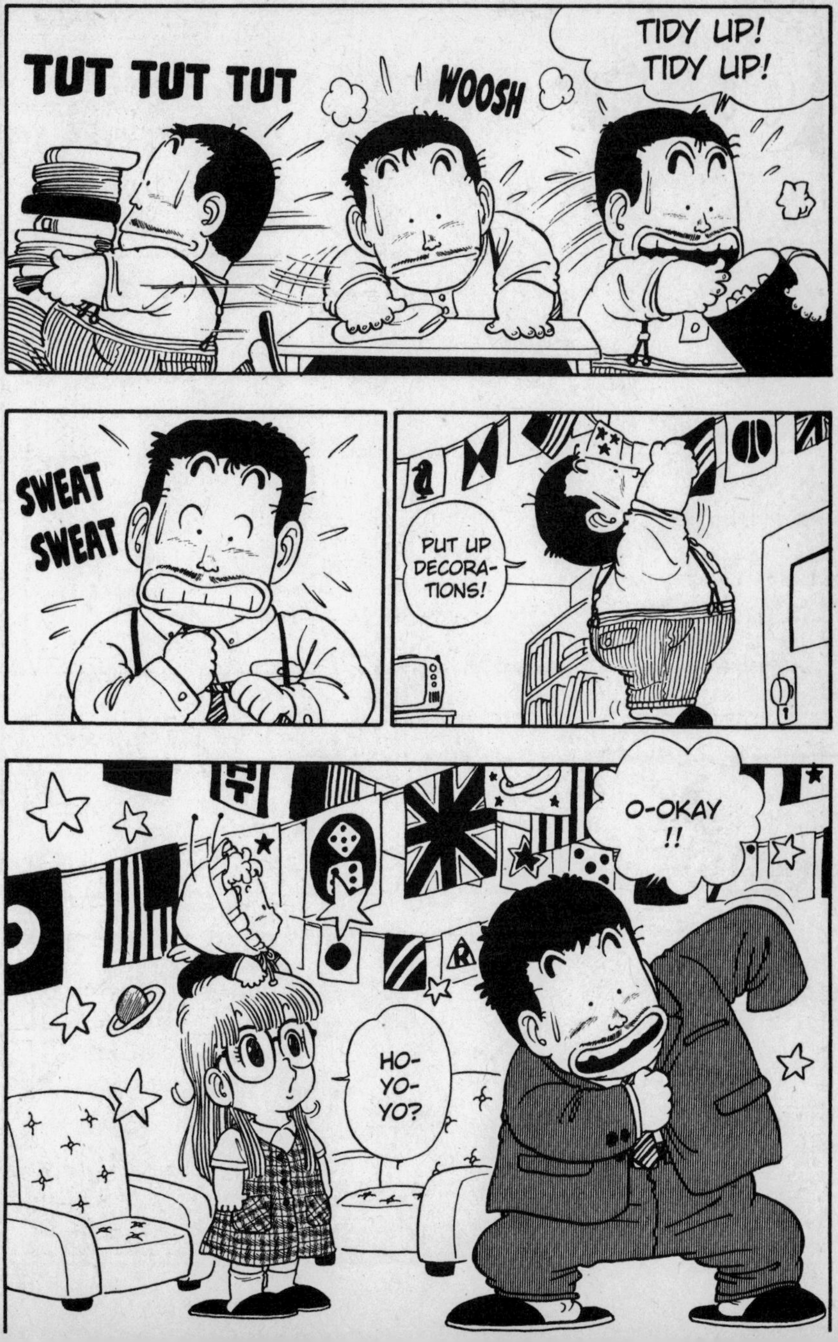
TIDY UP! TIDY UP!
WOOSH
TUT TUT TUT
PUT UP DECORA-TIONS!
SWEAT SWEAT
O-OKAY !!
HO-YO-YO?

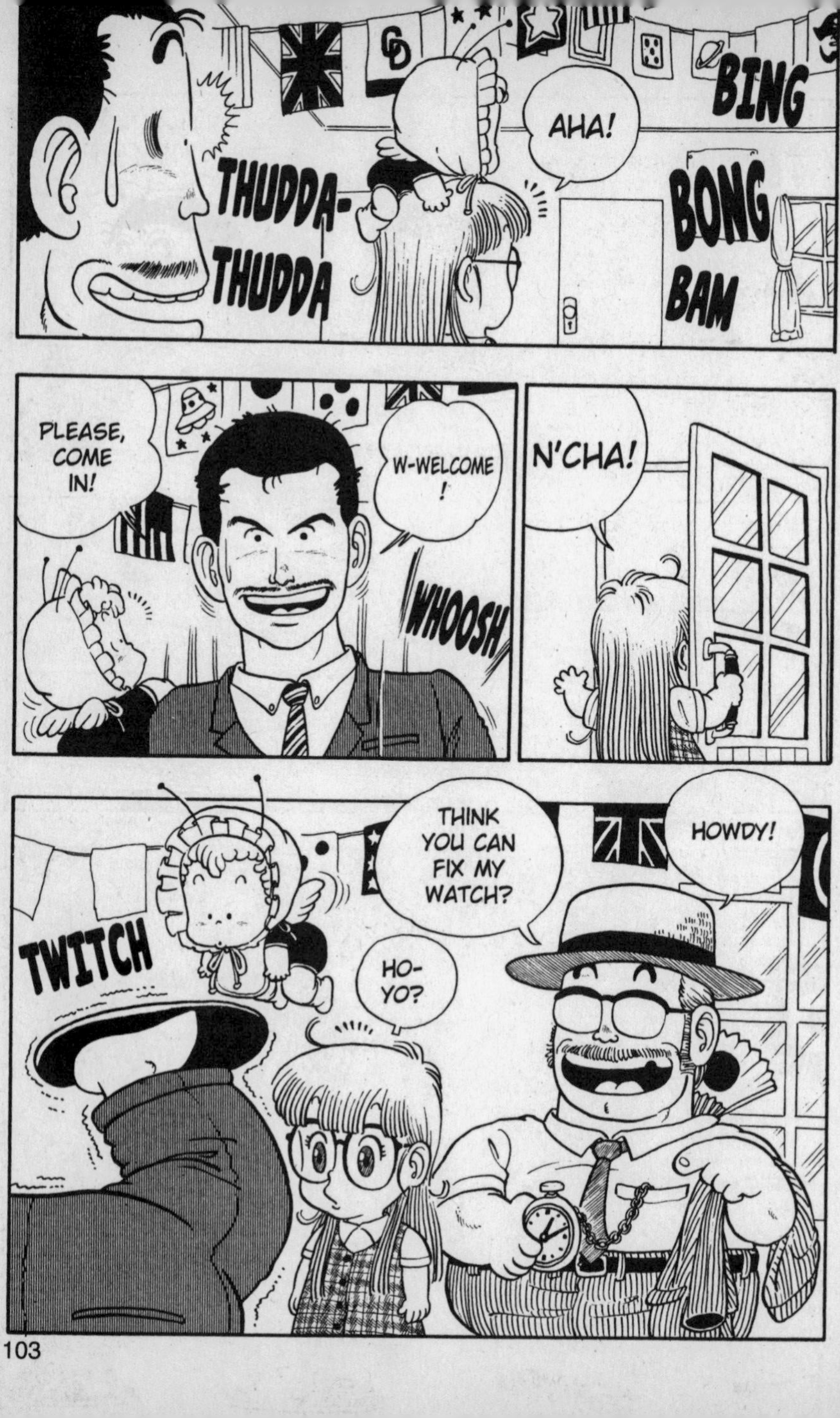
BING
AHA!
BONG
BAM
THUDDA-THUDDA
N'CHA!
W-WELCOME!
PLEASE, COME IN!
WHOOSH
HOWDY!
THINK YOU CAN FIX MY WATCH?
HO-YO?
TWITCH

SOME OF THE THINGS I USE TO DRAW

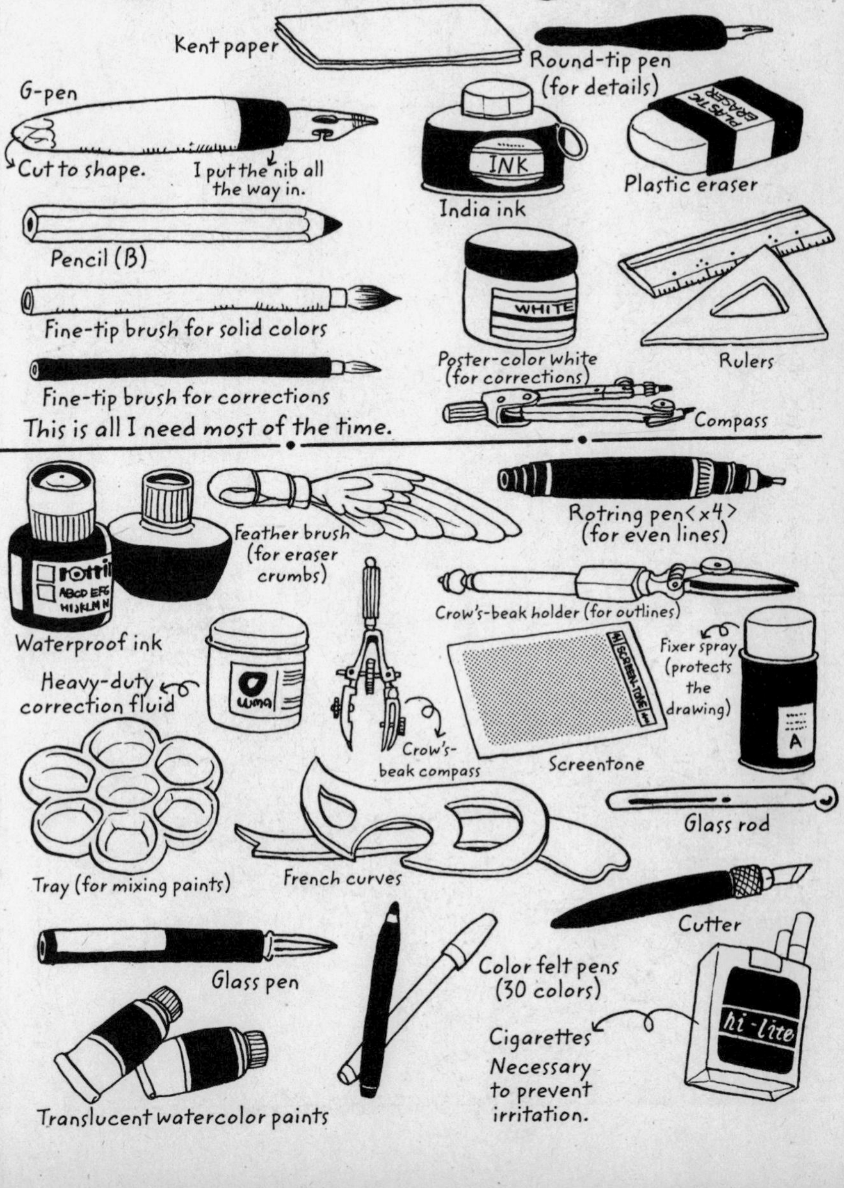
Kent paper
Round-tip pen (for details)
G-pen
Cut to shape.
I put the nib all the way in.
INK
India ink
PLASTIC ERASER
Plastic eraser
Pencil (B)
WHITE
Fine-tip brush for solid colors
Poster-color white (for corrections)
Rulers
Fine-tip brush for corrections
Compass
This is all I need most of the time.
Feather brush (for eraser crumbs)
Rotring pen<x4> (for even lines)
Waterproof ink
Crow's-beak holder (for outlines)
Heavy-duty correction fluid
SCREEN-TONE
Fixer spray (protects the drawing)
A
Crow's-beak compass
Screentone
Glass rod
Tray (for mixing paints)
French curves
Cutter
Glass pen
Color felt pens (30 colors)
hi-lite
Cigarettes Necessary to prevent irritation.
Translucent watercolor paints

The Ponpoko Morph Gun

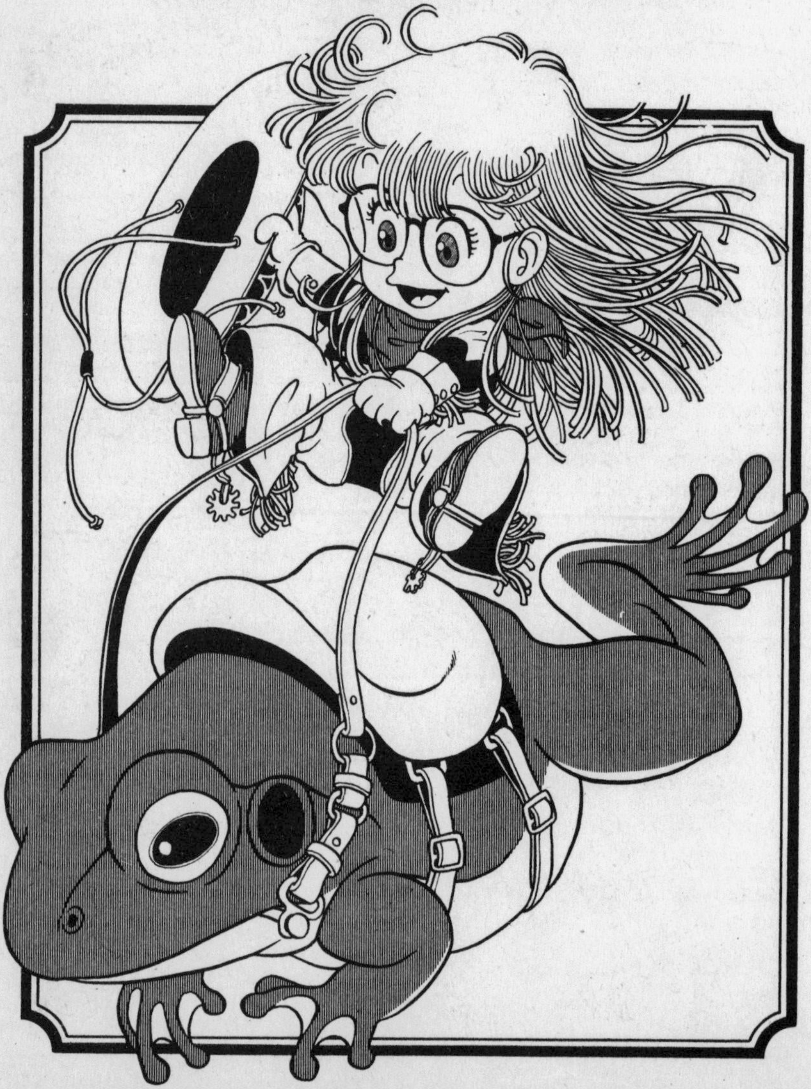

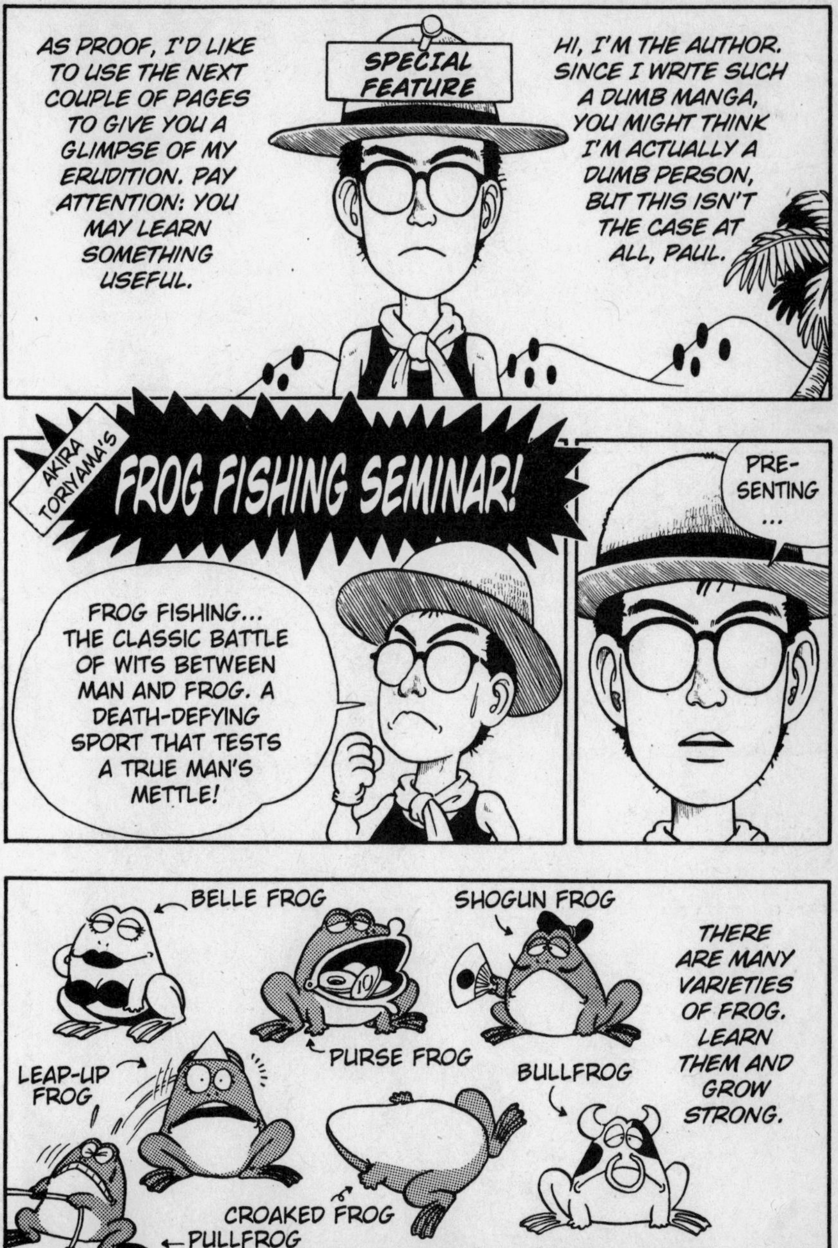
HI, I'M THE AUTHOR. SINCE I WRITE SUCH A DUMB MANGA, YOU MIGHT THINK I'M ACTUALLY A DUMB PERSON, BUT THIS ISN'T THE CASE AT ALL, PAUL.
SPECIAL FEATURE
AS PROOF, I'D LIKE TO USE THE NEXT COUPLE OF PAGES TO GIVE YOU A GLIMPSE OF MY ERUDITION. PAY ATTENTION: YOU MAY LEARN SOMETHING USEFUL.
PRE-SENTING ...
AKIRA TORIYAMA'S
FROG FISHING SEMINAR!
FROG FISHING... THE CLASSIC BATTLE OF WITS BETWEEN MAN AND FROG. A DEATH-DEFYING SPORT THAT TESTS A TRUE MAN'S METTLE!
THERE ARE MANY VARIETIES OF FROG. LEARN THEM AND GROW STRONG.
SHOGUN FROG
BULLFROG
PURSE FROG
BELLE FROG
CROAKED FROG
LEAP-UP FROG
PULLFROG

READ THIS WAY

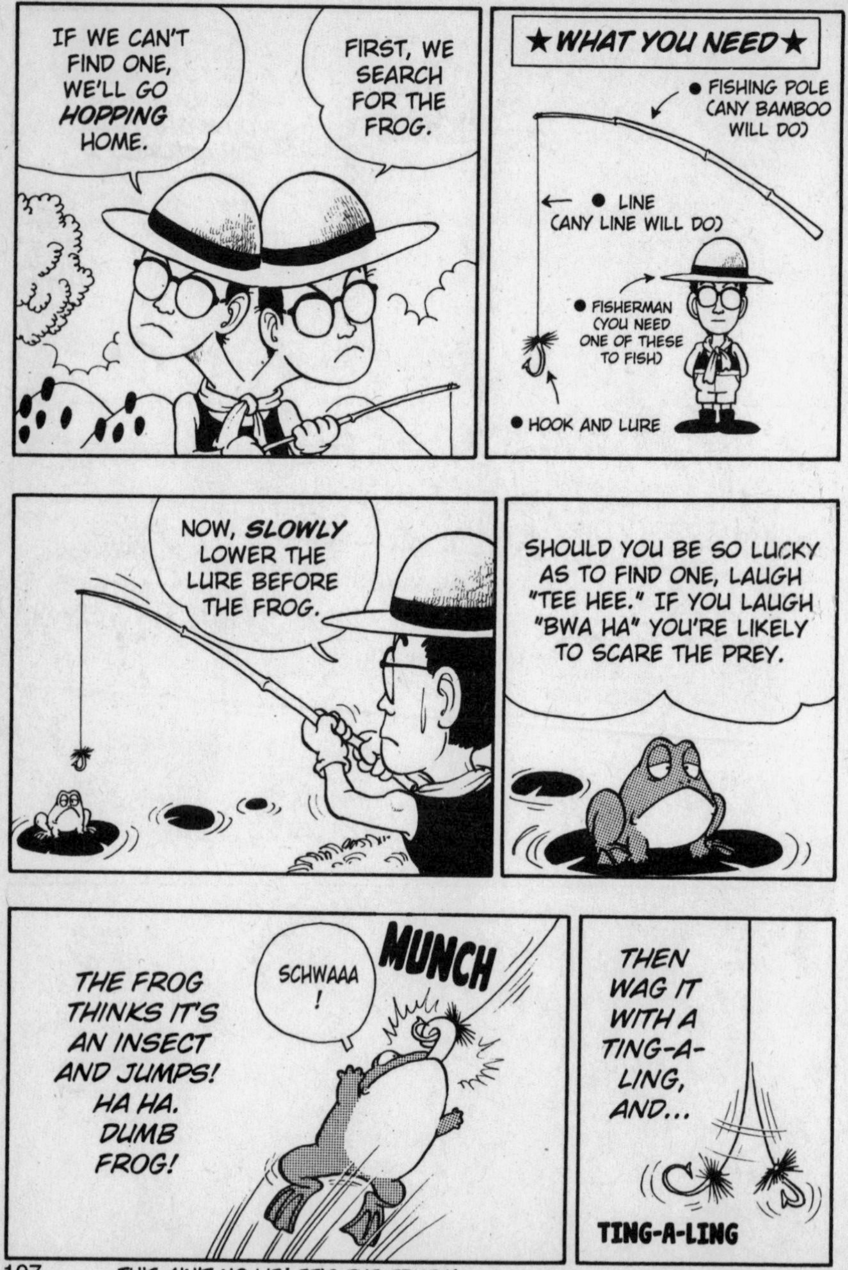
★WHAT YOU NEED★
● FISHING POLE (ANY BAMBOO WILL DO)
● LINE (ANY LINE WILL DO)
● FISHERMAN (YOU NEED ONE OF THESE TO FISH)
● HOOK AND LURE
FIRST, WE SEARCH FOR THE FROG.
IF WE CAN'T FIND ONE, WE'LL GO HOPPING HOME.
SHOULD YOU BE SO LUCKY AS TO FIND ONE, LAUGH "TEE HEE." IF YOU LAUGH "BWA HA" YOU'RE LIKELY TO SCARE THE PREY.
NOW, SLOWLY LOWER THE LURE BEFORE THE FROG.
THEN WAG IT WITH A TING-A-LING, AND...
TING-A-LING
MUNCH
SCHWAAA!
THE FROG THINKS IT'S AN INSECT AND JUMPS! HA HA. DUMB FROG!

THIS AIN'T NO LIE! IT'S THE TRUTH!
(MOSTLY US COUNTRY KIDS KNOW THIS TRICK.)

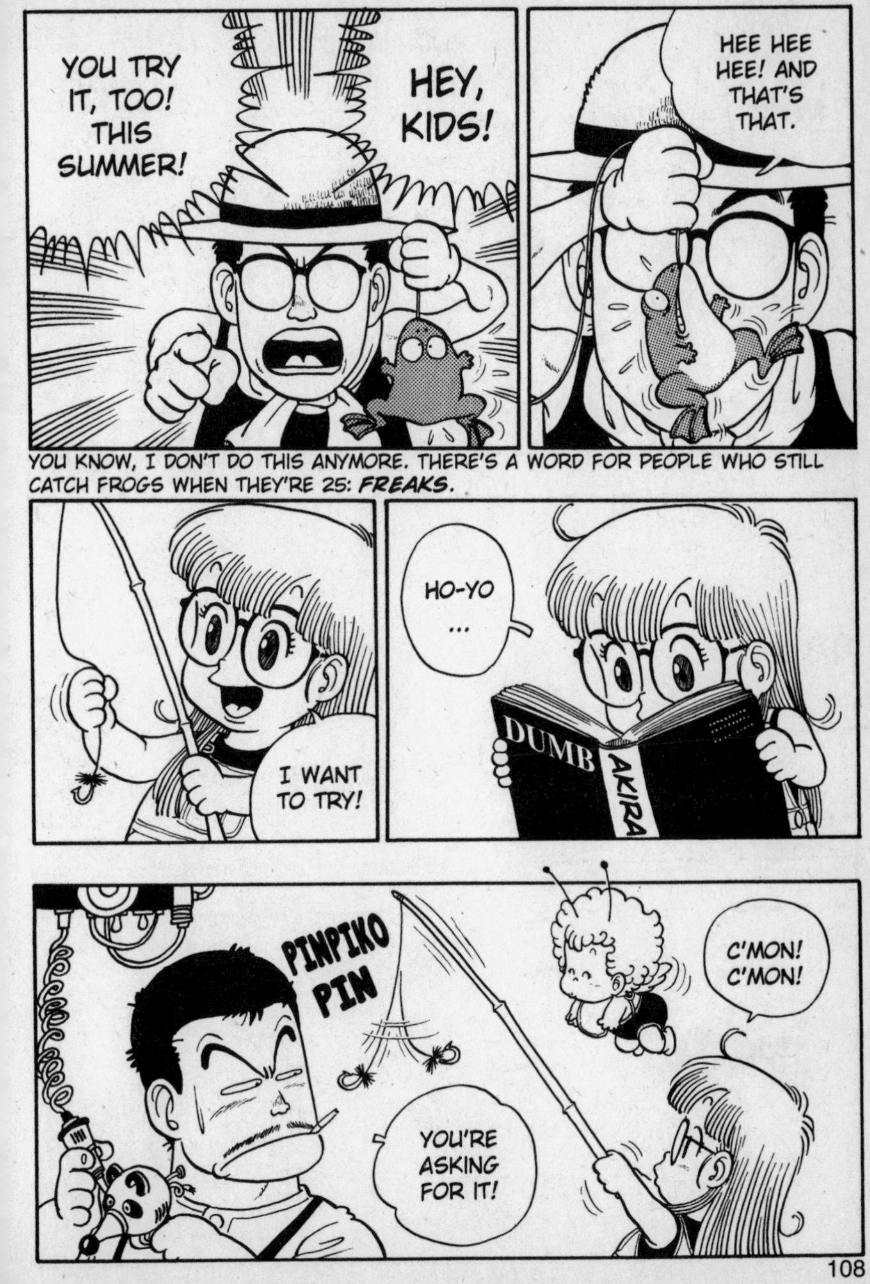
HEE HEE HEE! AND THAT'S THAT.
HEY, KIDS!
YOU TRY IT, TOO! THIS SUMMER!
YOU KNOW, I DON'T DO THIS ANYMORE. THERE'S A WORD FOR PEOPLE WHO STILL CATCH FROGS WHEN THEY'RE 25: FREAKS.
HO-YO ...
DUMB
AKIRA
I WANT TO TRY!
C'MON! C'MON!
PINPIKO PIN
YOU'RE ASKING FOR IT!

READ THIS WAY

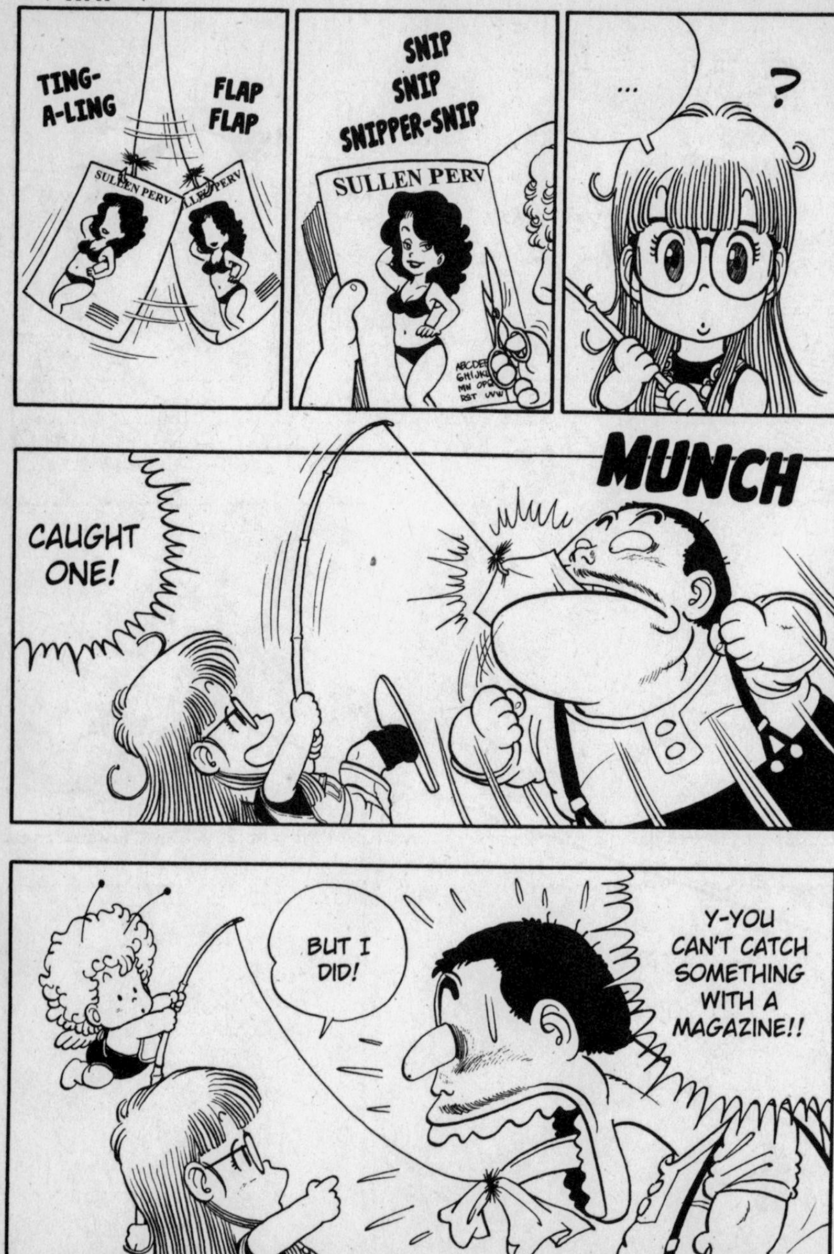

...
?
SNIP
SNIP
SNIPPER-SNIP
SULLEN PERV
TING-A-LING
FLAP FLAP
SULLEN PERV
SULLEN PERV
MUNCH
CAUGHT ONE!
Y-YOU CAN'T CATCH SOMETHING WITH A MAGAZINE!!
BUT I DID!

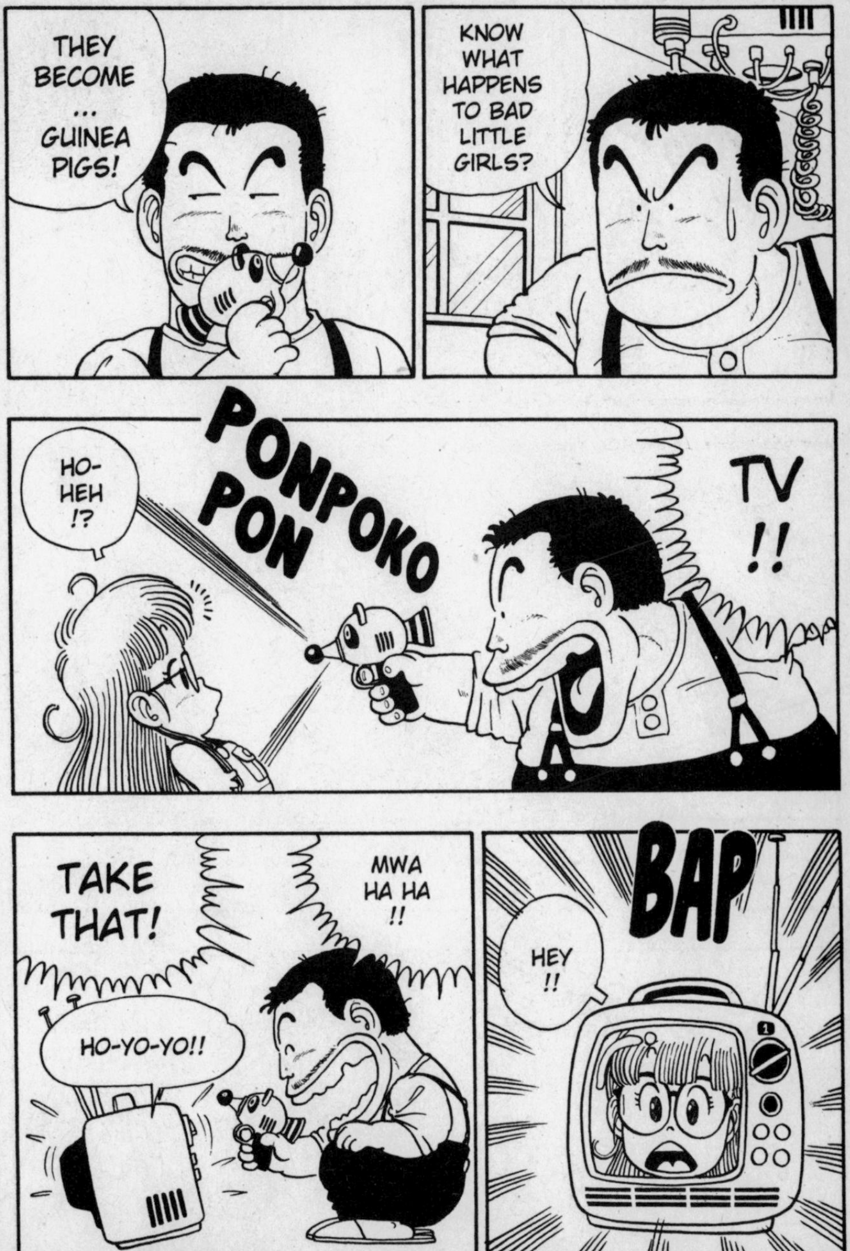
KNOW WHAT HAPPENS TO BAD LITTLE GIRLS?
THEY BECOME ... GUINEA PIGS!
TV !!
PONPOKO PON
HO-HEH !?
BAP
HEY !!
MWA HA HA !!
TAKE THAT!
HO-YO-YO!!

READ THIS WAY

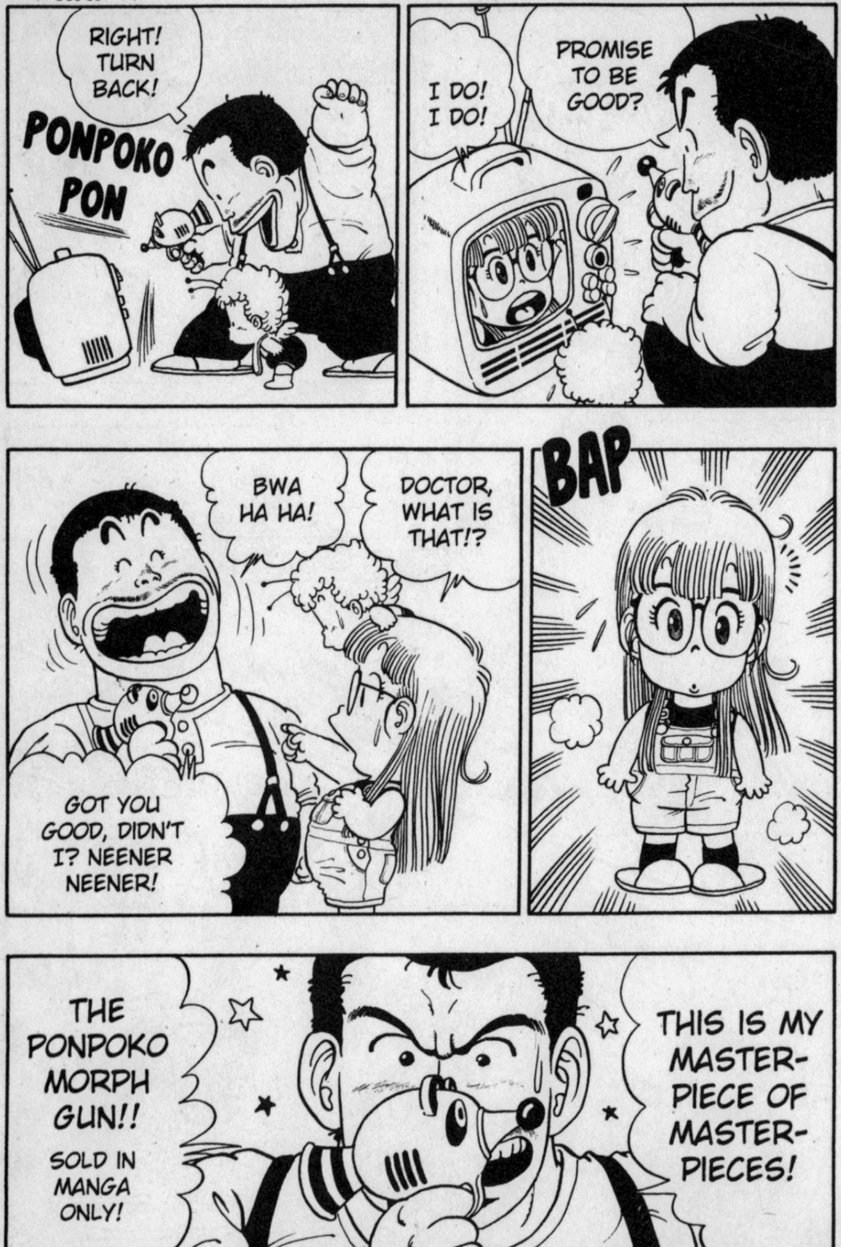
PROMISE TO BE GOOD?
I DO! I DO!
RIGHT! TURN BACK!
PONPOKO PON
BAP
DOCTOR, WHAT IS THAT!?
BWA HA HA!
GOT YOU GOOD, DIDN'T I? NEENER NEENER!
THIS IS MY MASTER-PIECE OF MASTER-PIECES!
THE PONPOKO MORPH GUN!!
SOLD IN MANGA ONLY!

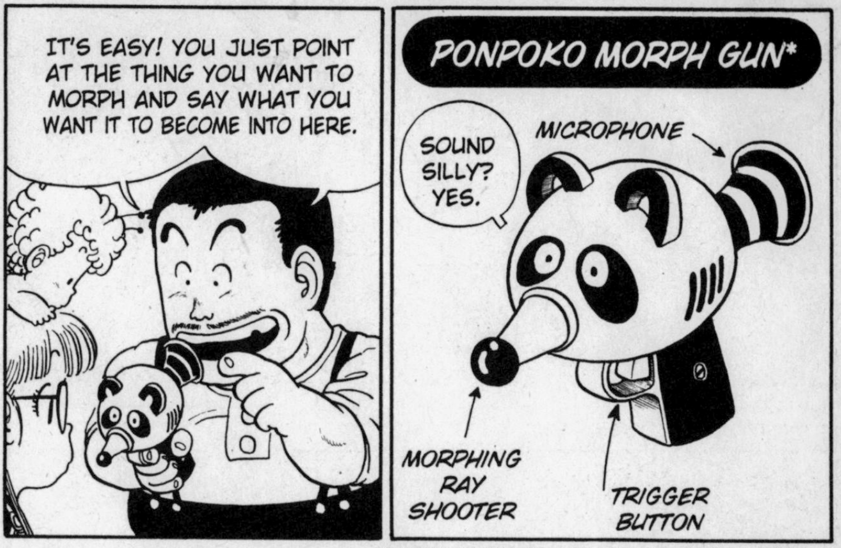
PONPOKO MORPH GUN*
SOUND SILLY? YES.
MICROPHONE
MORPHING RAY SHOOTER
TRIGGER BUTTON
IT'S EASY! YOU JUST POINT AT THE THING YOU WANT TO MORPH AND SAY WHAT YOU WANT IT TO BECOME INTO HERE.

*SHAPED LIKE *TANUKI* (SHAPE-CHANGING "RACCOON-DOGS"). "PONPOKO" IS THE SOUND THEY MAKE DRUMMING THEIR BELLIES.

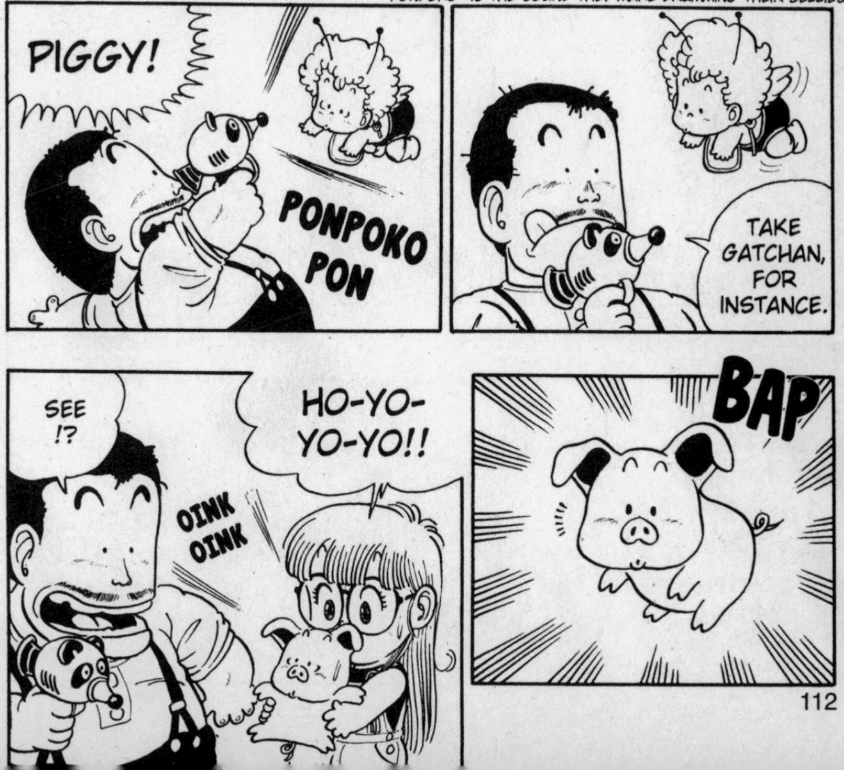
TAKE GATCHAN, FOR INSTANCE.
PIGGY!
PONPOKO PON
BAP
HO-YO-YO-YO!!
SEE !?
OINK OINK

READ THIS WAY

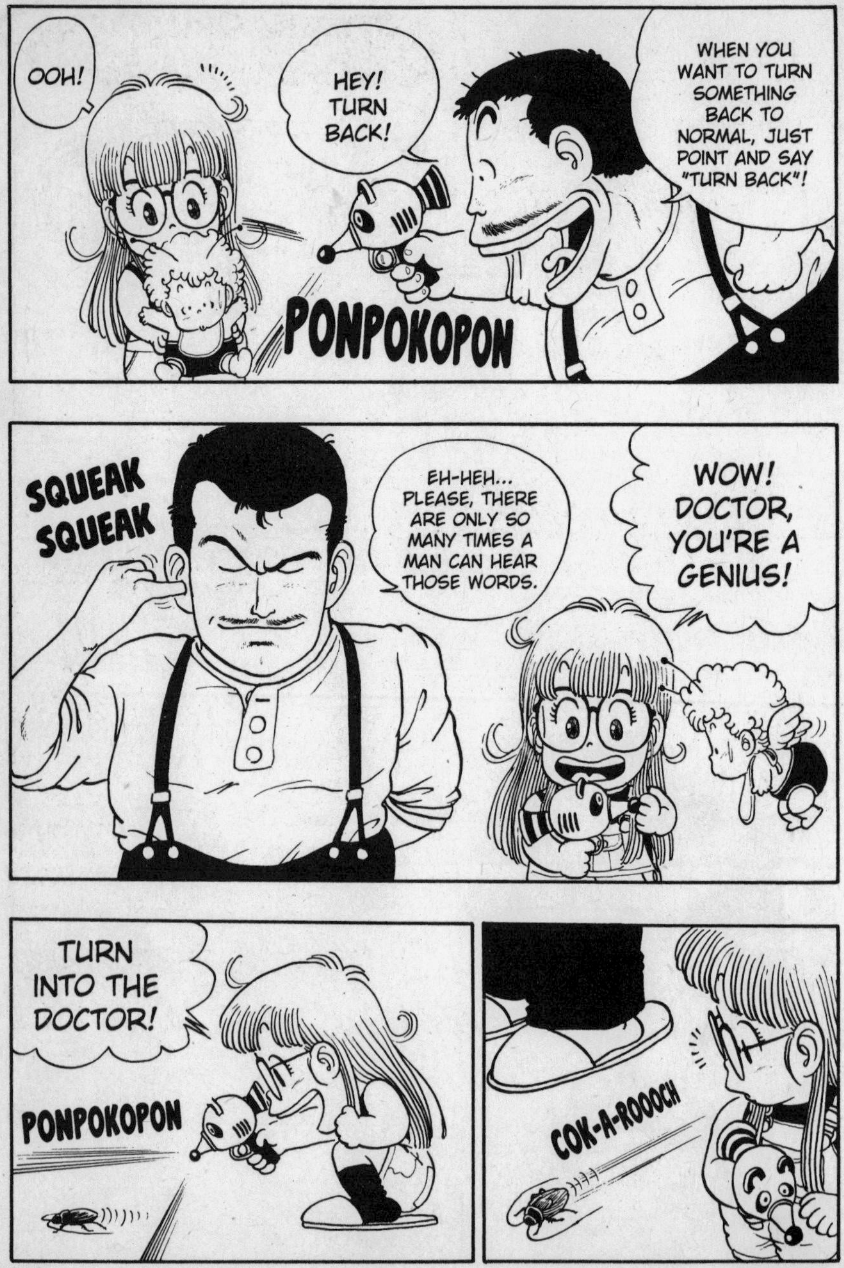

WHEN YOU WANT TO TURN SOMETHING BACK TO NORMAL, JUST POINT AND SAY "TURN BACK"!
HEY! TURN BACK!
OOH!
PONPOKOPON
WOW! DOCTOR, YOU'RE A GENIUS!
EH-HEH... PLEASE, THERE ARE ONLY SO MANY TIMES A MAN CAN HEAR THOSE WORDS.
SQUEAK SQUEAK
COK-A-ROOOCH
TURN INTO THE DOCTOR!
PONPOKOPON

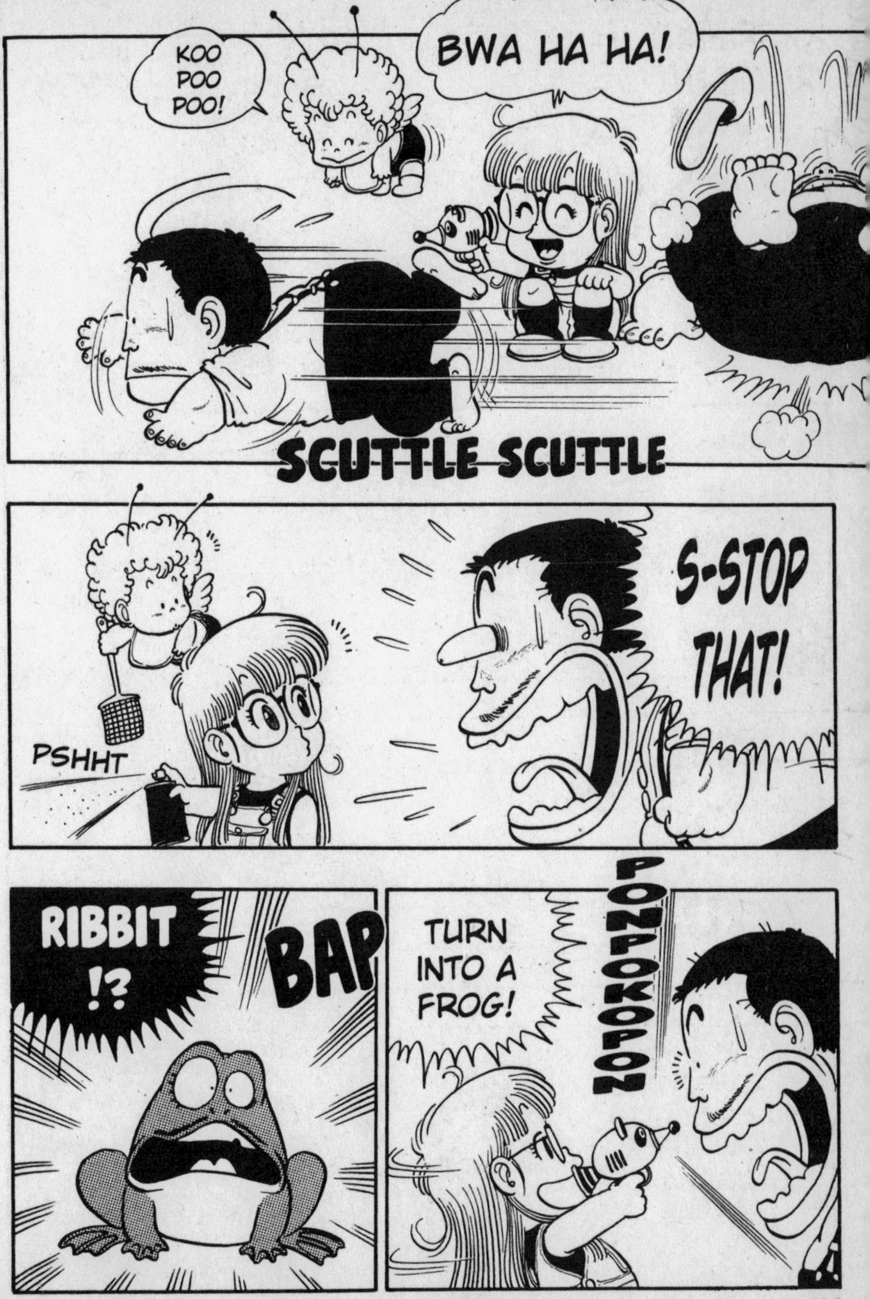
BWA HA HA!
KOO POO POO!
SCUTTLE SCUTTLE
S-STOP THAT!
PSHHT
PONPOKOPON
TURN INTO A FROG!
BAP
RIBBIT !?

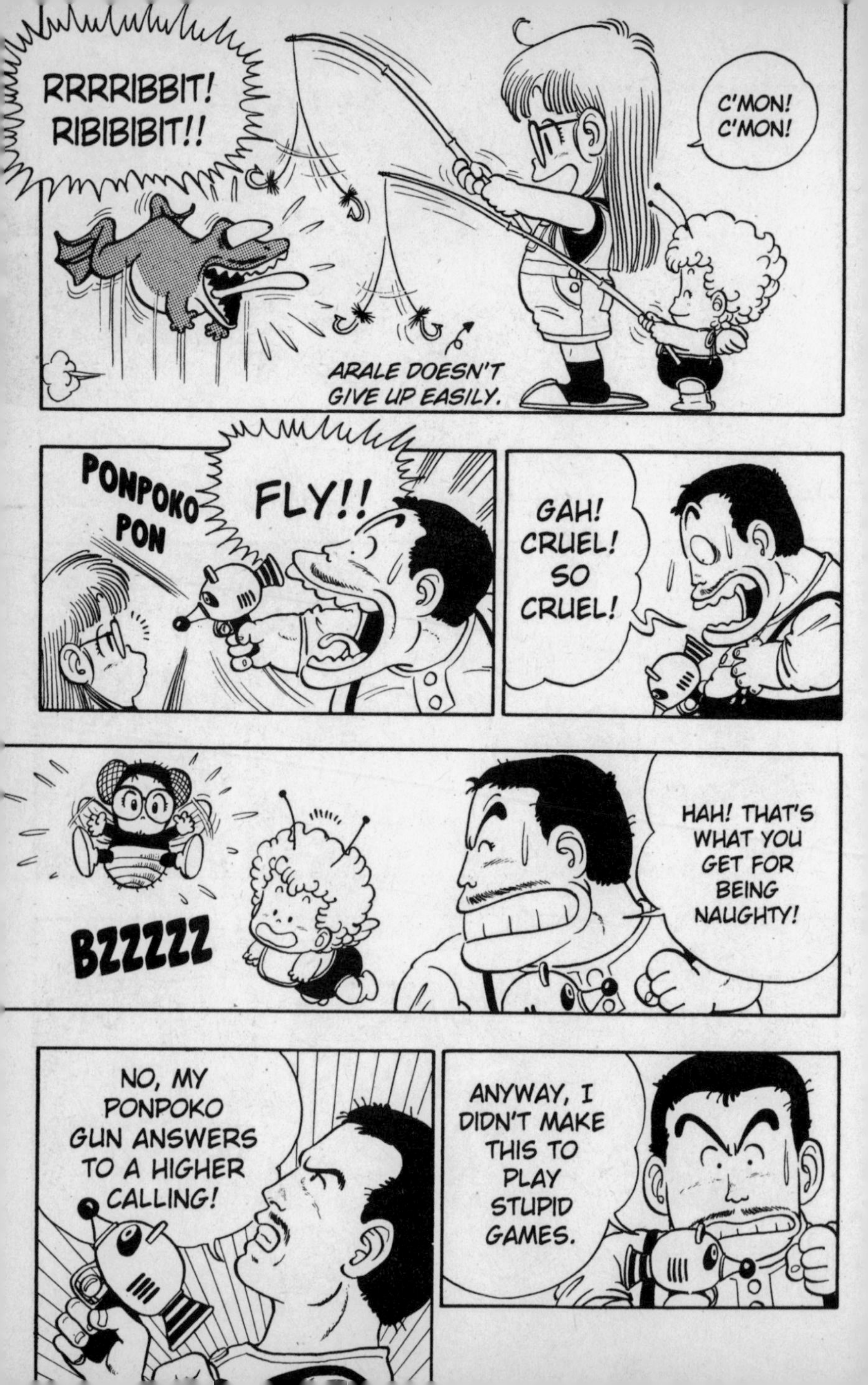
C'MON! C'MON!
RRRRIBBIT! RIBIBIBIT!!
ARALE DOESN'T GIVE UP EASILY.
GAH! CRUEL! SO CRUEL!
FLY!!
PONPOKO PON
HAH! THAT'S WHAT YOU GET FOR BEING NAUGHTY!
BZZZZZ
ANYWAY, I DIDN'T MAKE THIS TO PLAY STUPID GAMES.
NO, MY PONPOKO GUN ANSWERS TO A HIGHER CALLING!

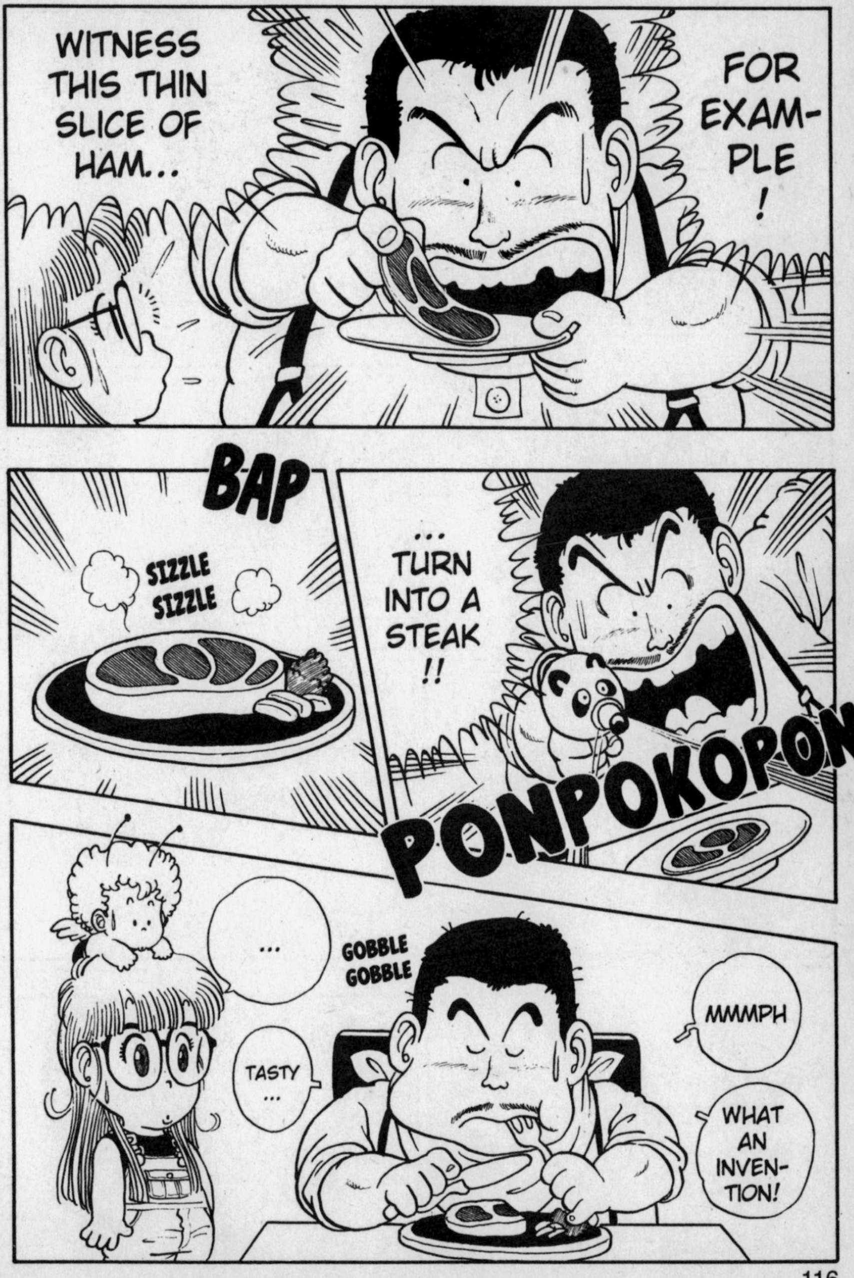
FOR EXAMPLE!
WITNESS THIS THIN SLICE OF HAM...
... TURN INTO A STEAK!!
PONPOKOPON
BAP
SIZZLE SIZZLE
MMMPH
WHAT AN INVENTION!
GOBBLE GOBBLE
TASTY ...
...

READ THIS WAY

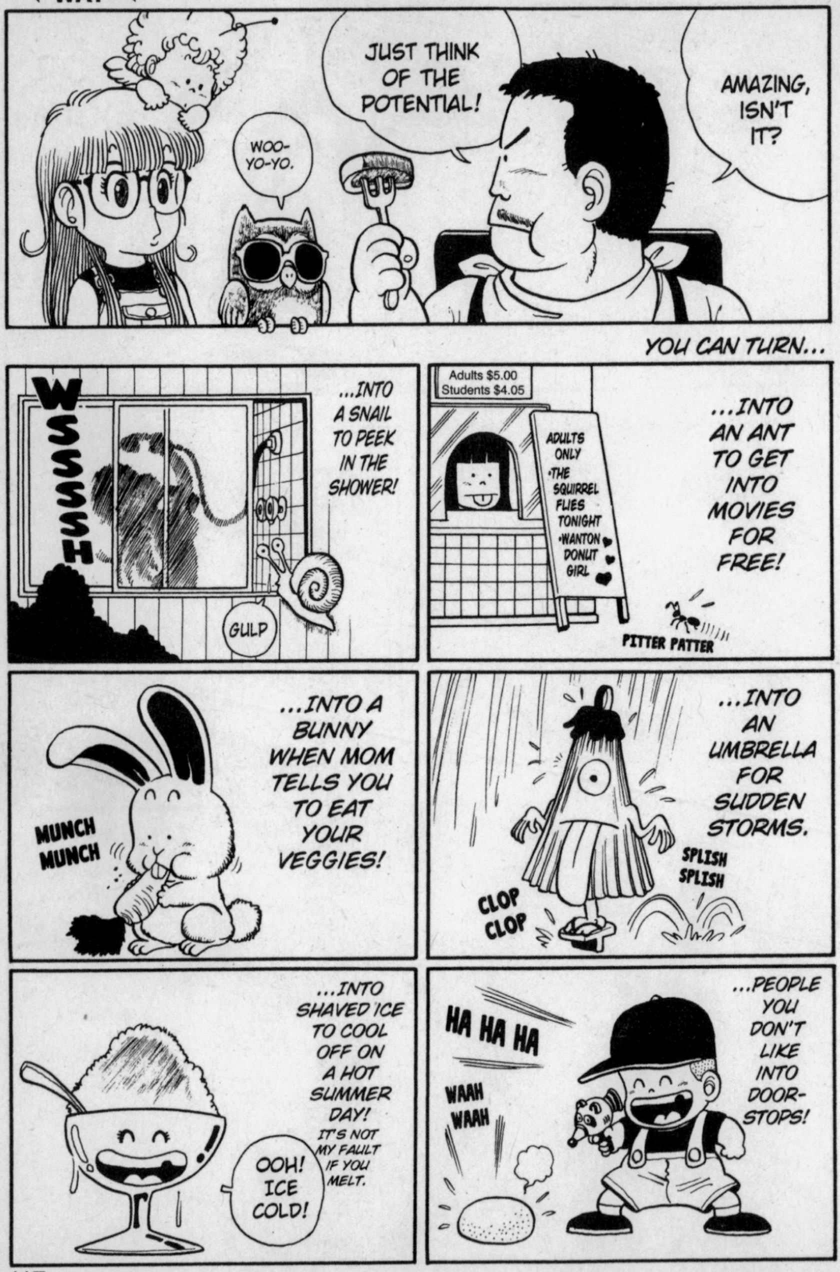
AMAZING, ISN'T IT?
JUST THINK OF THE POTENTIAL!
WOO-YO-YO.
YOU CAN TURN...
Adults $5.00
Students $4.05
...INTO AN ANT TO GET INTO MOVIES FOR FREE!
ADULTS ONLY
•THE SQUIRREL FLIES TONIGHT
•WANTON DONUT GIRL
PITTER PATTER
WSSSSH
...INTO A SNAIL TO PEEK IN THE SHOWER!
GULP
...INTO AN UMBRELLA FOR SUDDEN STORMS.
SPLISH SPLISH
CLOP CLOP
...INTO A BUNNY WHEN MOM TELLS YOU TO EAT YOUR VEGGIES!
MUNCH MUNCH
...PEOPLE YOU DON'T LIKE INTO DOOR-STOPS!
HA HA HA
WAAH WAAH
...INTO SHAVED ICE TO COOL OFF ON A HOT SUMMER DAY!
IT'S NOT MY FAULT IF YOU MELT.
OOH! ICE COLD!

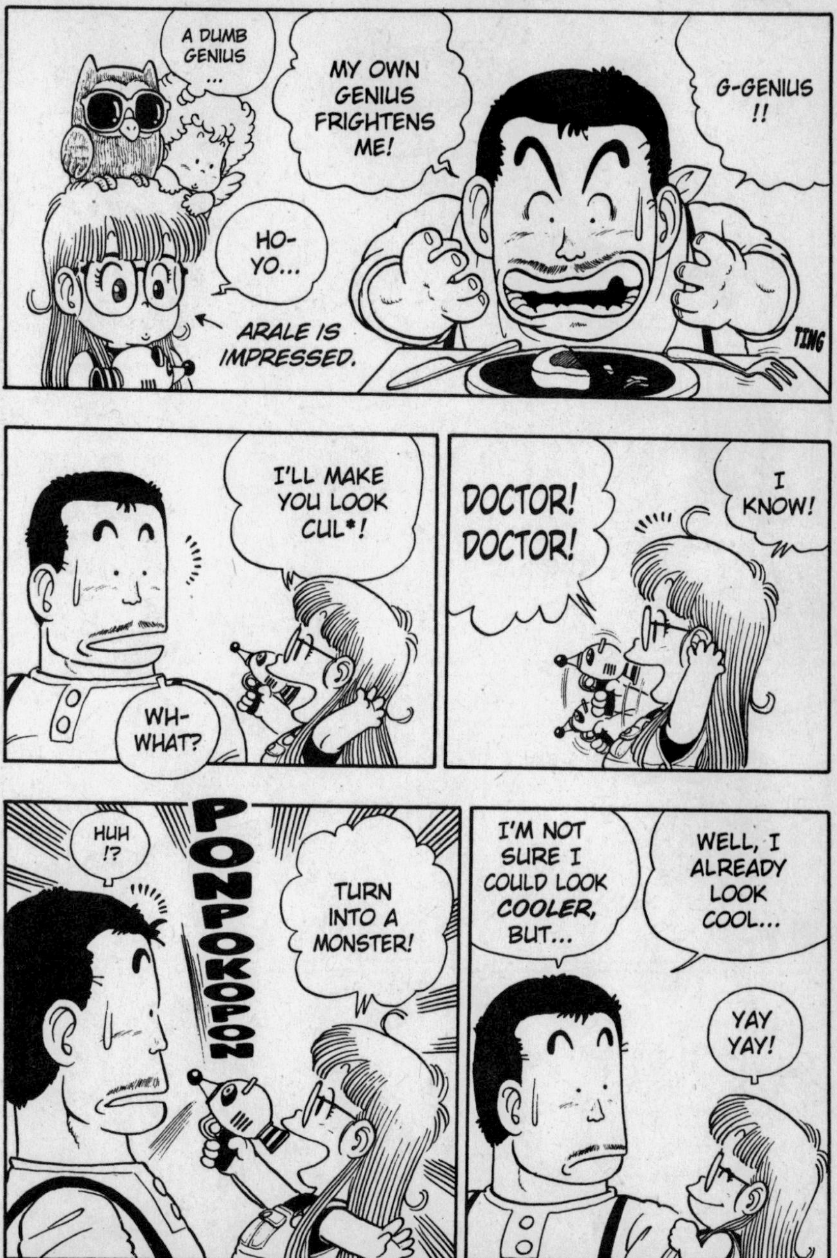
G-GENIUS !!
MY OWN GENIUS FRIGHTENS ME!
A DUMB GENIUS ...
TING
HO-YO...
ARALE IS IMPRESSED.
I KNOW!
DOCTOR! DOCTOR!
I'LL MAKE YOU LOOK CUL*!
WH-WHAT?
WELL, I ALREADY LOOK COOL...
I'M NOT SURE I COULD LOOK COOLER, BUT...
YAY YAY!
TURN INTO A MONSTER!
PONPOKOPON
HUH !?

*CUL = ARALE-ISM FOR "COOL." ARALE-SPEAK IS SWEEPING THE NATION! BAD SPELLERS AND LAZY TONGUES EVERYWHERE HAVE SENT GOOD WISHES AND THANKS FOR GIVING THEM HOPE FOR ACCEPTANCE IN SOCIETY AT LAST!

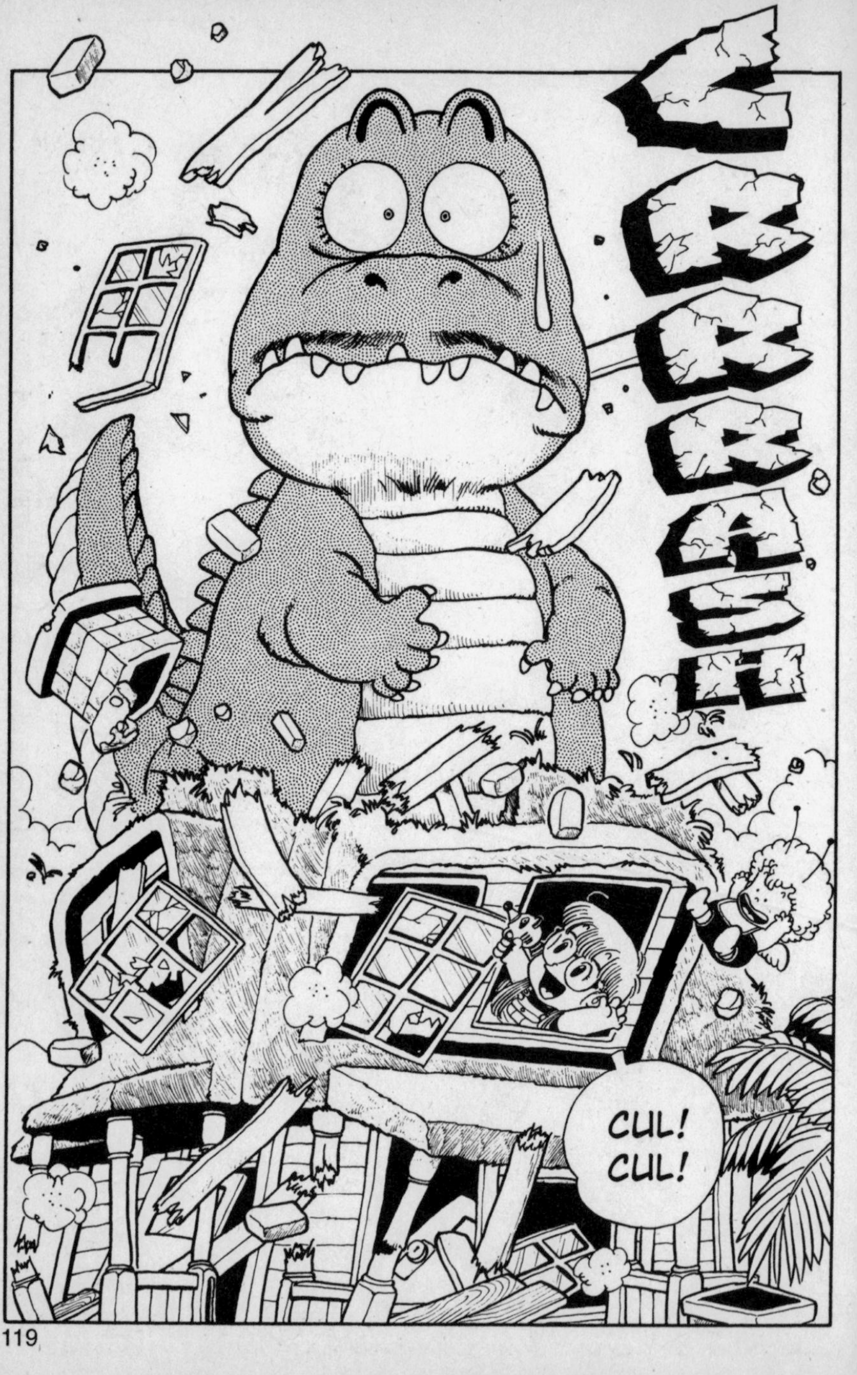
CRRRASH
CUL!
CUL!

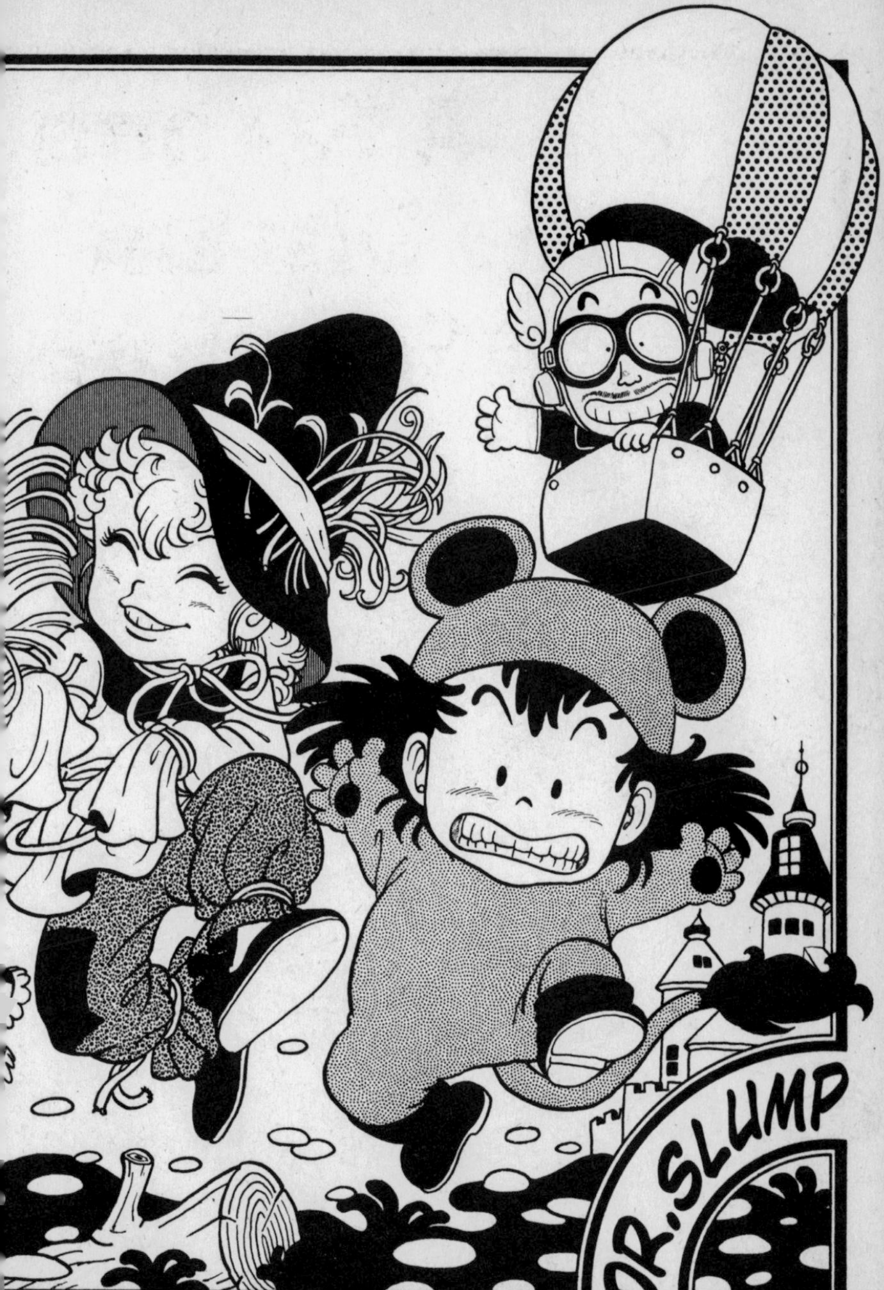
DR.SLUMP

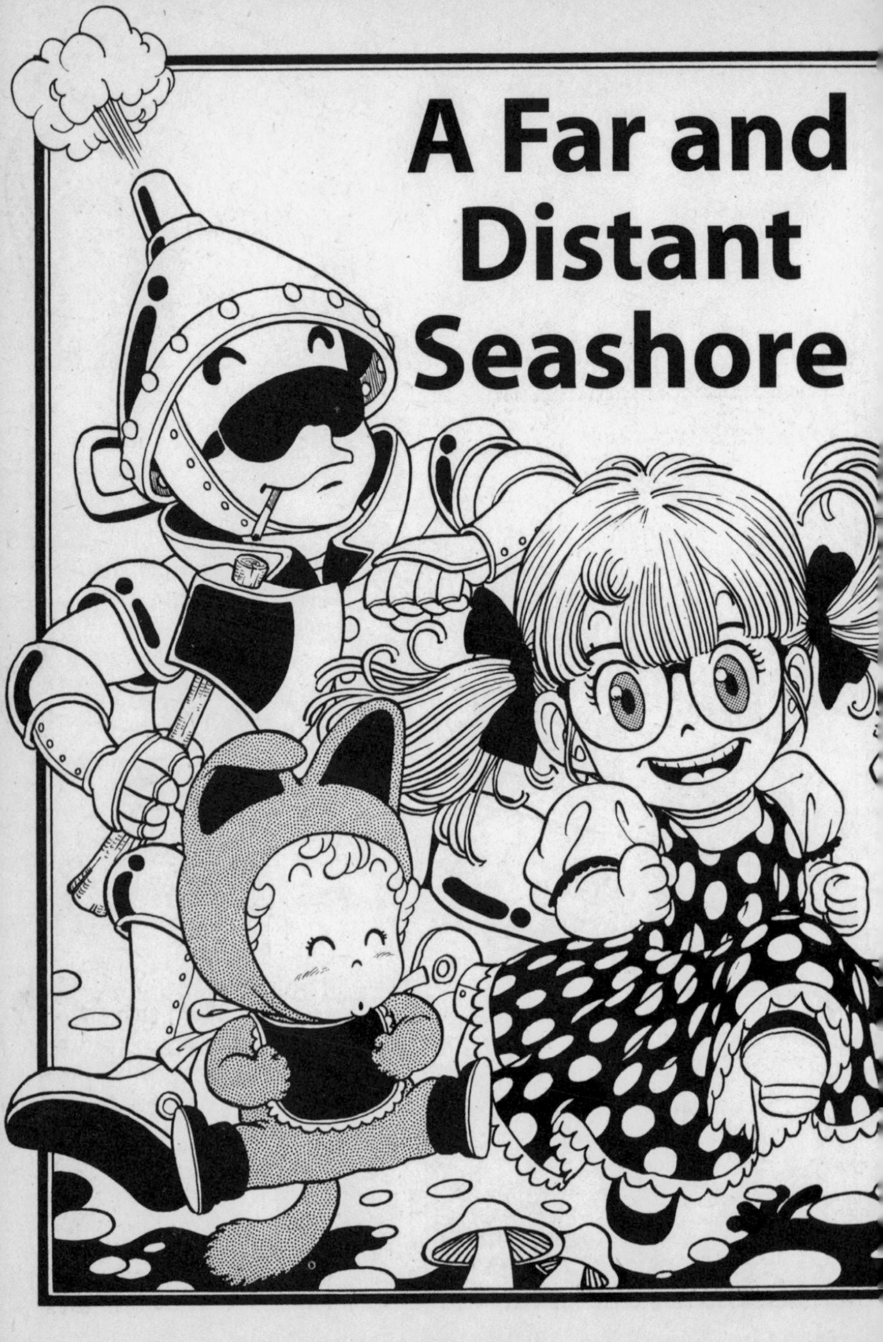
A Far and Distant Seashore

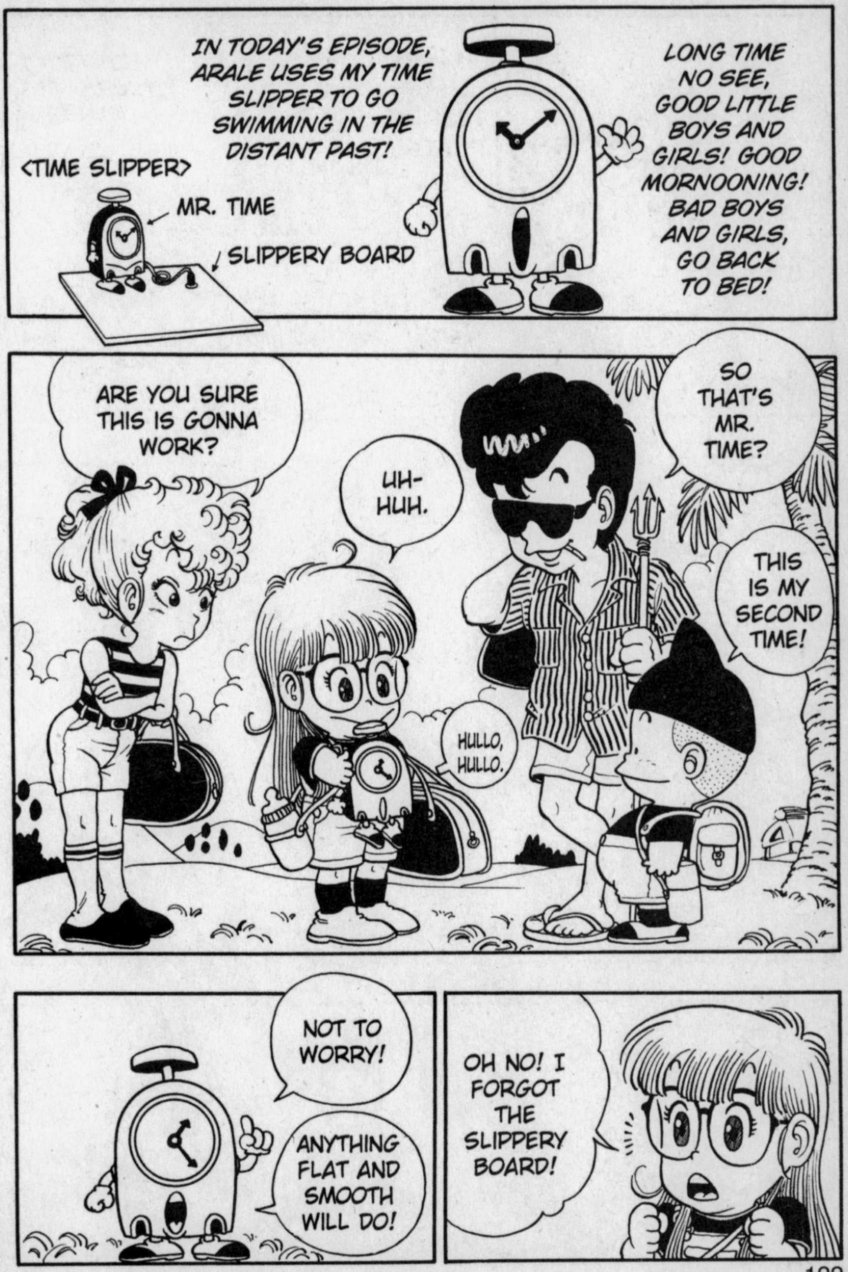
LONG TIME NO SEE, GOOD LITTLE BOYS AND GIRLS! GOOD MORNOONING! BAD BOYS AND GIRLS, GO BACK TO BED!
IN TODAY'S EPISODE, ARALE USES MY TIME SLIPPER TO GO SWIMMING IN THE DISTANT PAST!
<TIME SLIPPER>
MR. TIME
SLIPPERY BOARD
SO THAT'S MR. TIME?
THIS IS MY SECOND TIME!
ARE YOU SURE THIS IS GONNA WORK?
UH-HUH.
HULLO, HULLO.
OH NO! I FORGOT THE SLIPPERY BOARD!
NOT TO WORRY!
ANYTHING FLAT AND SMOOTH WILL DO!

READ THIS WAY

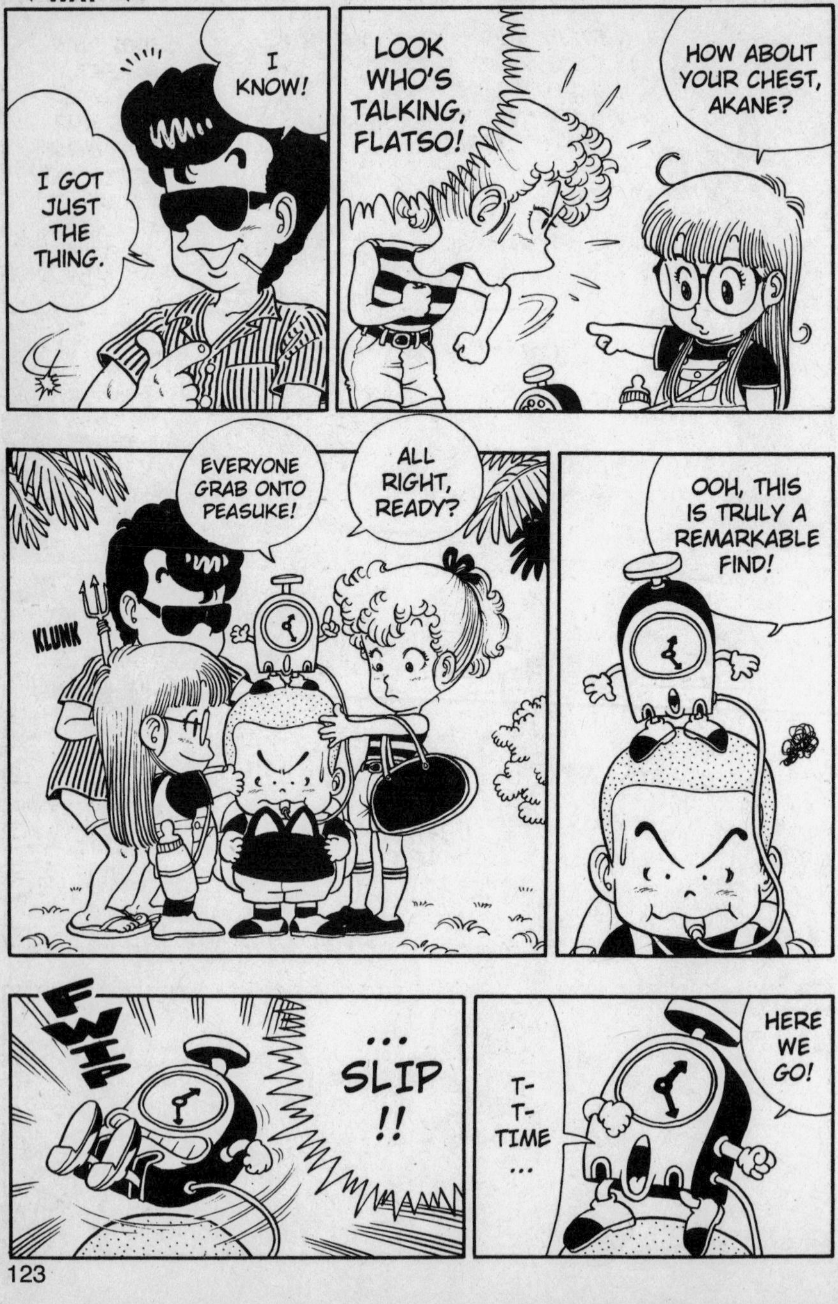
HOW ABOUT YOUR CHEST, AKANE?
LOOK WHO'S TALKING, FLATSO!
I KNOW!
I GOT JUST THE THING.
OOH, THIS IS TRULY A REMARKABLE FIND!
ALL RIGHT, READY?
EVERYONE GRAB ONTO PEASUKE!
KLUNK
HERE WE GO!
T- T- TIME ...
FWIP
... SLIP !!

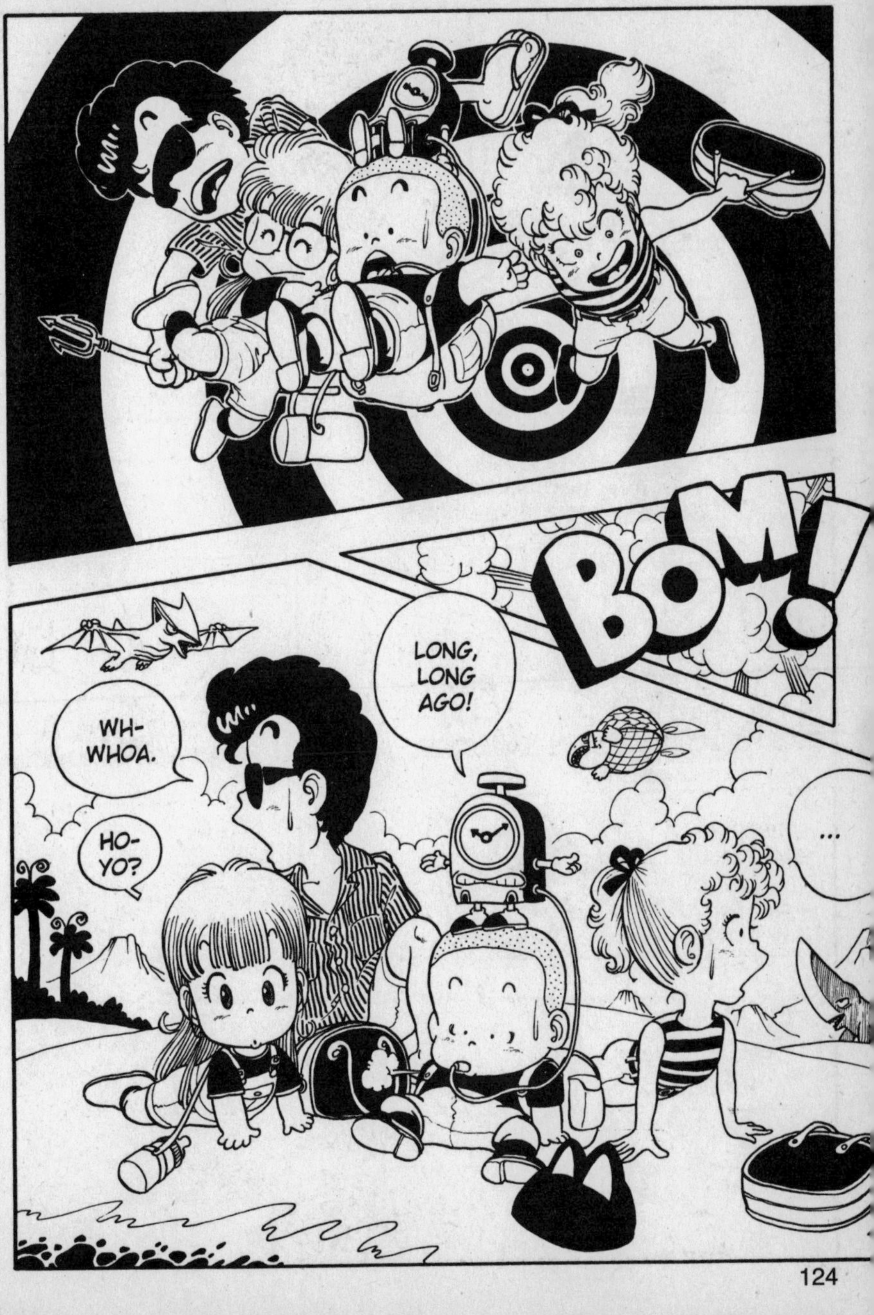
BOM!
...
LONG, LONG AGO!
WH- WHOA.
HO- YO?

READ THIS WAY

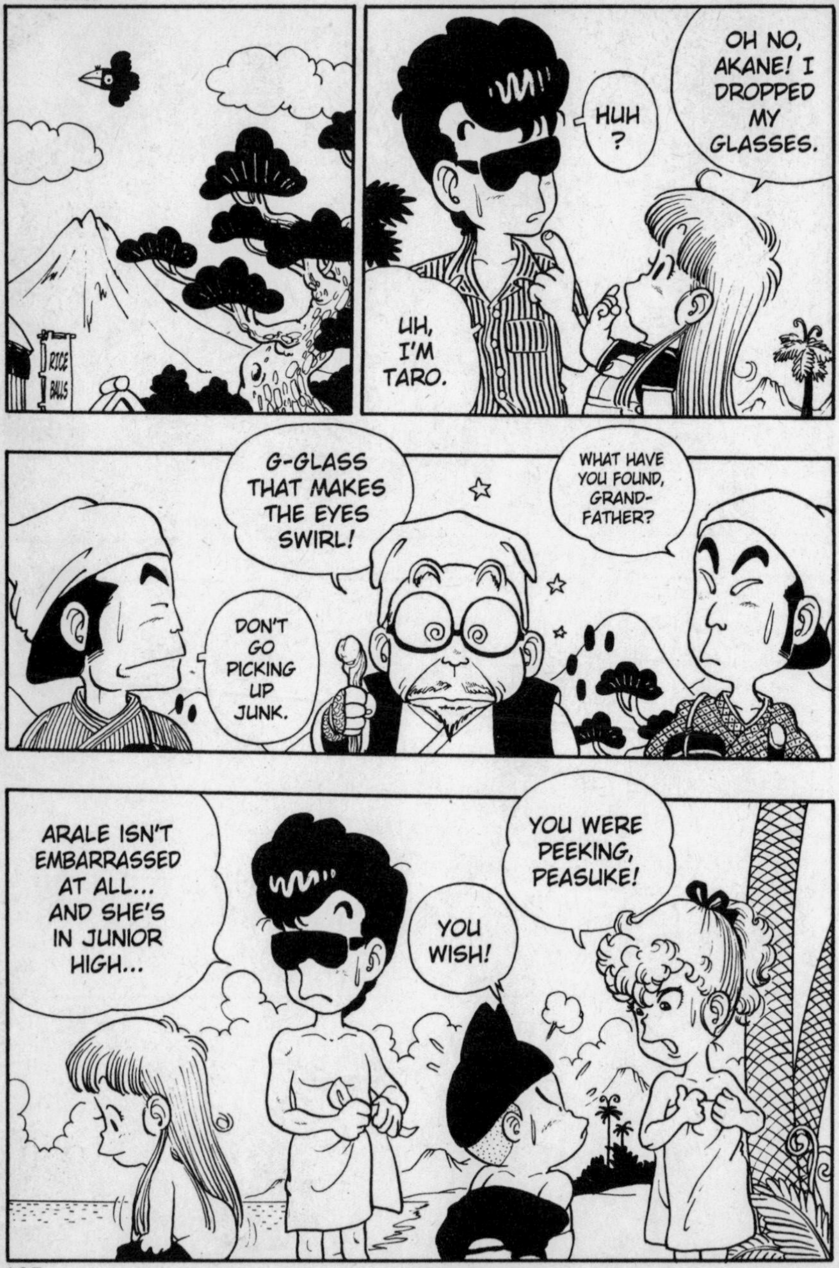
OH NO, AKANE! I DROPPED MY GLASSES.
HUH ?
UH, I'M TARO.
RICE BALLS
WHAT HAVE YOU FOUND, GRAND-FATHER?
G-GLASS THAT MAKES THE EYES SWIRL!
DON'T GO PICKING UP JUNK.
YOU WERE PEEKING, PEASUKE!
YOU WISH!
ARALE ISN'T EMBARRASSED AT ALL... AND SHE'S IN JUNIOR HIGH...

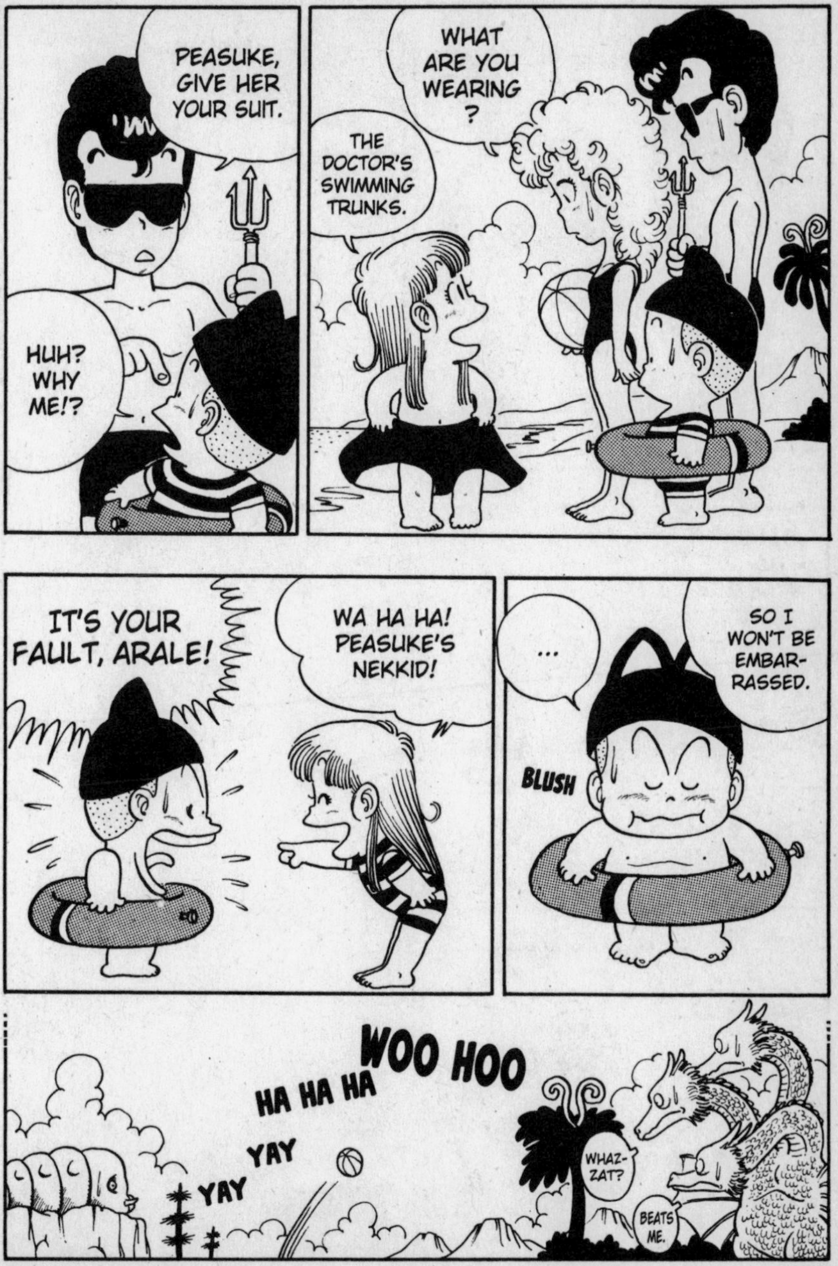
WHAT ARE YOU WEARING?
THE DOCTOR'S SWIMMING TRUNKS.
PEASUKE, GIVE HER YOUR SUIT.
HUH? WHY ME!?
SO I WON'T BE EMBARRASSED.
...
BLUSH
WA HA HA! PEASUKE'S NEKKID!
IT'S YOUR FAULT, ARALE!
WHAZ-ZAT?
BEATS ME.
WOO HOO
HA HA HA
YAY
YAY

READ THIS WAY

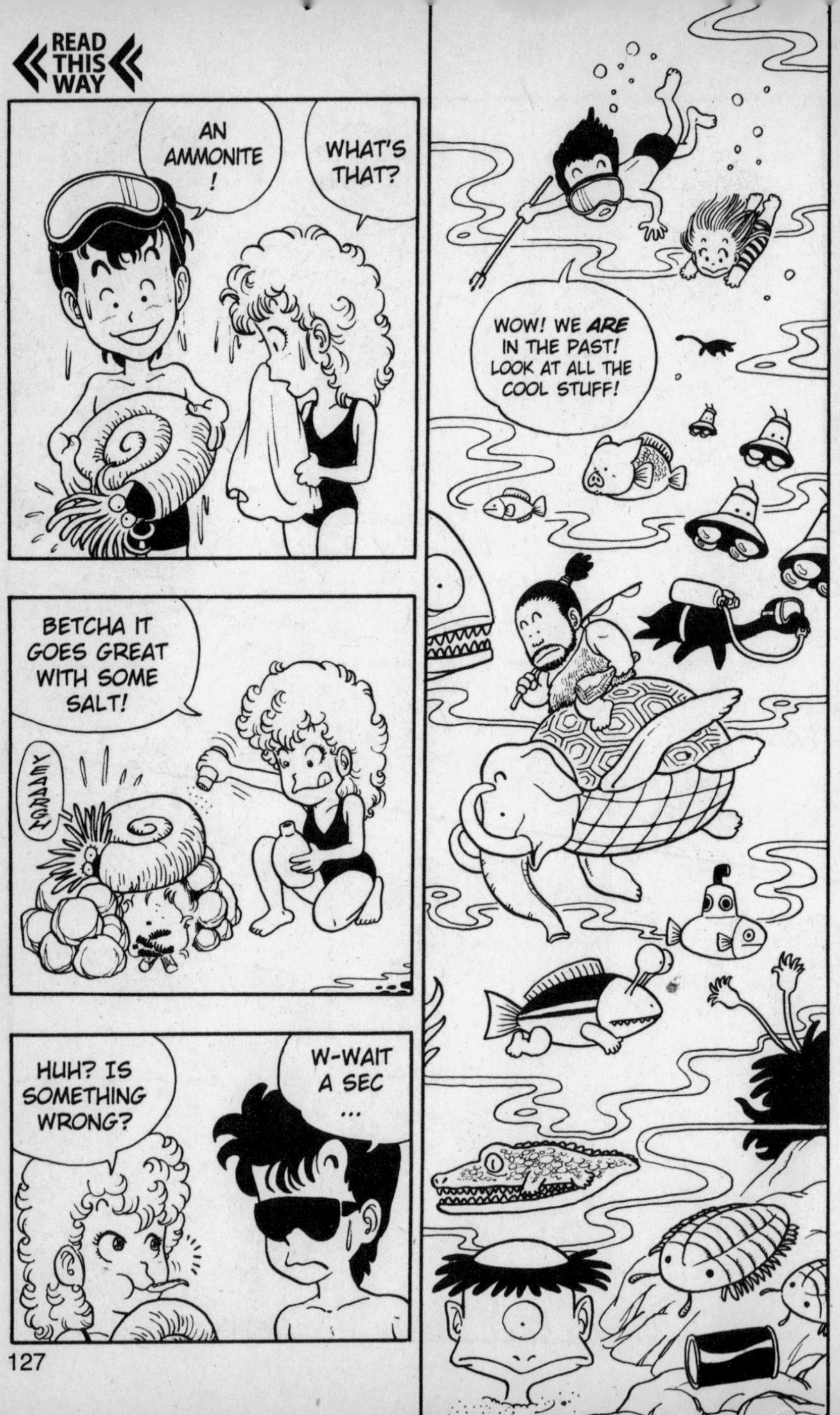
WOW! WE ARE IN THE PAST! LOOK AT ALL THE COOL STUFF!
WHAT'S THAT?
AN AMMONITE!
BETCHA IT GOES GREAT WITH SOME SALT!
YEAAARGH
W-WAIT A SEC ...
HUH? IS SOMETHING WRONG?

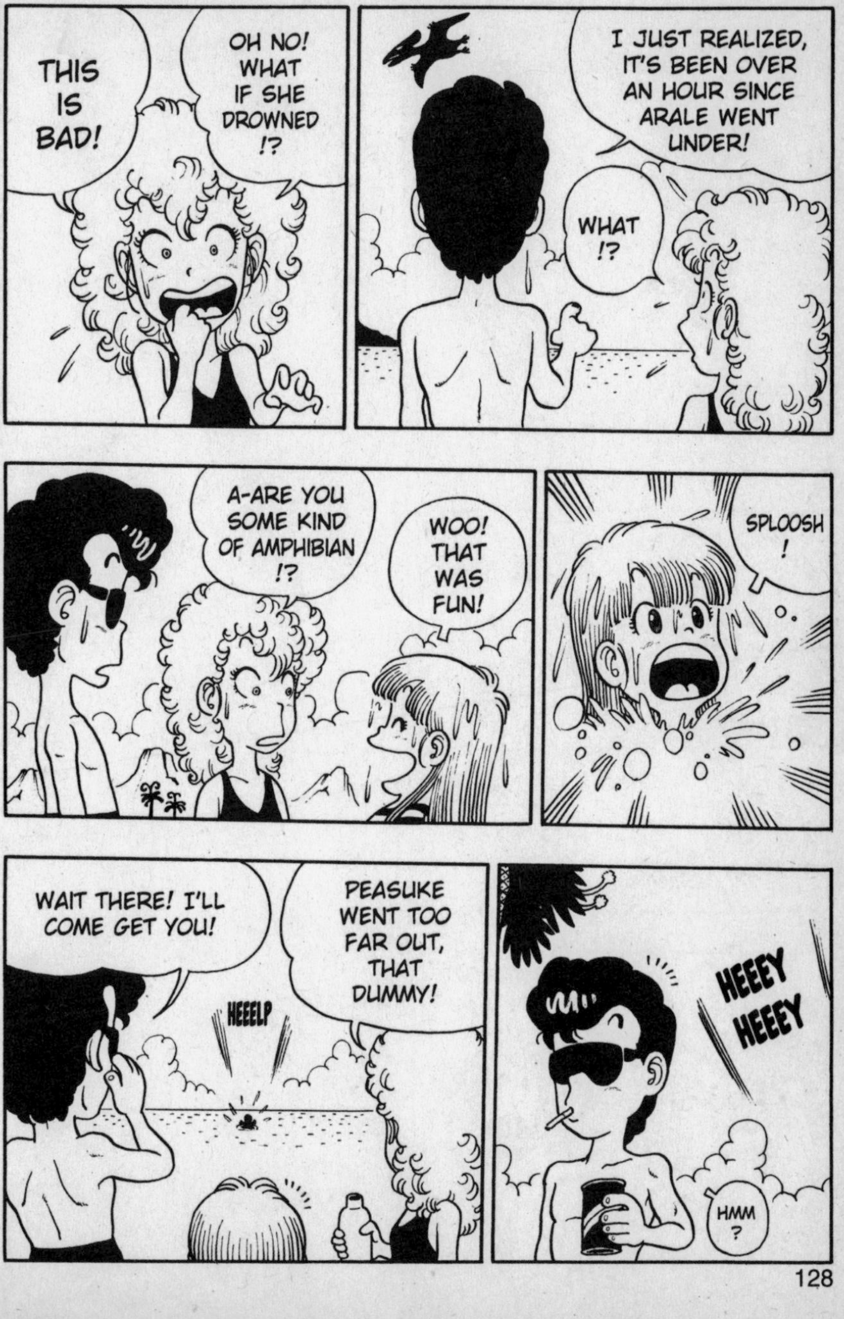
I JUST REALIZED, IT'S BEEN OVER AN HOUR SINCE ARALE WENT UNDER!
WHAT !?
OH NO! WHAT IF SHE DROWNED !?
THIS IS BAD!
SPLOOSH !
WOO! THAT WAS FUN!
A-ARE YOU SOME KIND OF AMPHIBIAN !?
HEEEY HEEEY
HMM ?
PEASUKE WENT TOO FAR OUT, THAT DUMMY!
HEEELP
WAIT THERE! I'LL COME GET YOU!

READ THIS WAY

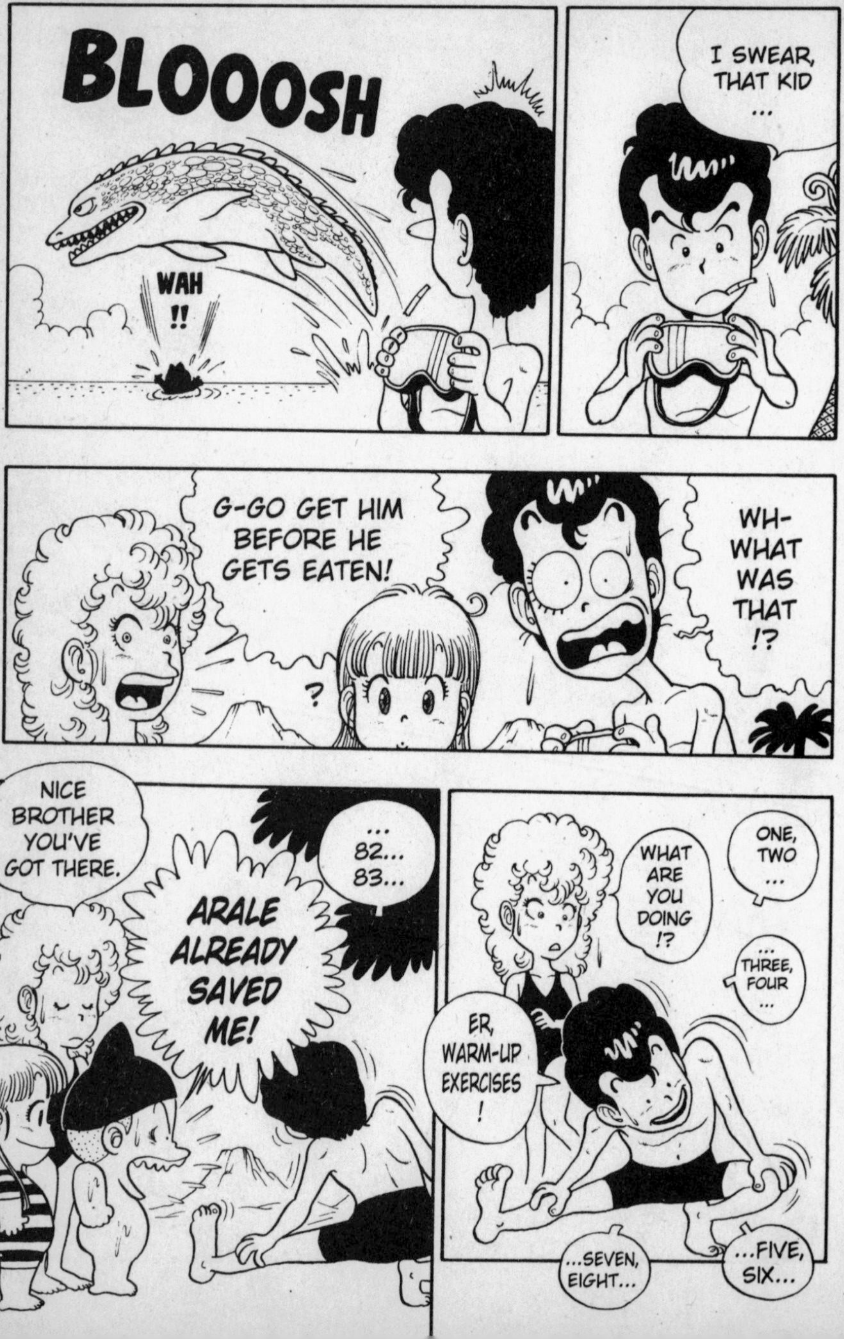

I SWEAR, THAT KID ...
BLOOOSH
WAH !!
WH-WHAT WAS THAT !?
?
G-GO GET HIM BEFORE HE GETS EATEN!
ONE, TWO ...
WHAT ARE YOU DOING !?
... THREE, FOUR ...
ER, WARM-UP EXERCISES !
...FIVE, SIX...
...SEVEN, EIGHT...
... 82... 83...
ARALE ALREADY SAVED ME!
NICE BROTHER YOU'VE GOT THERE.

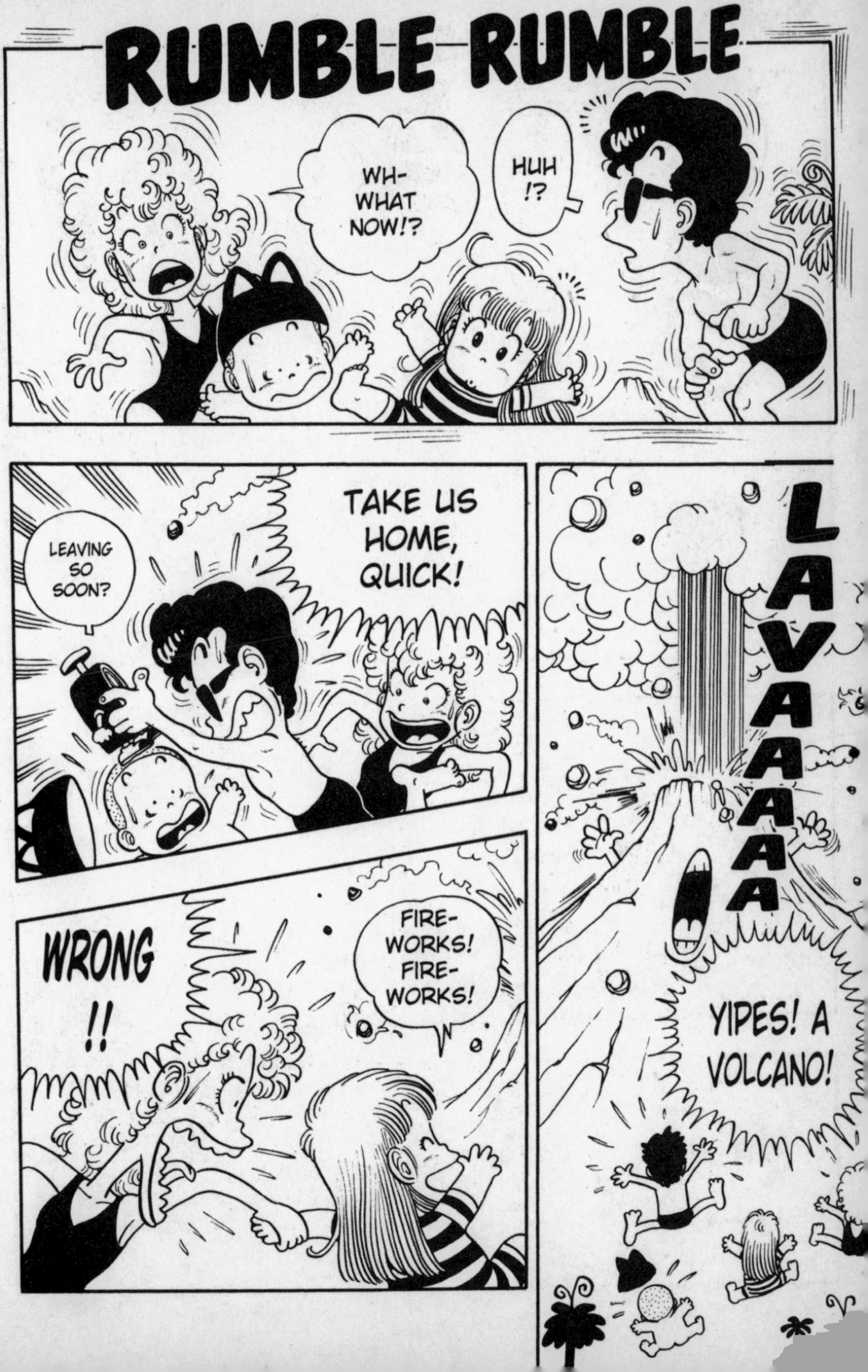
RUMBLE RUMBLE
HUH !?
WH- WHAT NOW!?
LAVAAAAAA
YIPES! A VOLCANO!
TAKE US HOME, QUICK!
LEAVING SO SOON?
FIRE-WORKS! FIRE-WORKS!
WRONG !!

READ THIS WAY

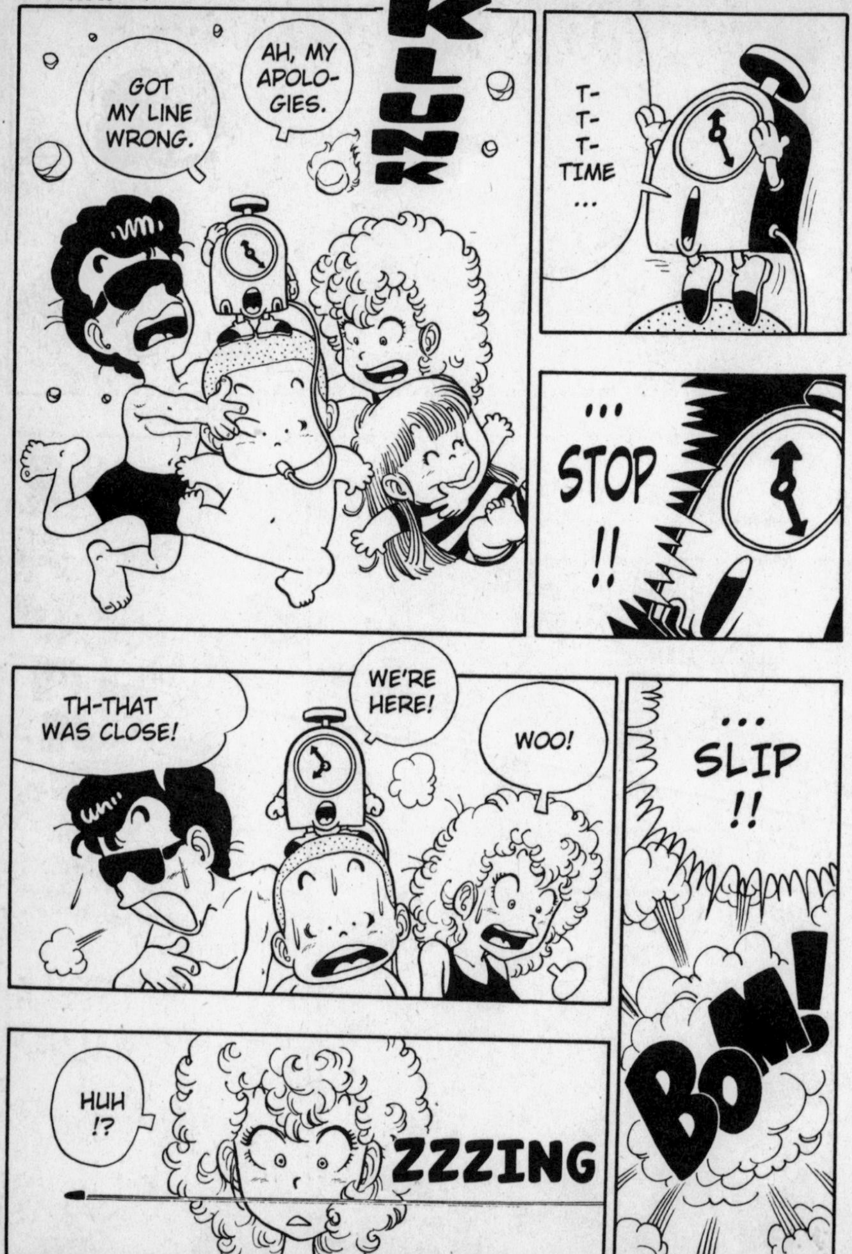

T-T-T-TIME...
... STOP !!
KLUNK
AH, MY APOLOGIES.
GOT MY LINE WRONG.
... SLIP !!
BOM!
WOO!
WE'RE HERE!
TH-THAT WAS CLOSE!
ZZZING
HUH !?

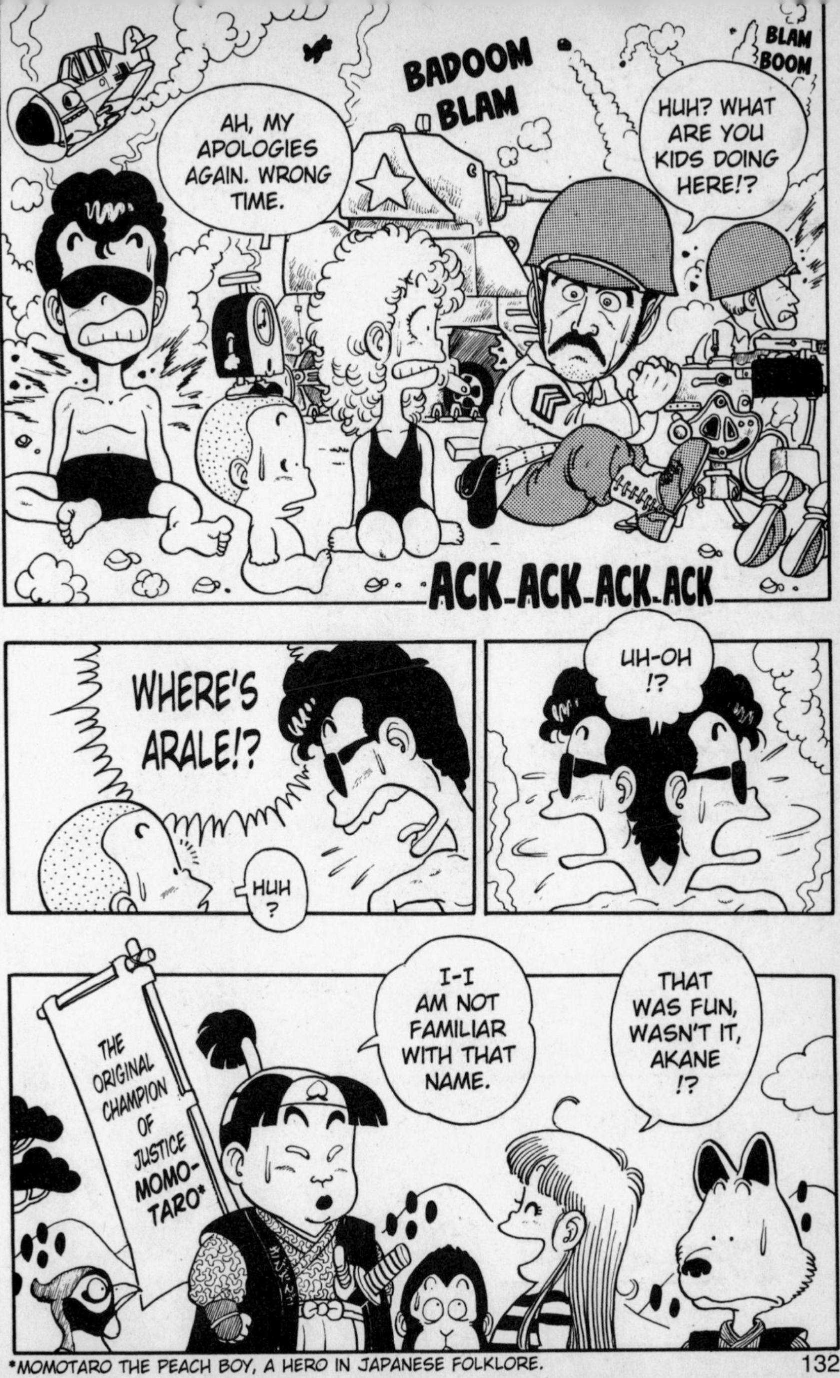
BLAM BOOM
HUH? WHAT ARE YOU KIDS DOING HERE!?
BADOOM BLAM
AH, MY APOLOGIES AGAIN. WRONG TIME.
ACK-ACK-ACK-ACK
UH-OH !?
WHERE'S ARALE!?
HUH ?
THAT WAS FUN, WASN'T IT, AKANE !?
I-I AM NOT FAMILIAR WITH THAT NAME.
THE ORIGINAL CHAMPION OF JUSTICE MOMO-TARO*

*MOMOTARO THE PEACH BOY, A HERO IN JAPANESE FOLKLORE.

THIS IS WHERE I SLAVE AWAY EVERY DAY-OOOH

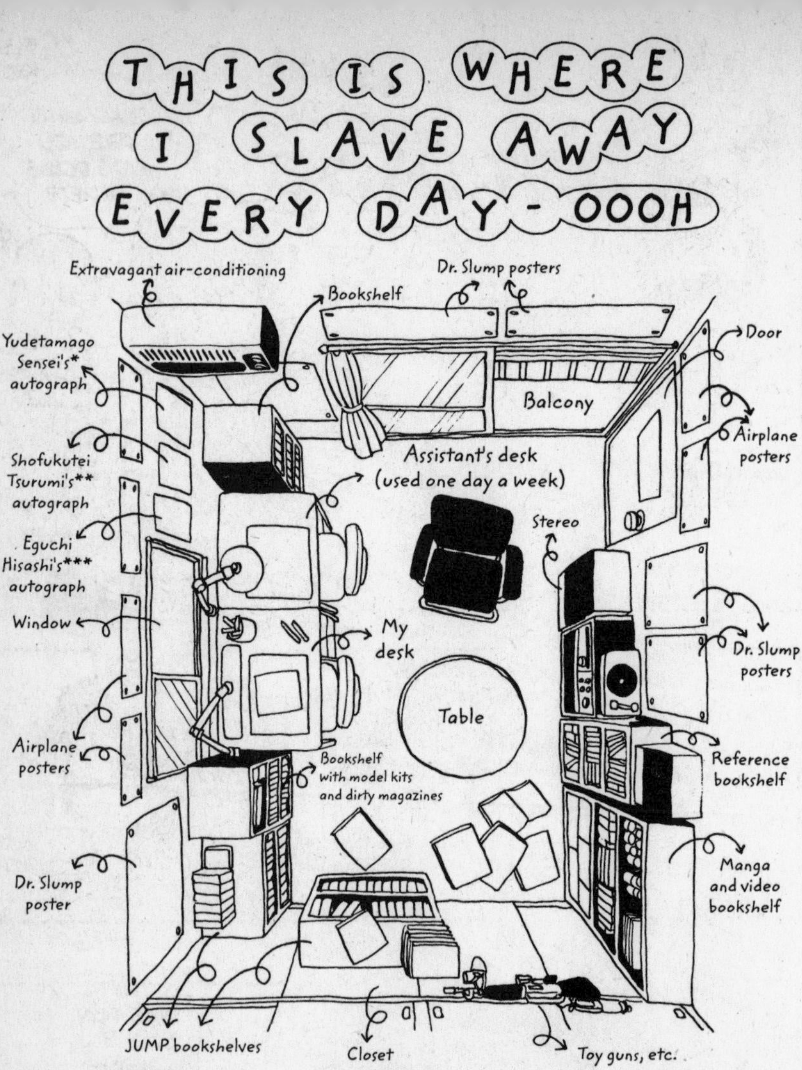

Extravagant air-conditioning
Dr. Slump posters
Bookshelf
Door
Yudetamago Sensei's* autograph
Balcony
Airplane posters
Assistant's desk (used one day a week)
Shofukutei Tsurumi's** autograph
Stereo
Eguchi Hisashi's*** autograph
Window
My desk
Dr. Slump posters
Table
Airplane posters
Bookshelf with model kits and dirty magazines
Reference bookshelf
Dr. Slump poster
Manga and video bookshelf
JUMP bookshelves
Closet
Toy guns, etc.

A small six-mat room in a small house set in the fields deep in the countryside of Aichi Prefecture (as of Sept. 1980).

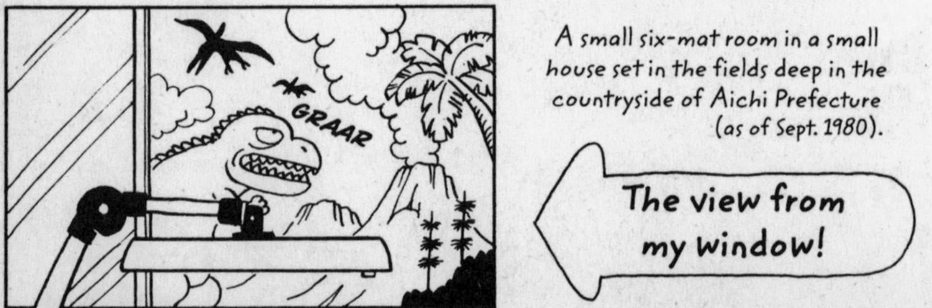

GRAAR

The view from my window!

*Manga artist, author of "Kinnikuman" ("Muscle Man")
**Popular TV comedian ***Humor manga artist

Barbershop Panic
Part 1

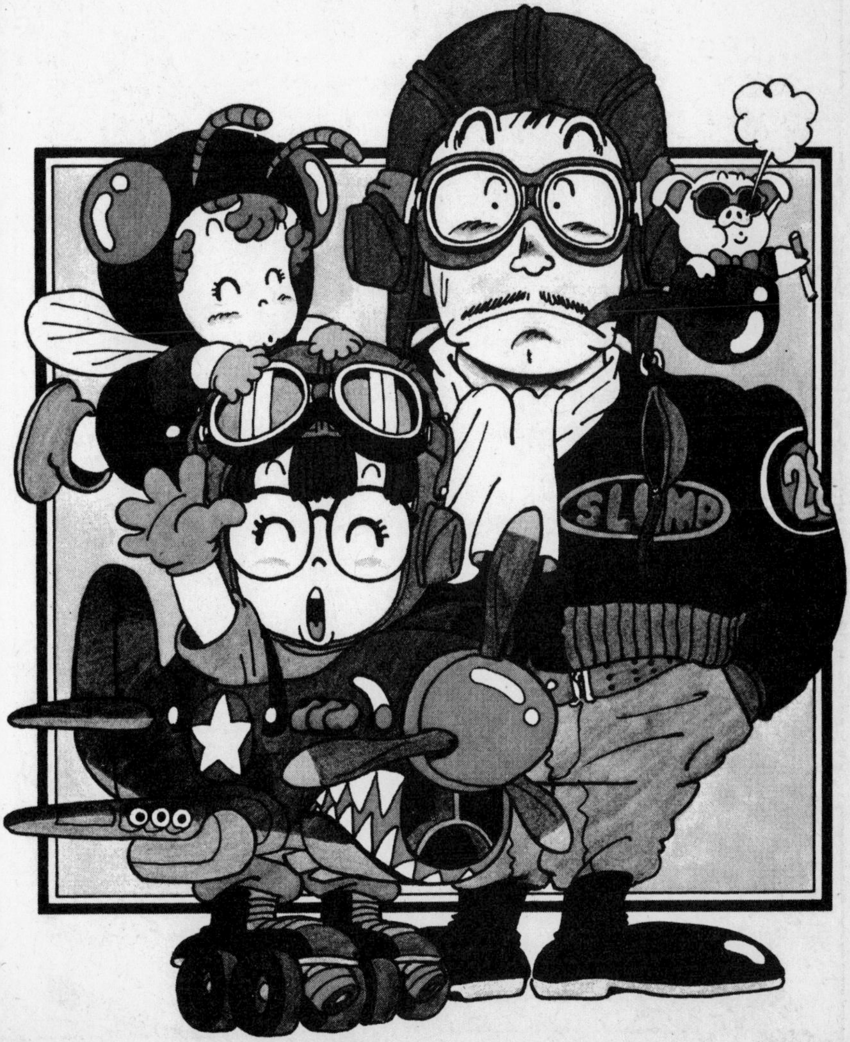
SLUMP

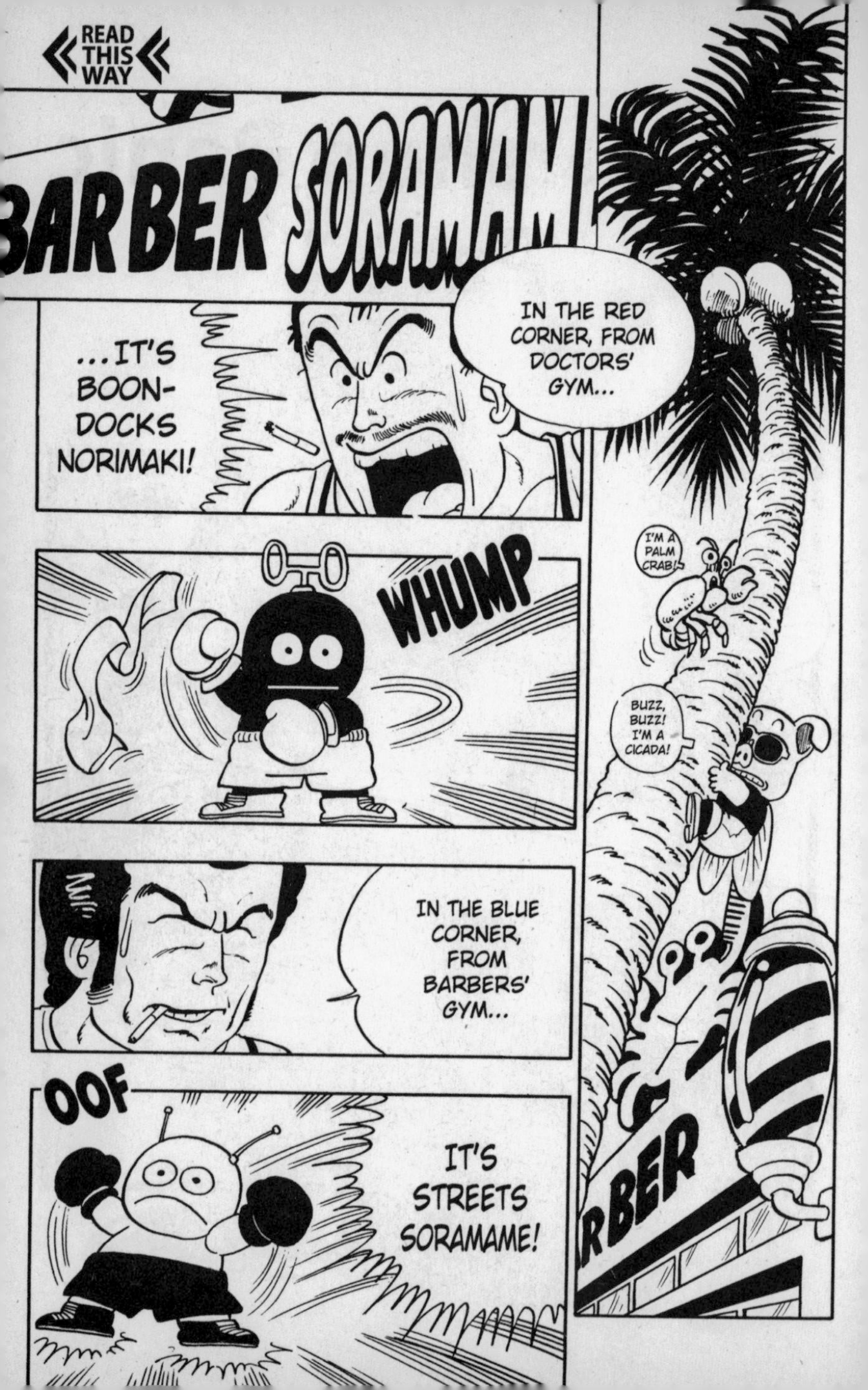
READ THIS WAY
I'M A PALM CRAB!
BUZZ, BUZZ! I'M A CICADA!
RBER
BARBER SORAMAM
IN THE RED CORNER, FROM DOCTORS' GYM...
...IT'S BOON-DOCKS NORIMAKI!
WHUMP
IN THE BLUE CORNER, FROM BARBERS' GYM...
OOF
IT'S STREETS SORAMAME!

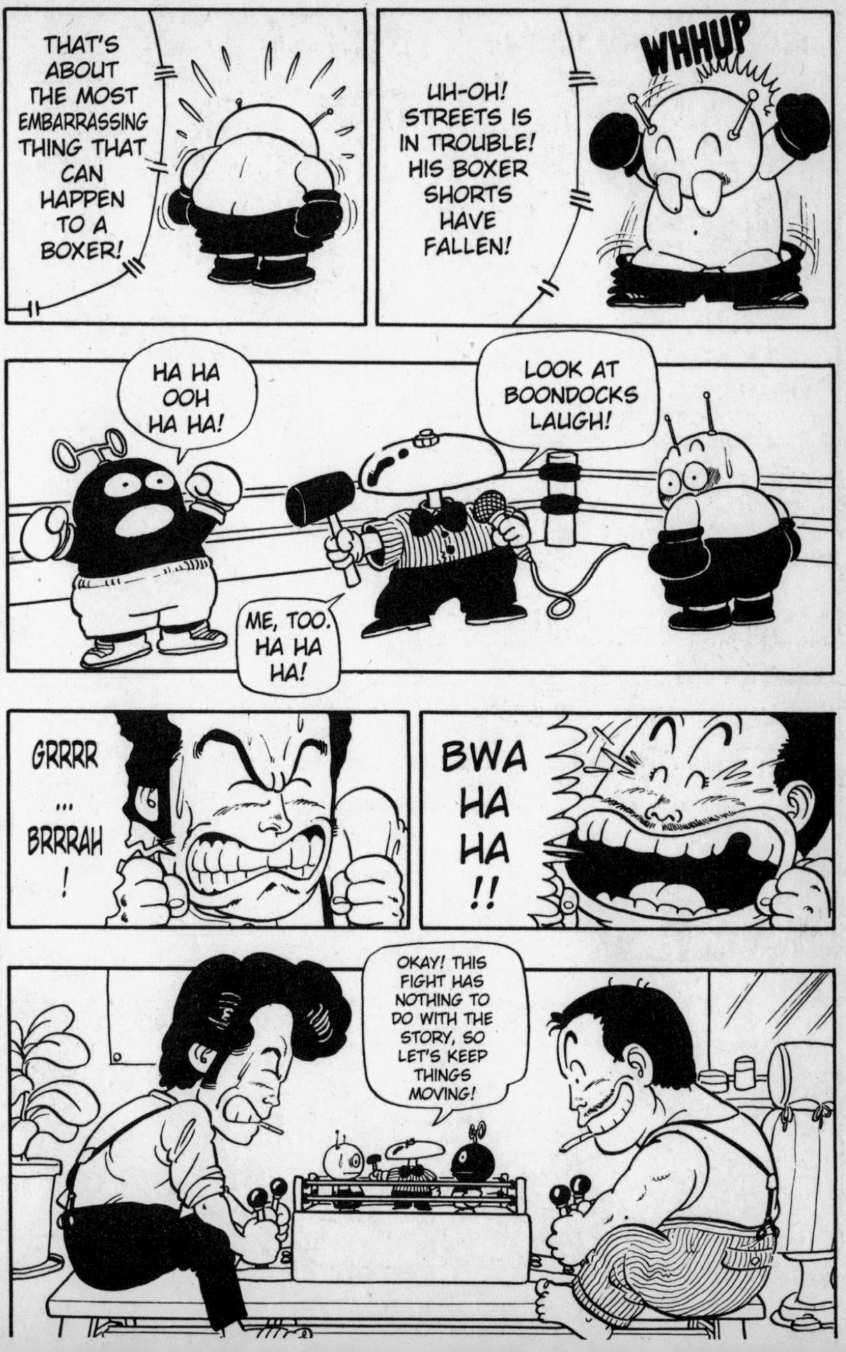
WHHUP
UH-OH! STREETS IS IN TROUBLE! HIS BOXER SHORTS HAVE FALLEN!
THAT'S ABOUT THE MOST EMBARRASSING THING THAT CAN HAPPEN TO A BOXER!
LOOK AT BOONDOCKS LAUGH!
HA HA OOH HA HA!
ME, TOO. HA HA HA!
BWA HA HA !!
GRRRR ... BRRRAH !
OKAY! THIS FIGHT HAS NOTHING TO DO WITH THE STORY, SO LET'S KEEP THINGS MOVING!

READ THIS WAY

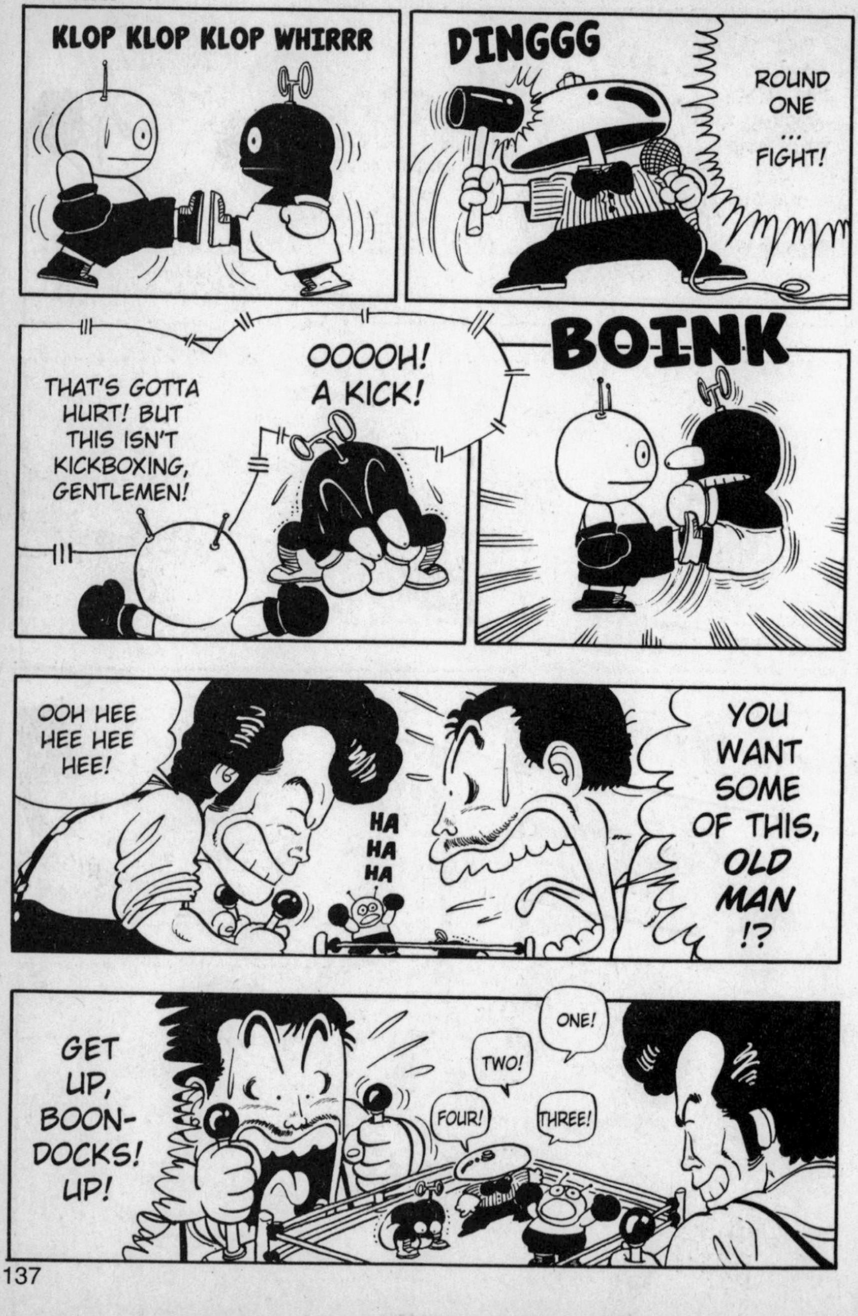
DINGGG
ROUND ONE ... FIGHT!
KLOP KLOP KLOP WHIRRR
BOINK
OOOOH! A KICK!
THAT'S GOTTA HURT! BUT THIS ISN'T KICKBOXING, GENTLEMEN!
YOU WANT SOME OF THIS, OLD MAN!?
HA HA HA
OOH HEE HEE HEE HEE!
ONE!
TWO!
THREE!
FOUR!
GET UP, BOON-DOCKS! UP!

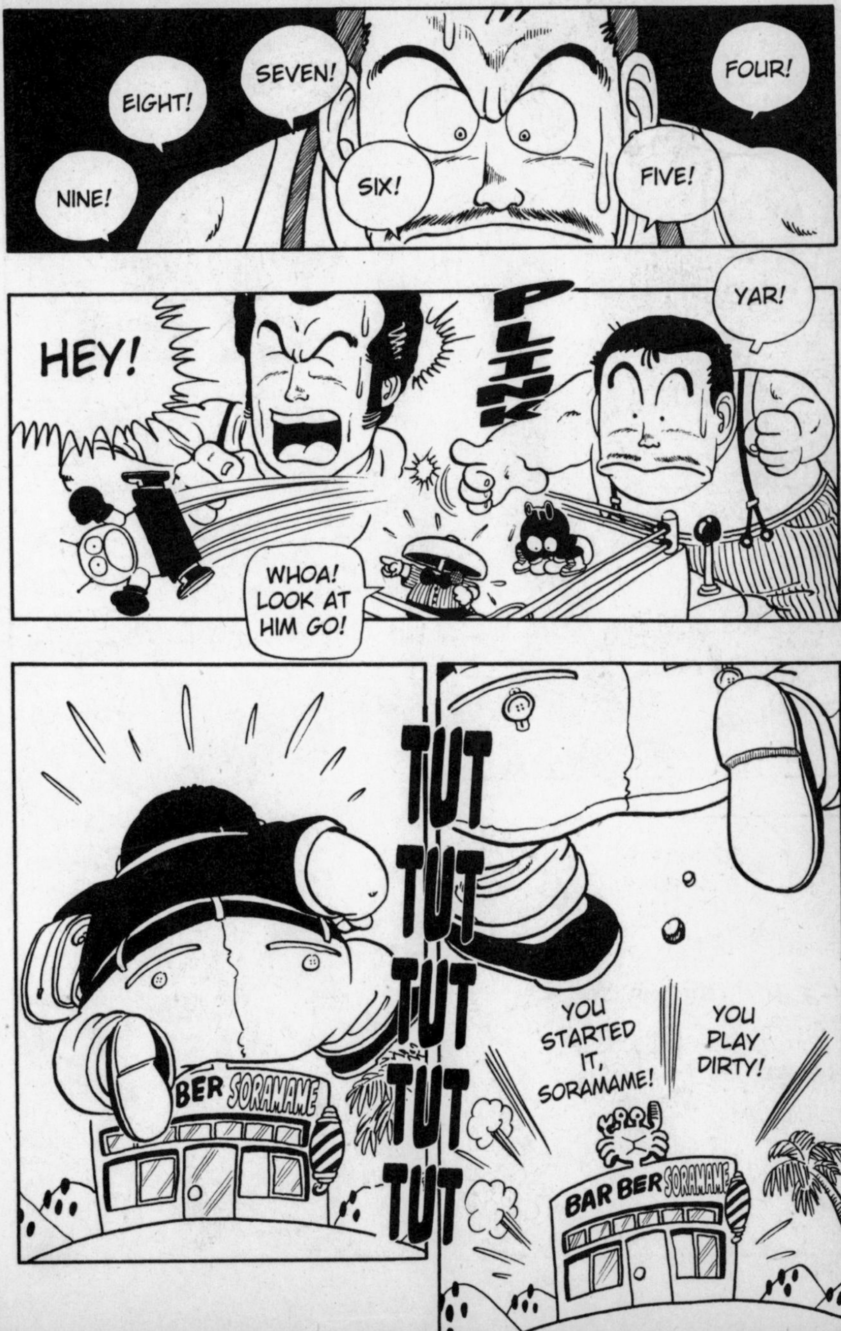
FOUR!
FIVE!
SIX!
SEVEN!
EIGHT!
NINE!
YAR!
PLINK
HEY!
WHOA! LOOK AT HIM GO!
YOU PLAY DIRTY!
YOU STARTED IT, SORAMAME!
BAR BER SORAMAME
TUT TUT TUT TUT TUT TUT
BER SORAMAME

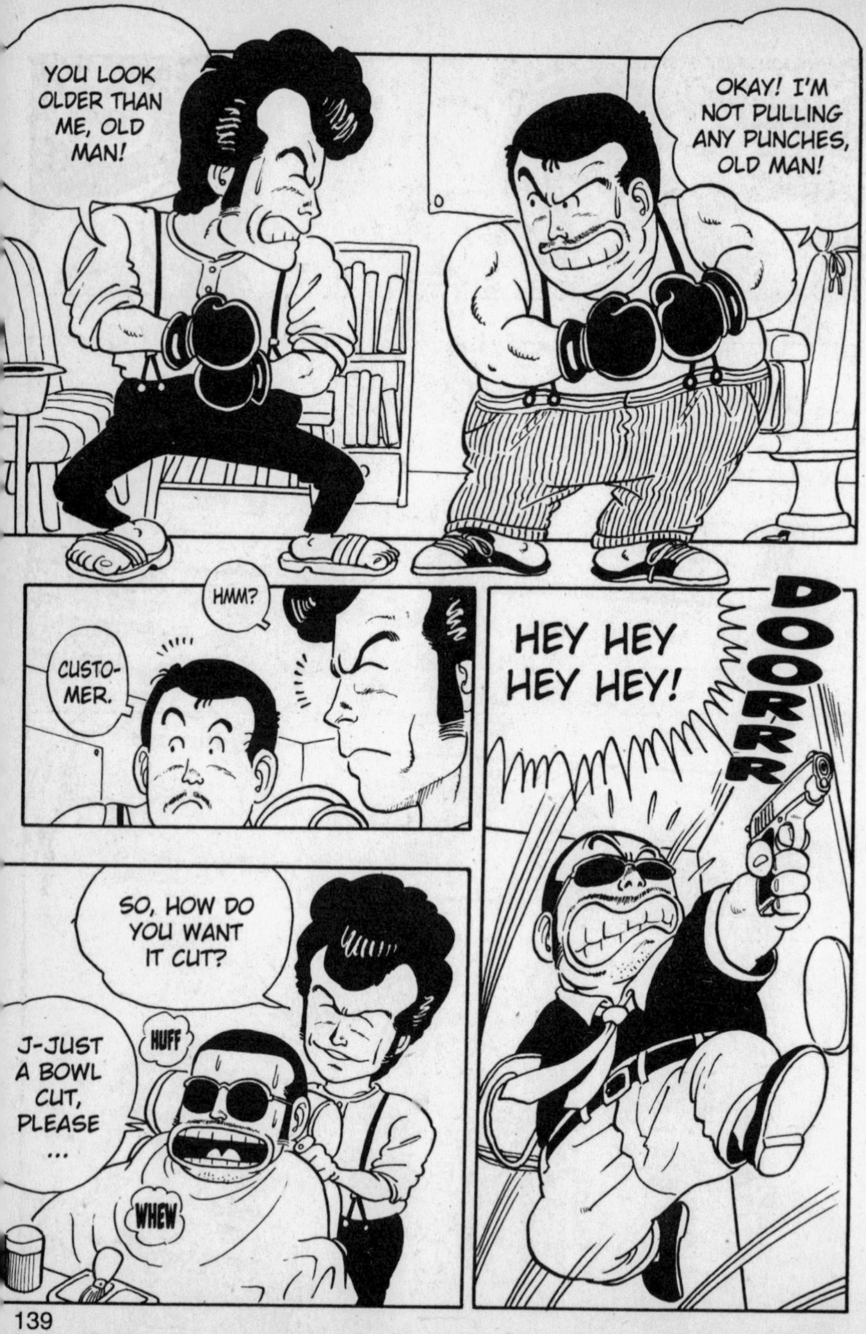
OKAY! I'M NOT PULLING ANY PUNCHES, OLD MAN!
YOU LOOK OLDER THAN ME, OLD MAN!
DOORRR
HEY HEY HEY HEY!
HMM?
CUSTOMER.
SO, HOW DO YOU WANT IT CUT?
HUFF
J-JUST A BOWL CUT, PLEASE ...
WHEW

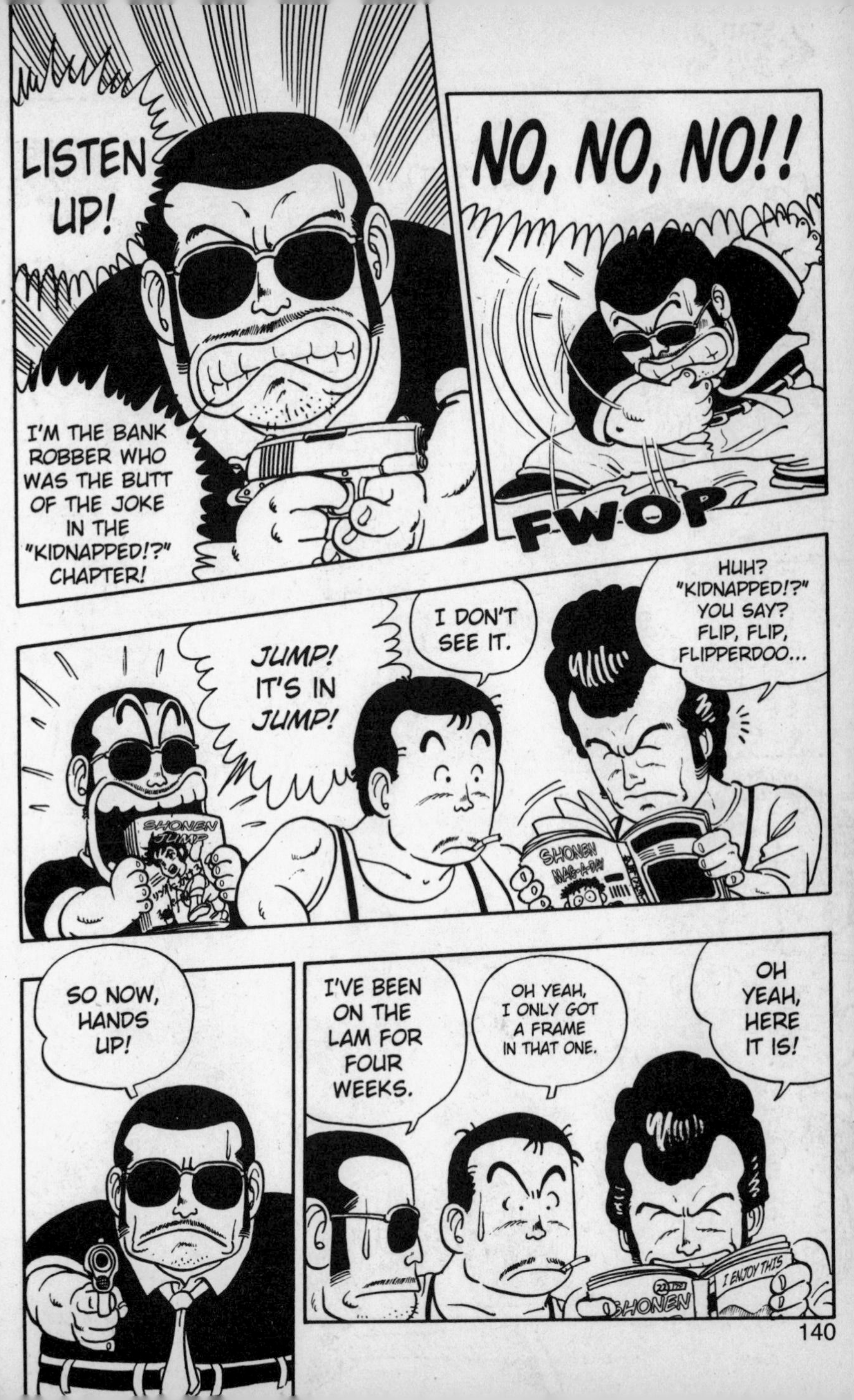
NO, NO, NO!!
FWOP
LISTEN UP!
I'M THE BANK ROBBER WHO WAS THE BUTT OF THE JOKE IN THE "KIDNAPPED!?" CHAPTER!
HUH? "KIDNAPPED!?" YOU SAY? FLIP, FLIP, FLIPPERDOO...
SHONEN MAG-A-DAY
I DON'T SEE IT.
JUMP! IT'S IN JUMP!
SHONEN JUMP
OH YEAH, HERE IT IS!
OH YEAH, I ONLY GOT A FRAME IN THAT ONE.
I ENJOY THIS
SHONEN
I'VE BEEN ON THE LAM FOR FOUR WEEKS.
SO NOW, HANDS UP!

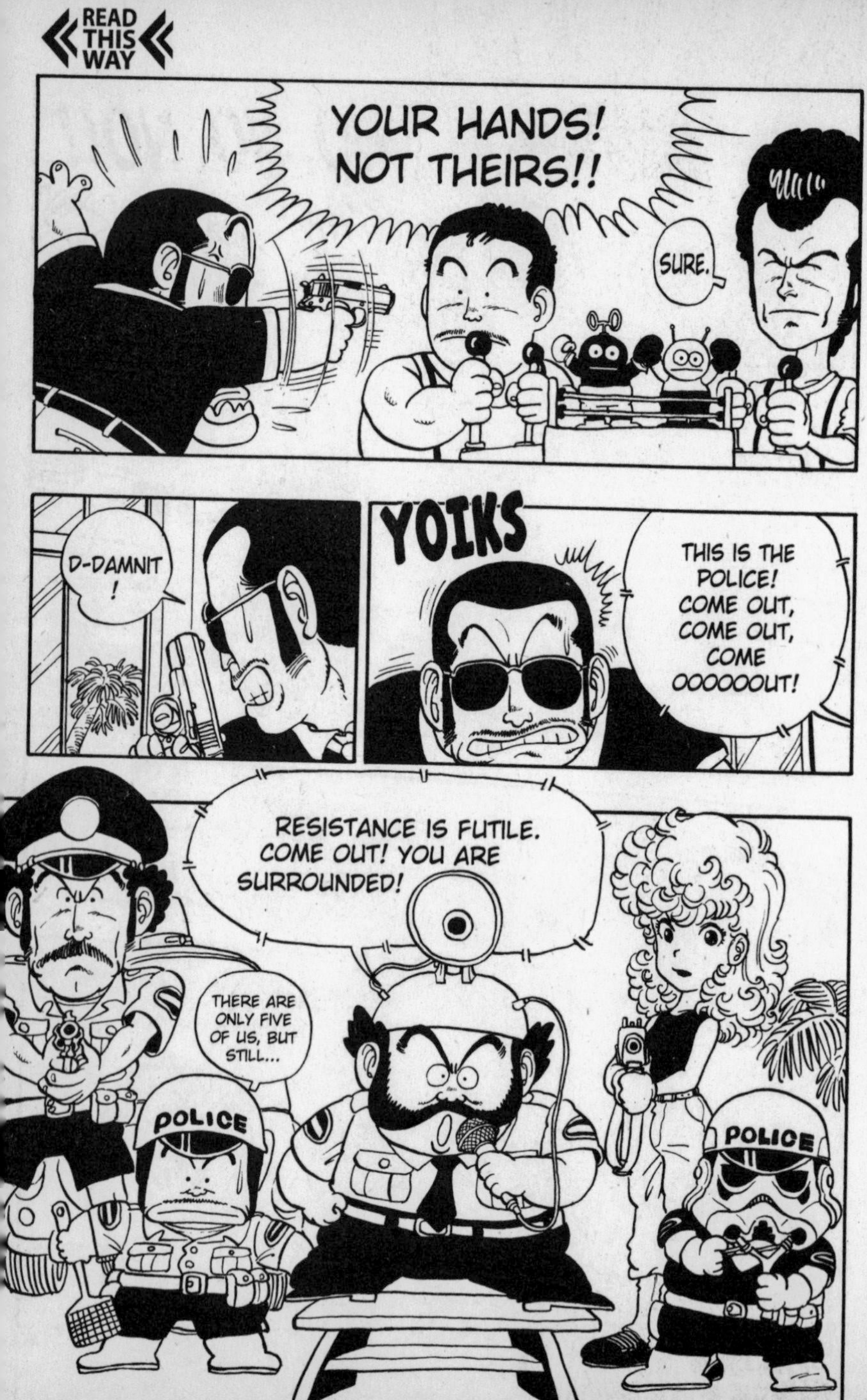
READ THIS WAY
YOUR HANDS! NOT THEIRS!!
SURE.
YOIKS
THIS IS THE POLICE! COME OUT, COME OUT, COME OOOOOOUT!
D-DAMNIT!
RESISTANCE IS FUTILE. COME OUT! YOU ARE SURROUNDED!
THERE ARE ONLY FIVE OF US, BUT STILL...
POLICE
POLICE

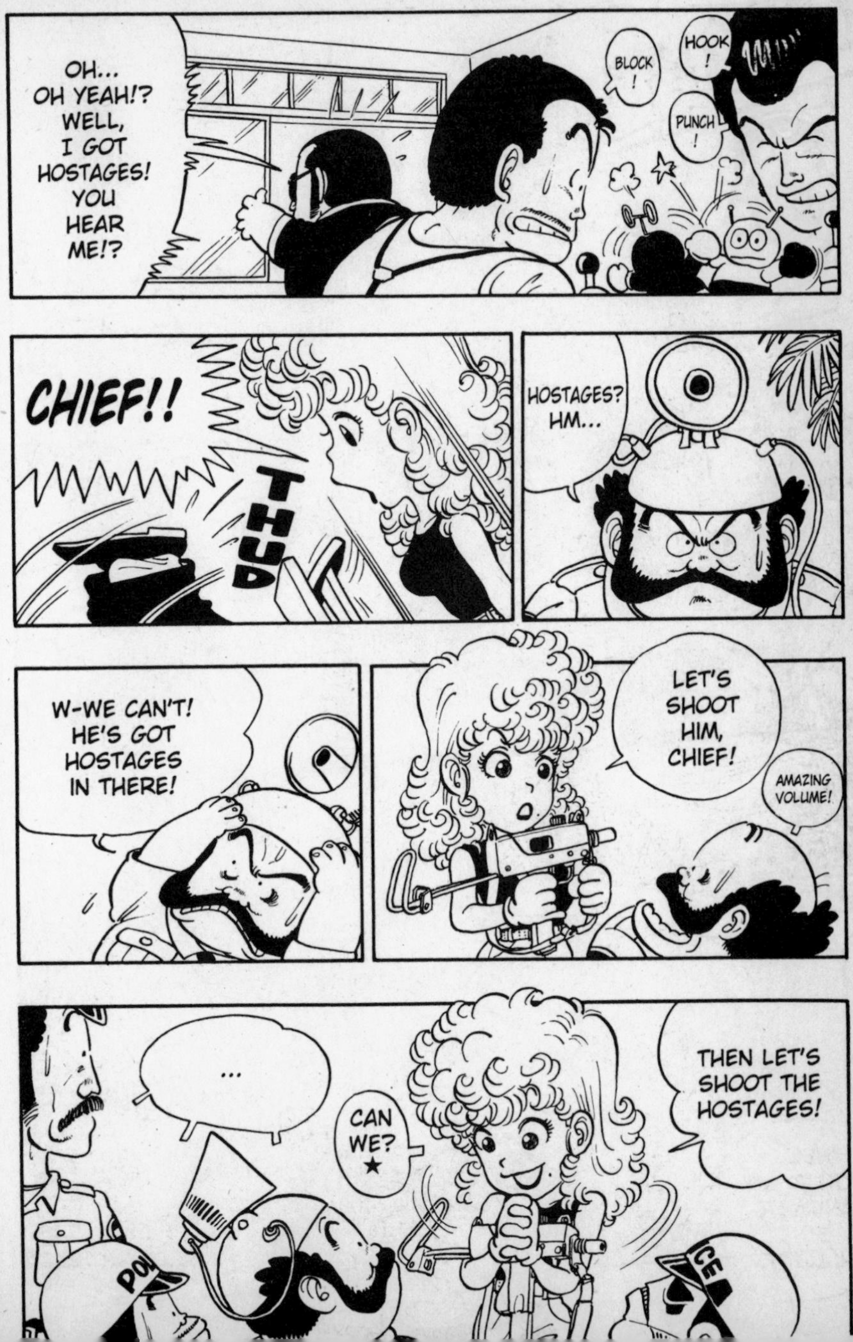
HOOK!
BLOCK!
PUNCH!
OH... OH YEAH!? WELL, I GOT HOSTAGES! YOU HEAR ME!?
HOSTAGES? HM...
CHIEF!!
THUD
LET'S SHOOT HIM, CHIEF!
AMAZING VOLUME!
W-WE CAN'T! HE'S GOT HOSTAGES IN THERE!
THEN LET'S SHOOT THE HOSTAGES!
CAN WE? ★
...

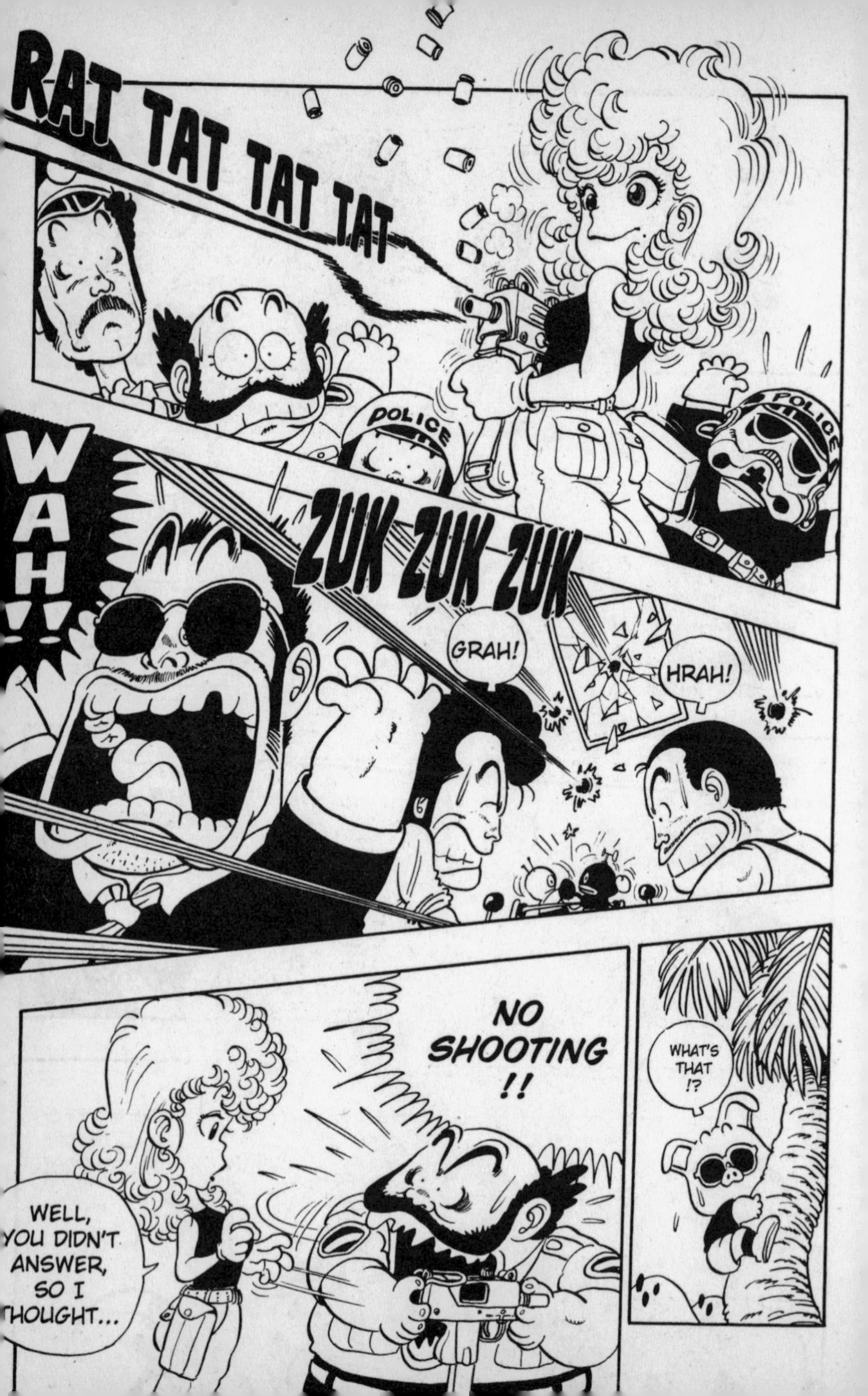
RAT TAT TAT TAT
ZUK ZUK ZUK
HRAH!
GRAH!
WAH!!
WHAT'S THAT !?
NO SHOOTING !!
WELL, YOU DIDN'T ANSWER, SO I THOUGHT...

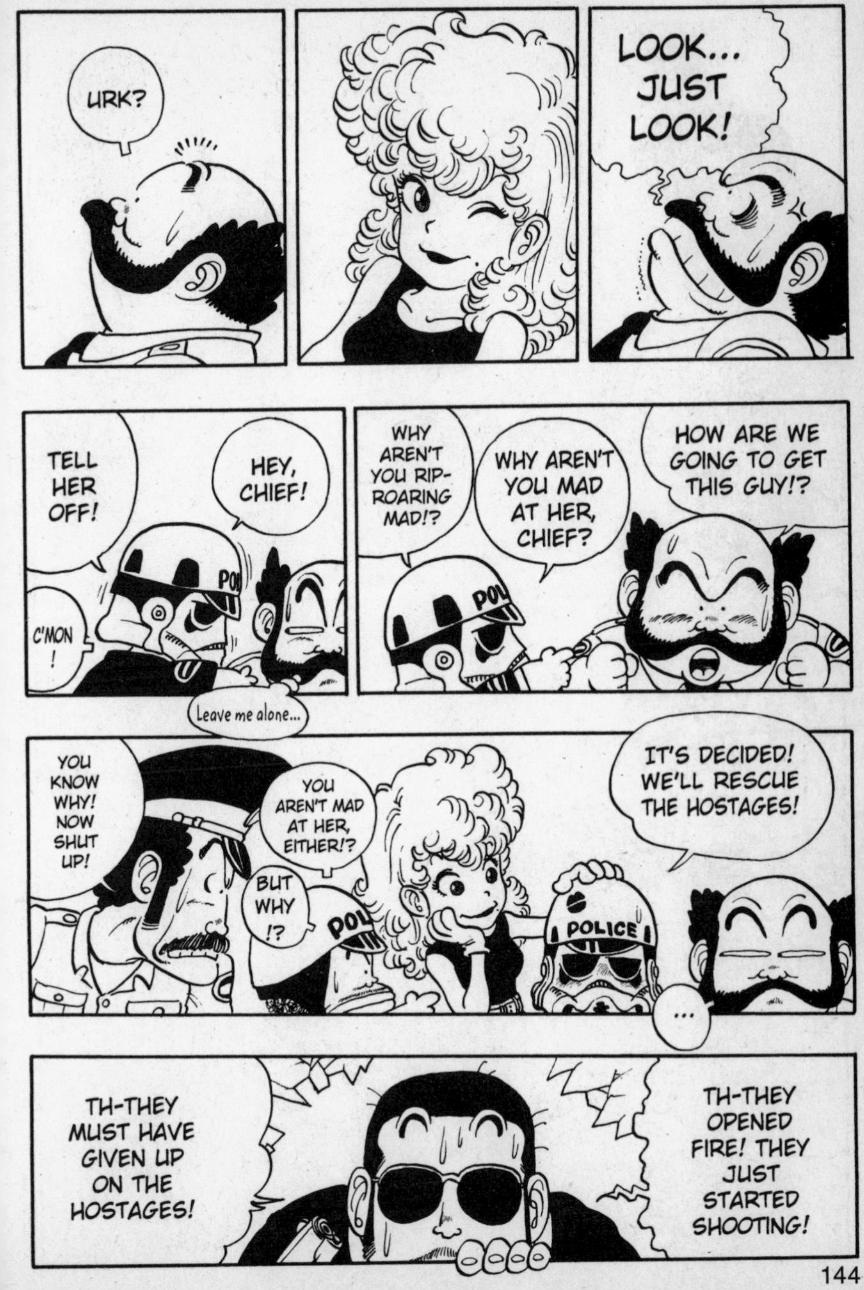

LOOK... JUST LOOK!
URK?
HOW ARE WE GOING TO GET THIS GUY!?
WHY AREN'T YOU MAD AT HER, CHIEF?
WHY AREN'T YOU RIP-ROARING MAD!?
HEY, CHIEF!
TELL HER OFF!
C'MON!
Leave me alone...
IT'S DECIDED! WE'LL RESCUE THE HOSTAGES!
...
YOU AREN'T MAD AT HER, EITHER!?
BUT WHY!?
YOU KNOW WHY! NOW SHUT UP!
TH-THEY OPENED FIRE! THEY JUST STARTED SHOOTING!
TH-THEY MUST HAVE GIVEN UP ON THE HOSTAGES!

READ THIS WAY

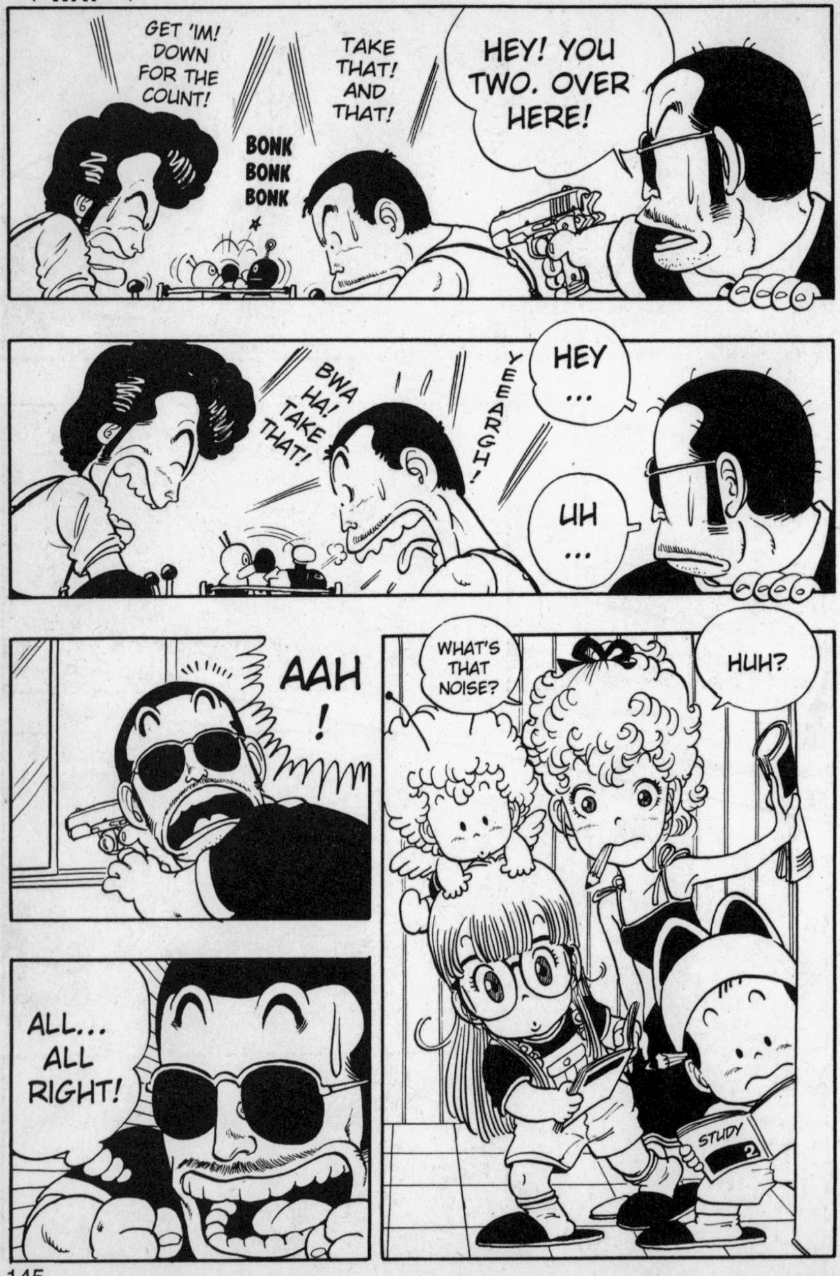

HEY! YOU TWO. OVER HERE!
TAKE THAT! AND THAT!
BONK BONK BONK
GET 'IM! DOWN FOR THE COUNT!
HEY ...
UH ...
YEEARGH!
BWA HA! TAKE THAT!
HUH?
WHAT'S THAT NOISE?
STUDY
AAH!
ALL... ALL RIGHT!

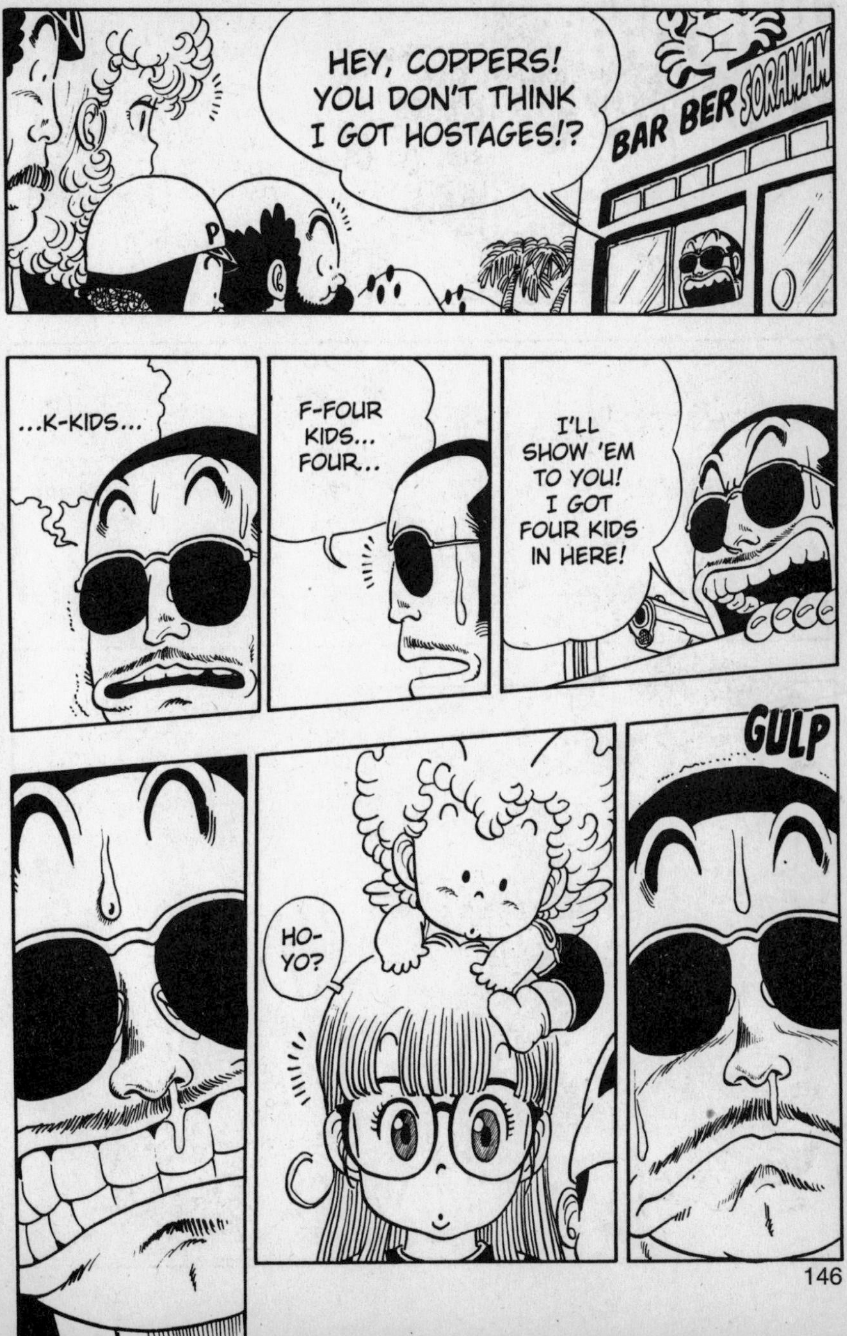
HEY, COPPERS! YOU DON'T THINK I GOT HOSTAGES!?
BAR BER SORAMAM
I'LL SHOW 'EM TO YOU! I GOT FOUR KIDS IN HERE!
F-FOUR KIDS... FOUR...
...K-KIDS...
GULP
HO-YO?

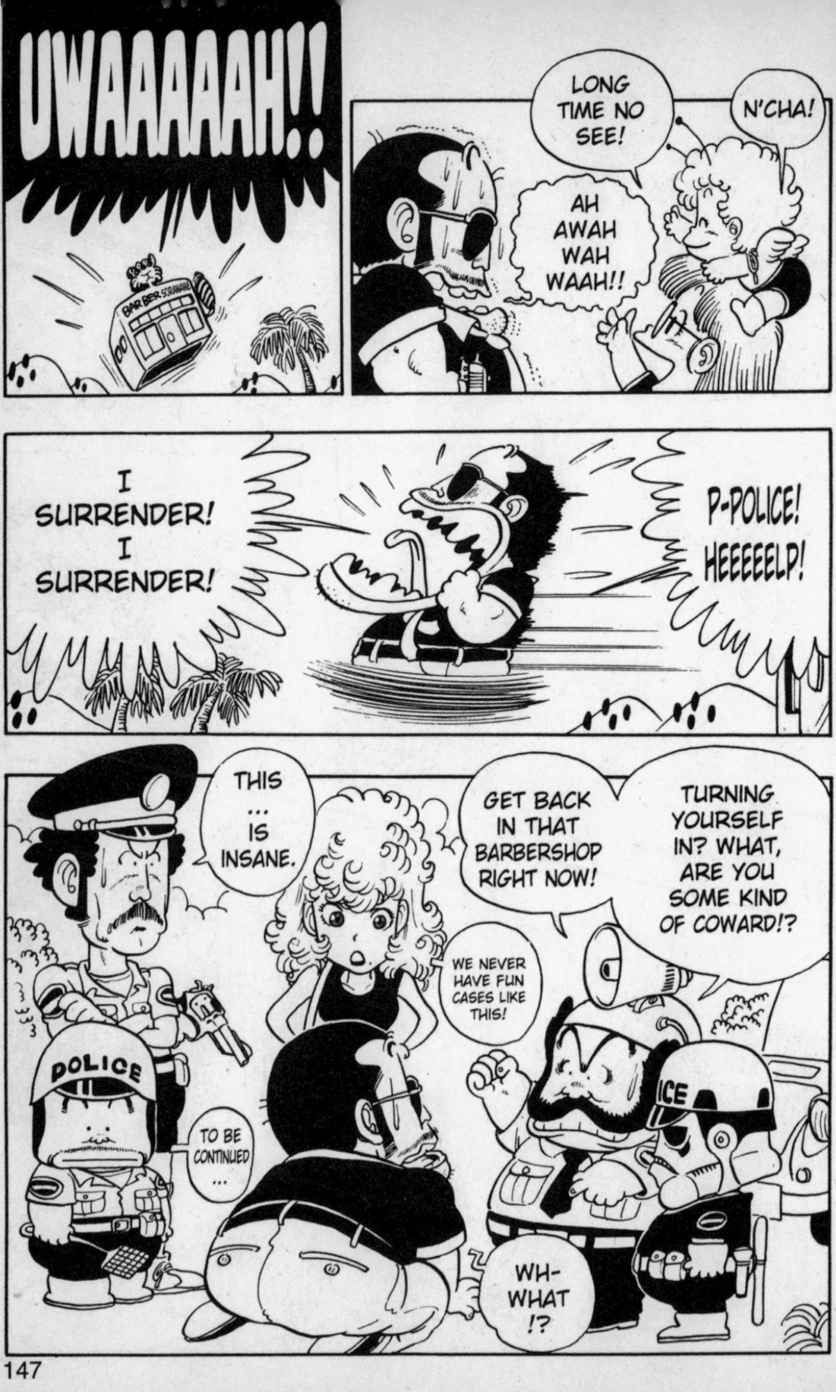
N'CHA!
LONG TIME NO SEE!
AH AWAH WAH WAAH!!
UWAAAAAH!!
P-POLICE! HEEEEELP!
I SURRENDER! I SURRENDER!
TURNING YOURSELF IN? WHAT, ARE YOU SOME KIND OF COWARD!?
GET BACK IN THAT BARBERSHOP RIGHT NOW!
THIS ... IS INSANE.
WE NEVER HAVE FUN CASES LIKE THIS!
ICE
POLICE
WH-WHAT!?
TO BE CONTINUED ...

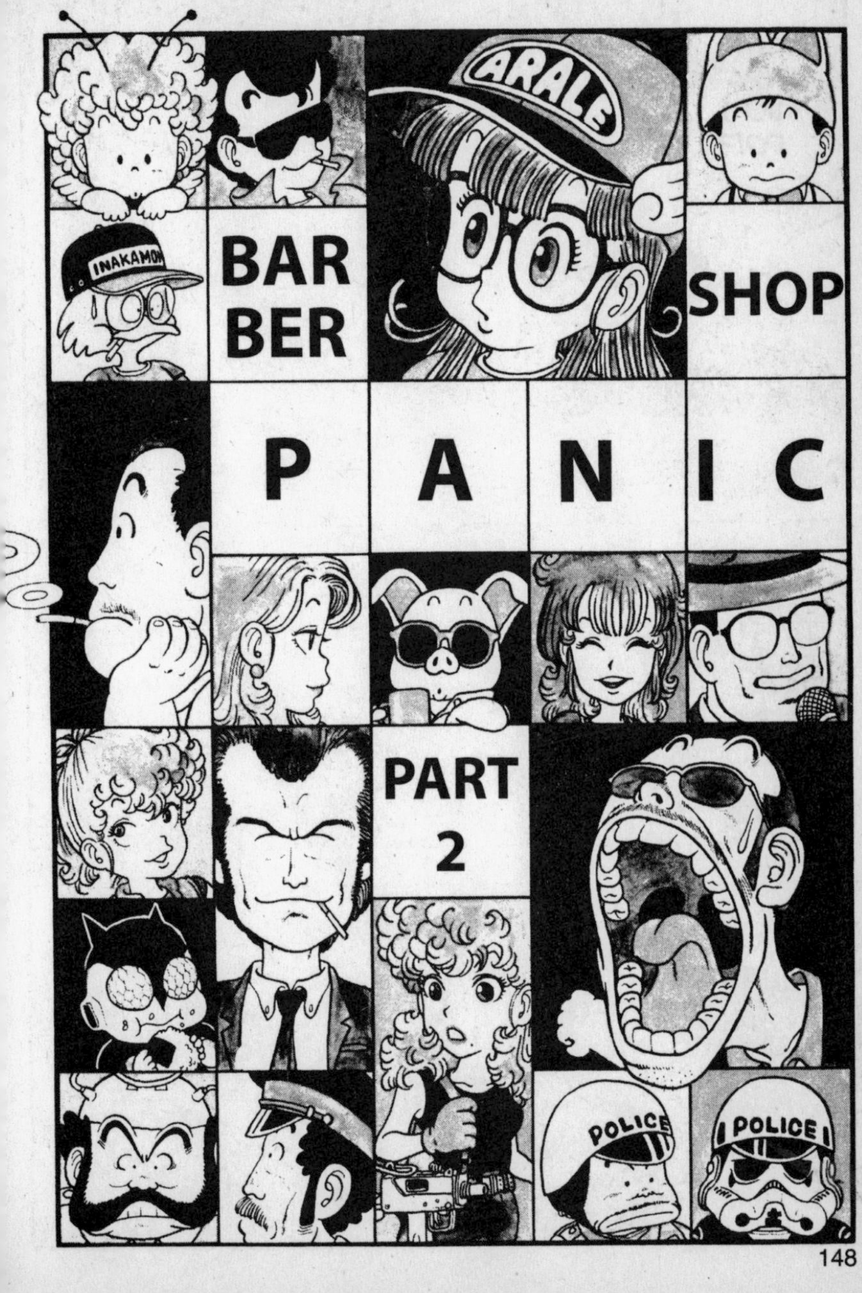
ARALE
BAR
BER
SHOP
INAKAMON
PANIC
PART
2
POLICE
POLICE

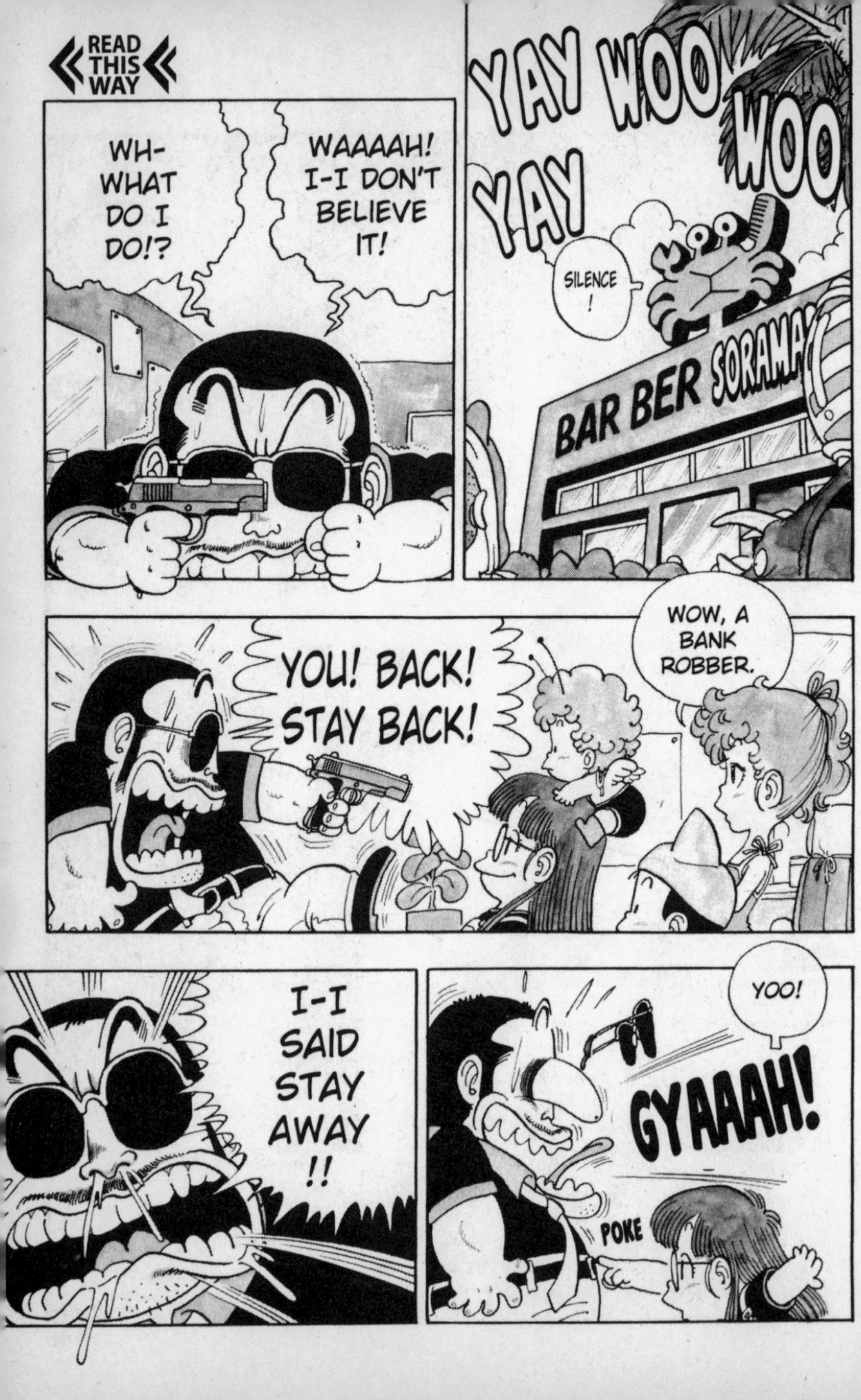
READ THIS WAY
YAY WOO
YAY WOO
SILENCE!
BAR BER SORAMA
WAAAAH! I-I DON'T BELIEVE IT!
WH-WHAT DO I DO!?
WOW, A BANK ROBBER.
YOU! BACK! STAY BACK!
YOO!
GYAAAH!
POKE
I-I SAID STAY AWAY!!

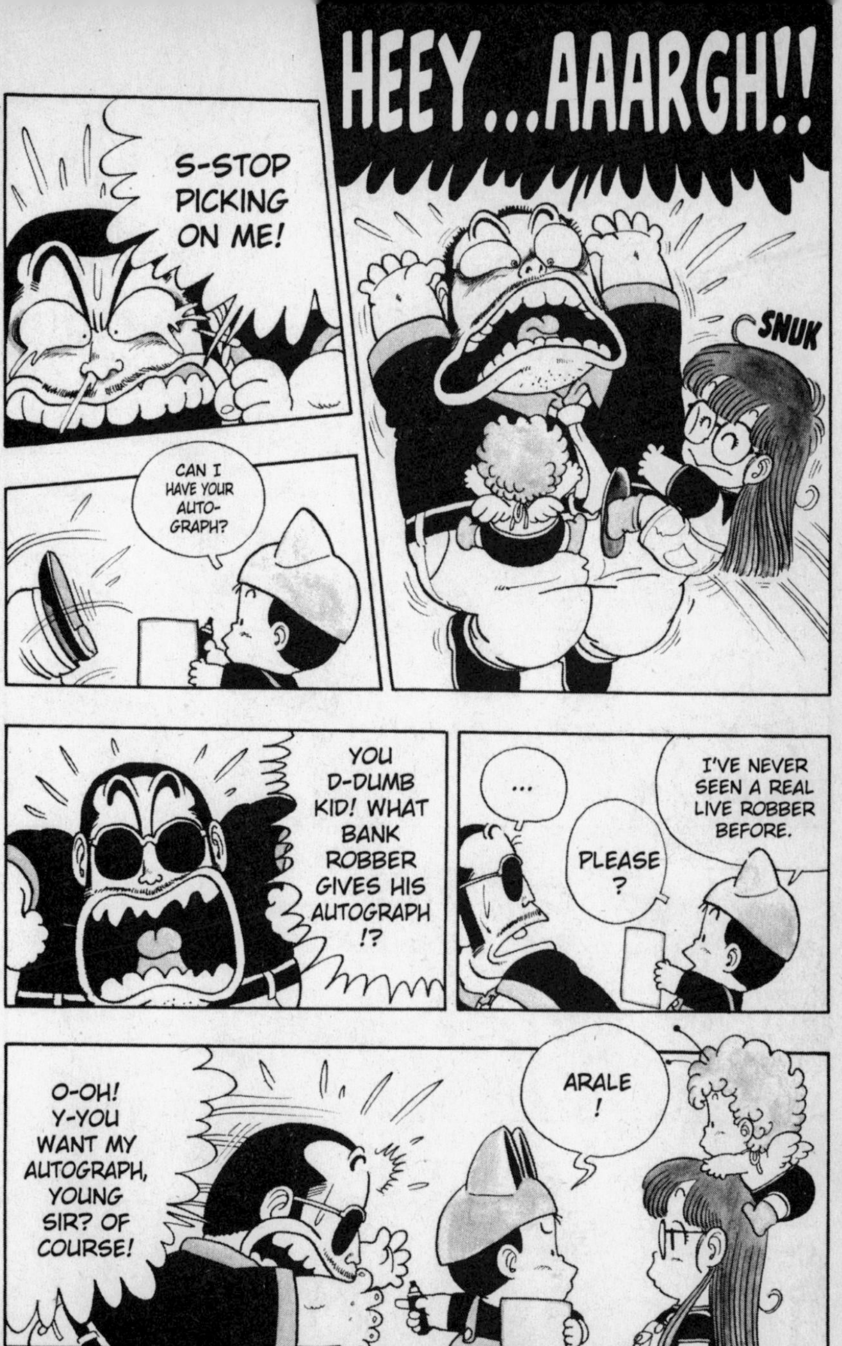
HEEY ...AAARGH!!
SNUK
S-STOP PICKING ON ME!
CAN I HAVE YOUR AUTO-GRAPH?
I'VE NEVER SEEN A REAL LIVE ROBBER BEFORE.
PLEASE?
...
YOU D-DUMB KID! WHAT BANK ROBBER GIVES HIS AUTOGRAPH!?
ARALE!
O-OH! Y-YOU WANT MY AUTOGRAPH, YOUNG SIR? OF COURSE!

READ THIS WAY

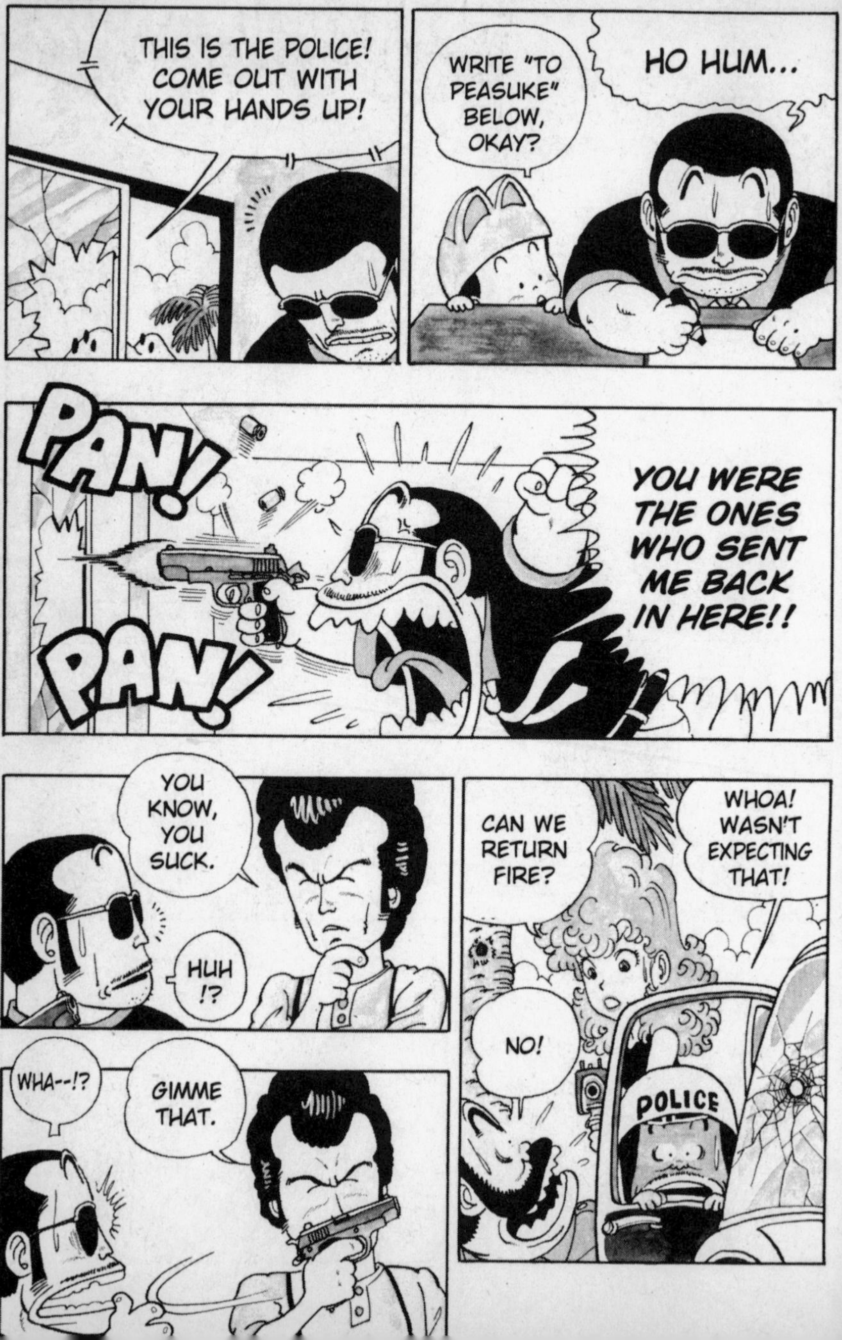
HO HUM...
WRITE "TO PEASUKE" BELOW, OKAY?
THIS IS THE POLICE! COME OUT WITH YOUR HANDS UP!
YOU WERE THE ONES WHO SENT ME BACK IN HERE!!
PAN!
PAN!
WHOA! WASN'T EXPECTING THAT!
CAN WE RETURN FIRE?
NO!
POLICE
YOU KNOW, YOU SUCK.
HUH!?
GIMME THAT.
WHA--!?

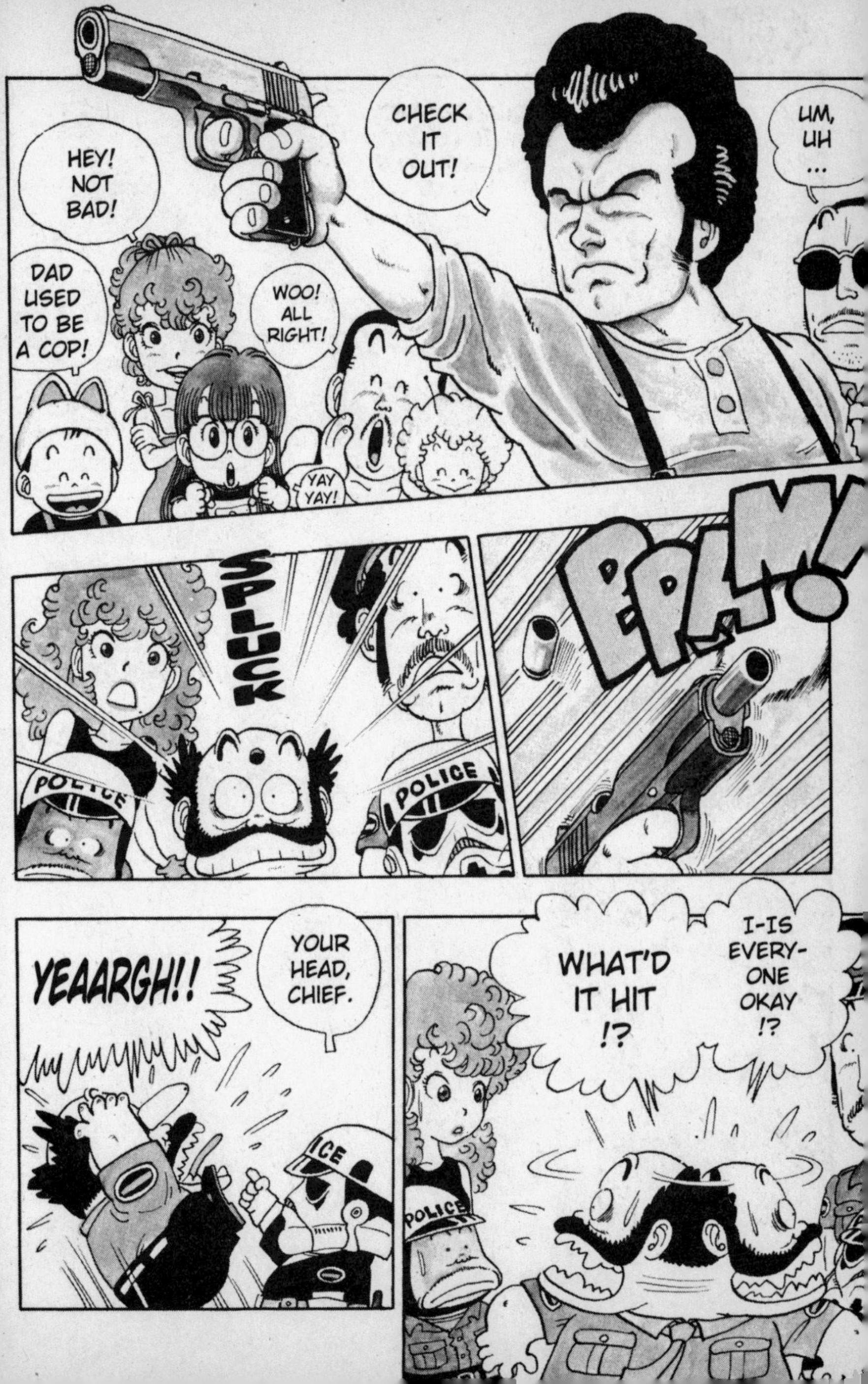
UM, UH ...
CHECK IT OUT!
HEY! NOT BAD!
WOO! ALL RIGHT!
DAD USED TO BE A COP!
YAY YAY!
BPLAM!
SPLUCK
POLICE
POLICE
I-IS EVERY-ONE OKAY !?
WHAT'D IT HIT !?
POLICE
YOUR HEAD, CHIEF.
YEAARGH!!
ICE

READ THIS WAY

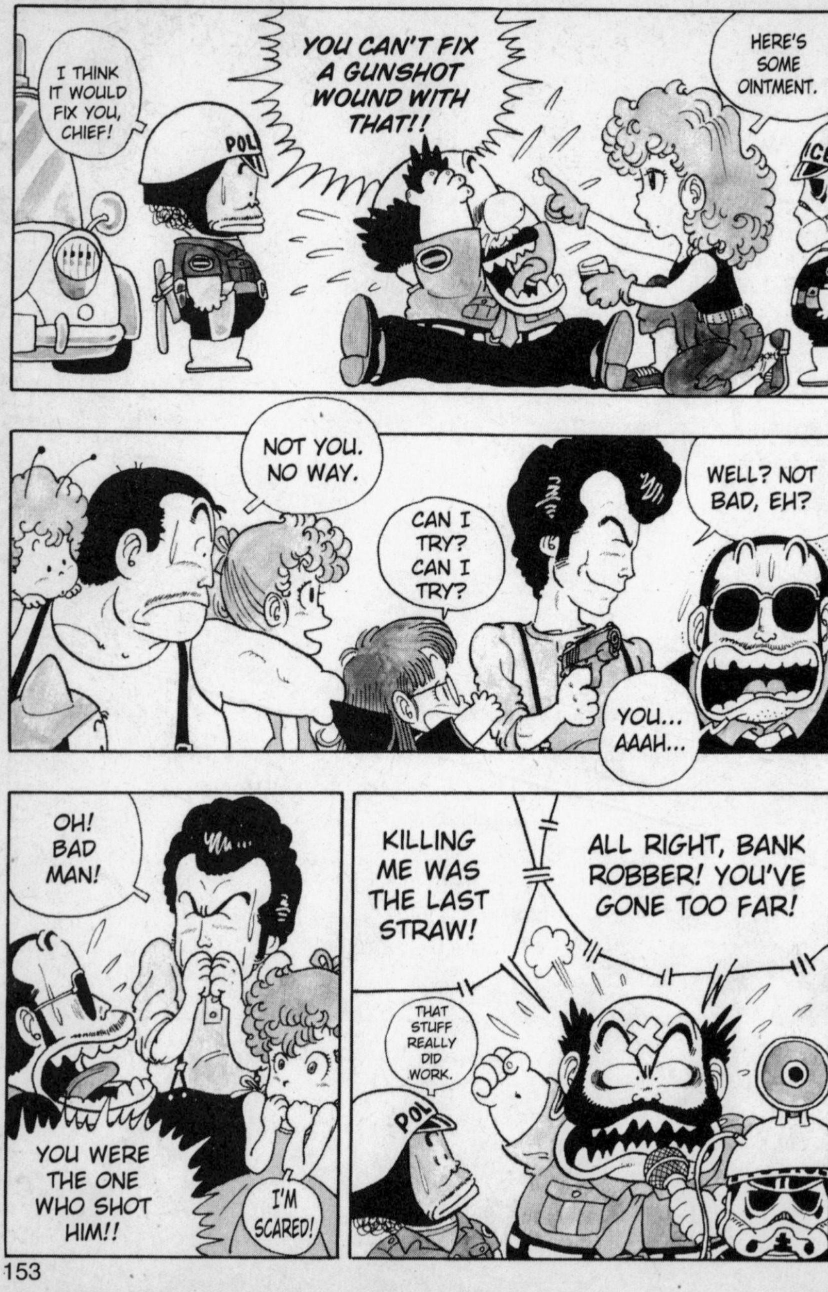

HERE'S SOME OINTMENT.
YOU CAN'T FIX A GUNSHOT WOUND WITH THAT!!
I THINK IT WOULD FIX YOU, CHIEF!
POL
ICE
WELL? NOT BAD, EH?
YOU... AAAH...
CAN I TRY? CAN I TRY?
NOT YOU. NO WAY.
ALL RIGHT, BANK ROBBER! YOU'VE GONE TOO FAR!
KILLING ME WAS THE LAST STRAW!
THAT STUFF REALLY DID WORK.
POL
OH! BAD MAN!
YOU WERE THE ONE WHO SHOT HIM!!
I'M SCARED!

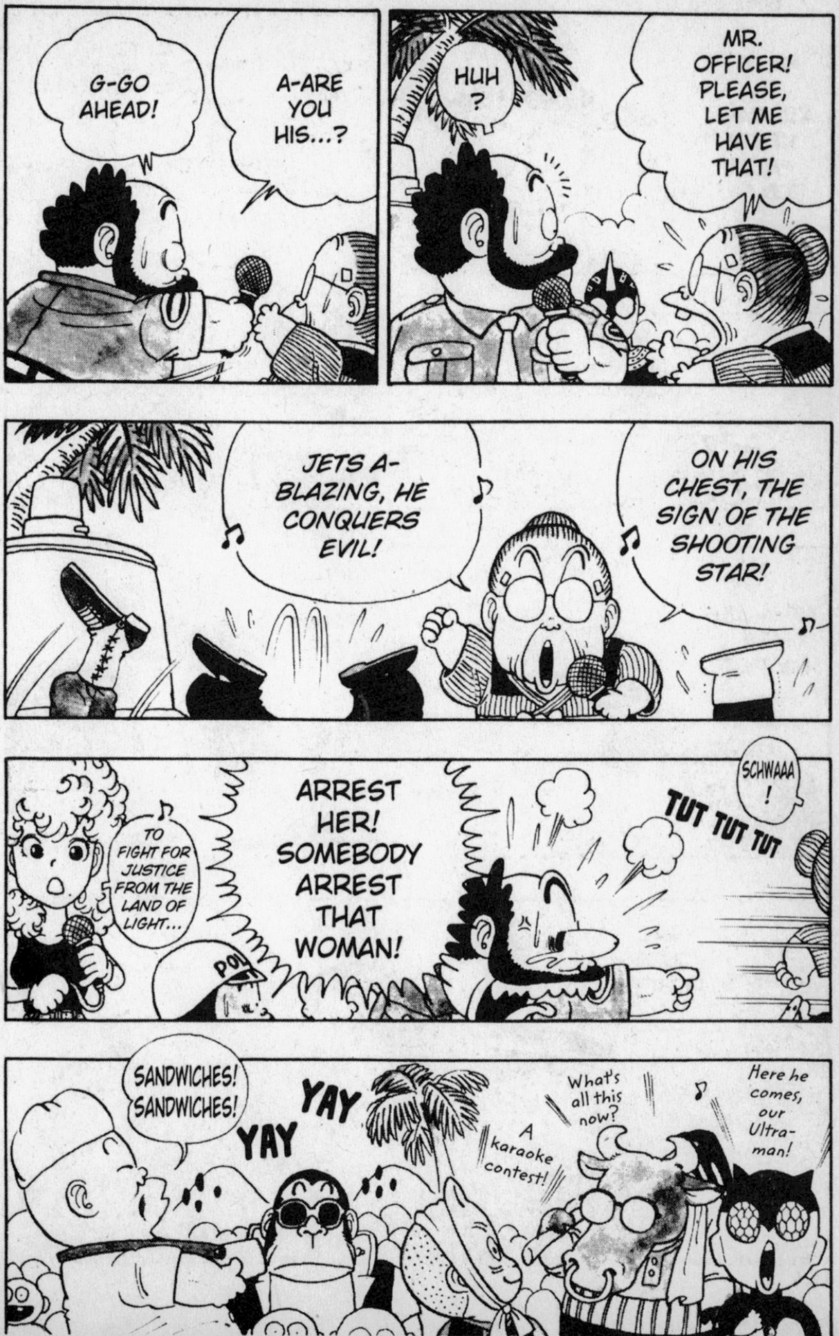
MR. OFFICER! PLEASE, LET ME HAVE THAT!
HUH?
A-ARE YOU HIS...?
G-GO AHEAD!
ON HIS CHEST, THE SIGN OF THE SHOOTING STAR!
JETS A-BLAZING, HE CONQUERS EVIL!
SCHWAAA!
TUT TUT TUT
ARREST HER! SOMEBODY ARREST THAT WOMAN!
TO FIGHT FOR JUSTICE FROM THE LAND OF LIGHT...
Here he comes, our Ultra-man!
What's all this now?
A karaoke contest!
YAY
YAY
SANDWICHES! SANDWICHES!

READ THIS WAY

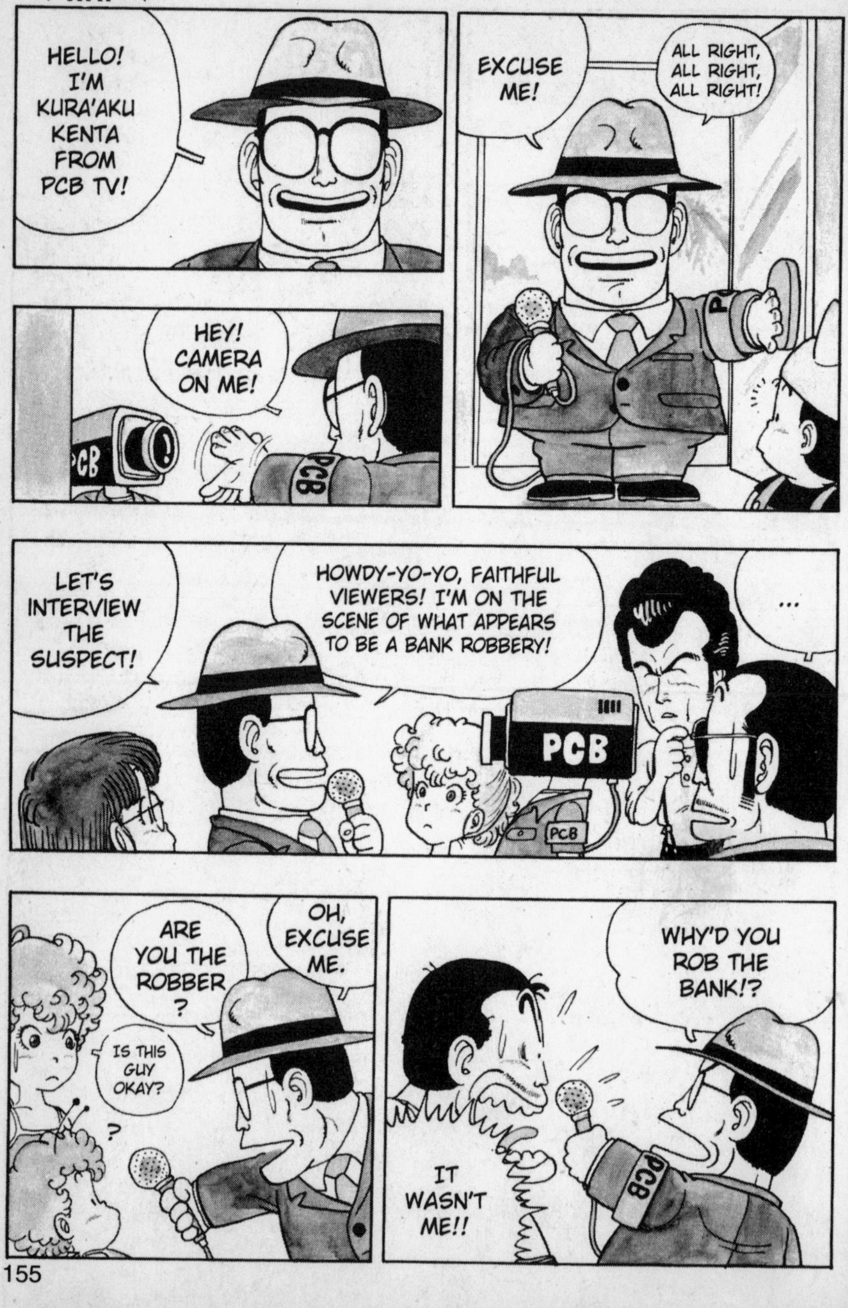

ALL RIGHT, ALL RIGHT, ALL RIGHT!
EXCUSE ME!
HELLO! I'M KURA'AKU KENTA FROM PCB TV!
HEY! CAMERA ON ME!
PCB
PCB
...
HOWDY-YO-YO, FAITHFUL VIEWERS! I'M ON THE SCENE OF WHAT APPEARS TO BE A BANK ROBBERY!
LET'S INTERVIEW THE SUSPECT!
PCB
PCB
WHY'D YOU ROB THE BANK!?
IT WASN'T ME!!
PCB
OH, EXCUSE ME.
ARE YOU THE ROBBER ?
IS THIS GUY OKAY?
?

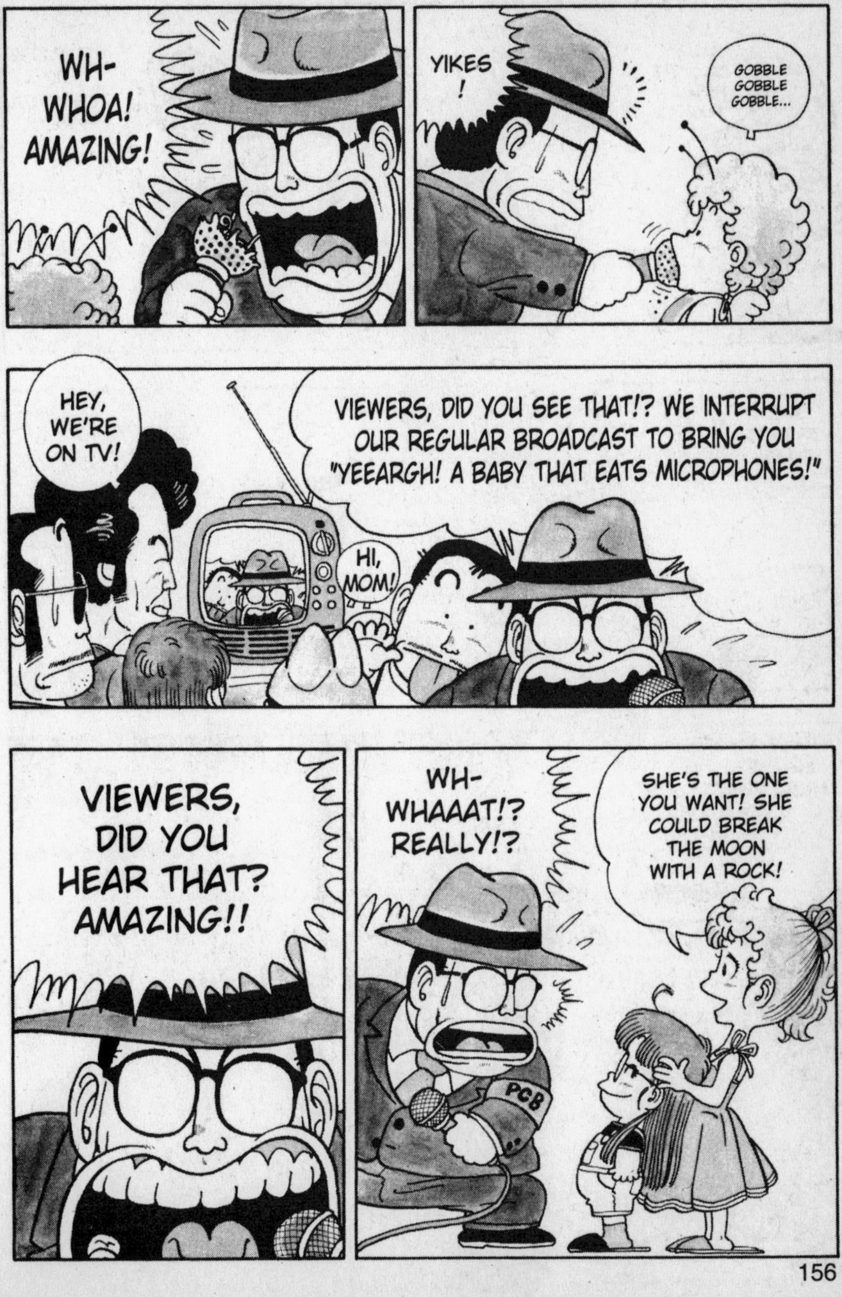
YIKES!
GOBBLE GOBBLE GOBBLE...
WH- WHOA! AMAZING!
VIEWERS, DID YOU SEE THAT!? WE INTERRUPT OUR REGULAR BROADCAST TO BRING YOU "YEEARGH! A BABY THAT EATS MICROPHONES!"
HEY, WE'RE ON TV!
HI, MOM!
PCB
SHE'S THE ONE YOU WANT! SHE COULD BREAK THE MOON WITH A ROCK!
WH- WHAAAT!? REALLY!?
VIEWERS, DID YOU HEAR THAT? AMAZING!!

READ THIS WAY

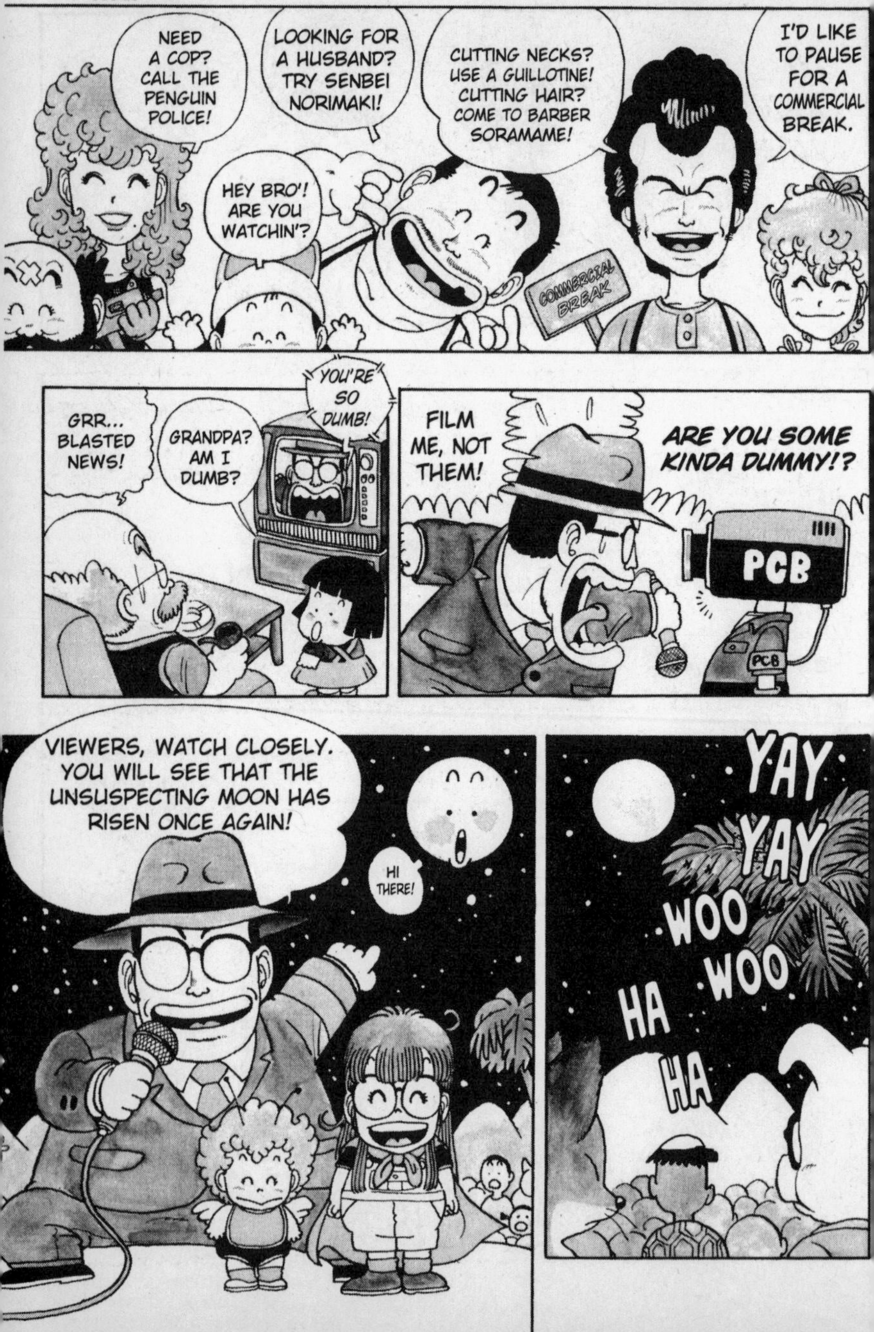

I'D LIKE TO PAUSE FOR A COMMERCIAL BREAK.
COMMERCIAL BREAK
CUTTING NECKS? USE A GUILLOTINE! CUTTING HAIR? COME TO BARBER SORAMAME!
LOOKING FOR A HUSBAND? TRY SENBEI NORIMAKI!
HEY BRO'! ARE YOU WATCHIN'?
NEED A COP? CALL THE PENGUIN POLICE!
ARE YOU SOME KINDA DUMMY!?
FILM ME, NOT THEM!
PCB
PCB
YOU'RE SO DUMB!
GRANDPA? AM I DUMB?
GRR... BLASTED NEWS!
YAY YAY
WOO WOO
HA HA
VIEWERS, WATCH CLOSELY. YOU WILL SEE THAT THE UNSUSPECTING MOON HAS RISEN ONCE AGAIN!
HI THERE!

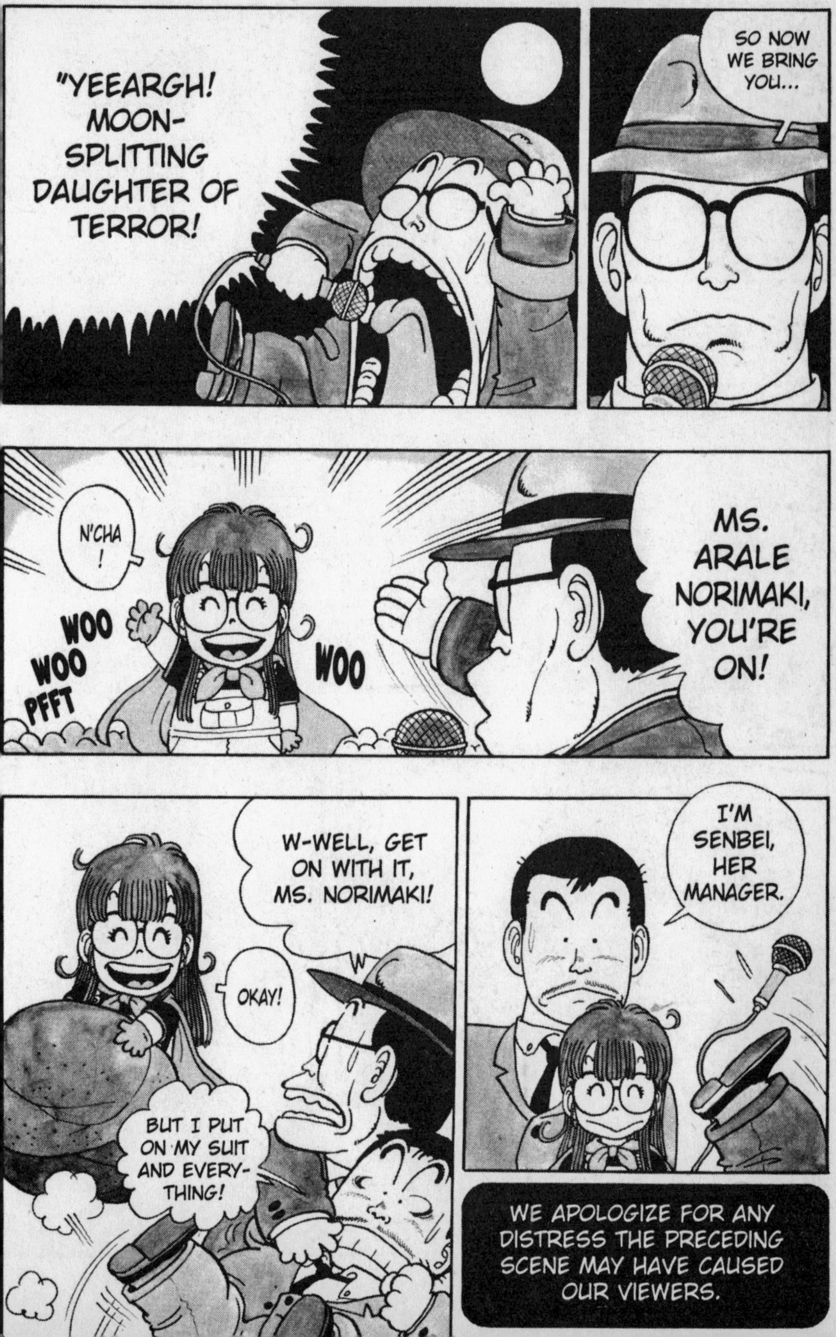
SO NOW WE BRING YOU...
"YEEARGH! MOON-SPLITTING DAUGHTER OF TERROR!
MS. ARALE NORIMAKI, YOU'RE ON!
WOO
N'CHA!
WOO
WOO
PFFT
I'M SENBEI, HER MANAGER.
WE APOLOGIZE FOR ANY DISTRESS THE PRECEDING SCENE MAY HAVE CAUSED OUR VIEWERS.
W-WELL, GET ON WITH IT, MS. NORIMAKI!
OKAY!
BUT I PUT ON MY SUIT AND EVERY-THING!

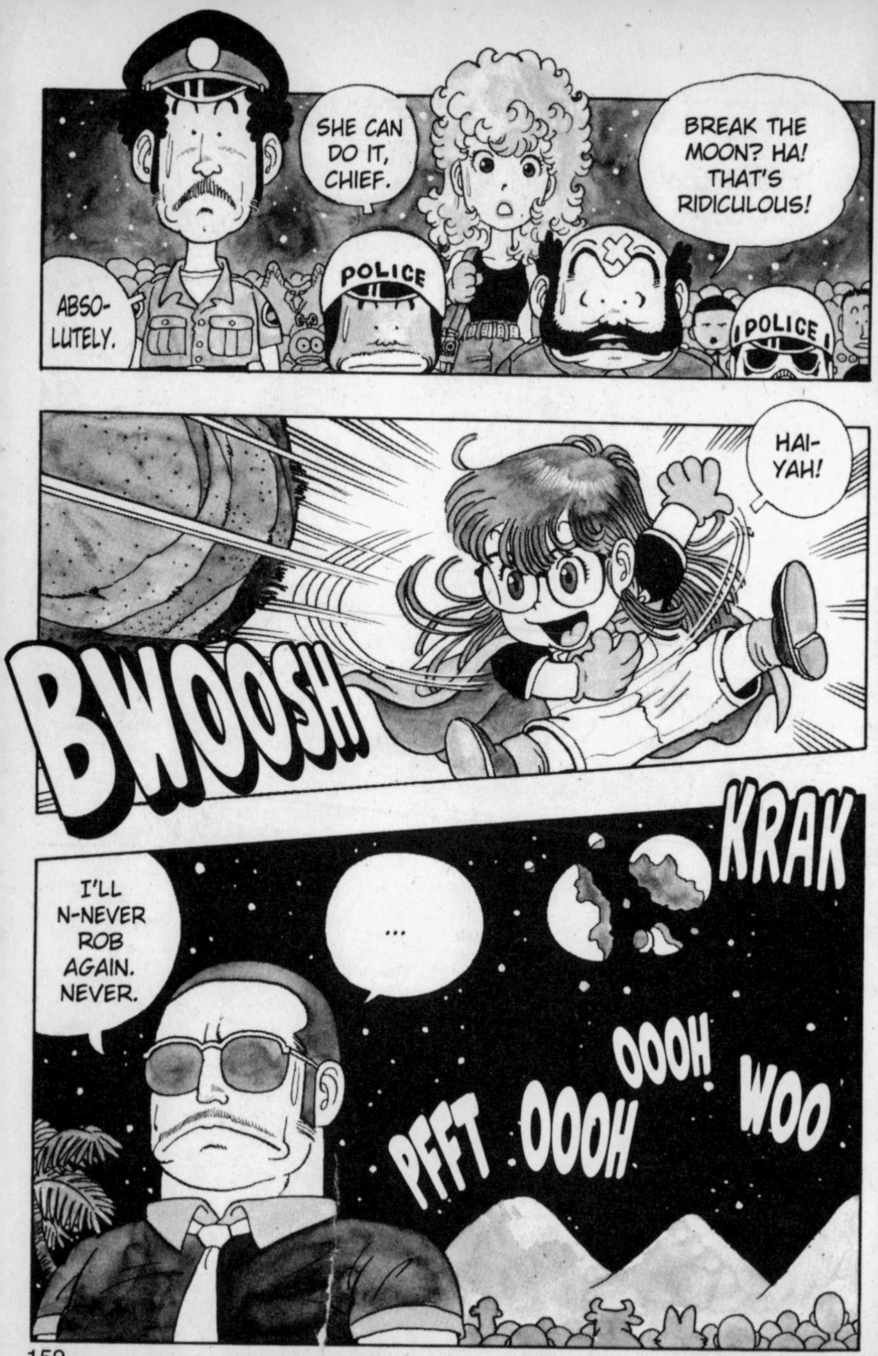
BREAK THE MOON? HA! THAT'S RIDICULOUS!
SHE CAN DO IT, CHIEF.
ABSO-LUTELY.
HAI-YAH!
BWOOSH
KRAK
...
WOO
OOOH
OOOH
PFFT
I'LL N-NEVER ROB AGAIN. NEVER.

The Great Strawberry Panties Caper Part 1

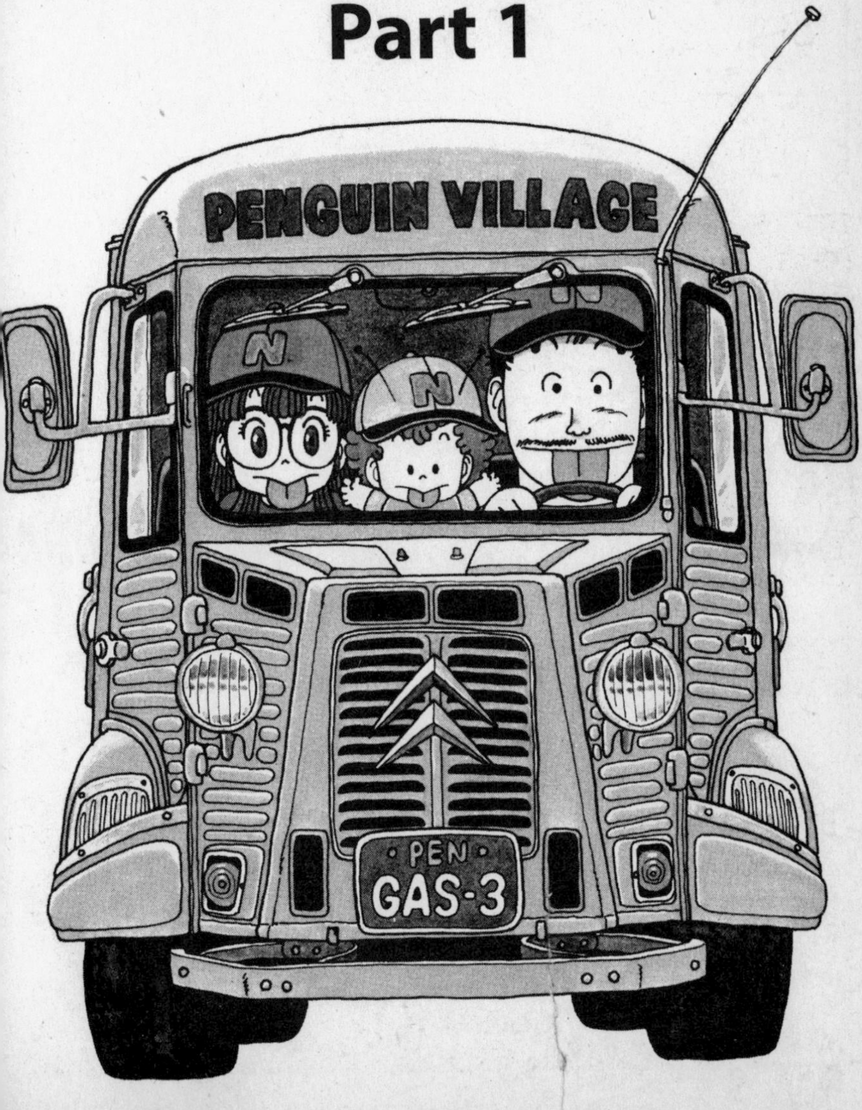
PENGUIN VILLAGE
PEN
GAS-3

READ THIS WAY

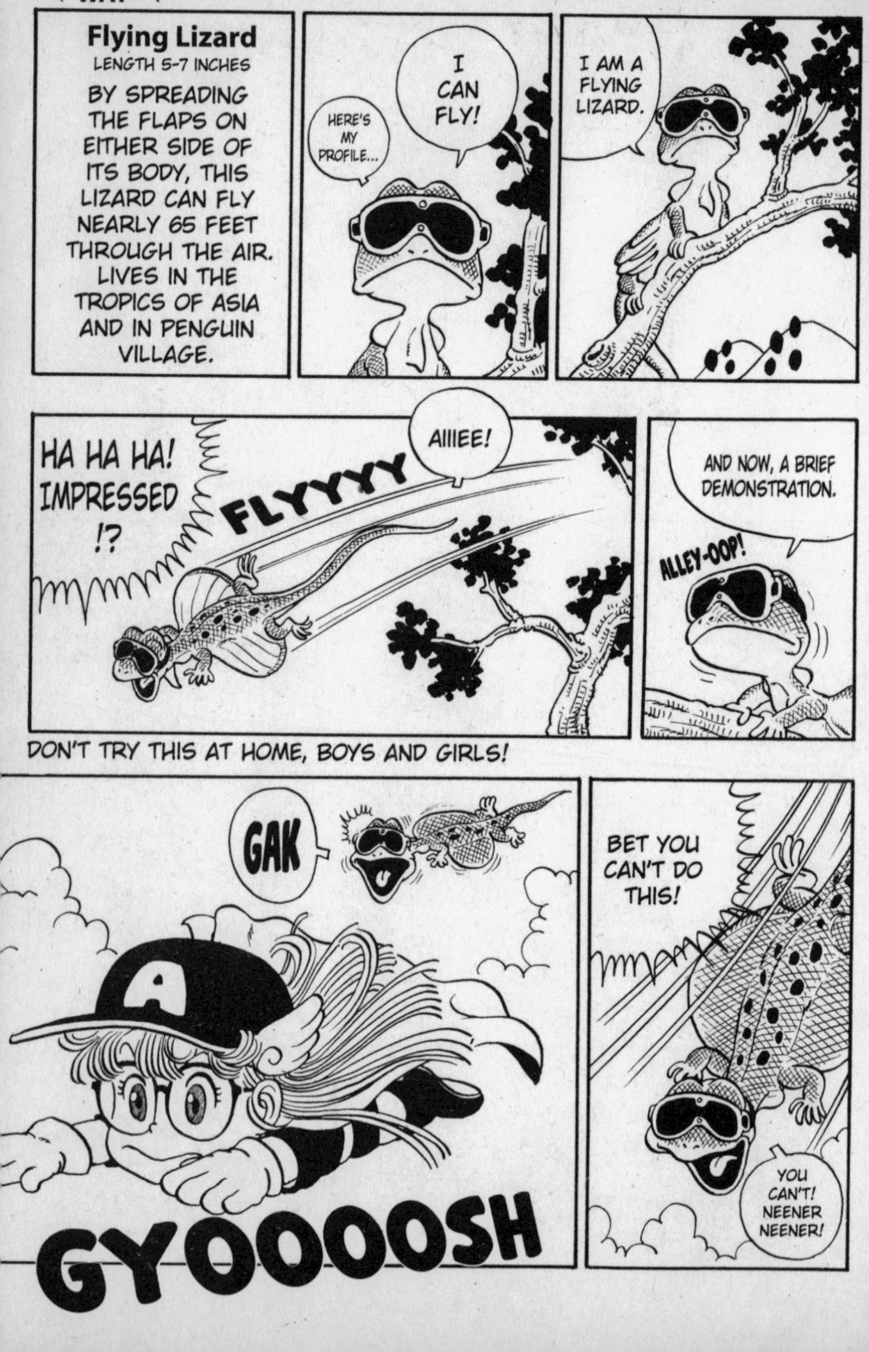
I AM A FLYING LIZARD.
I CAN FLY!
HERE'S MY PROFILE...
Flying Lizard
LENGTH 5-7 INCHES
BY SPREADING THE FLAPS ON EITHER SIDE OF ITS BODY, THIS LIZARD CAN FLY NEARLY 65 FEET THROUGH THE AIR. LIVES IN THE TROPICS OF ASIA AND IN PENGUIN VILLAGE.
AND NOW, A BRIEF DEMONSTRATION.
ALLEY-OOP!
AIIIEE!
FLYYYY
HA HA HA! IMPRESSED !?
DON'T TRY THIS AT HOME, BOYS AND GIRLS!
BET YOU CAN'T DO THIS!
YOU CAN'T! NEENER NEENER!
GAK
A
GYOOOOSH

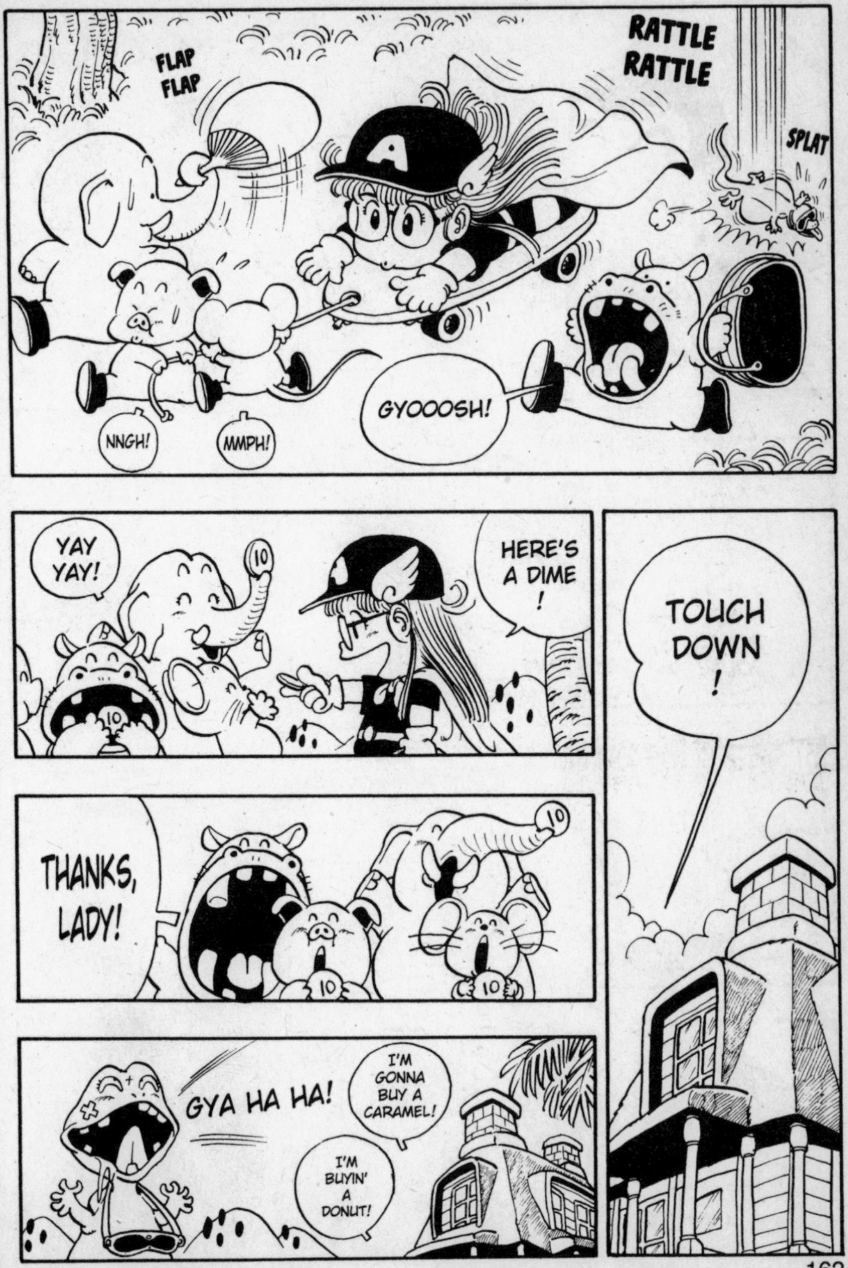
RATTLE RATTLE
SPLAT
FLAP FLAP
GYOOOSH!
MMPH!
NNGH!
TOUCH DOWN!
HERE'S A DIME!
YAY YAY!
THANKS, LADY!
I'M GONNA BUY A CARAMEL!
I'M BUYIN' A DONUT!
GYA HA HA!

READ THIS WAY

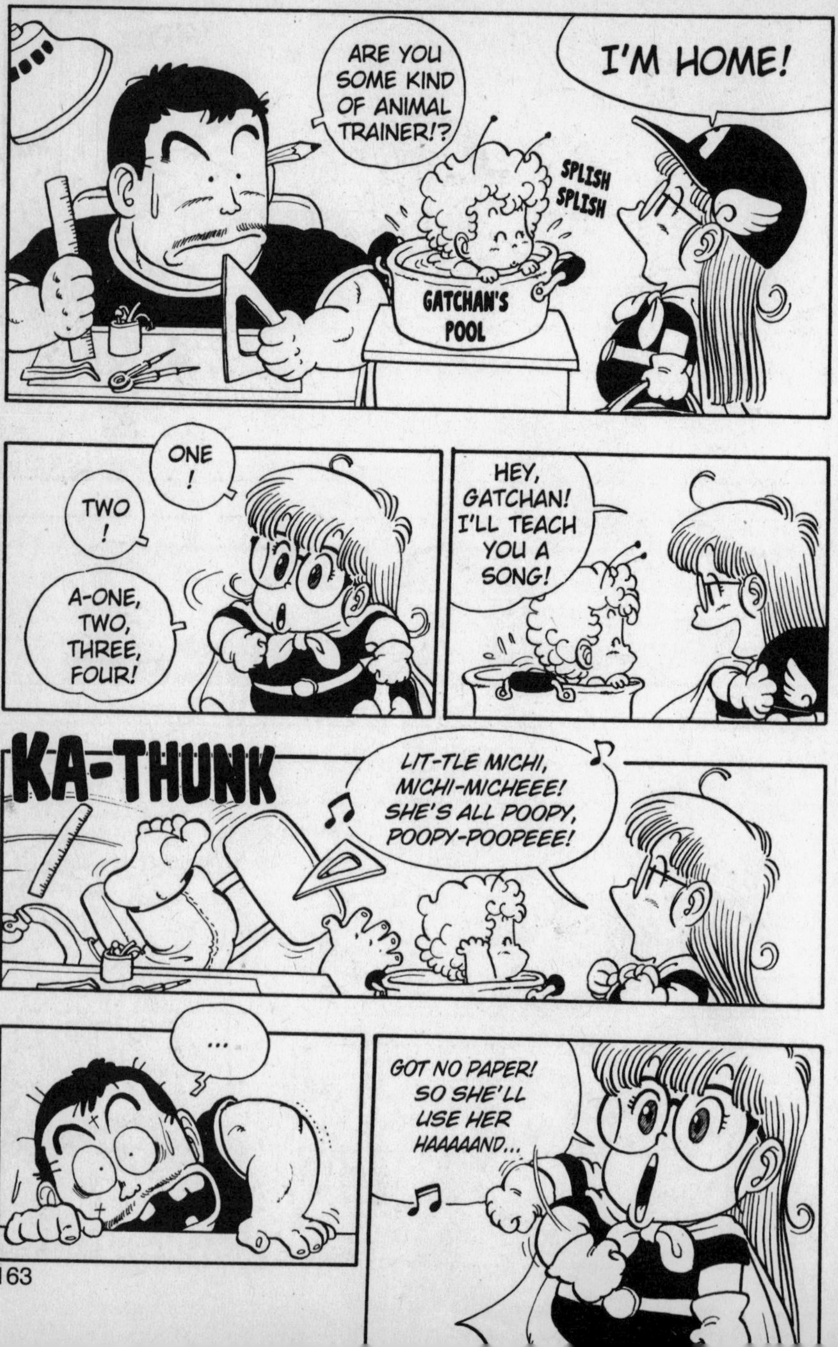

I'M HOME!
ARE YOU SOME KIND OF ANIMAL TRAINER!?
SPLISH SPLISH
GATCHAN'S POOL
HEY, GATCHAN! I'LL TEACH YOU A SONG!
ONE!
TWO!
A-ONE, TWO, THREE, FOUR!
LIT-TLE MICHI, MICHI-MICHEEE! SHE'S ALL POOPY, POOPY-POOPEEE!
KA-THUNK
GOT NO PAPER! SO SHE'LL USE HER HAAAAAND...
...

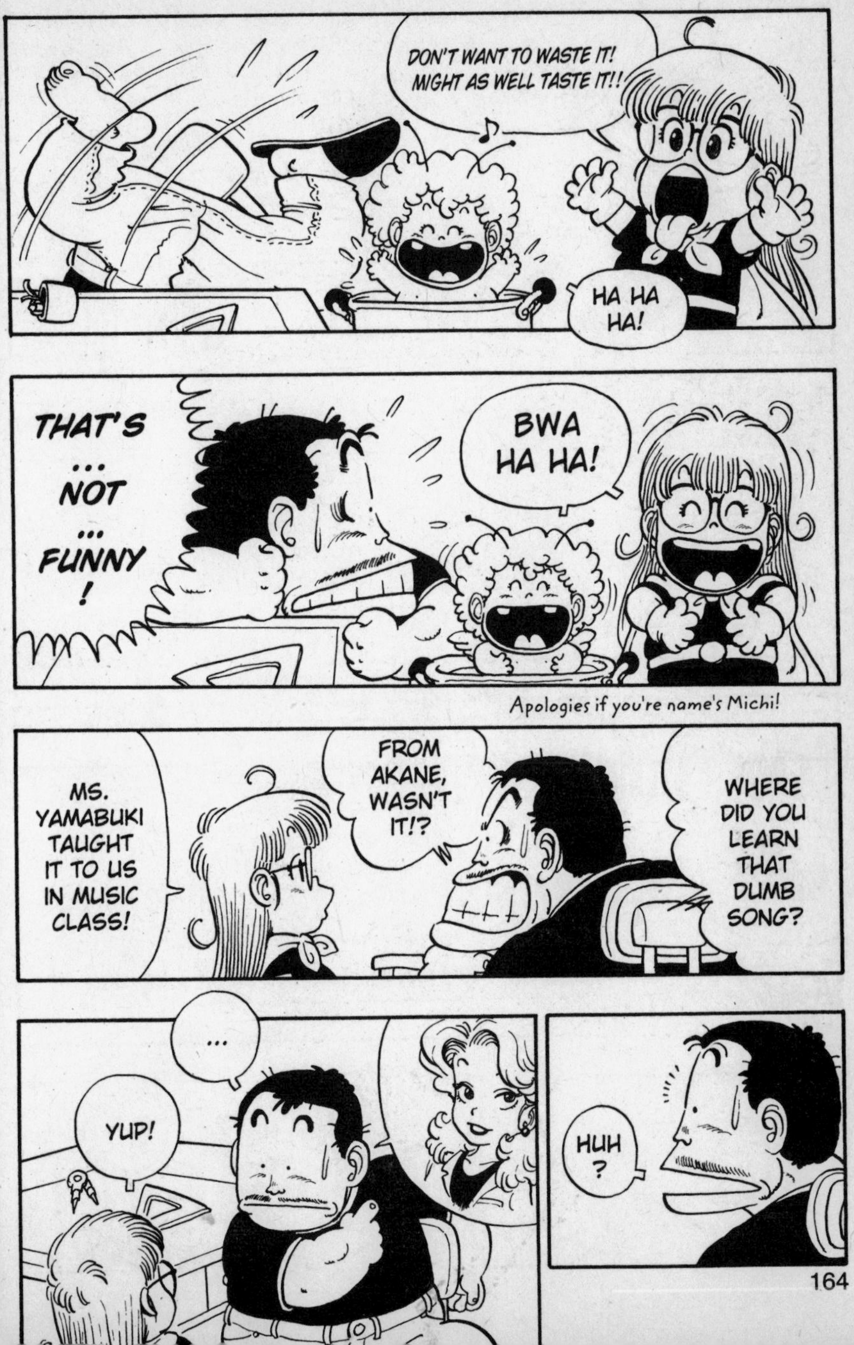
DON'T WANT TO WASTE IT! MIGHT AS WELL TASTE IT!!
HA HA HA!
BWA HA HA!
THAT'S ... NOT ... FUNNY!
WHERE DID YOU LEARN THAT DUMB SONG?
FROM AKANE, WASN'T IT!?
MS. YAMABUKI TAUGHT IT TO US IN MUSIC CLASS!
HUH?
...
YUP!

Apologies if you're name's Michi!

READ THIS WAY

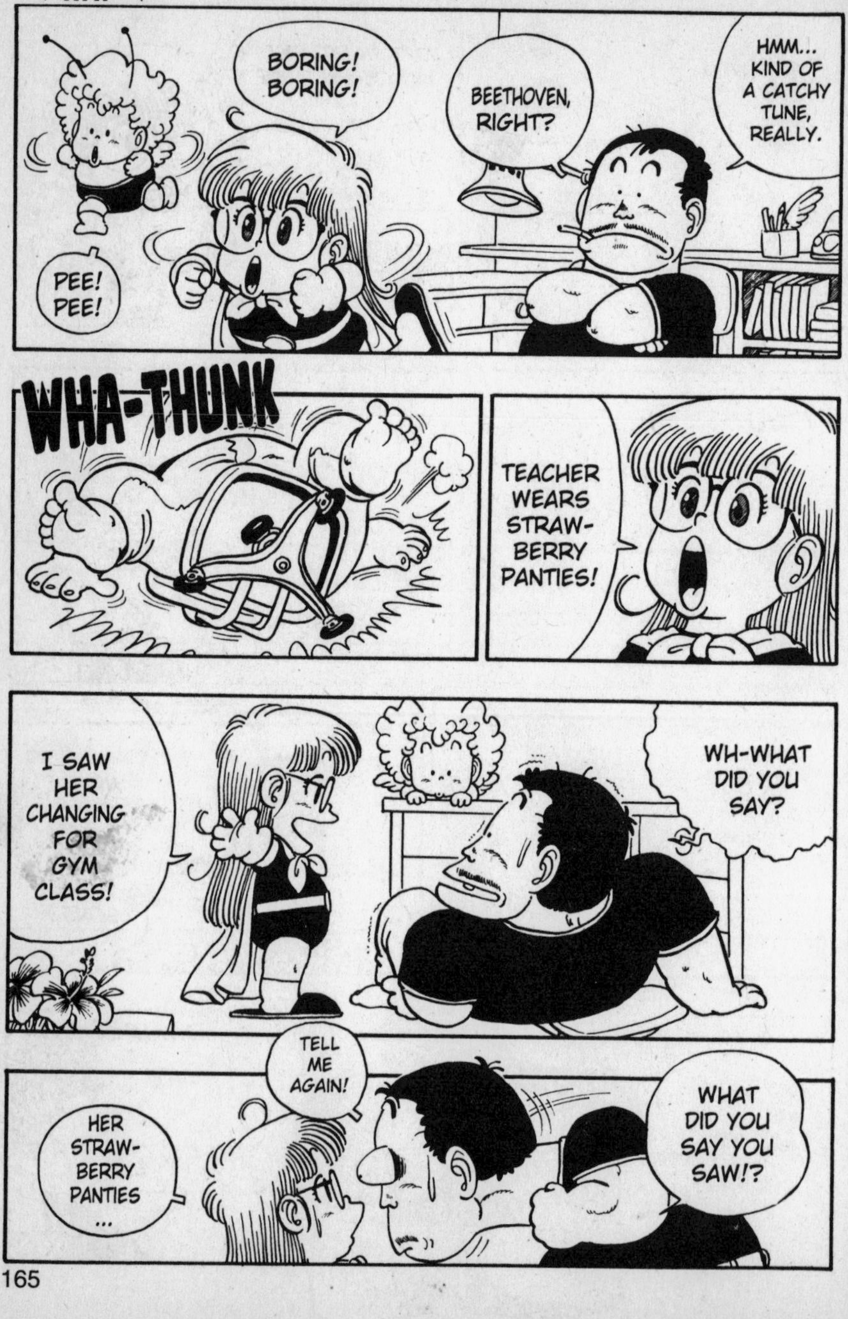

HMM... KIND OF A CATCHY TUNE, REALLY.
BEETHOVEN, RIGHT?
BORING! BORING!
PEE! PEE!
TEACHER WEARS STRAW-BERRY PANTIES!
WHA-THUNK
WH-WHAT DID YOU SAY?
I SAW HER CHANGING FOR GYM CLASS!
WHAT DID YOU SAY YOU SAW!?
TELL ME AGAIN!
HER STRAW-BERRY PANTIES ...

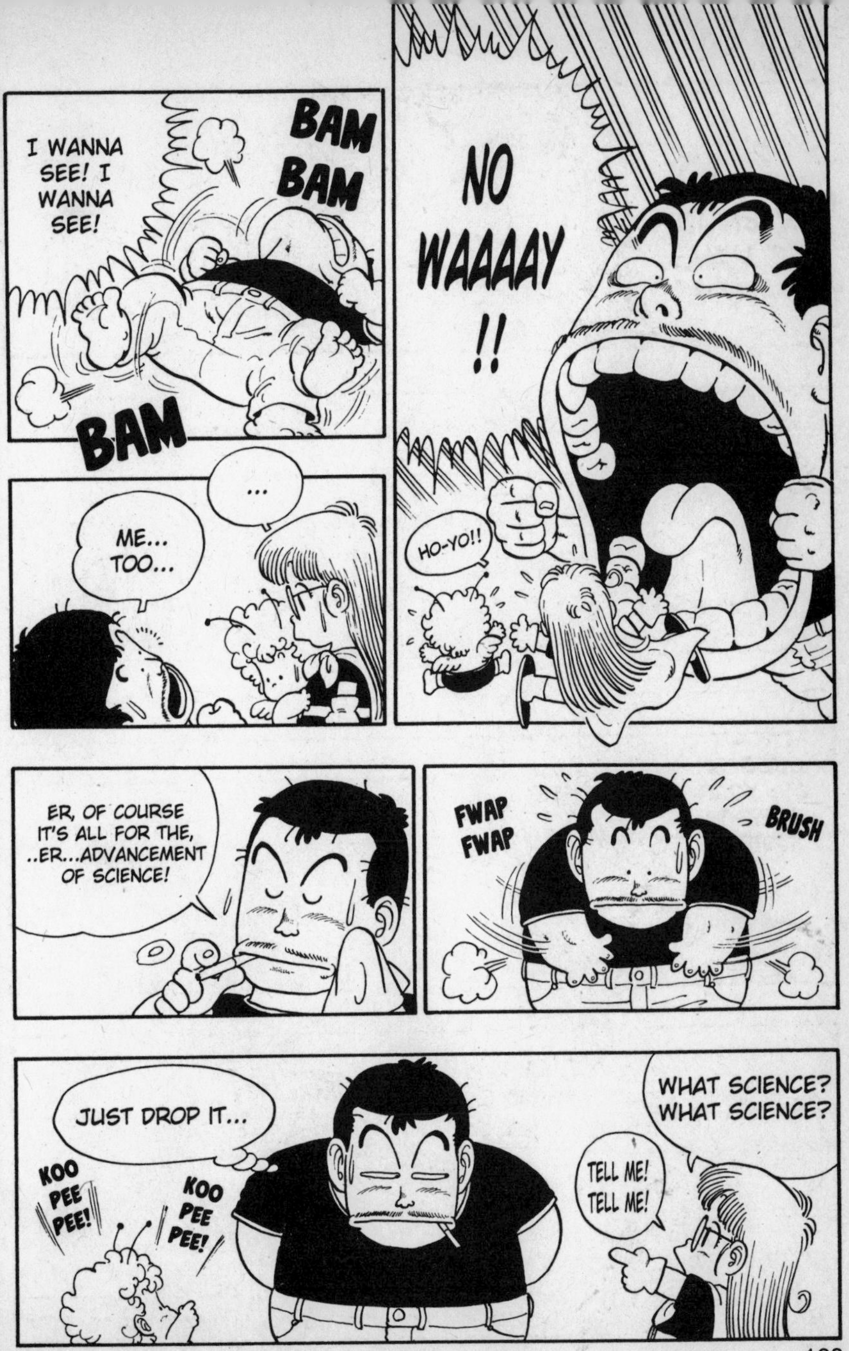
NO WAAAAY!!
HO-YO!!
BAM BAM
I WANNA SEE! I WANNA SEE!
BAM
...
ME... TOO...
BRUSH
FWAP FWAP
ER, OF COURSE IT'S ALL FOR THE, ..ER...ADVANCEMENT OF SCIENCE!
WHAT SCIENCE? WHAT SCIENCE?
TELL ME! TELL ME!
JUST DROP IT...
KOO PEE PEE!
KOO PEE PEE!

READ THIS WAY

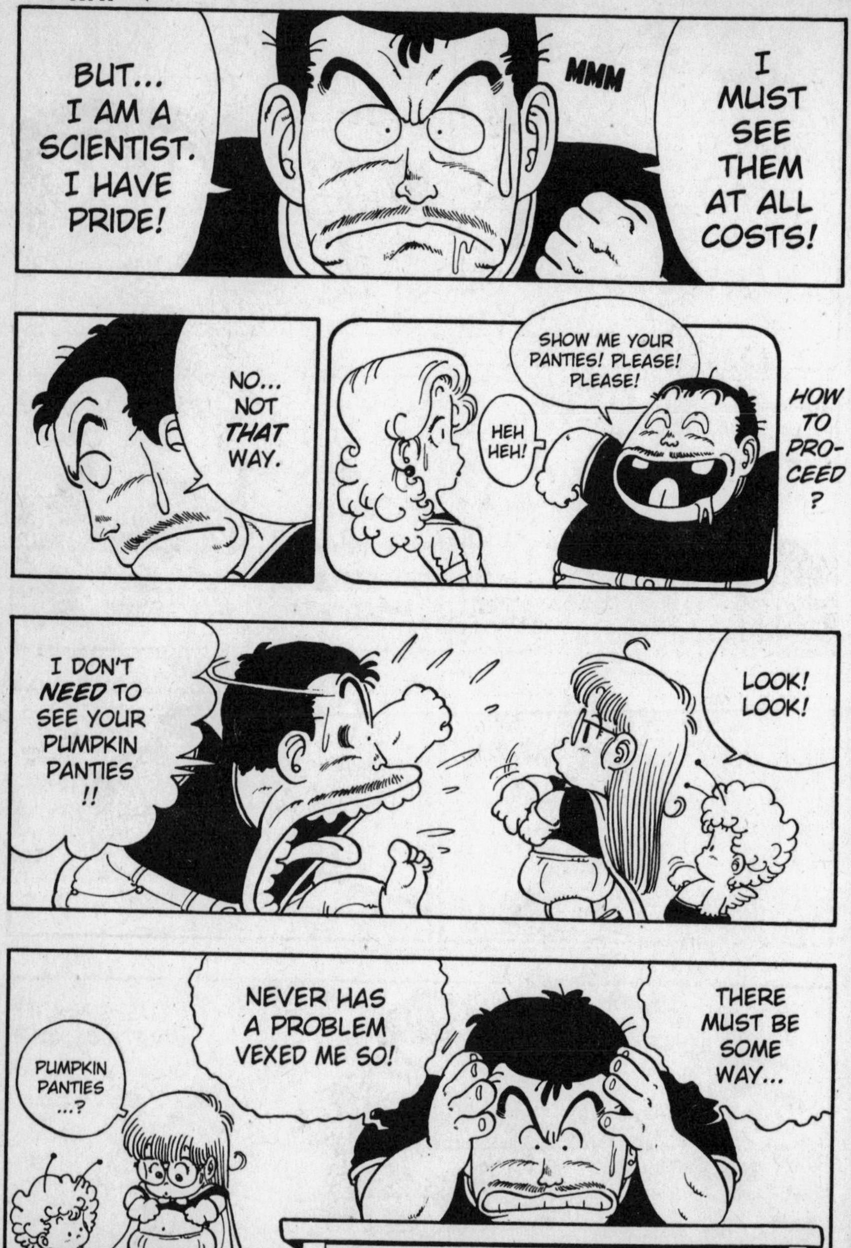

I MUST SEE THEM AT ALL COSTS!
MMM
BUT... I AM A SCIENTIST. I HAVE PRIDE!
HOW TO PRO-CEED?
SHOW ME YOUR PANTIES! PLEASE! PLEASE!
HEH HEH!
NO... NOT *THAT* WAY.
LOOK! LOOK!
I DON'T ***NEED*** TO SEE YOUR PUMPKIN PANTIES !!
THERE MUST BE SOME WAY...
NEVER HAS A PROBLEM VEXED ME SO!
PUMPKIN PANTIES ...?

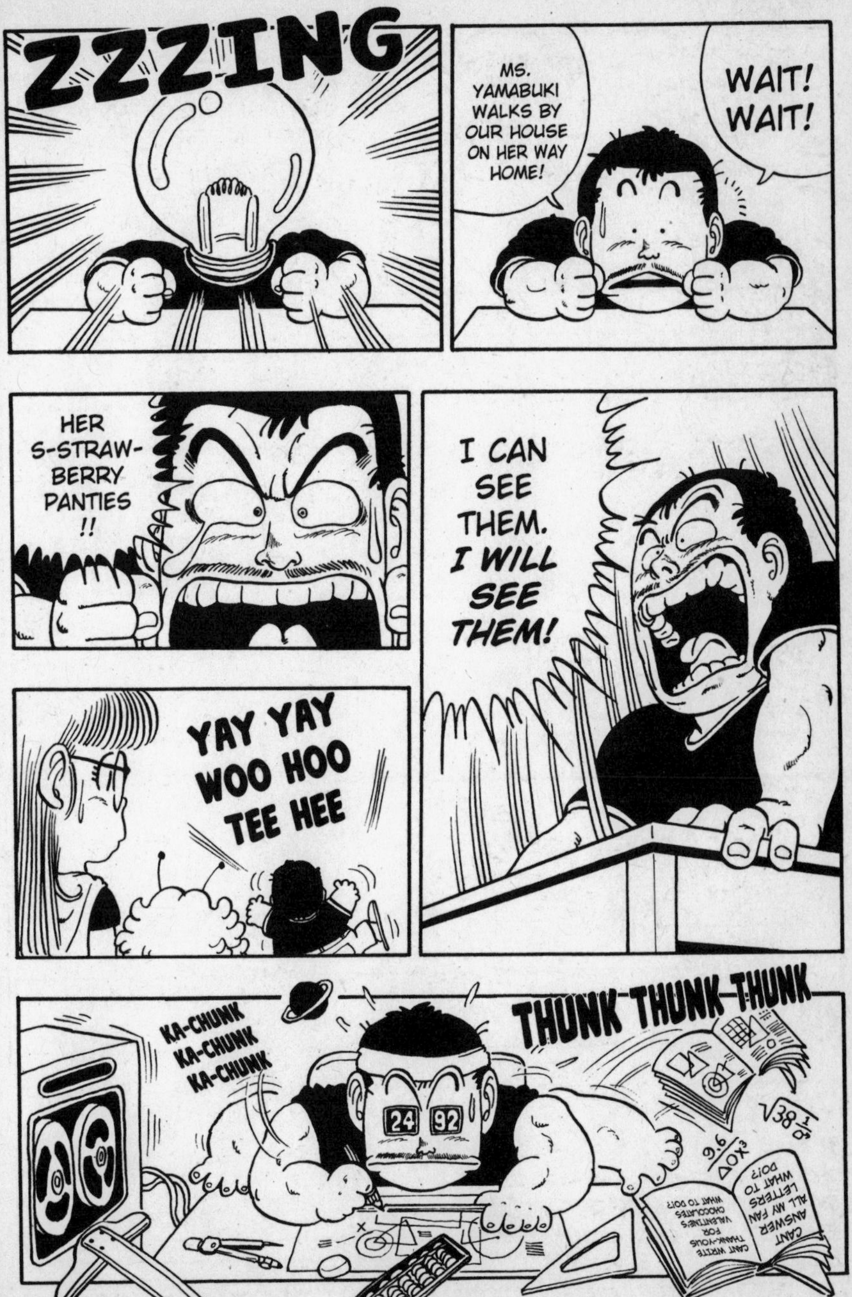
WAIT! WAIT!
MS. YAMABUKI WALKS BY OUR HOUSE ON HER WAY HOME!
ZZZING
I CAN SEE THEM. I WILL SEE THEM!
HER S-STRAWBERRY PANTIES !!
YAY YAY WOO HOO TEE HEE
THUNK THUNK THUNK
KA-CHUNK KA-CHUNK KA-CHUNK
24 92
CANT ANSWER ALL MY FAN LETTERS WHAT TO DO?
CANT WRITE THANK-YOUS FOR VALENTINE'S CHOCOLATES WHAT TO DO!?

READ THIS WAY

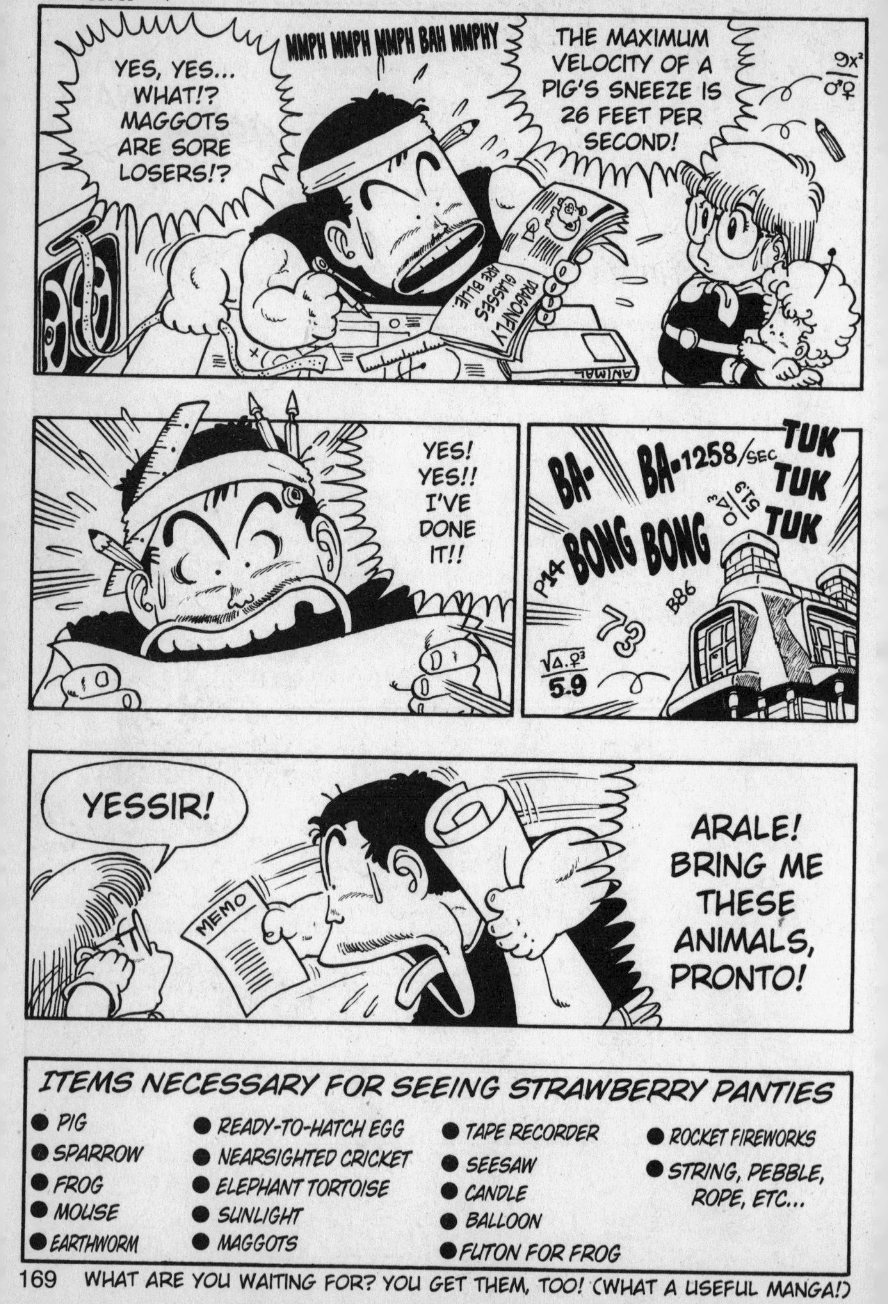

THE MAXIMUM VELOCITY OF A PIG'S SNEEZE IS 26 FEET PER SECOND!
MMPH MMPH MMPH BAH MMPHY
YES, YES... WHAT!? MAGGOTS ARE SORE LOSERS!?
DRAGONFLY GLASSES ARE BLUE
ANIMAL
TUK TUK TUK
BA- BA-1258/SEC
BONG BONG
P14
B86
73
5.9
YES! YES!! I'VE DONE IT!!
ARALE! BRING ME THESE ANIMALS, PRONTO!
YESSIR!
MEMO

ITEMS NECESSARY FOR SEEING STRAWBERRY PANTIES

- PIG
- SPARROW
- FROG
- MOUSE
- EARTHWORM
- READY-TO-HATCH EGG
- NEARSIGHTED CRICKET
- ELEPHANT TORTOISE
- SUNLIGHT
- MAGGOTS
- TAPE RECORDER
- SEESAW
- CANDLE
- BALLOON
- FUTON FOR FROG
- ROCKET FIREWORKS
- STRING, PEBBLE, ROPE, ETC...

 WHAT ARE YOU WAITING FOR? YOU GET THEM, TOO! (WHAT A USEFUL MANGA!)

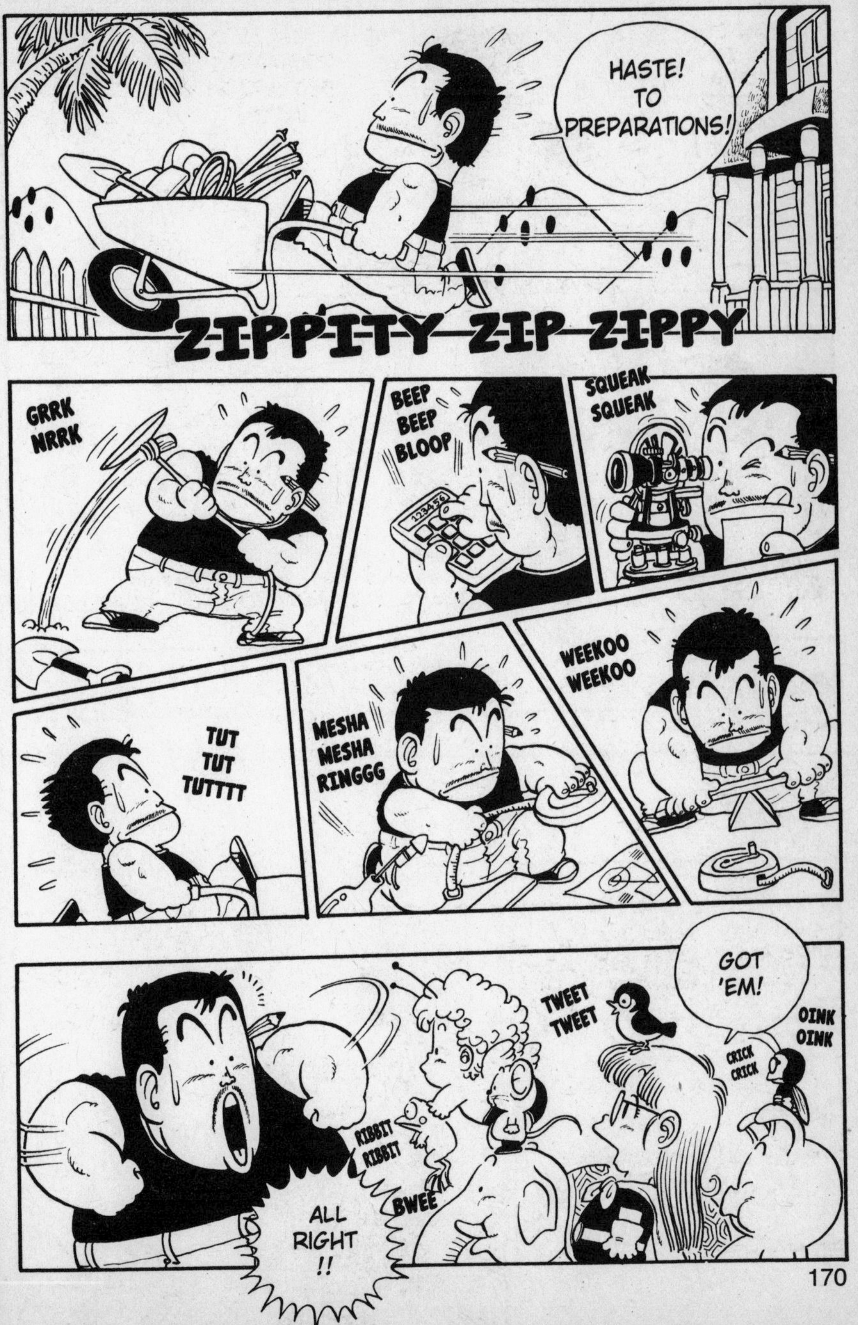
HASTE! TO PREPARATIONS!
ZIPPITY ZIP ZIPPY
SQUEAK SQUEAK
BEEP BEEP BLOOP
GRRK NRRK
WEEKOO WEEKOO
MESHA MESHA RINGGG
TUT TUT TUTTTT
GOT 'EM!
OINK OINK
CRICK CRICK
TWEET TWEET
RIBBIT RIBBIT
BWEE
ALL RIGHT !!

READ THIS WAY

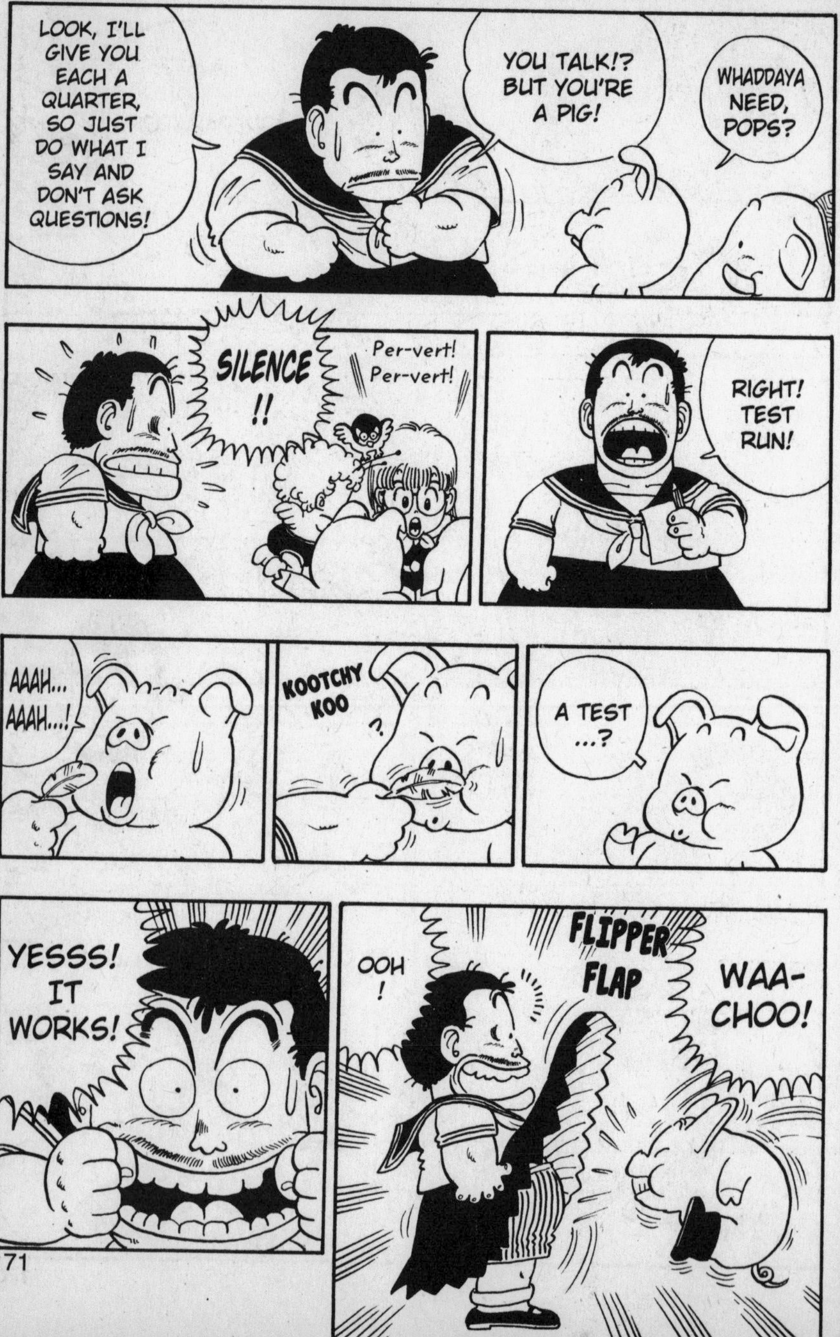
WHADDAYA NEED, POPS?
YOU TALK!? BUT YOU'RE A PIG!
LOOK, I'LL GIVE YOU EACH A QUARTER, SO JUST DO WHAT I SAY AND DON'T ASK QUESTIONS!
RIGHT! TEST RUN!
Per-vert! Per-vert!
SILENCE !!
A TEST ...?
KOOTCHY KOO
AAAH... AAAH...!
WAA-CHOO!
FLIPPER FLAP
OOH !
YESSS! IT WORKS!

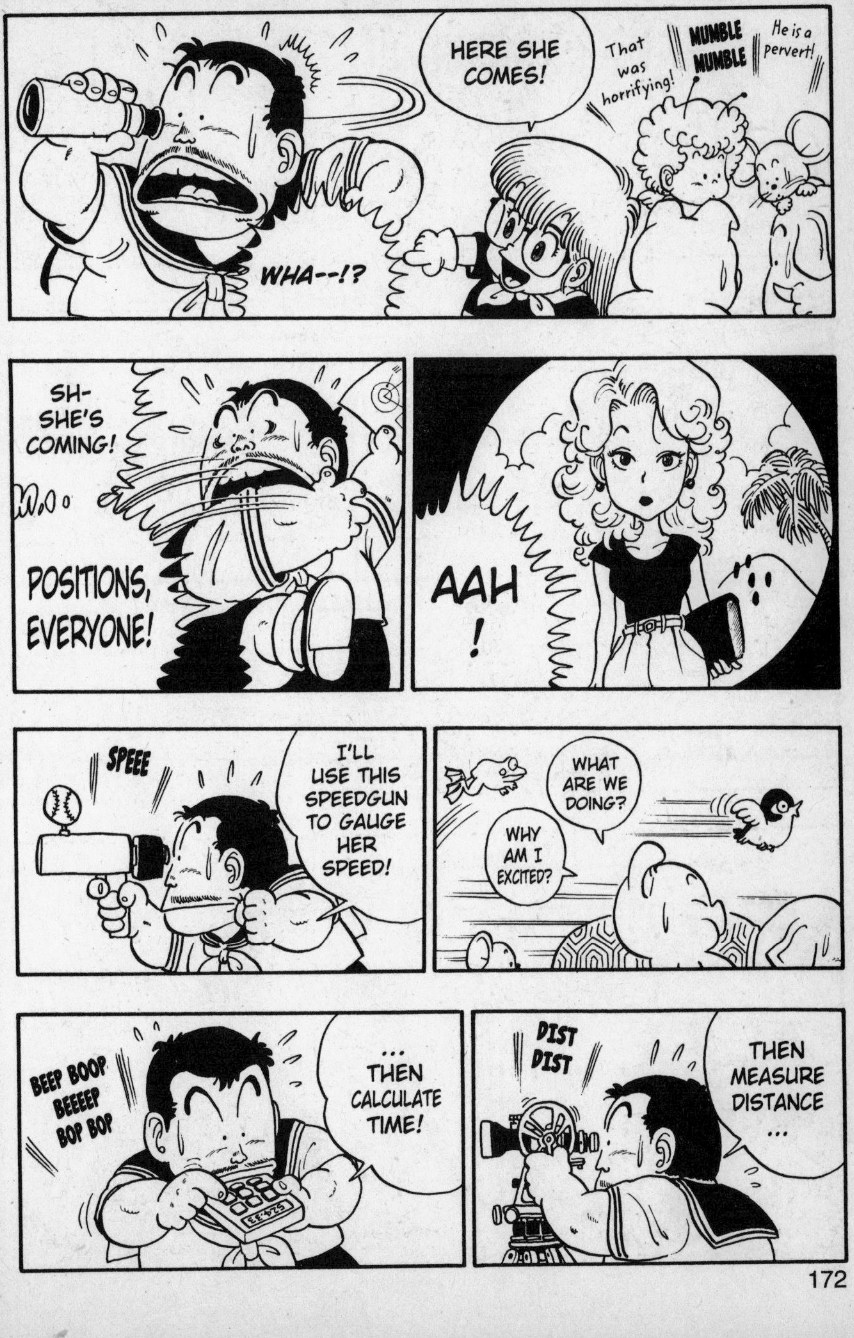
He is a pervert!
MUMBLE MUMBLE
That was horrifying!
HERE SHE COMES!
WHA--!?
AAH !
SH- SHE'S COMING!
POSITIONS, EVERYONE!
WHAT ARE WE DOING?
WHY AM I EXCITED?
I'LL USE THIS SPEEDGUN TO GAUGE HER SPEED!
SPEEE
THEN MEASURE DISTANCE ...
DIST DIST
... THEN CALCULATE TIME!
BEEP BOOP BEEEEP BOP BOP

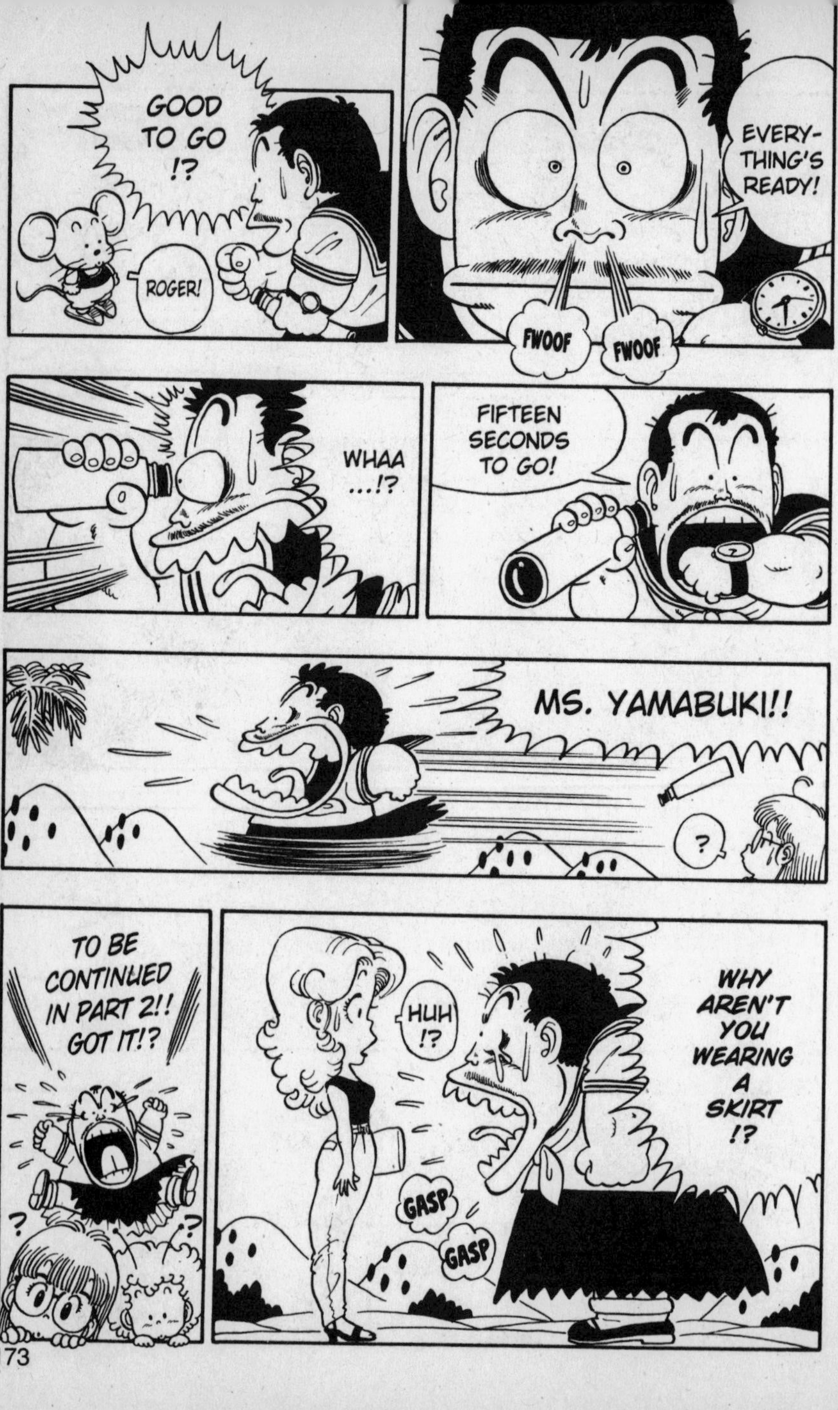
EVERY-THING'S READY!
FWOOF
FWOOF
GOOD TO GO !?
ROGER!
FIFTEEN SECONDS TO GO!
WHAA ...!?
MS. YAMABUKI!!
?
WHY AREN'T YOU WEARING A SKIRT !?
HUH !?
GASP
GASP
TO BE CONTINUED IN PART 2!! GOT IT!?
?
?

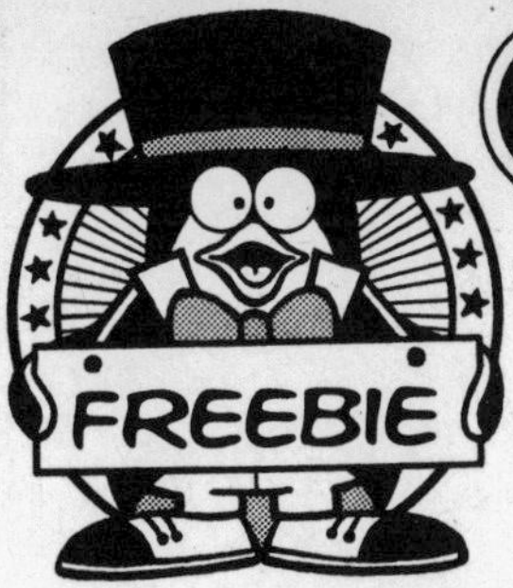
FREEBIE

Fault Finder

This one's **really** going to annoy you! There are over 30 differences in the two pictures! Find them ***if you dare!***

(Ink smears and rough lines don't count.)

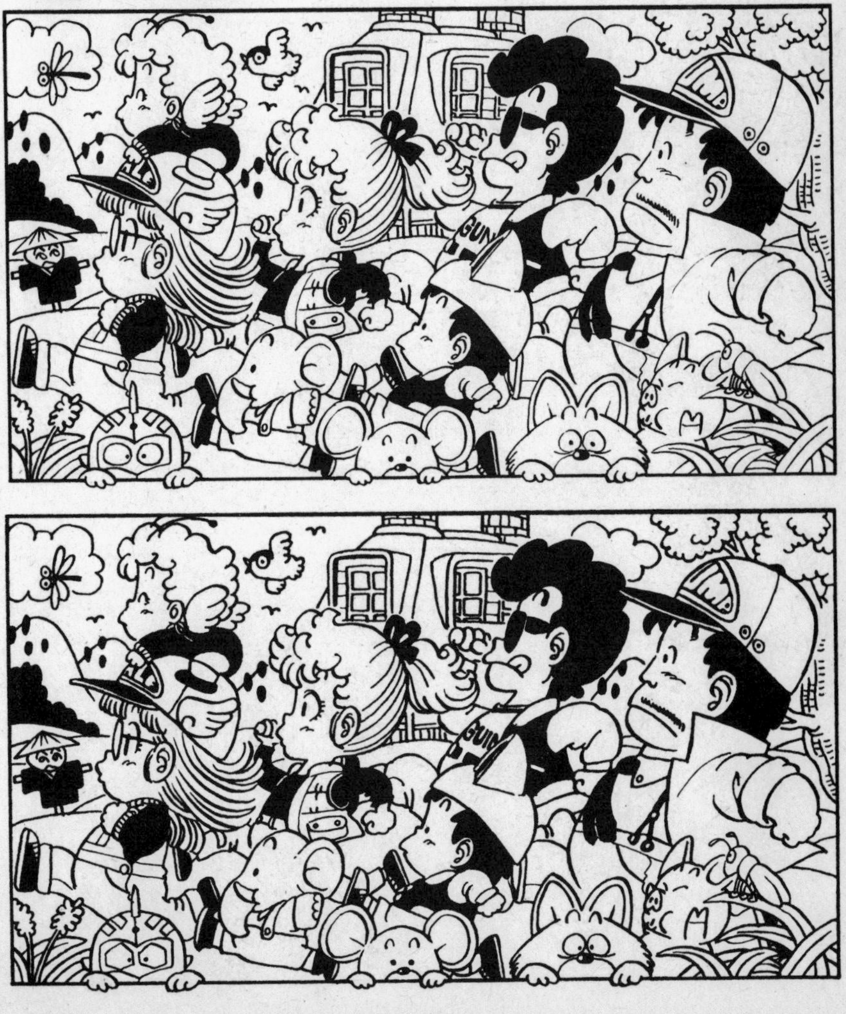

The Great Strawberry Panties Caper

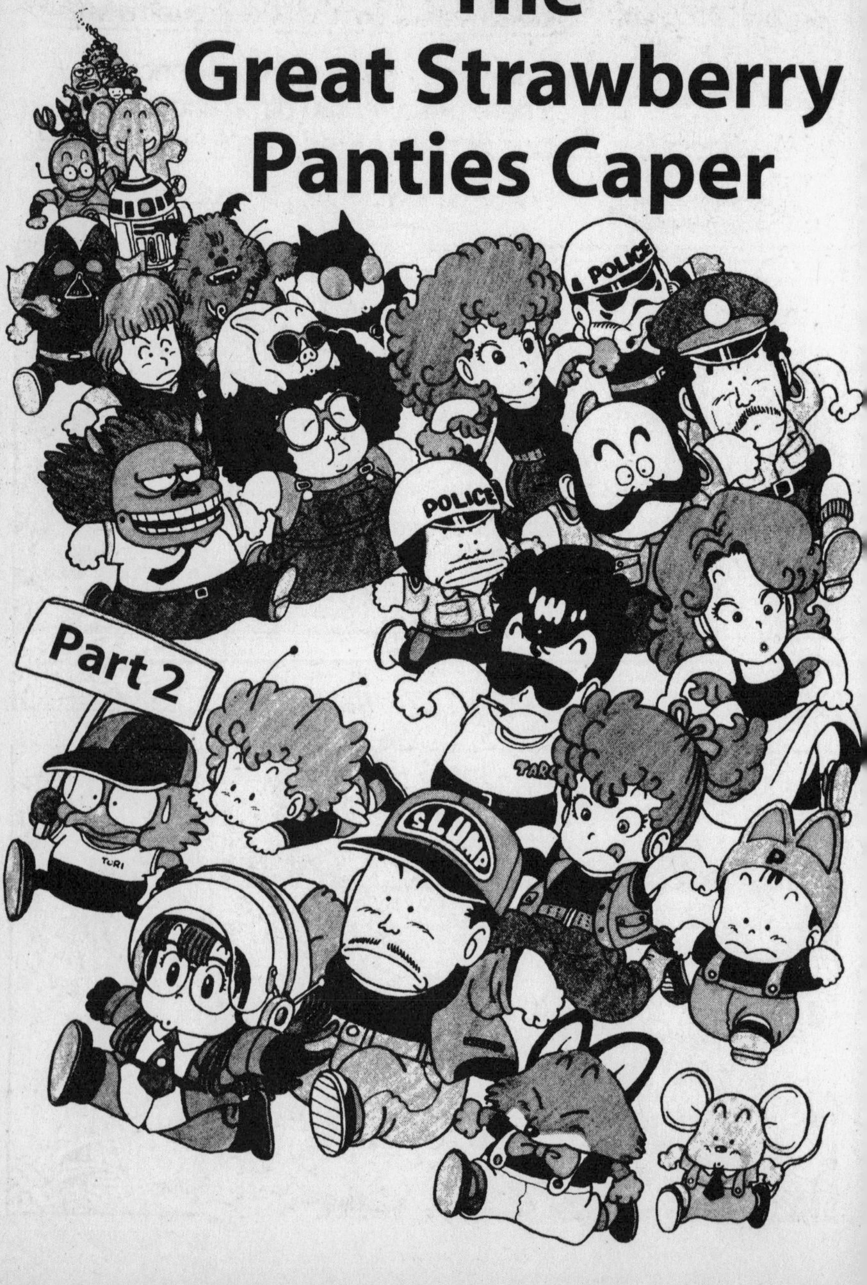
POLICE
POLICE
Part 2
SLUMP
TURI

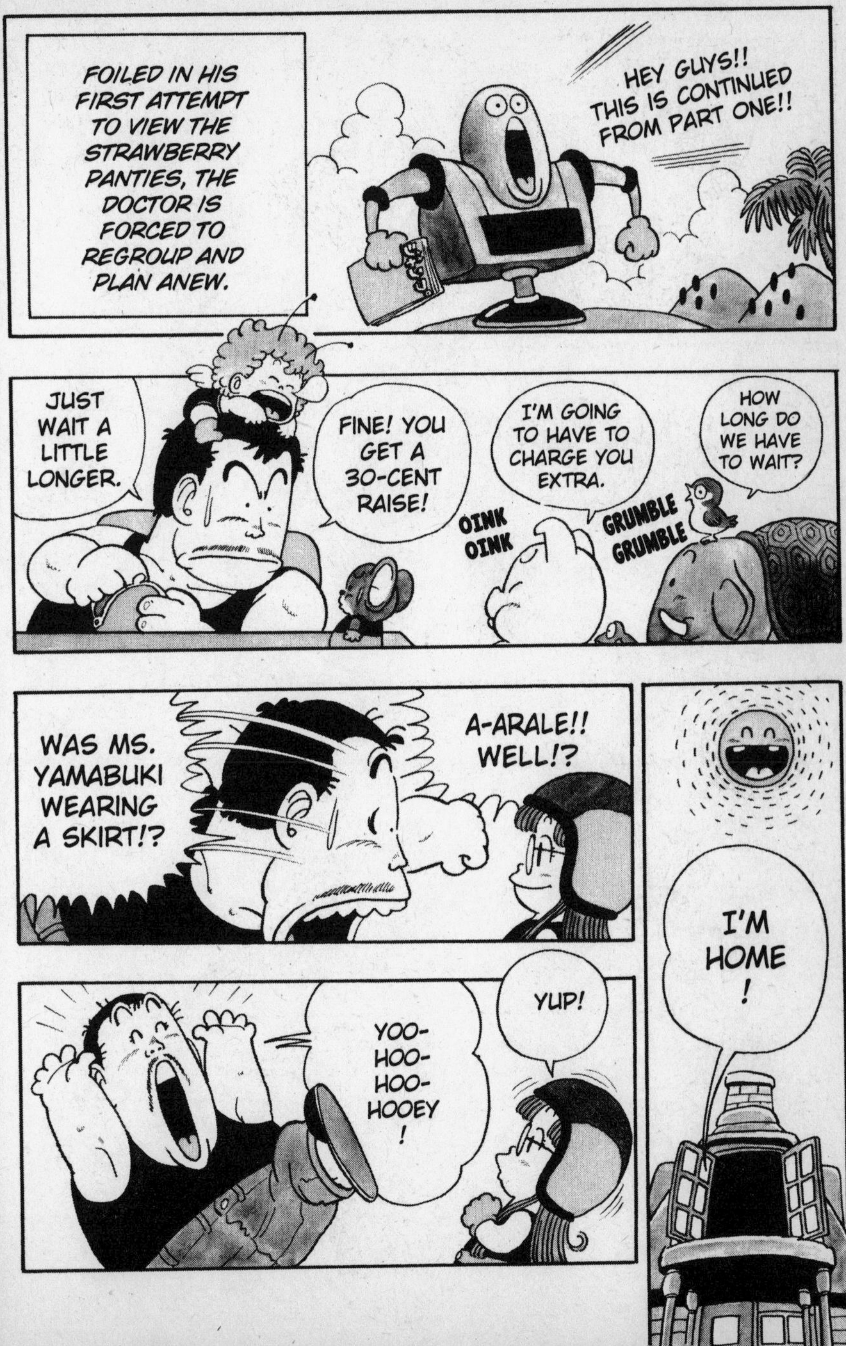
HEY GUYS!! THIS IS CONTINUED FROM PART ONE!!
FOILED IN HIS FIRST ATTEMPT TO VIEW THE STRAWBERRY PANTIES, THE DOCTOR IS FORCED TO REGROUP AND PLAN ANEW.
HOW LONG DO WE HAVE TO WAIT?
GRUMBLE GRUMBLE
I'M GOING TO HAVE TO CHARGE YOU EXTRA.
OINK OINK
FINE! YOU GET A 30-CENT RAISE!
JUST WAIT A LITTLE LONGER.
I'M HOME !
A-ARALE!! WELL!?
WAS MS. YAMABUKI WEARING A SKIRT!?
YUP!
YOO-HOO-HOO-HOOEY !

READ THIS WAY

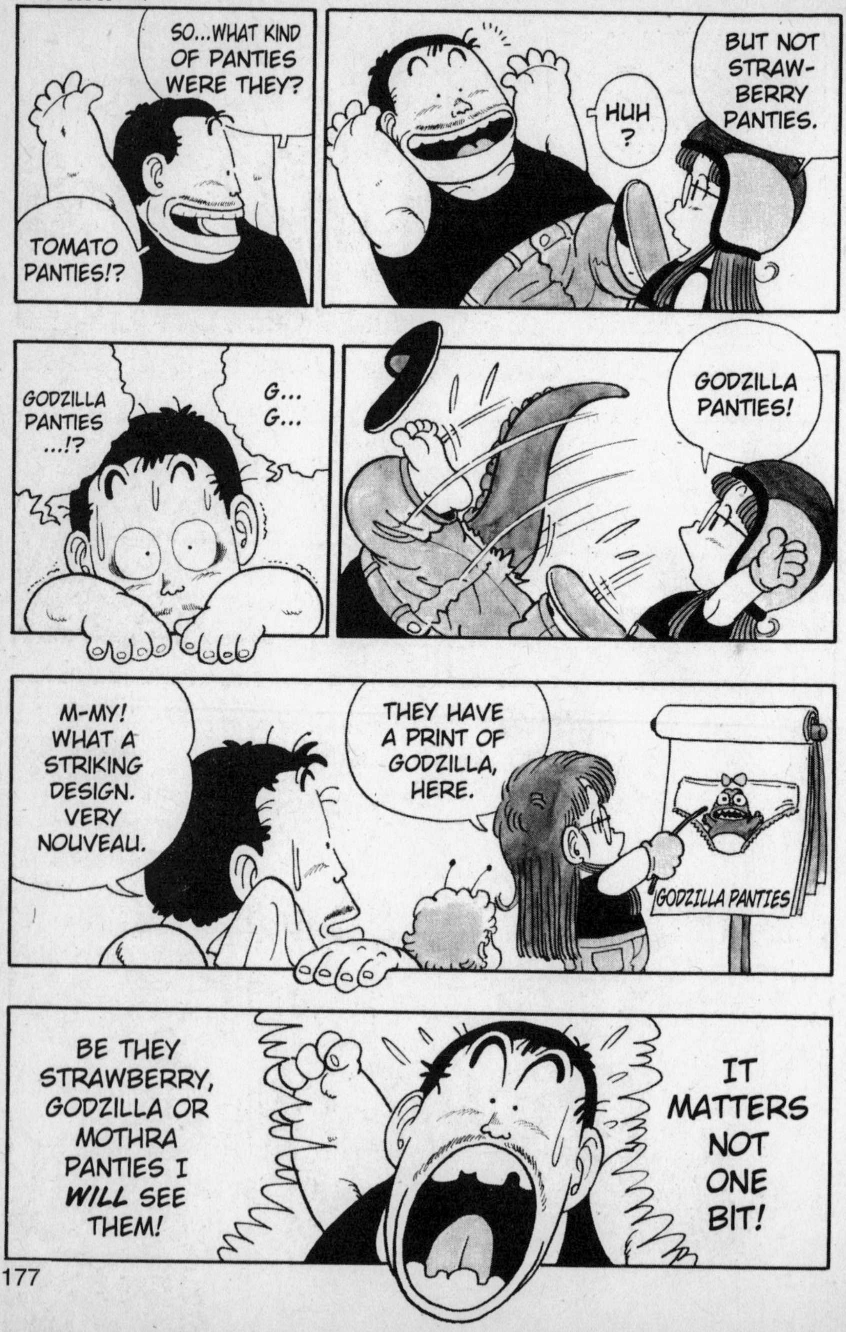

BUT NOT STRAW-BERRY PANTIES.
HUH?
SO...WHAT KIND OF PANTIES WERE THEY?
TOMATO PANTIES!?
GODZILLA PANTIES!
G... G...
GODZILLA PANTIES ...!?
GODZILLA PANTIES
THEY HAVE A PRINT OF GODZILLA, HERE.
M-MY! WHAT A STRIKING DESIGN. VERY NOUVEAU.
IT MATTERS NOT ONE BIT!
BE THEY STRAWBERRY, GODZILLA OR MOTHRA PANTIES I *WILL* SEE THEM!

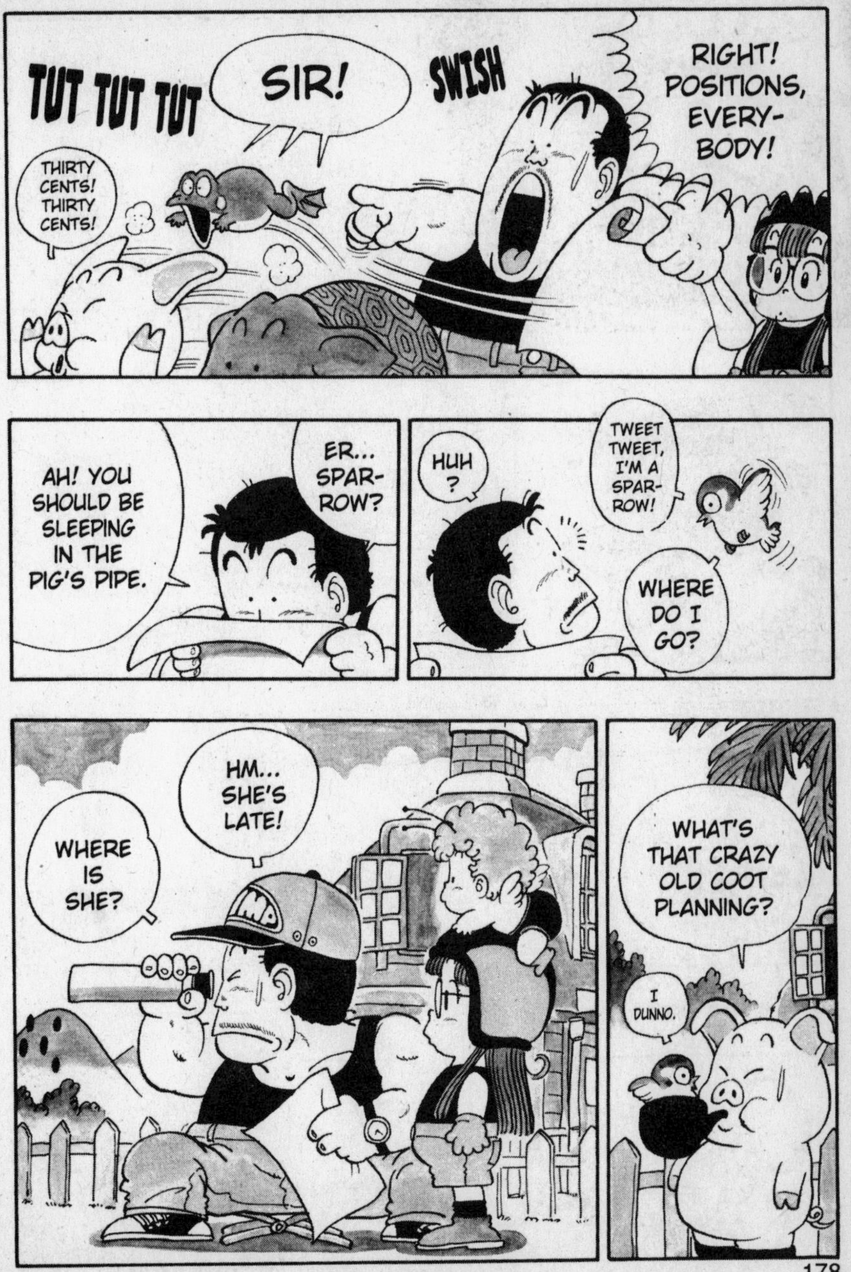
RIGHT! POSITIONS, EVERY-BODY!
SWISH
SIR!
TUT TUT TUT
THIRTY CENTS! THIRTY CENTS!
TWEET TWEET, I'M A SPAR-ROW!
WHERE DO I GO?
HUH ?
ER... SPAR-ROW?
AH! YOU SHOULD BE SLEEPING IN THE PIG'S PIPE.
WHAT'S THAT CRAZY OLD COOT PLANNING?
I DUNNO.
HM... SHE'S LATE!
WHERE IS SHE?

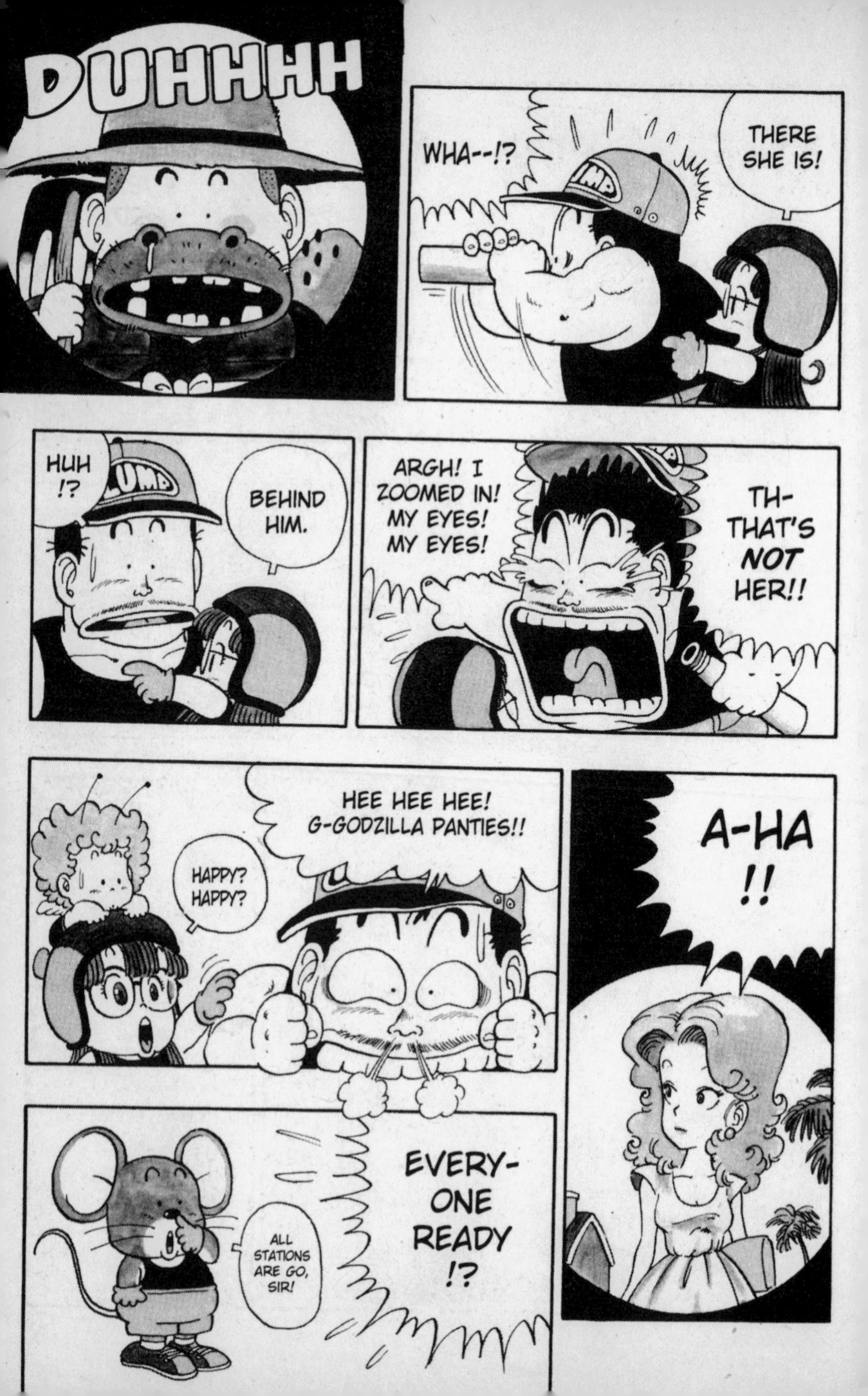
THERE SHE IS!
WHA--!?
DUHHHH
TH- THAT'S *NOT* HER!!
ARGH! I ZOOMED IN! MY EYES! MY EYES!
BEHIND HIM.
HUH !?
A-HA !!
HEE HEE HEE! G-GODZILLA PANTIES!!
HAPPY? HAPPY?
EVERY-ONE READY !?
ALL STATIONS ARE GO, SIR!

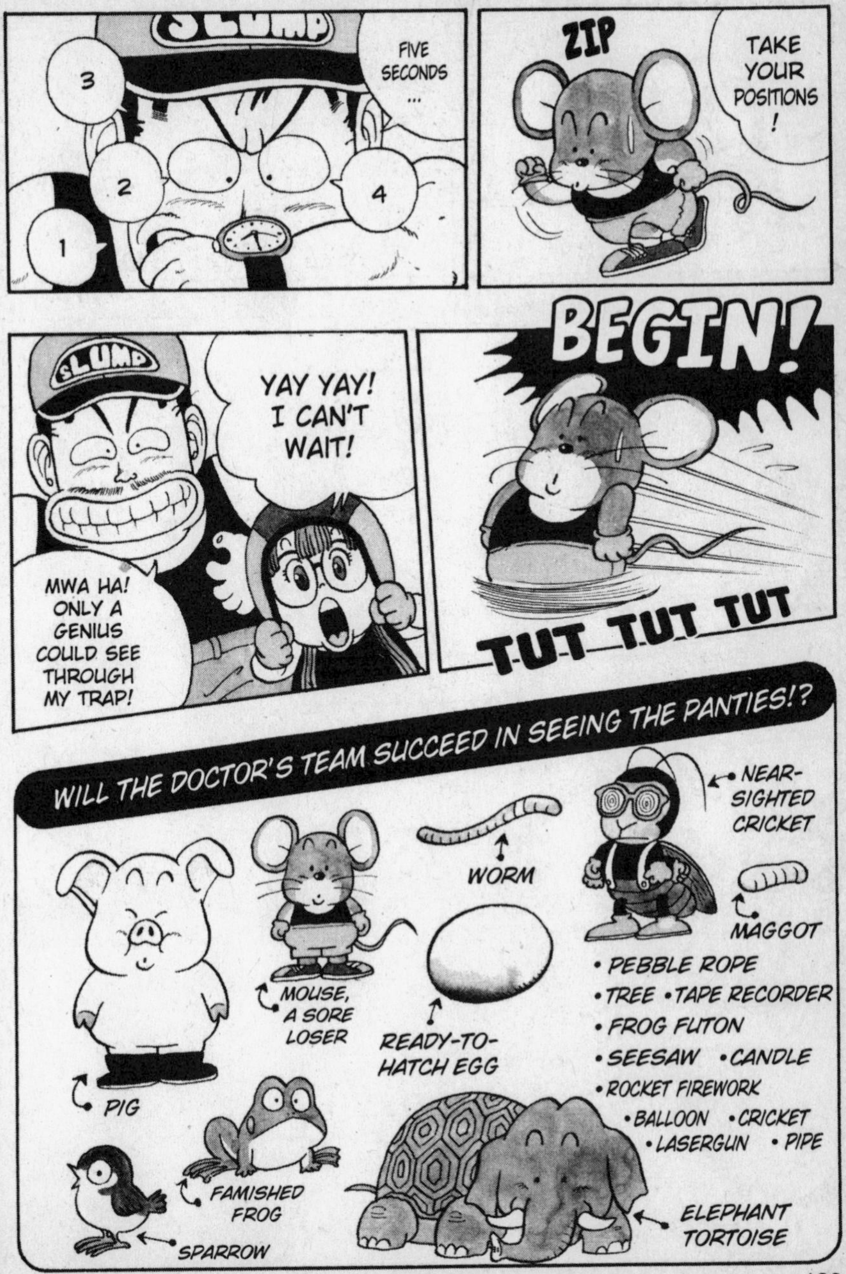
ZIP
TAKE YOUR POSITIONS!
FIVE SECONDS ...
4
3
2
1
BEGIN!
TUT TUT TUT
YAY YAY! I CAN'T WAIT!
MWA HA! ONLY A GENIUS COULD SEE THROUGH MY TRAP!
WILL THE DOCTOR'S TEAM SUCCEED IN SEEING THE PANTIES!?
NEAR-SIGHTED CRICKET
WORM
MAGGOT
• PEBBLE ROPE
• TREE • TAPE RECORDER
• FROG FUTON
• SEESAW • CANDLE
• ROCKET FIREWORK
• BALLOON • CRICKET
• LASERGUN • PIPE
MOUSE, A SORE LOSER
READY-TO-HATCH EGG
PIG
FAMISHED FROG
SPARROW
ELEPHANT TORTOISE

READ THIS WAY

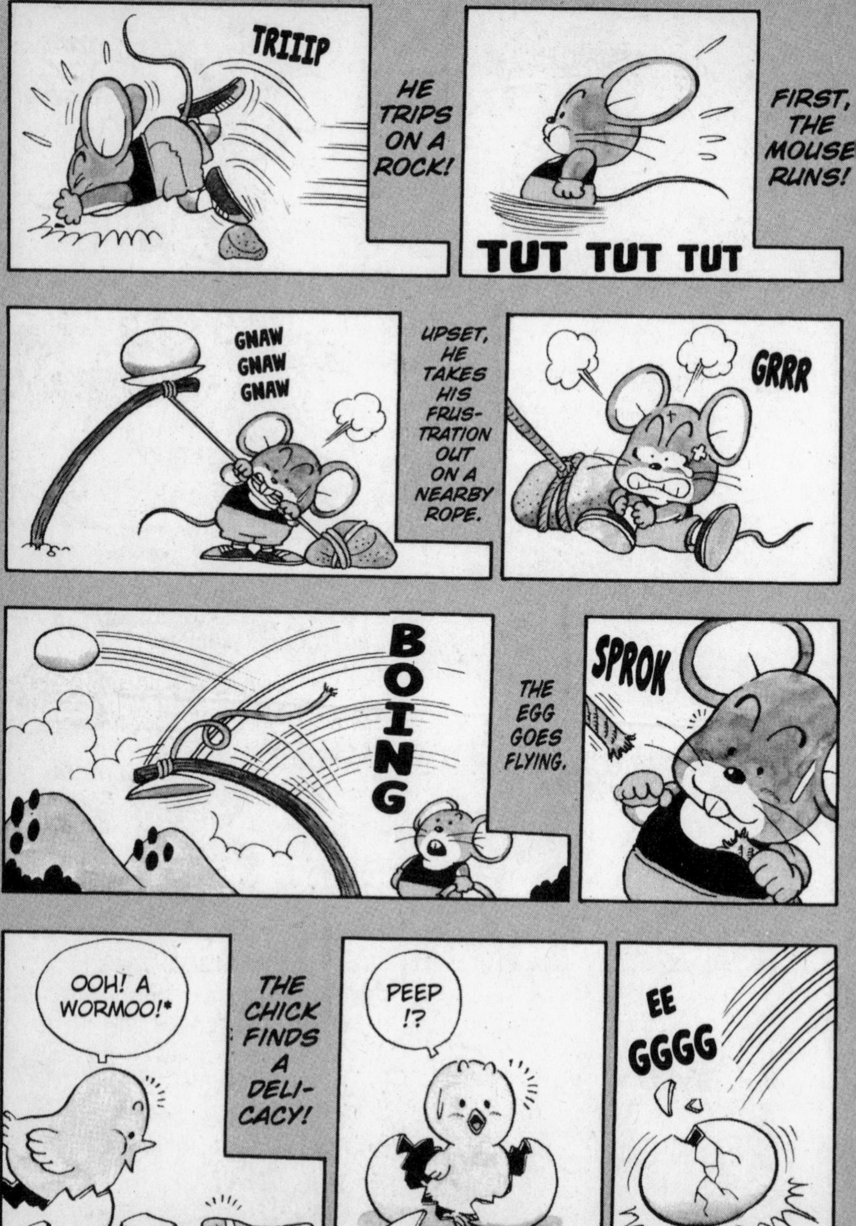

FIRST, THE MOUSE RUNS!
TUT TUT TUT
HE TRIPS ON A ROCK!
TRIIIP
GRRR
UPSET, HE TAKES HIS FRUSTRATION OUT ON A NEARBY ROPE.
GNAW GNAW GNAW
SPROK
THE EGG GOES FLYING.
BOING
EE GGGG
PEEP !?
THE CHICK FINDS A DELICACY!
OOH! A WORMOO!*

*THIS AUTHOR CALLS WORMS "WORMOOS," BUT NOTE THAT "WORMEES" AND WORMAS" ARE ACCEPTABLE VARIANTS.

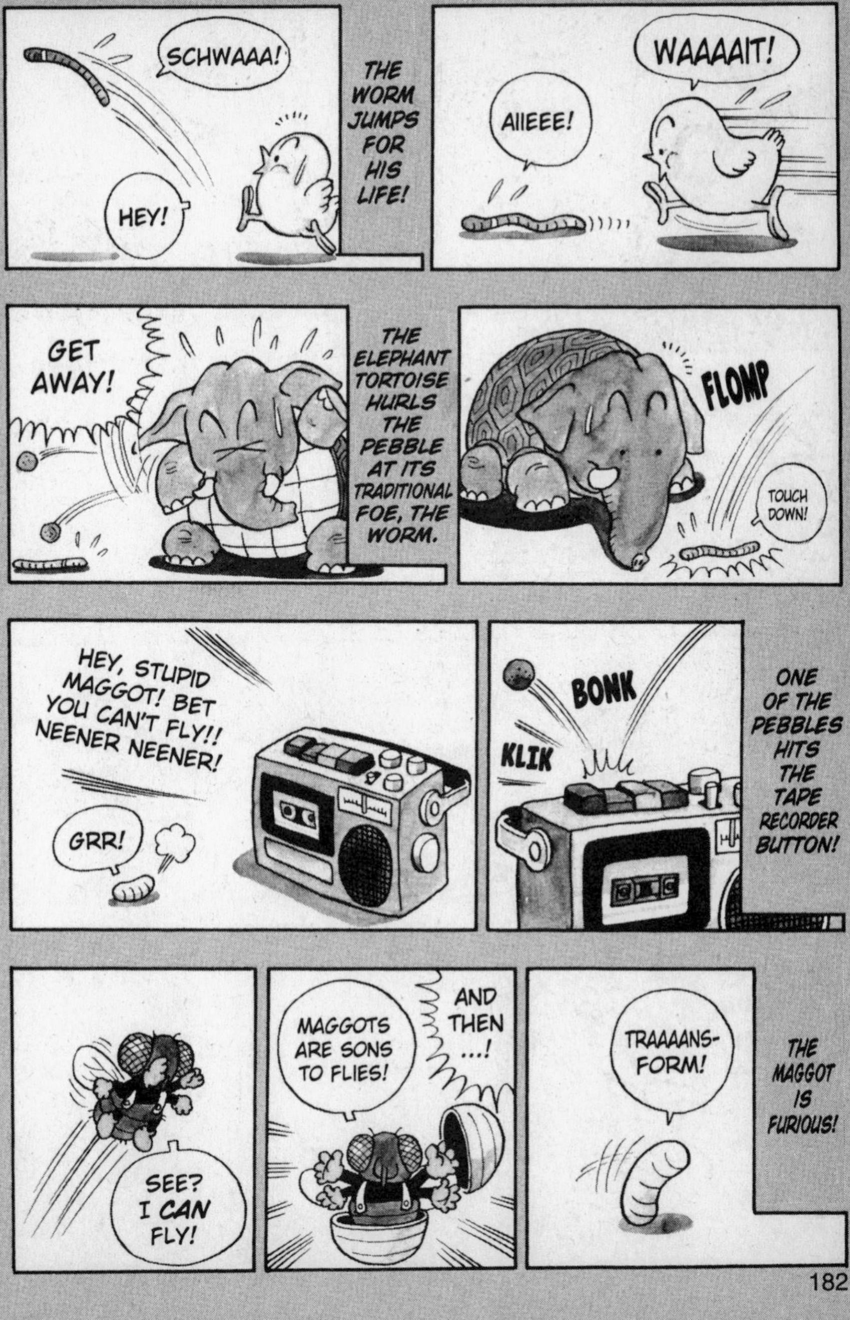
WAAAAIT!
AIIEEE!
THE WORM JUMPS FOR HIS LIFE!
SCHWAAA!
HEY!
FLOMP
TOUCH DOWN!
THE ELEPHANT TORTOISE HURLS THE PEBBLE AT ITS TRADITIONAL FOE, THE WORM.
GET AWAY!
ONE OF THE PEBBLES HITS THE TAPE RECORDER BUTTON!
BONK
KLIK
HEY, STUPID MAGGOT! BET YOU CAN'T FLY!! NEENER NEENER!
GRR!
THE MAGGOT IS FURIOUS!
TRAAAANS-FORM!
AND THEN ...!
MAGGOTS ARE SONS TO FLIES!
SEE? I CAN FLY!

READ THIS WAY

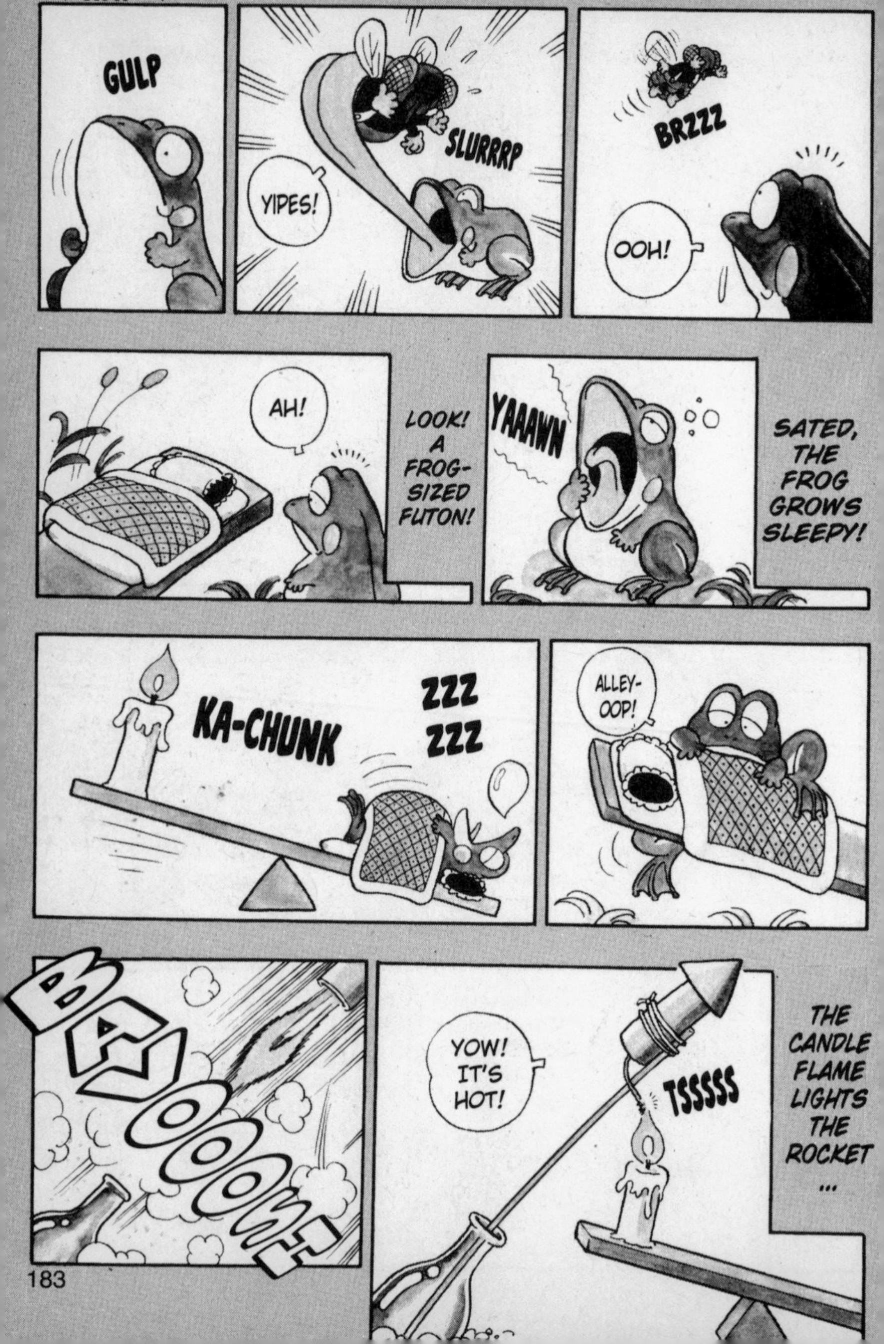

BRZZZ
OOH!
SLURRRP
YIPES!
GULP
SATED, THE FROG GROWS SLEEPY!
YAAAWN
LOOK! A FROG-SIZED FUTON!
AH!
ALLEY-OOP!
ZZZ ZZZ
KA-CHUNK
THE CANDLE FLAME LIGHTS THE ROCKET ...
TSSSSS
YOW! IT'S HOT!
BA-OOOM!

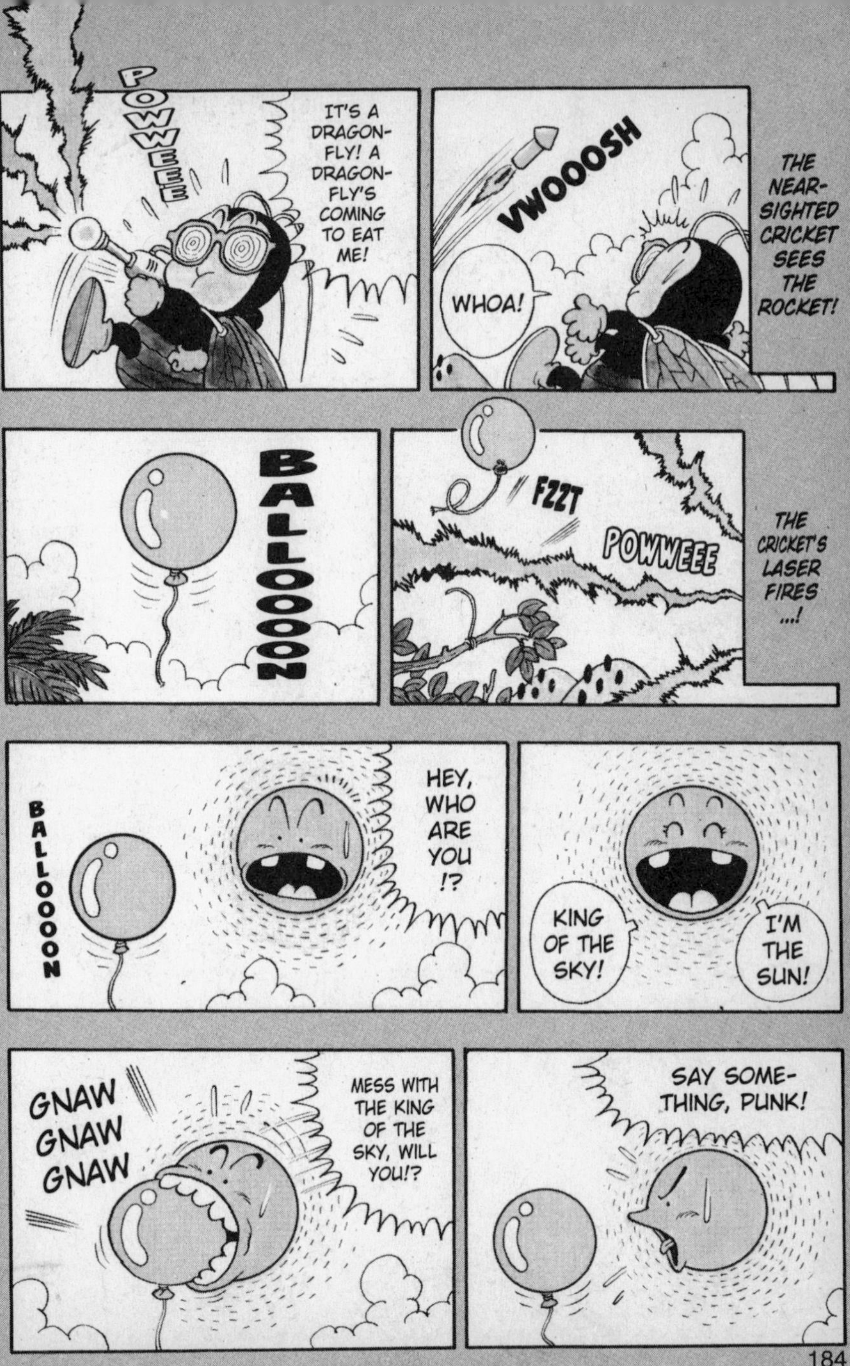
THE NEAR-SIGHTED CRICKET SEES THE ROCKET!
VWOOOSH
WHOA!
POWWEEE
IT'S A DRAGON-FLY! A DRAGON-FLY'S COMING TO EAT ME!
THE CRICKET'S LASER FIRES ...!
FZZT
POWWEEE
BALLOOOOON
I'M THE SUN!
KING OF THE SKY!
HEY, WHO ARE YOU !?
BALLOOOON
SAY SOME-THING, PUNK!
MESS WITH THE KING OF THE SKY, WILL YOU!?
GNAW GNAW GNAW

READ THIS WAY

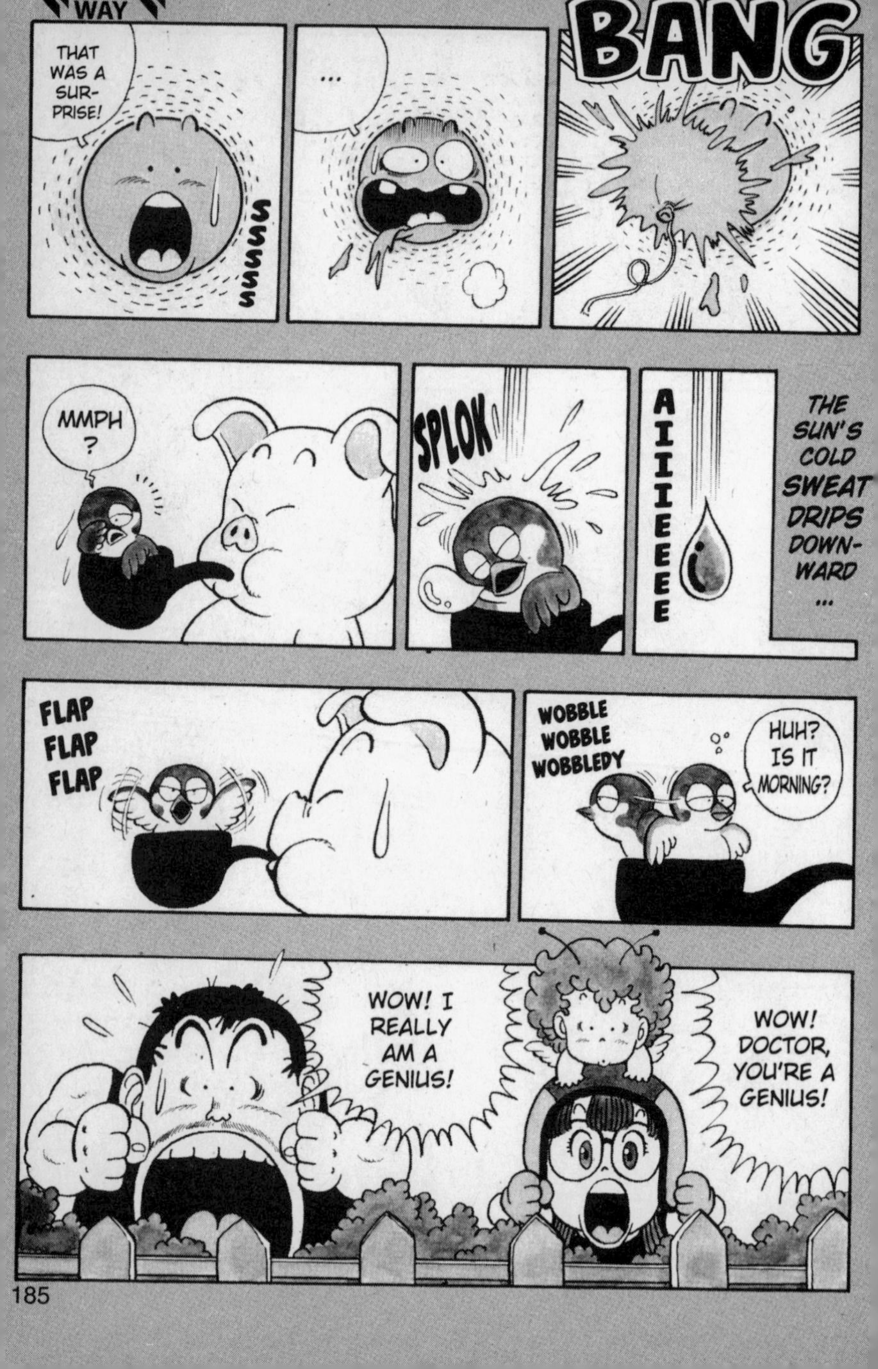
BANG
...
THAT WAS A SUR-PRISE!
SSSSSS
AIIIEEEE
THE SUN'S COLD SWEAT DRIPS DOWNWARD ...
SPLOK
MMPH ?
WOBBLE WOBBLE WOBBLEDY
HUH? IS IT MORNING?
FLAP FLAP FLAP
WOW! DOCTOR, YOU'RE A GENIUS!
WOW! I REALLY AM A GENIUS!

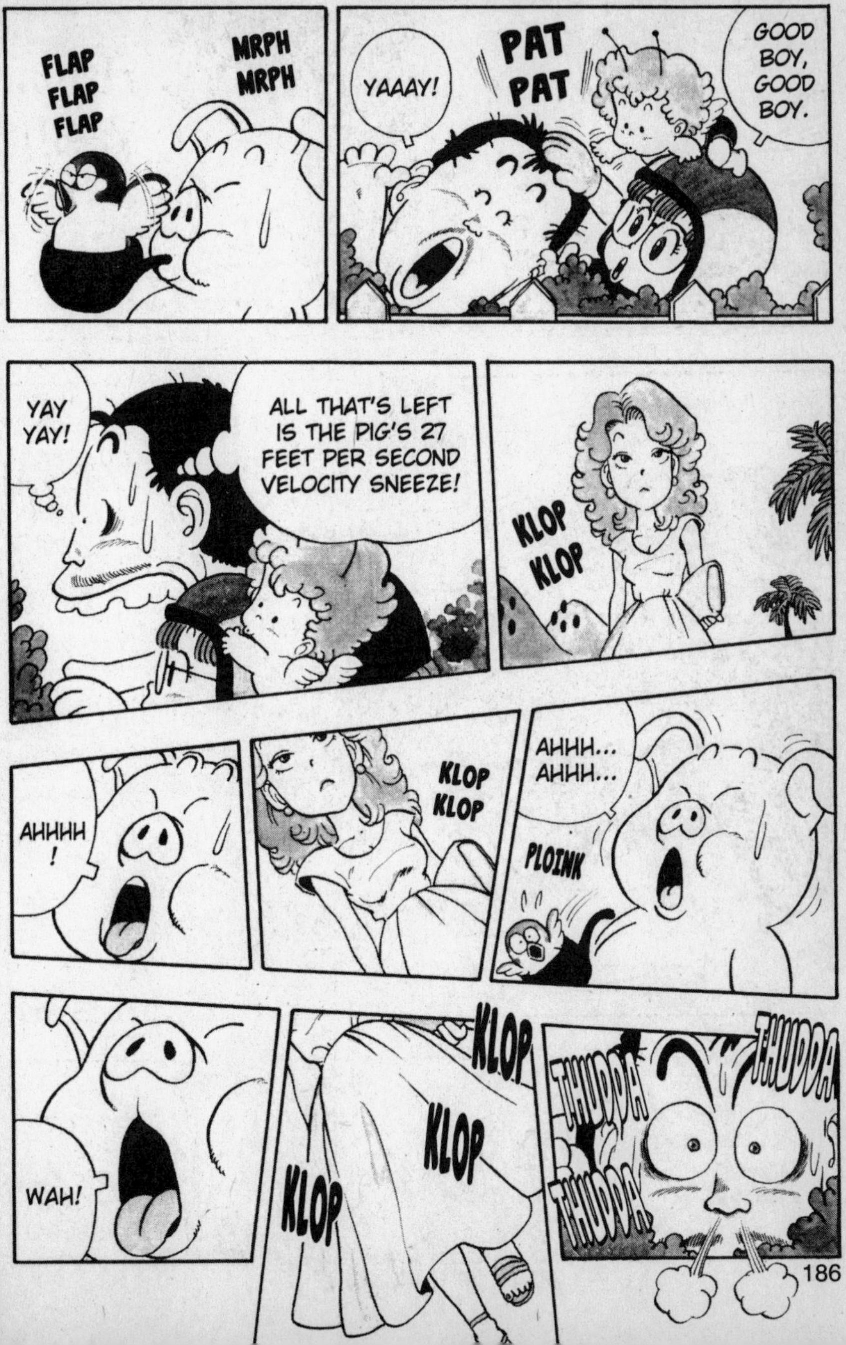
GOOD BOY, GOOD BOY.
PAT PAT
YAAAY!
MRPH MRPH
FLAP FLAP FLAP
KLOP KLOP
ALL THAT'S LEFT IS THE PIG'S 27 FEET PER SECOND VELOCITY SNEEZE!
YAY YAY!
AHHH... AHHH...
PLOINK
KLOP KLOP
AHHHH!
THUDDA
THUDDA
THUDDA
KLOP
KLOP
KLOP
WAH!

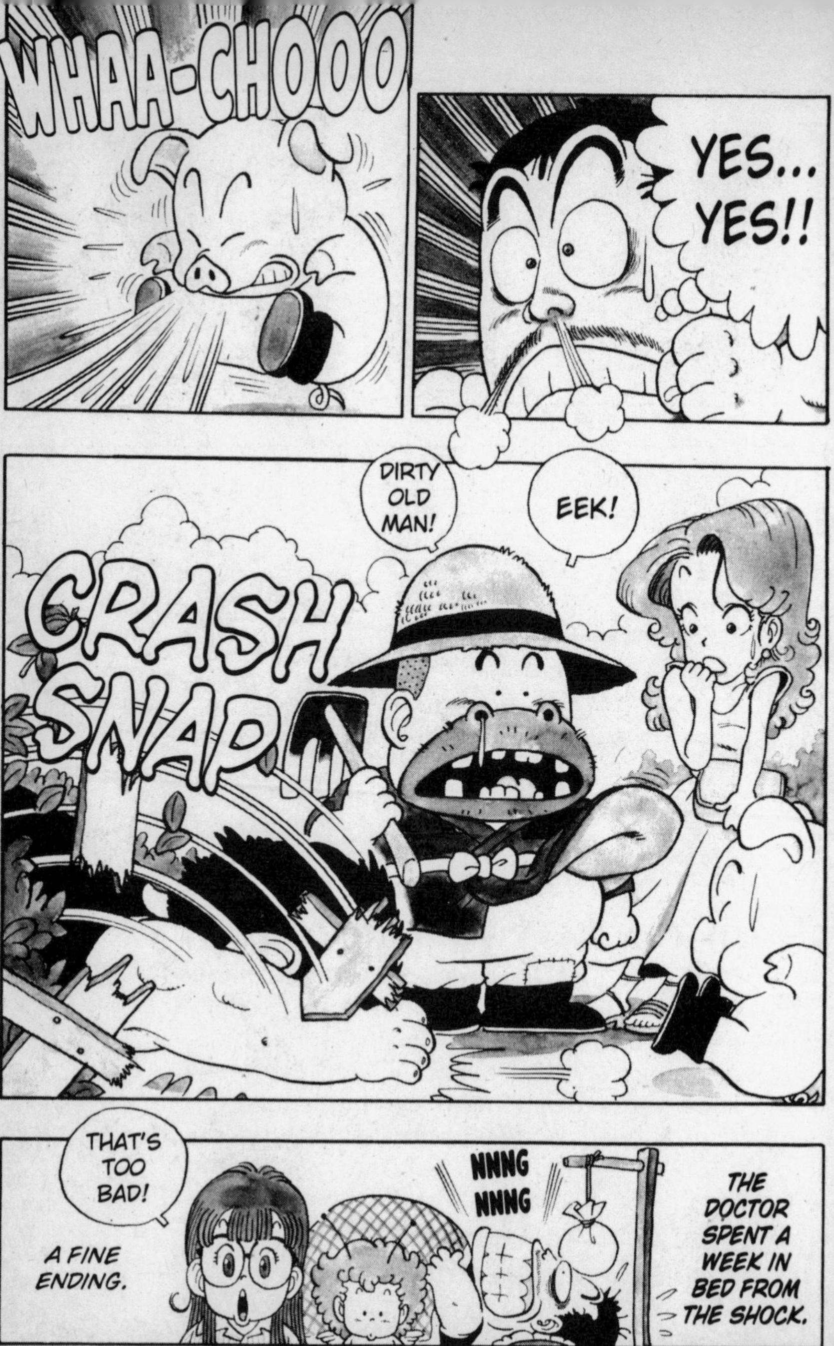
YES... YES!!
WHAA-CHOOO
EEK!
DIRTY OLD MAN!
CRASH SNAP
THE DOCTOR SPENT A WEEK IN BED FROM THE SHOCK.
NNNG NNNG
THAT'S TOO BAD!
A FINE ENDING.

END OF VOLUME 2

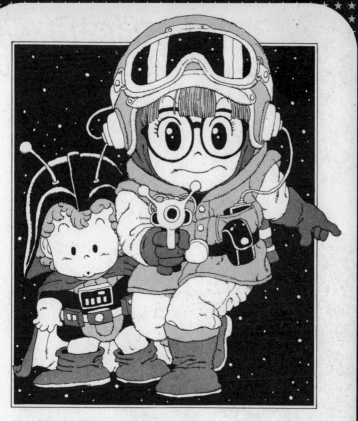

In The Next Volume

In volume 3 of **Dr. Slump**, Arale single-handedly averts an alien invasion of Earth by making fun of the visitors from outer space... Also making his appearance is Penguin Village's very own superhero, "Suppaman," who transforms from a regular businessman to the feeble Suppaman by eating sour pickled plums! And, in a bizarre twist, Akane poses as Ms. Yamabuki, and Senbei does his best to impress her!

Available in September 2005!

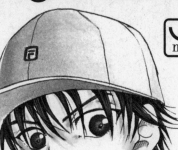
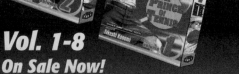

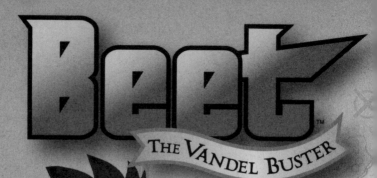
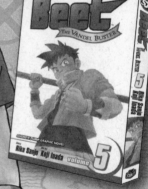

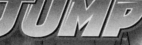

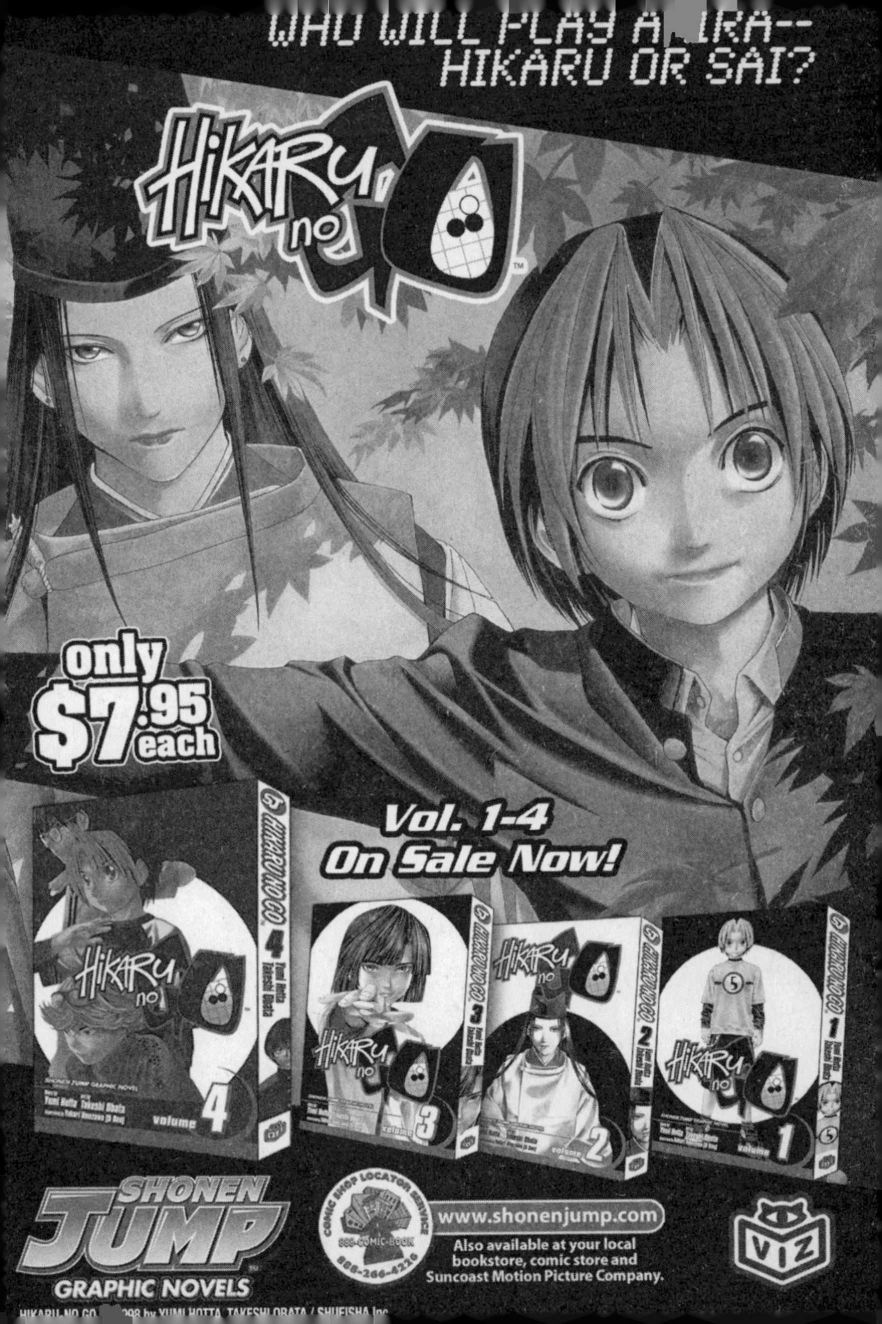
WHO WILL PLAY A IRA--
HIKARU OR SAI?
HIKARU no GO
only $7.95 each
Vol. 1-4
On Sale Now!
SHONEN JUMP
GRAPHIC NOVELS
COMIC SHOP LOCATOR SERVICE
888-COMIC-BOOK
888-266-4226
www.shonenjump.com
Also available at your local bookstore, comic store and Suncoast Motion Picture Company.
VIZ
HIKARU NO GO 998 by YUMI HOTTA, TAKESHI OBATA / SHUEISHA Inc.

SHONEN JUMP™
THE WORLD'S MOST POPULAR MANGA

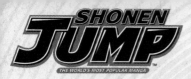

COMPLETE OUR SURVEY AND LET US KNOW WHAT YOU THINK!

☐ Please do NOT send me information about VIZ and SHONEN JUMP products, news and events, special offers, or other information.

☐ Please do NOT send me information from VIZ's trusted business partners.

Name: ______________________________

Address: ______________________________

City: ______________ **State:** ________ **Zip:** ______________

E-mail: ______________________________

☐ **Male** ☐ **Female** **Date of Birth** (mm/dd/yyyy): ____/____/________ (**Under 13? Parental consent required**)

1 Do you purchase SHONEN JUMP Magazine?

☐ Yes ☐ No **(if no, skip the next two questions)**

If **YES**, do you subscribe?

☐ Yes ☐ No

If **NO**, how often do you purchase SHONEN JUMP Magazine?

☐ 1-3 issues a year

☐ 4-6 issues a year

☐ more than 7 issues a year

2 Which SHONEN JUMP Graphic Novel did you purchase? **(please check one)**

☐ Beet the Vandel Buster ☐ Bleach ☐ Dragon Ball

☐ Dragon Ball Z ☐ Dr. Slump ☐ Eyeshield 21

☐ Hikaru no Go ☐ Hunter x Hunter ☐ I"s

☐ Knights of the Zodiac ☐ Legendz ☐ Naruto

☐ One Piece ☐ Rurouni Kenshin ☐ Shaman King

☐ The Prince of Tennis ☐ Ultimate Muscle ☐ Whistle!

☐ Yu-Gi-Oh! ☐ Yu-Gi-Oh!: Duelist ☐ YuYu Hakusho

☐ Other ______________________________

Will you purchase subsequent volumes?

☐ Yes ☐ No

3 How did you learn about this title? **(check all that apply)**

☐ Favorite title ☐ Advertisement ☐ Article

☐ Gift ☐ Read excerpt in SHONEN JUMP Magazine

☐ Recommendation ☐ Special offer ☐ Through TV animation

☐ Website ☐ Other ______________________________

4 **Of the titles that are serialized in SHONEN JU... Graphic Novels?**

- [ ] Yes
- [ ] No

W9-CMD-260

If **YES**, which ones have you purchased? (check all that apply)

- [ ] Dragon Ball Z
- [ ] Hikaru no Go
- [ ] Naruto
- [ ] One Piece
- [ ] Shaman King
- [ ] Yu-Gi-Oh!
- [ ] YuYu Hakusho

If **YES**, what were your reasons for purchasing? (please pick up to 3)

- [ ] A favorite title
- [ ] A favorite creator/artist
- [ ] I want to read it in one go
- [ ] I want to read it over and over again
- [ ] There are extras that aren't in the magazine
- [ ] The quality of printing is better than the magazine
- [ ] Recommendation
- [ ] Special offer
- [ ] Other

If **NO**, why did/would you not purchase it?

- [ ] I'm happy just reading it in the magazine
- [ ] It's not worth buying the graphic novel
- [ ] All the manga pages are in black and white unlike the magazine
- [ ] There are other graphic novels that I prefer
- [ ] There are too many to collect for each title
- [ ] It's too small
- [ ] Other ______________

5 **Of the titles NOT serialized in the Magazine, which ones have you purchased?**
(check all that apply)

- [ ] Beet the Vandel Buster
- [ ] Bleach
- [ ] Dragon Ball
- [ ] Dr. Slump
- [ ] Eyeshield 21
- [ ] Hunter x Hunter
- [ ] I"s
- [ ] Knights of the Zodiac
- [ ] Legendz
- [ ] The Prince of Tennis
- [ ] Rurouni Kenshin
- [ ] Whistle!
- [ ] Yu-Gi-Oh!: Duelist
- [ ] None
- [ ] Other ______________

If you did purchase any of the above, what were your reasons for purchase?

- [ ] A favorite title
- [ ] A favorite creator/artist
- [ ] Read a preview in SHONEN JUMP Magazine and wanted to read the rest of the story
- [ ] Recommendation
- [ ] Other

Will you purchase subsequent volumes?

- [ ] Yes
- [ ] No

6 **What race/ethnicity do you consider yourself?** **(please check one)**

- [ ] Asian/Pacific Islander
- [ ] Black/African American
- [ ] Hispanic/Latino
- [ ] Native American/Alaskan Native
- [ ] White/Caucasian
- [ ] Other

THANK YOU! Please send the completed form to:

VIZ Survey
42 Catharine St.
Poughkeepsie, NY 12601

All information provided will be used for internal purposes only. We promise not to sell or otherwise divulge your information.